Jim KETNER,
   Thanks for y
Soldiers in Iraq.

        Steadfast & Loyal,

        Bob Babcock

M000251051

Operation Iraqi Freedom I: A Year in the Sunni Triangle

Operation Iraqi Freedom I: A Year in the Sunni Triangle

The History of the 4th Infantry Division and Task Force Ironhorse in Iraq

April 2003 to April 2004

Robert O. Babcock

St. John's Press
Tuscaloosa, AL

ALL RIGHTS RESERVED—No part of this book may be reproduced in any form or by any electronic or mechanical means including information storage and retrieval systems without permission in writing from the author, except by a reviewer who may quote brief passages in a review.

First printed by US Government, June 2005

Grateful acknowledgment is made to Mike Hedges of the The Houston Chronicle, Rowan Scarborough of the Washington Times, and the American Forces Press Service for permission to reprint news articles relating to the 4th Infantry Division and Task Force Ironhorse during Operation Iraqi Freedom I.

Photograph: The 173rd Airborne jump into Bashur by Joe Dietz—by permission

Writings, diary entries, and song lyrics by LTC Steve Russell—by permission

The photographs and facsimile maps for this volume were obtained from the 4th Infantry Division Public Affairs Office and the private collections of individuals serving in Task Force Ironhorse—used here with permission.

Printed in the United States of America
Published by St. John's Press, Tuscaloosa, AL
Book cover design by Charles J. Boyle
Author's Photograph by Kenny Ames

First Edition, 2005

Books are available in quantity for promotional or premium use. For information write Task Force Ironhorse Book, PO Box 682222, Marietta, GA 30068.

Catalog in Publication Data (Pending) - First Printing
The 4th Infantry Division and Task Force Ironhorse/Babcock, Robert O.—1943
Operation Iraqi Freedom I: A Year in the Sunni Triangle, The History of the 4th Infantry Division and Task Force Ironhorse in Iraq — April 2003 to April 2004
ISBN 0-9710551-8-1

1. War in Iraq—2003-2004 2. United States Army—The 4th Infantry Division - Task Force Ironhorse—History

For the Soldiers of Task Force Ironhorse and their families

Contents

Introduction

Military history has been my passion since I was a young boy growing up in Oklahoma during the Korean War. That passion became very focused on the history of the 4th Infantry Division (4ID) after I served as a rifle platoon leader with Bravo Company, 1st Battalion, 22nd Infantry Regiment of the 4ID during the early part of the Vietnam War. When the 4ID and Task Force (TF) Ironhorse were alerted for deployment to Iraq, I started collecting information from the internet and 4ID Soldiers to preserve what I knew would become another important chapter in the proud history of the 4ID.

In May 2003, I began producing a daily "*4ID Update from Iraq*" email newsletter that chronicled the daily events of TF Ironhorse and sent it out to several thousand family members and friends of our Soldiers. It became my full time focus for the next eleven months. I knew that we had to preserve this rich history of our TF Ironhorse Soldiers during the period from January 2003 through April 2004 by putting it in book form.

COL Don Campbell, 4ID and TF Ironhorse Chief of Staff, wholeheartedly agreed with my idea, as did MG Ray Odierno, Commanding General of 4ID and TF Ironhorse. Under contract to the Army, I began work on this book project in April 2004. Despite Soldiers moving to new assignments, getting themselves and their units ready for future deployments, and the many other demands on their time, every leader and Soldier I asked found the time to contribute to this history of an important year in the lives of many American patriots.

Included in this book is the original work that I did for the 4ID plus a few minor additions. I thank the 4ID for giving me permission to use that material in this book. The intent of this work is to preserve the history for our Soldiers and their families, and to make it available to anyone who wants to learn more about TF Ironhorse's operations in Iraq. When our TF Ironhorse Soldiers sit with their grandchildren in the future, this will authenticate their role in the Global War on Terror. Future historians may write a more in depth history of the TF Ironhorse actions, but it is unlikely any will cover the broad scope of the operation as this one does.

Bob Babcock
May 2005

Acknowledgments

LTG Ray Odierno, 4ID/TF Ironhorse Commanding General, and COL (P) Don Campbell, 4ID/TF Ironhorse Chief of Staff, showed great vision and foresight in deciding to preserve the history of TF Ironhorse while it was still fresh. I am forever grateful for their leadership and sense of history and pride in their unit and for giving me the opportunity to write this history.

Special thanks go to MAJ Joe Cox, the 4ID Information Officer who tirelessly served as my liaison officer with the 4ID and insured that I was provided the information that I needed. MAJ Josslyn Aberle, former Deputy Public Affairs Officer of TF Ironhorse provided all the press releases and pictures that she had in her files, plus was a valued sounding board as I worked through the project—without her help, the work would have been much less complete. Commanders, staff, and Soldiers from all units of TF Ironhorse sent documents and pictures, took time for personal interviews, and responded to questions as the work progressed. LTC Steve Russell, CO of my old unit, 1-22 Infantry, added greatly to the book by providing his historical diaries for our use. Major General J. D. Thurman, current Commanding General of 4ID, and his Chief of Staff, COL Curtis Potts, and Deputy Chief of Staff, LTC John Novalis, have given great support through all phases of this work.

Chuck Boyle of St. John's Press, my editor for my previous "War Stories—Utah Beach to Pleiku" book on the 4ID, again was an endless source of knowledge and help to make this history as good as we know how to make it. Two friends, Grace Kidwell and Mike May, gave valuable civilian viewpoints as we attempted to make the history of interest to both military and civilian audiences.

Without the support of my wife, Jan, and my family, this work would never have been completed. I am forever indebted to them for their patience in allowing me to follow my passion.

To all who helped make this book a reality, to the Soldiers, families, and friends of the 4ID and TF Ironhorse, to those who will forever carry the scars of war, and to the memories of those who made the ultimate sacrifice while serving with TF Ironhorse, I remain—Steadfast and Loyal.

Bob Babcock
May 2005

Raymond T. Odierno
Commanding General, 4th Infantry Division
24 Oct 2001 - 18 Jun 2004

Foreword

IT WAS AN HONOR TO LEAD THE OFFICERS, NCOS, and Soldiers of the 4th Infantry Division and Task Force Ironhorse in Operation Iraqi Freedom I. I have never worked with a finer group of men and women—all true American heroes. Their dedication, discipline, spirit, and sense of team is what made them successful in a very complex environment. Their strength to execute every day was heroic. This is not just an historic document, but also a collection of their lessons learned.

The capture of Saddam Hussein was the most acclaimed accomplishment of the 4th Infantry Division and Task Force Ironhorse in Iraq, but only a small part of the significant endeavors accomplished. From our historic deployment to our rapid transition into combat and our execution of a campaign plan to simultaneously rebuild Iraq and conduct counter-insurgency operations, this task force set the standard for future operations in the 21st Century.

Task Force Ironhorse has many highlights that are preserved here, and many more individual and unit accomplishments that will be told at a later time. Among the things I am most proud of are moving a heavy armored task force from the United States into combat in record time, conducting eleven major offensive operations, maintaining a constant offensive spirit from the day we arrived in Iraq until the day we departed, and maintaining a laser focus on improving the lives of the Iraqi people. We left our portion of Iraq in much better condition than it was in when we arrived.

We could not have accomplished so much without the continuous support of our families and rear detachment Soldiers. This history is as much about the wives, parents, families, and friends of our Task Force Ironhorse Soldiers as it is about those who served on the ground in Iraq.

We will never forget those who made the ultimate sacrifice in this Global War on Terror, nor those who will forever wear the scars suffered while answering our nation's call.

This deployment has added another chapter to the proud history of the 4th Infantry Division and to all of the units that made up Task Force Ironhorse. Like the veterans before us in World War I, World War II, and Vietnam, we will proudly wear the Ivy Leaf patch on our right shoulder as a symbol of our accomplishments during this very significant year in our lives.

The Global War on Terror is not over, and the 4th Infantry Division will be called on to perform other missions and make more sacrifices in the future. I have no doubt that the Soldiers and families of the "Steadfast and Loyal" Division will answer that call and set the standard of performance for everyone to emulate.

Steadfast and Loyal,
Raymond T. Odierno
Commanding General, TF Ironhorse
December 2004

I

The Army's Leading Edge

Force XXI overview, First year of command for MG Odierno
October 2001 to November 2002

O CTOBER 24, 2001. UNDER A BRIGHT AUTUMN SUN at Fort Hood, Texas, Major General Ray Odierno assumed command of the 4th Infantry Division (Mechanized) and became the 53rd commanding general in the 84-year history of the division.

Only 43 days earlier, on September 11, the attacks on the World Trade Center and the Pentagon had plunged our country fully into the Global War on Terror. MG Odierno's charter was to quickly move the 4th Infantry Division from the experimental Force XXI mission it had so ably conducted since 1995 (and had recently completed), into the most lethal fighting force in the world, ready to deploy where needed and on short notice.

The 4th Infantry Division had last heard the sound of battle before it returned to Fort Carson, Colorado from Vietnam in December 1970. From 1971 to 1995, it had become a mechanized division, adopted the name of "Ironhorse" and had waited in the wings for wartime duty. Sadly, the division had become known in the Army as the "Go Nowhere" division.

On December 15, 1995, as part of the downsizing of the U.S. Army to ten divisions, the 2nd Armored Division was deactivated and the 4th Infantry Division (Mechanized) was moved to Fort Hood, Texas. One brigade, the 3rd Brigade, remained at Fort Carson, Colorado. The newly reorganized 4th Infantry Division (4ID) took on responsibility as the test division for the Army, known as Force XXI.

As they had done in the early 1940s when called on to test a motorized division concept at the beginning of World War II, the 4ID was tasked with the critically important job of testing the equipment, organization, tactics, and digitization which would lead the Army into the 21st century.

1

Over the next six years, under the leadership of four different commanding generals, the 4th Infantry Division led the Army in its movement to change itself to meet the challenges of the 21st century. Much of the new technology that came into the Army was tested first with the 1st "Raider" Brigade of the 4ID and then passed throughout the 4ID for further testing.

Force XXI was the Army's approach to dealing with a smaller force, down a half-million personnel from 1989 and an active duty strength of ten divisions, down from eighteen in 1989.

In the early 1990s, Army Chief of Staff General Gordon R. Sullivan realized the edge the Army would need in the future. "Information is power!" he said. "The power of information will enable a small, CONUS-based, force projection Army to master the challenges ahead. That's because tomorrow's military successes will result from rapid and accurate decision-making. Having the most potent weapon systems does not matter if you can't get them quickly to the right place at the right time, and faster than the enemy can."

Modern information-age equipment was provided to the 4ID during Force XXI testing. Through multiple "war fighter" experiments at the National Training Center, results were evaluated and modifications made in the technology and the units' organization, doctrine, tactics, and techniques—all based on improving the availability of information to commanders and Soldiers, so lethal force could be brought to bear quickly. This process continued until the final "war fighter" exercise was conducted in the early fall of 2002.

Examples of Force XXI capabilities included providing a terminal map display to vehicle commanders showing friendly locations and enemy equipment, and the user's position relative to them. Spot reports and instructions were transmitted in seconds, not minutes, to lower and higher echelons without voice communication. Scouts were equipped with helmet-mounted digital image systems, which enabled them to send video images of the enemy along with accurate grid locations for indirect fire. Unmanned Aerial Vehicles (UAVs), mounted with digital video capability, became key force multipliers as they ranged far in front of the friendly forces and pinpointed exact locations of the enemy.

Key to the situational awareness that the new capabilities offered was the FBCB2 (Force XXI Battle Command Brigade-and-Below) system. It instantly provided forces answers to:

Where am I? Where are my buddies? Where is the enemy? Where are the danger areas? This capability, along with the tactical internet (down to the platoon level) made available expanded ranges of operation and it coordinated night maneuvers in bad weather. It reduced uncertainty in decision-making; decreased incidents of fratricide; and increased lethality of the force.

Brigade TOCs (Tactical Operations Center) looked nothing like in previous wars. Computer displays; situational awareness constantly updated down to the vehicle level; information about friend and foe available to all levels of command; and the ability to engage the enemy at long range were beyond any capability ever known before. Through the use of digital technology, the 4ID had become the most lethal division in the world.

During the last two years of Force XXI, the 4ID carried out three major missions: complete the Force XXI experiment; reorganize the division to implement the lessons learned during the early test phases; and be prepared to deploy on demand to meet any crisis in Korea. Few outside the division realized how thinly stretched they were.

Coming off the Force XXI mission and focusing on future combat missions, MG Odierno published his Commander's Intent. This became the foundation as the division again became part of the main army force structure. That commander's intent remained the same throughout MG Odierno's tenure as CG. It read:

 ## 4ID(M) Commander's Intent

TRAINING READINESS
- Ruthless Devotion to Effective Training
- To Standard BN & CO Training Meetings
- Individual Training Readiness
  - Individual MOS Proficiency
  - Physically & Mentally Fit
  - Small Arms Mastery
  - NBC Readiness
- Collective Training Readiness (METL Based)
  - Lethal Maneuver PLTs & CO/TMs
  - Competent Battle Staffs
  - Leverage Situational Dominance
  - Combined Arms Synchronization

FORCE WELL BEING
- Safety of our Soldiers & Families
  - On & Off Duty
- Dignity & Respect (The Golden Rule)
- Predictability for Soldiers & Families
- Maintain Balance – Family & Readiness
- First Class Facilities – Pride
- Environment that Allows Growth – Individually & Collectively
- A Fun Place to Work & Be Assigned

LEADER DEVELOPMENT
- Competent, Caring, Physically & Mentally Fit Leaders
- Clear Communication Up & Down the Chain of Command
- Empowered Leaders at the Lowest Level
- Will Underwrite Risk to Grow Leaders
- A Sense of Teamwork (Non-negotiable)
- Social & Professional Mentorship at all Levels
- Enforcement of Standards
- Professionalism & Selfless Service

DEPLOYMENT READINESS
- Deployment Mindset Everyday by Every Leader & Soldier
- Individual Soldier Readiness
- Family Readiness
- Unit Deployment Readiness
- Continuous Material Readiness
- Force Protection

Command Climate

Readiness — Leaders — Soldiers — Families

MG Odierno and his leadership team quickly set out to change the mindset of the 4ID Soldiers—from one of testing concepts to that of warriors, ready to fight any time and any place. The leaders knew it was not "if" the 4ID would be called to combat, it was more a question of "how soon and where." Training intensified, leader development was stepped up, and the division's planners built contingency plans for all potential threats that the 4ID might be called upon to fight. Training focused on deployment and pre-deployment, specifically oriented on individual and collective training readiness and the well-being of Soldiers and their families. Developing the physical and mental toughness for combat operations was stressed in all units. From 1 November 2001 through January 2003, the 4ID was designated within FORSCOM (Forces Command) to have the Division Ready Brigade poised for deployment within 18 hours of callup.

Brigade level training exercises at the National Training Center in Fort Irwin, CA consistently set new levels of excellence as the energized 4ID team soundly defeated every aggressor that came its way in the realistic desert training environment.

Programs were put into place to teach the old and new Soldiers about the proud fighting history of the 4th Infantry Division. Twelve 4ID veterans from the D-Day landing in Normandy, France in WWII were brought to Fort Hood on June 6, 2002 to tell the Soldiers first hand about their experiences fighting across Europe. All Soldiers coming into the division spent an afternoon in the 4ID museum and were introduced to their proud legacy. Pride in one's unit—a pride that was strong in our WWI, WWII, and Vietnam veterans—was being restored to Soldiers of the 4ID.

Seemingly small, but subtly important things, were added to the 4ID routine. The Soldiers Creed, the Army Values, and the 4ID Song were read and sung regularly in meetings of Soldiers and family members, and their principles were woven into the very fabric of the division's soul. The changes could be felt; a seriousness and strong sense of purpose was building in the 4th Infantry Division. The 4ID was no longer going to be known as the "Go Nowhere" division, it was building on its heritage and taking its place as the most aggressive and lethal Army division in the world.

The Soldiers Creed

I am an American Soldier.

I am a Warrior and a member of a team. I serve the people of the United States and live the Army Values.

I will always place the mission first.

I will never accept defeat.

I will never quit.

I will never leave a fallen comrade.

I am disciplined, physically and mentally tough, trained and proficient in my warrior tasks and drills. I always maintain my arms, my equipment and myself.

I am an expert and I am a professional.

I stand ready to deploy, engage, and destroy the enemies of the United States of America in close combat.

I am a guardian of freedom and the American way of life.

I am an American Soldier.

Army Values

Loyalty: Bear true faith and allegiance to the U.S. Constitution, the Army, your unit, and other Soldiers.

Duty: Fulfill your obligations.

Respect: Treat people as they should be treated

Selfless-Service: Put the welfare of the nation, the Army, and your subordinates before your own.

Honor: Live up to all the Army values.

Integrity: Do what's right, legally and morally.

Personal Courage: Face fear, danger, or adversity (Physical or Moral).

II

Our Proud Heritage

To acquaint our readers with the 4ID heritage, this chapter covers the history of the 4ID from 1917 to 2001

ALTHOUGH THE 4TH INFANTRY DIVISION HAD NOT seen combat since December 1970, they had a proud history in three shooting wars and the Cold War as they prepared for the deployment to Iraq. Quietly performing their mission with minimal attention from the press, the 4th Infantry Division built a record of which few Americans were aware. In summary form, the following few pages cover the highlights of the first 84 years of the 4th Infantry Division's history.

On November 17, 1917, the same year that America entered World War I, the 4th Division was formed at Camp Greene, North Carolina to begin its long tradition of service to our country. Filled with draftees, the Fourth Division, whose insignia had been adopted by its first commanding general, Major General George H. Cameron, became known as the "Ivy" division. Its insignia consisted of four green ivy leaves on a khaki background. The Division also derived its numerical designation from the Roman numeral IV (4 and IV mean the same thing); hence the nickname, "Ivy" division. Also, in the language of flowers, ivy means "Steadfast and Loyal" —the division's motto.

In April 1918, the Ivy Division's doughboys embarked aboard a number of ships—all 29,180 officers and men—en route to fight in France. The first casualties of the division were suffered as the ship carrying men of the 58th Infantry Regiment was hit by a German torpedo, killing 56 men. After a brief layover in England, the Ivy division landed at Calais, Bordeaux, and Brest, en route to the front lines. By mid June the mighty Aisne-Marne campaign was shaping up, and the Ivy Doughboys were sent to bolster the French 6th Army. Unbeknownst to the men of the Division, their movements were beginning to create a historic precedent. By the

7

time the "Great War" ended some months hence, the Ivy Division would serve with distinction. They were the only American combat force to serve with both the French and the British in their respective sectors, as well as with all Corps in the American sector.

When the war ended on November 11, 1918, the Ivy Division had earned battle streamers with the names of Aisne-Marne, St. Mihiel, Meuse Argonne, Defensive Sector, and Army of Occupation emblazoned on them. A price had been paid: 69 officers and 2,000 men killed in action, and total casualties of killed and wounded added up to 499 officers and 13,150 men. The Ivy Division had fought and defeated sixteen enemy divisions. Nine days after the end of the war, the Fourth Division marched into Germany to take on occupation duties. It wasn't until August 1919 that the Ivy Division's Doughboys returned to the United States and the division was soon deactivated. France had been their first battlefield. A generation later, a new breed of Ivy Division Soldiers would again fight in France.

As war clouds engulfed Europe, the 4th Division was reactivated on June 1, 1940 at Fort Benning, Georgia as America began to increase the size of our armed forces. Selected as an experimental unit for the development of methods recently demonstrated by the German blitz through Belgium and France, the 4th Motorized Division began a three-year, wide-open experiment. From August 1940 through August 1943, the division participated in the Louisiana Maneuvers, then moved to the newly opened Camp Gordon, Georgia where they participated in the Carolina Maneuvers, and finally moved to Fort Dix, New Jersey before being redesignated as the 4th Infantry Division. A move in September 1943 to Camp Gordon Johnston, Florida gave the division realistic amphibious training in preparation for the assault on fortress Europe.

January 18, 1944 saw the Ivy Division embark from the port of New York en route to a final training phase in England. Chosen as the spearhead amphibious division of the D-Day landing on the Normandy coast of France, the men of the 4th Infantry Division stormed ashore at H-Hour (0630 hours) on a stretch of the French coast named—for this operation and forever after—Utah Beach. It was for his actions that day that Brigadier General Theodore Roosevelt, Jr., Assistant Division Commander, earned the first Medal of Honor of the division.

8

After their successful D-day landing, the men of the Ivy division fought through the hedgerows of the Cotentin Peninsula, taking the critically important port of Cherbourg on June 25, 1944. The division was in continuous action during the period of June 6 to June 28 when the last resistance around Cherbourg was eliminated. During this period, the 4th Infantry Division sustained over 5,450 casualties and had over 800 men killed.

With hardly a pause to catch their breath, the Ivymen continued to attack through the hedgerow country and, along with the 2nd Armored Division, spearheaded the breakthrough at St. Lo on July 25, 1944. Exploiting the break in the German lines, the division continued the attack across France. On August 25, 1944 they, along with the French 2nd Armored Division, were the troops who earned the distinction of liberating Paris from four years of Nazi rule. Passing through the wildly applauding Parisians, the Ivymen left the victory parade to outfits following in their wake and continued to pursue the Germans.

On September 11, 1944, a patrol from the 4th Infantry Division became the first Allied ground force to enter Germany. Fighting in the Siegfried Line followed. Mid November found the division in the bloodiest battle of its history. The most grueling battle in Europe was fought in the Hurtgen Forest. Fighting in the cold rain and snow and in a forest of pine and fir trees 150 feet in height, the Ivymen slugged it out yard-by-yard and day-by-day against determined German artillery and infantry resistance. By early December, the division had fought through what had become a twisted mass of shrapnel-torn stumps and broken trees and had accomplished its mission. Casualties in the Hurtgen often exceeded 150 percent of original rifle company strength.

With the Hurtgen Forest behind them, the division moved into a defensive position in Luxembourg and was soon engaged in the Battle of the Bulge. General George S. Patton wrote to Major General Raymond Barton of the 4th Infantry Division: "Your fight in the Hurtgen Forest was an epic of stark infantry combat; but, in my opinion, your most recent fight—from the 16th to the 26th of December—when, with a depleted and tired division, you halted the left shoulder of the German thrust into the American lines and saved the City of Luxembourg, and the tremendous supply establishments and road nets in that vicinity, is the most outstanding accomplishment of yourself and your division."

As the German push was halted in the Bulge, the Ivy Division resumed the attack and continued the pursuit through the Siegfried Line—the same location it had crossed in September—and fought across Germany as the war ground on in the first four months of 1945. When the war ended on May 8, 1945, the 4th Infantry Division had participated in all of the campaigns from the Normandy Beach through Germany. Five more battle streamers were added to the 4th Infantry Division colors and personnel of the Division during this period wear the five campaign stars of Normandy, Northern France, Rhineland, Ardennes, and Central Europe. The division suffered almost 22,000 battle casualties and over 34,000 total casualties, including over 5,000 who were killed or died of injuries, during their eleven months of fighting across Europe. For 199 straight days, the 4th Infantry Division was in constant contact with the Germans.

On July 11, 1945, the Ivy Division returned to New York harbor to begin preparing at Camp Butner, North Carolina, for the invasion of Japan. Fortunately, the war ended before that was required.

The Cold War found the 4th Infantry Division again standing tall in defense of freedom. While others fought the Communists in Korea, the Ivy Division returned to Germany in 1950 and for the next six years stood strong against the Communist threat to Western Europe. After returning to the States in 1956, the division trained at Fort Lewis, Washington, for the next time they would be called into battle. The next time was in Vietnam in the late summer of 1966, twenty-two years and two months after the Ivymen landed on Utah Beach.

Led in August 1966 by the 2nd Brigade, the Ivy Division headquarters closed into the central highlands of Vietnam on September 25, 1966. Their combat assignment against the North Vietnamese would not end until December 7, 1970.

Eleven additional battle streamers would be added to the 4th Infantry Division colors as the Ivy Soldiers fought in places such as the Ia Drang Valley, Plei Trap Valley, Fire Base Gold, Dak To, the Oasis, Kontum, Pleiku, Ben Het, An Khe, and Cambodia. With the largest assigned area of operations of any division in Vietnam, the Ivy division was charged with screening the border of South Vietnam as the first line of defense against infiltration down the Ho Chi Minh trail through Laos and Cambodia, and to preempt any offensive on the more populated lowlands. Triple canopy jungles, extreme heat, and seasonal monsoons were constant challenges to the division as were the North Vietnamese Regulars and Viet Cong. By the time the Ivy Division completed is assignment in Vietnam and returned to Fort Carson, Colorado at the end of 1970, 2,497 Ivy Soldiers had been killed and 15,229 hade been wounded. Eleven Ivy Division Soldiers earned the Medal of Honor during that period.

Resuming training and Cold War missions, the 4th Infantry Division remained stationed at Fort Carson, Colorado from 1970 through 1995. During this period, the division was converted to a Mechanized organization and frequently sent units to Europe to continue the Cold War mission of standing against the Communist threat. It was during their time in Fort Carson that the division assumed the nickname, "Ironhorse".

In December 1995, the Ivy Division was moved to Fort Hood, Texas when the 2nd Armored Division was deactivated as part of the downsizing of the Army. Combining five armor battalions of the 2nd Armored Division with four mechanized infantry battalions of the 4th Infantry Division, the Ivy Division again became the experimental division of the Army, as it had been in the early 1940s. Until completing the mission in October 2001, the Ivy men and women led the United States Army into the twenty-first century under the banner of Force XXI. They developed and tested state-of-the-art digital communications equipment, night fighting gear, advanced weaponry, organization, and doctrine to prepare the United States Army for wars in the new century, in addition to being ready to deploy to any hot spot in the world.

That hot spot was to be the country of Iraq. We will read about that new chapter in the 4th Infantry Division's history in the remainder of this book. Names like Sunni Triangle, Tikrit, Bayji, Kirkuk, Baqubah, Balad, Samarra, Ad Dawr, and others would join the list of places where the 4th Infantry Division has fought with distinction and honor.

MG George H. Cameron
First Commanding General of 4th Division
3 Dec 1917 - 16 Aug 1918

MG Raymond O. Barton
Commanding General
4th Infantry Division
1 Jul 1942 - 26 Dec
1944

4ID Soldiers on operation along Cambodian border - Vietnam - Nov 1966

III

Alert for Iraq

**Planning, TF Ironhorse concept and plan, Initial plan and objectives
November 2002 to January 2003**

MAJOR GENERAL ODIERNO, HIS STAFF AND HIS Soldiers stayed very busy during all of 2002. Beginning with assumption of the Division Ready Brigade mission in November 2001, a reinforced company was always fully packed and ready to deploy anywhere in the world on eighteen hours notice. Quarterly equipment load-out exercises were conducted in each battalion—insuring they were ready to deploy with minimal delay when the call came. Deployable CONEX containers were acquired, surplus equipment was eliminated, and all the necessary repair parts for deployment were packed and ready for shipment. Leader terrain walks through the Fort Hood and Fort Carson deployment staging facilities and the ports in Corpus Christi, Galveston, and Beaumont, Texas were conducted between December 2001 and September 2002.

In April 2002, MG Odierno was summoned to a meeting, along with the CGs of the 3rd Infantry Division, 1st Cavalry Division, and 1st Armored Division, with General Tommy Franks, CENTCOM Commander, and General Eric Shinsecki, Chief of Staff of the Army. At that meeting they were told to be prepared for future operations in the Mideast. He flew to various other high level meetings when it became increasingly apparent the division met the needs for deployment if needed. Planning had already begun for the massive logistical challenge of moving what would become a 32,000-person task force, with all associated equipment, from the United States to Turkey and on to Iraq.

Each Brigade of the 4ID, 1st, 2nd, 3rd, and 4th, along with the Division Cavalry Squadron (1-10 Cavalry), completed two rotations through the National Training Center desert training site at Fort Irwin, California.

14

As part of his schedule, MG Odierno made it to the National Training Center at Fort Irwin, CA in October 2002 to observe his 3rd Brigade go through battle exercises. While there, he received an urgent call telling him that there were several contingency plans developed, one of which the 4ID would be part of an operation that would attack into Iraq from the north. He was to leave immediately to fly to Germany to discuss the plan with LTG Scott Wallace, V Corps commander. Talking to the key leaders before he left, he said, "Take this training seriously. If we send forces to the Mideast, the 4ID will be one of the units deployed. Get yourself and your troops ready."

In the meeting in Germany, it became more apparent that 4ID would not be part of V Corps, but would be a separate major command, to be called Task Force Ironhorse (TF Ironhorse). The force would include the 173rd Airborne Brigade out of Italy plus other active duty, reserve, and National Guard units to make up a force of over 32,000 Soldiers—double the normal strength of the 4th Infantry Division.

The staff Warfighter exercise, originally planned for December 2002, was moved forward to November with focus on the attack into Iraq from Turkey. For two weeks the 4ID leaders and staff, including leaders from 173rd Airborne Brigade, 555th Engineer Group, and other units to be attached, worked on the plan that would very likely be executed in the not too distant future.

As 2002 came to an end, the 4ID leaders and planners continued to refine an OPLAN that could be executed when the official word came to deploy. After many long days and nights working in secure rooms in 4ID HQ, the plan was in place, ready to be implemented.

In addition to the tactical plan, the logistics plan to move the heavy mechanized task force, complete with all the engineers and bridging equipment to meet whatever obstacles might lie in their path, was meticulously developed. That plan had begun taking shape in the summer of 2002 at a joint meeting at Scott Air Force Base outside St. Louis, MO.

The mission of TF Ironhorse was to attack through Turkey to defeat enemy forces in their Area of Operations (AO) and secure a lodgment in northern Iraq. This would threaten the regime of Saddam Hussein from the north. They were to secure the key oil infrastructure near Kirkuk in order to prevent its destruction and attack south to isolate Tikrit from Baghdad.

Critical to the leadership style of MG Odierno, which was to allow maximum flexibility for subordinate leaders, he spelled out the results he expected, both in the operations order and in his briefing with his commanders:

"Our decisive operation is seizing key oil infrastructure located within the vicinity of Kirkuk in order to prevent its destruction and protect against further environmental disaster. We will begin this operation by rapidly penetrating into Iraq using combat force packages to create sufficient maneuver space within a lodgment in order to rapidly and decisively achieve our objectives and exert continuous pressure on the Iraqi regime while continuing to build combat power.

"I see two decisive points within this operation: breach of the Tigris River in the north which supports the establishment of a lodgment within northern Iraq, and seizure of bridges crossing the Tigris River in the vicinity of Qayyarah in order to enable the rapid seizure of key oil infrastructure.

"In the combat assault phase, we will move quickly across the Tigris River, establish our lodgment, and then prepare for decisive operations toward Kirkuk. I want to maintain continuous pressure on the Iraqi regime by defeating the Adnan Division, as we build combat power within our lodgment. Next, we must aggressively attack to seize the Qayarrah Bridge intact. Essential to our momentum is the linkup of 173rd Airborne Brigade and 3rd Brigade Combat Team (3BCT) to rapidly establish a bridgehead line east of the Tigris River.

"Throughout this operation, we will proactively defeat all chemical capable enemy artillery units, mechanized forces, enemy counter-mobility and Air Defense Artillery (ADA) assets that could slow the Task Force's momentum. We must rapidly penetrate through our Area of Operation (AO) and force the enemy to fight on multiple fronts making it difficult to mass his organic fires and ground maneuver capability. We must maximize shaping operations with indirect fires, CAS, AI, attack aviation, and IO to enable our ground maneuver to engage at maximum range with direct fire systems. Essential to capitalizing on our shaping operations is placing artillery assets well forward into our formations to maximize both range and the effects of shaping.

"Key to our momentum is our ability to fix enemy units within urban areas while controlling key terrain with reconnaissance forces. Maneuver Brigades can bypass dismounted infantry company-size forces, but will destroy all enemy tanks, Armored Personnel Carriers (APCs), and mobile Anti-Tank (AT) systems outside of urban areas within our AO. We must aggressively conduct information operations to penetrate the enemy's decision-making cycle. More specifically, I want to separate enemy Soldiers from their weapon platforms, and systematically degrade the enemy C4I network. The Task Force must be prepared to ensure the safety of displaced civilians and EPWs (Enemy Prisoners of War).

"Initially, we will assume risk with the Task Force's extended Lines of Communication (LOCs) by protecting critical resupply convoys to permit uninterrupted logistics flow. Finally, key to our success is the ability to move bulk petroleum rapidly forward to sustain the Task Force's momentum.

"End state is for designated sensitive sites and key oil infrastructure around Kirkuk to be secured, and Task Force Ironhorse is prepared to attack south to isolate Tikrit and secure key oil infrastructure in the vicinity of Bayji."

A key part of the plan was to establish Force Packages with all the required personnel and equipment to complete the assigned mission. Force Package One, led by COL Don Campbell, was made up of the 1st "Raider" Brigade—1st Battalion, 22nd Infantry Regiment; 1st and 3rd Battalions, 66th Armor Regiment; 299th Engineer Battalion, 4th Battalion, 42nd Field Artillery Regiment; and 4th Forward Support Battalion—with attachments of 1st Squadron, 10th Cavalry Regiment; 1st Battalion, 8th Infantry Regiment; and 1st Battalion, 17th Artillery Regiment; plus the engineering, transportation, supply and other support units required to accomplish their spearhead mission. Elements of the 1st and 2nd Battalions, 4th Aviation Regiment; 2nd Battalion, 20th Field Artillery Regiment; and the 4ID Assault Command Post were also included in Force Package One. By early December, the commanders of all the Force Package One units had been alerted to their role. Follow-on Force Packages were established and briefed on their missions.

Movement through Turkey presented a challenge. Ships had to arrive at several ports—ammunition into one, equipment into others. "Simultaneously, the troops will fly into two airfields," the operations order declared. All personnel and equipment faced a movement across 700 kilometers of rough terrain: their destination—the first stage of combat—the Division Assembly Area. Equipment would move by rail and Heavy Equipment Transports (HETs) over a rail and road network not designed for this level of heavy equipment. Both military and civilian transportation were built into the troop movement plan. Operational projections assumed two and a half days of travel across an unfamiliar land before all elements moved into the assembly area.

As the planners and commanders planned the attack into Iraq, the Soldiers continued to train and handle the personal challenges that an overseas combat deployment necessitated. Married Soldiers asked each other, "Should my family stay in the Fort Hood (Fort Carson, etc.,) areas or should they go home to be closer to family?" Unmarried men and women wondered: "Where will my personal belongings be stored? Will I ever see them again?" Similar questions busied the minds of 4ID Soldiers and their families as 2002 ended.

On Friday, January 17, 2003, MG Odierno received the order to deploy. On Sunday, January 19, 2003, all unit commanders at Fort Hood and Fort Carson (by secure video teleconference) were assembled for the alert order they had been expecting. The 4th Infantry Division and TF Ironhorse were headed for Iraq; their preparation was over. It was time to execute the plan. The next day, Monday, January 20, 2003, the news hit the press:

Bush Deploys 'Iron Horse' Of Army To Gulf
By Rowan Scarborough, The Washington Times
The Bush administration yesterday rolled out its most-advanced land combat division for a war against Iraq, ordering the Army's 4th Infantry Division to deploy to the Persian Gulf from Fort Hood, Texas.

The deployment of the "Iron Horse" division marks the second of the Army's "heavy" divisions, along with the 3rd Infantry at Fort Stewart, Ga., to be tapped for a possible desert showdown.

More Army deployments of tank-heavy units are expected to follow as President Bush weighs a decision to order an invasion, perhaps in late February, to oust Iraqi leader Saddam Hussein.

"Task Force Iron Horse," comprising 16,000 Soldiers from the 4th Infantry and 20,000 supporting troops from 10 bases, is deploying as a special unit to confront Iraq. By month's end, as many as 100,000 American troops may be positioned in the region. A total force of more than 200,000 Soldiers, sailors, airmen and Marines is expected to be in place, or on the way, by late February.

"Within weeks we can be over there," said Lt. Col. Dan Baggio, Public Affairs Officer (PAO) for III Corps at Fort Hood.

Tanks and other armored vehicles will move by rail to ports in Beaumont and Corpus Christi, Texas. Soldiers will board cargo jets for the trip to Kuwait in one or two weeks and unite there with their heavy weapons.

Britain, America's strongest ally in this face-off with Baghdad, announced yesterday that 26,000 troops had received orders to go to the region.

Of the Army's 10 active divisions, the 4th is its laboratory for systems developed in the 1990s. As a result, it will take new tools to battle: the advanced M1-A2 battle tank, a digitized system of communicating from a brigade commander to individual tanks and to Bradley Fighting Vehicles, and a new spy drone, the Shadow 200 RQ-7A. The division also boasts Apache attack helicopters, which proved effective in the 1991 Gulf war by destroying Iraqi tanks from a safe range. The 4th is one of the few divisions to operate the more advanced AH-64D Longbow Apache helicopter. Improvements include "fire-and-forget" Hellfire antitank missiles and digital communications.

The 4th is commanded by Maj. Gen. Raymond T. Odierno, a West Point graduate and artillery officer with the 3rd Armored Division in the Gulf war. His division will join a burgeoning air, land and sea force assembling for what would be a lightning strike on Iraq from the south, east and north to seize Baghdad.

Eventually, Army sources say, the 1st Cavalry Division, also at Fort Hood, plus the 101st Airborne Division at Fort Campbell, Ky., and two heavy divisions in Germany also will deploy. Elements of the European-based units may head to bases in Turkey, from where they can activate a northern front against Iraq. Gen. Richard B. Myers, Joint Chiefs of Staff chairman, was in Turkey yesterday discussing basing rights. The United States desires as many as 80,000 troops, but Ankara wants to keep the deployment to fewer than 20,000, Turkish press reports say.

Turkey at first balked at letting the United States use Incirlik Air Base to strike Iraq in 1991, but then relented, permitting Air Force F-111 long-range fighters to launch missions.

Mr. Bush earlier this month traveled to Fort Hood and gave a rousing pep talk to 4th Infantry and 1st Cavalry Soldiers, who responded with enthusiastic "hoo-ahs"—the infantry's unique shout of approval.

The president seemed close to tears as he concluded his speech. The president, who has been briefed several times on war plans, knew that many in the audience would be leaving soon for a possible war.

"We are ready. We're prepared," Mr. Bush told the Soldiers Jan. 3. "And should the United States be compelled to act, our troops will be acting in the finest traditions of America, should we be forced to act. Should Saddam Hussein seal his fate by refusing to disarm, by ignoring the opinion of the world, you will be fighting not to conquer anybody, but to liberate people."

A senior U.S. Official told The Washington Times last week that the administration was looking at a time window of February 21-28 to launch an attack.

Defense Secretary Donald H. Rumsfeld is one of several senior officials arguing that a "smoking gun" need not be disclosed to the world to justify an invasion. He believes sufficient justification lies in Iraq's long pattern of thwarting inspectors and failing to disclose weapons to be destroyed, as ordered by a series of U.N. Security Council resolutions.

Yesterday, Mr. Rumsfeld told a symposium of the Reserve Officers Association, "No one wants war, but, as the president has said, Iraq will be disarmed, and the decision between war and peace will be made not in Washington, D.C., and not in the United Nations in New York, but rather in Baghdad. It is their decision. Either they will cooperate or they won't, and it will not take months to determine whether or not they are cooperating."

U.S. Central Command yesterday continued its low-grade air war against Iraq. Jets struck communications feeding into Iraq's network of air defense radars, batteries and command centers.

Central Command, which runs U.S. Military operations in the Gulf region, said aircraft targeted eight "cable repeater sites" around 7 a.m. EST. The targets sit between al-Kut, 95 miles south of Baghdad, and an-Nasiriyah, 170 miles southeast of Baghdad.

IV

Ready to Go – But Delayed

Logistics of deployment, Family Readiness Groups and Rear Detachment support, Personnel preparation, TF Ironhorse comes to life, Problem with Turkey, Frustration of waiting, Planning continues, Embedded media

20 January 2003 to 25 March 2003

O ONCE THE ORDER TO DEPLOY TO IRAQ WAS RE-ceived, TF Ironhorse and the 4ID sprang into action. For the last half of 2003, MG Odierno had been strongly focused to insure the units were prepared to load out for deployment. Plan and rehearse, then make adjustments and do it again. All across Fort Hood and Fort Carson the 4ID troops continued to refine their loads, eliminating items that were not considered necessary, added new items as the need became known, and practicing, practicing, practicing. When the order came to move, all units began implementing what had become second nature to them.

Bradley Fighting Vehicles, M1 Abrams tanks, and other vehicles and containers of all types and shapes were loaded and ready to go. They moved to the Deployment Ready Reaction Field, were inspected, weighed, and then moved to the other side of the field awaiting a call to the railhead.

"Paperwork is the hard part when it comes to transporting something on rail or a boat," LTC Mark Woempner, battalion commander of 1-22 Infantry said. Detailed inspection, checking, and documentation were required for everything—what was in the vehicle, how it was packed, and what it weighed. With all equipment in good order and the paperwork completed, the monotonous waiting began.

With long lines of empty flatcars constantly coming into Fort Hood, Fort Carson, and other debarkation points around the country, work continued day and night. Tanks and Bradleys were driven across the concrete aprons onto the flatcars and chained down. Railroad inspectors came to assess each vehicle's security on the car. Chilly nights at Fort Hood—in the 40s—were easy compared to the snowstorm that hit the Fort Carson troops during their loading process. Despite being on the fringe of safety considerations for loading in snow and icy conditions, the Fort Carson troops persisted in loading vehicles and equipment so trains could head for Texas ports on the Gulf of Mexico.

Less than three weeks after receiving the order to deploy, the 4ID motor pools at Fort Hood and Fort Carson were empty and the equipment was headed to Turkey. One thousand, eight hundred and five rail cars left Fort Hood with tracked vehicles, metal containers, and hundreds of other pieces of equipment. Tractor trailers, 912 of them, took the remainder of the gear to the ports of Corpus Christi, Beaumont, and Galveston. From Fort Hood alone, over 9,000 vehicles and other equipment—including nearly 600 M1 Abrams tanks, Bradley Fighting Vehicles, and M109 Paladin howitzers—were loaded and shipped. Thanks to the hard work of 4ID and TF Ironhorse Soldiers, and the Army's investment in Power Projection Platforms at Fort Hood and Fort Carson, the 4ID deployed a reinforced heavy division in one-third the time it took during Operation Desert Storm. Never in history had such a large force moved out so quickly.

Frequently, the post was moving equipment out faster than the ports could accept it. Long lines of equipment laden rail cars filled the spur tracks around the port cities, waiting to be loaded. Within ten days of the deployment order, the first ships headed toward Turkey. Many years of moving equipment to the National Training Center and other deployment sites provided the valuable experience that allowed this rapid deployment to succeed.

With the equipment loaded, inventoried, and forwarded to the port cities, Task Force Ironhorse personnel then went through the Soldiers Readiness Process, insuring they were ready for deployment. Over 18,000 Soldiers processed at Fort Hood and Fort Carson. Smallpox vaccinations were given and other medical requirements for each Soldier were fulfilled. Wills, powers of attorney, and other legal documents were finalized and filed. Personal vehicles and personal belongings of unmarried Soldiers were taken to the storage facilities that had been established. Barracks and other battalion and brigade facilities were emptied and prepared for use by other units. Non-deployable Soldiers were assigned other duties—either with the rear detachment of their own unit or with another unit that was not deploying. Similar events were taking place around the country where active duty, reserve, and National Guard units were preparing for deployment with TF Ironhorse.

Family Readiness Groups and Rear Detachments Spring Into Action
Family Readiness Groups (FRGs) and Rear Detachments began a new level of operations to look out for the needs of those family members left behind. At Division level, an *Ironhorse Readiness Guide*, with information and phone numbers for virtually any challenges that might come up, was developed and distributed throughout the division. In October 2002, when it became apparent that deployment was imminent, the division put together a *Dealing with Crisis* handbook, an *FRG Leader Guide*, and a *Family Member Deployment* handbook. Units at Division, Brigade and Battalion Levels worked very hard at updating unit rosters, phone trees, and detailed family information sheets which were required in all units with constant focus on keeping them current, as well as a system to disseminate information by email and phone.

A war game exercise was conducted in early December which included all commanders, rear detachment personnel, and FRG leaders from battalion and higher level units. At this time, COL Jim Moore was named and introduced as the Division Rear Detachment Commander and from that point on was responsible to the CG for the planning and execution of all Rear Detachment activities in the Division. Topics covered included role playing of challenges that FRG and rear detachment leaders might face, introduction of all key players so they could get to know each other and understand the responsibilities and interactions between the FRG's and the rear detachment at Division, Brigade and Battalion levels. There was a workshop on dealing with the media, and other topics also.

In December, MG Odierno met with the police chiefs and mayors of Killeen, Copperas Cove, Harker Heights, and Temple to explain the deployment and help them understand 4ID's mission. He also asked them to tell him what resources they had in place for spouses who lived off post. In January, he met with local school districts and principals to explain the deployment and the importance of being trained in dealing with children of deployed parents and the challenges the children would have.

On 22 January, when the official deployment announcement was made, a planning and brainstorming session was conducted with all spouses of brigade commanders and above. At both that meeting and a 5 February Ivy League meeting, where all Taskforce Ironhorse unit representatives were included, MG Odierno briefed the spouses on the upcoming deployment. Weekly steering committee meetings began in late January at Division and Brigade and Battalion Levels where FRG and Rear Detachment leaders came together to discuss issues of the week and topics of importance. On 27 March, the Family Assistance Center, supported by Army Community Services, on and off post community services, and volunteers, opened at Fort Hood.

It was obvious that 4ID and TF Ironhorse leaders understood the importance of communicating and taking care of their families during the deployment. These and other 4ID FRG and Rear Detachment innovations set the tone that would be followed by many other units in subsequent deployments.

Waiting and Continued Training

With ships loaded and already at sea, the 1st Brigade advance party was scheduled to fly from Fort Hood to Turkey on the weekend of February 15, but the order didn't come. Political problems in Turkey slowed the deployment. High level State Department and military officials worked feverishly with Turkish leaders to try to break the logjam. At Fort Hood and Fort Carson and other posts around the country, TF Ironhorse Soldiers wrapped up loose ends, preparing for their imminent deployment.

The delay and uncertainty began to wear on the leaders and Soldiers. One battalion commander was told by his friend, a general, "You have the toughest leadership challenge now. What do you do to keep your troops engaged with their major equipment on ships?"

The answer was simple: keep training. That included physical training, road marches, and plenty of time on firing ranges with individual weapons. Close Combat Training simulators, where crews of Bradley fighting vehicles could hone their skills in desert and village environments, were operational day and night.

Both at Fort Hood and Fort Carson, the infantry units used the Military Operations in Urban Terrain (MOUT) villages to continue to improve their skills on clearing rooms and houses. Empty motor pools and buildings at Fort Hood and Fort Carson became MOUT training areas to augment the formal training sites. Training focused on the individual Soldier, fire team, and squad, while the company and battalion commanders worked on the bigger picture of the deployment. As the attack through Turkey became less and less probable, attention of the leadership turned toward planning for an attack from Kuwait into Iraq.

Despite the uncertainty and frequent changes, the truth remained—if a Soldier is well trained, he or she will be successful regardless of the mission. Whether attacking through Turkey or through Kuwait, a skilled Soldier's job remained basically the same. Reception, Staging, Onward Movement, and Integration (RSOI) is the same whether it is done in Turkey or Kuwait. The techniques for clearing a room in a house in Iraq remained the same whether the building was approached from the south (Kuwait) or from the north (Turkey). Every battalion in the 4th Infantry Division was exceptionally well trained. All had successfully completed tours at the National Training Center, Fort Irwin, CA within the past year. Many of the commanders and key NCOs had experience from Desert Storm, Panama, Bosnia, Kosovo, or similar areas earlier in their careers.

Although a farewell ceremony was held at Fort Carson on February 19, the troops remained there. The days became weeks and the Soldiers and their families remained in limbo. Most of them had accepted that deployment would happen and they were ready to "just get on with it."

Single Soldiers did not have it easy, either. Personal belongings such as stereos, computers, civilian clothes, and TV's from their barracks had been in storage for weeks. Stored vehicles were retrieved and documents prepared to quickly return them to fenced parking lots when the deployment orders came.

Soldiers got creative with ways to spend their spare time. Bowling became more popular and units initiated athletic competition to help fill the idle time. Preparation for combat continued and physical training intensified. Empty motor pools turned into working training areas. Motor pool buildings made excellent MOUT instruction facilities.

By early March, rumors circulated in the national press that the 4ID would not deploy. Although quickly discounted by the 4ID Public Affairs Officer, the rumors added another degree of uncertainty to what had become a life of monotonous anticipation. Most Soldiers shrugged off the rumors, as did General Tommy Franks, commander of Central Command, as he discredited the press reports.

On March 18, the 720th Military Police Battalion, consisting of about 300 Soldiers, and later to become part of TF Ironhorse, deployed from Fort Hood to Southwest and Central Asia; exact destination not announced. TF Ironhorse Soldiers and their destiny were still unknown. State Department officials continued to work with the Turkish government as Turkey's top political leaders and generals urged their government to allow in U.S. troops. At Fort Hood and Fort Carson, desert camouflage uniforms (DCUs) were issued—a sure sign of impending battle in the deserts of Iraq.

Important Role of Women in Task Force Ironhorse
For the first time in 4ID combat history, female Soldiers played a major role in their ranks. Women had played key roles in the Army for many years and had long been accepted as critical and important parts of the team. For most 4ID and TF Ironhorse Soldiers, working alongside women was as normal as it had been for generations in the civilian world. Although excluded by law from infantry, armor, and artillery units, women were in virtually all other units. Female Soldiers were truck drivers, medics, technicians, mechanics, chemical specialists, MPs, engineers, helicopter pilots, military intelligence specialists, doctors, nurses, and many other specialists. Women commanded units, were key NCOs in others, came from active Army, Reserve, and National Guard components, and held key staff positions in battalions, brigades, and 4ID HQ. The spokesperson for TF Ironhorse, MAJ Josslyn Aberle, was quoted in the news virtually every day of the deployment.

Women would regularly participate in convoys, patrols, and checkpoints. With all of Iraq as a battlefield, women suffered wounds and injuries along with their male counterparts, including some who were killed in combat. Clearly, women were equal players who performed significant roles in the TF Ironhorse team.

Embedded Media

A new phenomenon of Operation Iraqi Freedom I was the presence of embedded media. In World War II, the press was censored and reported only what the military approved for them to report. By the Vietnam War, there had developed a strong disagreement in many cases between the Army and the media on what should and should not be reported. The Gulf War in 1991 and CNN changed the news format to a 24-hour per day news cycle, not just two to three times a day as it had been in the past. After working with officers of the Vietnam era who had a hands-off policy toward the media, the Army began bringing officers from a variety of different branches into the Public Affairs Officer (PAO) role. Finally, the Army was starting to get the right skills mix for the Public Affairs Office.

An interview with the 4ID PAO, LTC Bill McDonald, and the 4ID Deputy PAO, MAJ Josslyn Aberle, revealed the comprehensive training given to embedded media personnel:

In January 2003, immediately upon alert that a deployment order was imminent, plans began in earnest to handle the embedded media that were set to descend on the 4th Infantry Division. Taking a proactive approach, the 4ID invited media to come to join TF Ironhorse. The Department of Defense desired to have equal representation from all types of national media, plus local and regional news teams. Some news organizations had the ability to send reporters but others did not have the financial resources. The press was housed, clothed, and fed by the military. With the dangerous assignment and the high cost of combat zone insurance, buying insurance coverage forced some news sources to decline the opportunity to send a reporter.

Although the local Killeen newspaper did not send a reporter, there was plenty of representation from local affiliates in Dallas, San Antonio, Austin, Colorado Springs, and Denver. The position of MG Odierno was that if the media wanted to go with TF Ironhorse, he would try to take them—a welcome change from old attitudes. Since there were more requests than TF Ironhorse could accommodate, they established a cutoff of 75 national news groups that could be embedded.

When the media arrived at Fort Hood for training and indoctrination, they were given a packing list of what they would need in order to accompany the TF. A complete set of paperwork regarding security rules, shipment details, personal identification photographs, prisoner of war behavior if captured, medical condition and location of records, plus a multitude of similar items had to be signed and authenticated before the reporters could qualify as embedded media. Ground rules were given to them to read, agree to, and sign. If the media would not agree with the policies, they were not allowed to accompany the TF. The TF Ironhorse PAO team met with two or three individuals at a time to have waivers signed on riding on government transportation, release of liability of the government, and to explain the history of the unit to which they would be assigned.

A conference room was set up in a Killeen hotel where embedded media were given mandatory training. Topics included an overview of the 4ID, who the PAO personnel were and what their roles were, what they could expect, a little about the military (Military 101), the chain of command, the TF expectations of them, and what they could expect from the TF. During the three days of training, the CG took time to talk with them, as did the Chief of Staff. The Judge Advocate gave a class on military law to insure they understood that the military follows rules of law. Also covered were rules of engagement, how the military follows them, what "no fire zones" are; things the Army views as important when operating in a foreign theater—all to insure the media understood this was not law enforcement they were going in to; it was combat. A proactive, not defensive, approach was taken to insure the media knew the TF was engaging a hostile enemy according to laws of war.

At the conclusion of the classroom briefings, combat engineers set up land mine training lanes for the media to go through. Each reporter went to the Central Issue Facility to draw protective equipment and went through NBC (Nuclear, Biological, and Chemical) training. Among other tasks, each of them had to open a decontaminant packet; a very comprehensive program to insure they were qualified to deal with potential NBC conditions.

Along with the training and combat gear, Fort Hood offered to give the media immunizations. This was one of only a few places in the world where the media could get all immunizations. Some took it, some didn't—but it was offered to them all.

When the journalist's training was complete, their assigned units were given a brand new Soldier to add to their rolls.

The PAO team had plenty of help from the Brigade and Battalion staffs to pull this off. In each subordinate organization, a military liaison was identified to help the PAO team work with their assigned reporter. These key personnel were given two days of training to help understand the correspondent's profession and their tasks; how to mutually benefit from them; and how to resolve problematic issues should they arise. Such foresight proved to be invaluable when TF Ironhorse arrived in the theater of operations. The PAO team always had help in communication with the news groups, managing their safety and well being, and helping them as needed.

As the delay with Turkey caused time to drag on, the PAO staff worked with the CG and Chief of Staff to figure out how to best utilize the media talents and keep them engaged, ready to deploy on short notice. The decision was made to get them all to Fort Hood and have them ready to go. As the next 45 days passed, some news organizations wanted to put them onto other assignments. A 48-hour recall program was designed, complete with an alert roster to get news personnel back quickly if their specific unit was ready to deploy.

Overall, the foresight, planning, and training by TF Ironhorse for the embedded correspondent's program went very well. They learned how outstanding the men and women of TF Ironhorse Soldiers were. Blending quickly into their units, they became part of it, getting to know the people very well. They did physical training with the Soldiers, dressed in DCUs, and even got short haircuts. The general physical condition of these newsmen and women was first-class. One of the qualifying requirements for the reporters was that they be physically able to do their mission. The physical training they did with the troops put them into even better condition, as they wanted to be part of the team. Only a very few of these journalists were unsuited for the mission: that came from poor attitudes or negative views of the military. Most of the press wanted to deploy more than the Soldiers. The war was underway and they were not there, frustrating them in their desire to make their mark in their profession. Before long, however, they would be in the thick of the action along with the Soldiers in TF Ironhorse.

On March 19, 2003, President Bush went on national television to address the nation. A summary of his remarks:

War Begins; Coalition Aircraft Attack Iraqi Targets
By Jim Garamone, American Forces Press Service
WASHINGTON, March 19, 2003—Operations to disarm Iraq have begun, President Bush announced during a speech to America tonight.

The president confirmed the early stages of military operations to disarm Iraq, to free its people and to defend the world.

News reports from Baghdad showed anti-aircraft artillery streaming into the sky. Western reporters spoke of hearing bombs drop in the western part of the city—which is home to many government buildings.

"On my orders, coalition forces have begun striking selected targets of military importance to undermine Saddam Hussein's ability to wage war," the president said from the Oval Office at 10:15 p.m. Eastern time. Bush stressed this will be a broad and concerted campaign.

He said the coalition—35 nations contributing in a variety of ways—is moving to disarm Hussein and put a stop to his murderous rule. "Every nation in this coalition has chosen to bear the duty and share the honor of sharing in our common defense," Bush said.

Bush had direct words to the more than 250,000 U.S. service members in the area of operations. "The peace of a troubled world and the hopes of an oppressed people now depend on you," the president said. "That trust is well-placed. The enemies you confront will soon know your skill and bravery. The people you liberate will witness the honorable and decent spirit of the American military."

He said that once again Saddam Hussein has placed innocent civilians amid military targets. He assured the world that coalition forces will do all they can to minimize Iraqi casualties.

Bush observed the conflict will be dangerous, but U.S. commitment to the Iraqi people will not end with victory. He promised America will help feed the population of Iraq and rebuild the infrastructure of the oil-rich land.

But even then, the United States will not stay in the nation one second longer than necessary. "We have no ambition in Iraq except to remove a threat and restore control of that country to its own people," Bush said.

The president also spoke of the sacrifice made by the relatives

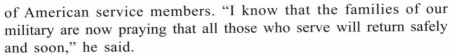
of American service members. "I know that the families of our military are now praying that all those who serve will return safely and soon," he said.

"Millions of Americans are praying with you for the safety of your loved ones and for the protection of the innocent. For your sacrifice, you have the gratitude and respect of the American people. And you can know our forces will be coming home as soon as their work is done."

Bush pointed out that now is the time to confront the threat Saddam Hussein has become. Waiting will only make things worse, he said. "We will not live at the mercy of an outlaw regime that threatens the peace with weapons of mass murder. We will meet that threat now with our Army, Air Force, Navy, Coast Guard and Marines, so we will not have to meet it later with armies of firefighters, and police and doctors on the streets of our cities."

He stressed the U.S. military will apply decisive force to ensure a speedy campaign. "I assure you this will not be a campaign of half-measures and we will accept no outcome but victory."

Two days later, the following announcement was made:

"The Army's storied 'Rock of the Marne' division out of Fort Stewart, Ga., started moving across southern Iraq 'largely unopposed.' The offensive began at 10 P.M. in Washington, 6 A.M. March 21 in Baghdad.

"The 3rd ID is comprised of nearly 20,000 Soldiers, 300 tanks and a similar number of Bradley fighting vehicles."

Final Decision and Casing of Colors Ceremony
Frustration grew greater in the leadership of TF Ironhorse. The war had started and they were still sitting in the US—waiting.

On Saturday afternoon, 22 March, the decision was finally announced on the status of TF Ironhorse going through Turkey.

The TF Ironhorse ships that had been waiting off the coast of Turkey were redirected to Kuwait. U.S. hopes to use Turkish bases to move into northern Iraq had ended. The 37 ships carrying the 4ID and TF Ironhorse equipment were moving through the Suez Canal by Sunday, 23 March. It was expected that ships would begin arriving in Kuwait by 30 March, with all to be fully unloaded by 10 April. The work of the hundreds of 4ID and European based Soldiers who had been in southern Turkey preparing for the arrival turned out to be wasted effort.

With the announcement, 4ID troops at Fort Lewis, Fort Carson, and other bases around the United States and Europe erupted with new activity as they knew their time had finally come to get into the fight. Within days the first troops would be headed for Kuwait, and three days later the 173rd Airborne Brigade would be making a combat assault into northern Iraq to join the Special Operations forces already on the ground.

Even before the official press announcement was made public, MG Odierno had assembled his commanders into the secure room in 4ID HQ where they had been working on the southern entry plan. "We're going through Kuwait, get ready," was his simple order. The decision was confirmed to the press by III Corps Commander, LTG Tom Metz: "As people have seen in the media, the 4th Infantry Division decision has been made. They won't go through Turkey; they'll go in a different route in the area of responsibility." For security reasons, the timetable of the troop movement was not announced.

MG Odierno also decided to conduct a Casing of the Colors ceremony on Cameron Field, the 4ID parade ground in front of 4ID HQ, on the morning of 27 March. "Whenever a unit moves locations we case our colors and take them with us," said MAJ Josslyn Aberle, 4ID deputy public affairs officer. "It's a great morale booster for everyone and it's an opportunity for our commanding general to talk to the Soldiers and families."

In his speech at the Colors Casing Ceremony, MG Odierno said, "The Ironhorse has been summoned, and we will answer that calling. It is not a calling we answer for money, easy work or glory. But rather it's a calling from deep within our hearts to protect you, our families and each other. It is the calling for the love of a country, defending our way of life for the next generation of Americans." He went on to say, "Each and every Soldier has voluntarily raised his right hand and took an oath to support and defend the Constitution of the United States against all enemies, foreign and domestic. I admire them for their bravery and courage and I am humbled to serve in their ranks."

In closing, he said, "Ladies and gentlemen, we have a non-negotiable contract with the people of America to fight and win our nation's wars. We pray for peace and do not wish for war, but we train to fight in order to protect our families, each other, and our country. Our cause is right and our resolve is unwavering.

Almost sixty years ago our colors liberated Paris from the grips of a vile and tyrannical rule. Once again we have been called upon, and I assure you the magnificent Soldiers of this powerful task force will continue the long, proud legacy of the Ironhorse Division."

The ceremony closed with the singing of the 4th ID song:

Steadfast and Loyal
We're Fit to fight!
The Nation's Finest Soldiers
Keep Liberty's Light
Our Soldiers ROAR for Freedom
We're Fit for any Test
The Mighty 4th Division
AMERICA'S BEST!

The wait was over. The 4th Infantry Division was ready to embark on their biggest test since returning from Vietnam at the end of 1970. Within days, lead elements were flying to Kuwait.

MG Ray Odierno and CSM Charles Fuss Casing the 4ID Colors at Fort Hood, Texas - 27 March 2003

TF Ironhorse Representative Units

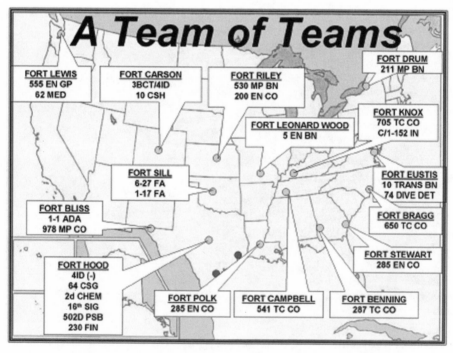

US origins of TF Ironhorse units – Team of Teams

COL Don Campbell Addressing 1-22 Infantry Troops - 11 Feb 2003

Vehicles from Task Force Ironhorse staged at Fort Hood rail head for loading on trains - 31 Jan 2003

M1A2SEP Tank with mine plow from 2BCT, Warhorse Brigade Combat Team, moving to the Fort Hood DRF - 1 Feb 2003

Equipment from 1BCT, Raider Brigade Combat Team, loaded on trains for rail movement to the SPOE - 31 Jan 2003

Trains loaded with combat equipment from Task Force Ironhorse staged at Fort Hood for movement to the SPOE - 1 Feb 2003

4ID Soldiers and families at Starker gym awaiting departure to Kuwait

V

Deployed — Finally

Change of mission, Ships rerouted to Kuwait, Troops fly to Kuwait, RSOI in Kuwait, 173rd jumps into Iraq, Final preparations for attack into Iraq

26 March 2003 to 14 April 2003

T HE POLITICAL DEBATE WITH TURKEY OVER THE movement of TFIronhorse continued as their leaders and planners labored in the secure rooms of 4ID HQ to develop the contingency plans for movement into Iraq from Kuwait. Several options had always been in the overall plan, so despite the frustration of the uncertainty with Turkey, it was not a major problem to focus on an alternate attack plan. Until mid February, focus continued on the northern plan. Later, it shifted to Kuwait.

BG Steve Speakes, ADC-Support of 4ID, flew to Kuwait to prepare for the advance party and to coordinate plans for the potential arrival of TF Ironhorse Soldiers. MG Odierno and his staff soon followed to temporarily work from Kuwait, and then returned to Fort Hood. The mission changed daily—both from the uncertainty with Turkey and from the fluid battle situation and lines of communications after the attack into Iraq had begun. Exactly how TF Ironhorse would deploy remained a question.

In early March, still anticipating movement through Turkey, the 173rd Airborne Brigade moved its equipment by rail to the Italian seaport city of Livorno, to be loaded when the Turkish issue was resolved. When it became clear that Turkey was not going to cooperate, the equipment was moved back on 18 March to the Aviano air base where it was hastily reconfigured for air movement, and in some cases, to be air dropped.

Operations Order for Attack Through Kuwait

On 22 March, when the final decision was made that TF Ironhorse would not move through Turkey, the mission officially changed. The new operations order read as follows:

Mission: On order, TF Ironhorse attacks to destroy enemy forces in the vicinity of Taji and Balad in order to establish a secure forward operating base. On order, neutralize remaining enemy forces in order to allow corps movement along Highway 1 and occupy positions in the vicinity of Tikrit in order to establish a presence and deter aggression.

Concept of the Operation: This combat operation is divided into two sub phases. The first phase is to seize Taji and clear Highway 1. Second phase is to clear Highway 1 and establish a presence in the vicinity of Tikrit.

Phase 1: On order, TF Ironhorse conducts a tactical movement to a forward assembly area in order to forward position the Task Force for future combat operations deep inside Iraq to facilitate the destruction of non-compliant forces and remaining symbols of Regime power. A TF Ironhorse advanced security and command and control (C2) element moves from the Camp Areas to Tactical Assembly Area (TAA) Ironhorse to conduct passage of lines with 3rd Brigade, 3rd Infantry Division to facilitate the passage of the entire Task Force. This initial security and C2 clears any non-compliant enemy forces along Highway 1 and Highway 8 from the Camp Areas in Kuwait to TAA Ironhorse and the assault routes to the TF Ironhorse AO. Follow-on force packages from each BCT and TF troops flow sequentially from the Kuwait Camp area to TAA Ironhorse (HET download site) to download combat vehicles and move to assigned attack positions. Simultaneously during the flow of the TF into its AO, combat operations are ongoing with attacks planned against enemy forces vicinity the Taji airfield and any directed missions from V Corps. On order the TF is prepared to attack north to destroy non-compliant forces along Highway 1, isolate Tikrit, or attack towards Kirkuk in order to secure key oil infrastructure.

Scheme of Maneuver: The movement of the TF will commence approximately 14 April 2003 with the first lift led by 1-10 CAV (OPCON to 1BCT), 1-17 FA, 1BCT TAC/1BRT, MP PLT/4 MP CO, and the TF Assault CP. On order the first lift mounts their vehicles onto HETs and convoys from the Kuwait Camp Area to TAA Ironhorse south of Baghdad. 1-10 CAV secures TAA

Ironhorse which enables the downloading of HETs and the emplacement of the 1-44 ADA BN CP in a secure environment. On order, 1-10 CAV, 1-17 FA, 1 BCT TAC move along designated routes and conduct passage of lines with 3BDE/3ID. On order, 1BCT conducts passage of lines with 3ID, attacks to the Taji airfield, and clears the military complex of non-compliant forces in order to support the forward positioning of 11AHR (11th Attack Helicopter Regiment). 1BCT prepares to continue the attack and secures a Tigris River crossing to enable movement across the river to secure the Balad airfield. On order, 3BCT(-) moves via HETs to TAA Ironhorse in order to forward position forces for movement into the TF AO. On order, 3BCT clears Highway 1in order to allow coalition movement north along Highway 1 and is prepared to seize Balad to enable establishment of a corps logistical base and/or to enable east-west movement across the Tigris River. 3BCT is prepared to continue attack north of Samarra Canal to clear Highway 1 to vicinity Tikrit to enable coalition movement north along Highway 1. On order, 2BCT HETs to TAA Ironhorse and moves forward as the TF reserve. 2BCT is prepared to conduct combat operations and defeat non-compliant forces in the AO or follow and assume 3BCT attack to clear Highway 1 from Samarra to Tikrit. 2BCT is also prepared to conduct a tactical road march from Kuwait to the north of the East-West canal. On order, 4BCT initially co-locates with 3ID or 101st Aviation and prepares to conduct close shaping in support of BCT attacks in AO. On order, occupy FOB in vicinity of Balad.

End state is enemy forces in AO destroyed and the Taji and Balad airfields are secured. The TF is prepared to continue the attack to the north to clear the remainder of Highway 1 to Tikrit or east to secure Kirkuk oil infrastructure. 1BCT continues to defend in AO along Tigris River, 1-10 CAV and 3BCT secures crossing sites along the Samarra Canal, and 2BCT closes to attack position to advance as required.

Phase 2: The TF conducts an attack to destroy remaining enemy forces, clear Highway 1 and establish a presence in the vicinity of Tikrit. The 3BCT follows 1-10 CAV as the initial TF main effort, breaches the Samarra Canal then attacks to complete the defeat of enemy forces in the Tikrit area. 3BCT then isolates

Tikrit from the south and clears Highway 1 from Samarra to Tikrit. 3BCT is prepared to breach Tigris River and defeat forces east of Tikrit. 3BCT is also prepared to conduct operations in and around Tikrit and Samarra to destroy non-compliant forces. The 2BCT crosses the Samarra Canal and envelopes Bayji from the west. On order, 2BCT clears Bayji of non-compliant forces to enable movement along Highway 1 by V Corps sustainment convoys. On order, isolate Tikrit from the north and clear Highway 1 to Bayji. Be prepared to conduct operations in and around Tikrit to destroy non-compliant forces. Be prepared to secure key oil infrastructure in the vicinity of Bayji. 1BCT maintains an Armor Battalion TF at Taji to secure the airfield. 1BCT (-) as the TF reserve prepare to cross the Tigris river and defeat enemy forces east of Tikrit and isolate Tikrit from the south. Be prepared to link up with the 101st west of Kirkuk. 4BCT attacks to defeat enemy field artillery and armor, vicinity of Samarra. Be prepared to defeat enemy field artillery within other parts of the AO.

End state: The TF is prepared to conduct operations into Tikrit to destroy non-compliant forces or continue attack to clear remainder of Highway 1 or secure Kirkuk oil infrastructure.

With the plan in place, TF Ironhorse was ready to move. The ships that had been circling off the coast of Turkey for several weeks steamed south toward Kuwait. Final good-byes were made as the advance party of TF Ironhorse boarded planes for immediate departure to Kuwait. There they prepared for arrival of the ships and the planes with the main body of Soldiers. After over six weeks of uncertainty, TF Ironhorse was about to take their first actions in the Global War on Terror.

173rd Airborne Enters the War
The 173rd Airborne Brigade had already made its assault into Iraq. Although not yet officially under the command of TF Ironhorse, Sky Soldiers of the 173rd Airborne Brigade had boarded C-17 airplanes at Aviano Air Base, near their home station of Vicenza, Italy during the afternoon of 26 March. After focusing from October through February on a sea deployment and subsequent operation through Turkey, the Sky Soldiers quickly adapted to their airborne mission. The advance party from

the 74th Long Range Surveillance Detachment had struggled for several days with terrible weather in northern Iraq but had finally been inserted to prepare the way for the remainder of the brigade. Weather continued to be problematic in northern Iraq but a gutsy Air Force meteorologist "guaranteed" on 18 March that there would be a clear window for the airborne drop at 2000 hours on 26 March.

On 25 March, when seventeen C-17 airplanes were seen sitting on the apron of the Aviano airfield, the Sky Soldiers knew this was not a practice—it was serious business. They were slated to add a new chapter to Airborne history with the largest airborne combat jump into a single drop zone since World War II. Their mission, code named "Operation Northern Delay," was designed to defeat anti-coalition efforts and destroy non-compliant forces in the At Tamin Province in order to maintain a secure operational environment.

The successful establishment of a northern front was essential to the Coalition battle plan. Without a northern front, six Iraqi divisions arrayed in northern Iraq remained free to move south. There they could reinforce Baghdad and stop, disrupt, or delay the onslaught of the 3rd Infantry Division and Marine Forces and the inevitable fall of the regime. Fast moving Coalition forces were closing on Baghdad with the expectation of having to capture the capitol from three defensively arrayed Iraqi divisions. Six additional Iraqi divisions streaming from the north could dramatically affect the balance of power around Baghdad.

Another critical factor was the oil rich area of Kirkuk. The oil wealth of that area would be crucial to rebuilding Iraq, but the Iraqi army had shown a willingness to destroy their country's future simply to spite the coalition. Securing the oil fields and air bases of Kirkuk was assigned to the 173rd Airborne Brigade. Several airfields were considered for the drop until it was decided the Bashur airfield, 150 kilometers north of Kirkuk, would be the objective. Deciding factors were that it was controlled by friendly Kurdish and American Special Forces personnel; that it appeared to be capable of handling heavy aircraft loads; and it was just north of the no-fly zone line where allied airplanes had patrolled since the end of Operation Desert Storm.

As the Air Force meteorologist had predicted, the sleet and rain that had been falling on the drop zone stopped at 1830 hours and the 74th Long Range Surveillance (LRS) Commander, CPT Tom McNally, already on the ground, radioed to the planes that the weather was a "go" for the jump. Troopers had been briefed that the area was Kurdish controlled and was expected to offer little resistance. That did little to alleviate the concerns running through their minds as the white lights in the plane were replaced with red lights, allowing their eyes to become accustomed to the darkness they would be jumping into. Another worry was the predicted muddy drop zone. It could break a man's leg, or worse, if he could not control his landing.

At 2000 hours, on a pitch-black night with no moon or stars, fifteen C-17 aircraft (two of the original 17 C-17s were for backup) delivered 20 heavy platforms of equipment and 959 Sky Soldiers onto Bashur Drop Zone near Bashur in northern Iraq. By 2030 hours, the sleet and rain had resumed. Units involved were HHC, 173rd Airborne Brigade; 1st Battalion (Airborne), 508th Infantry Regiment; 2nd Battalion (Airborne), 503rd Infantry Regiment; 74th Long Range Surveillance Detachment; D Battery, 319th Airborne Field Artillery Regiment; 173rd Combat Support Company; 501st Forward Support Company; 250th Forward Surgical Team; 2nd Battalion, 10th Special Forces Group; 4th ASOG (USAF); and the 86th Expeditionary Response Group (-) (USAF). The C-17's were from the 62nd and 446th Airlift Wings from McChord AFB, Washington, and the 437th Airlift Wing and 315th Reserve Airlift Wing from Charleston, AFB, SC. This was the first combat airborne insertion ever conducted with the C-17.

Coming through hostile territory and with the drop zone nestled in a valley, the C-17's were forced into a steep dive, plunging from 30,000 feet to 800, the drop altitude. When the green "jump" light flashed, COL Bill Mayville, Brigade Commander, a veteran of the 75th Ranger's combat jump into Grenada in 1983, was the first man out the door, followed closely by Command Sergeant Major William Gunter. Others, most of whom had never experienced a combat jump, quickly spilled out the doors as the C-17's climbed back up into the sky, clearing the valley walls. This marked the first combat jump for the 173rd since they had performed the only major combat jump of the Vietnam War—during Operation Junction City in February 1967.

The landing was unopposed but muddier than expected. Using their night vision goggles to locate guidance beacons, the paratroopers moved to their unit assembly areas and established a secure area for additional forces to land. Within two hours the Sky Troopers had secured the airfield. Although some Soldiers were scattered from four to five kilometers short or long of the intended drop zone, they quickly moved to the airfield as planned. Fewer than twenty Soldiers had been injured in the drop—none of them life threatening. Daylight found the 173rd established in northern Iraq.

From 27 March to 9 April, the 173rd conducted air/land operations to build combat power and posture for the attack on Kirkuk and seizure of the oil fields. Over four consecutive nights, forty-seven C-17 flights landed at the Bashur airfield and brought in an additional 1,165 Soldiers, 253 vehicles, 113 special equipment vehicles, and 97 pallets to build a partially motorized combined arms Brigade Task Force. The first heavy units, from TF 1-63 AR, were flown in and added to the force on the ground.

On 2 April, 1-508 IN (-) was given the mission to move 45 kilometers to Irbil airfield to conduct raids on enemy forces. Unlike other airborne units, the 173rd had twelve Humvees assigned to each company. Moving in the Humvees and five ton trucks, the battalion seized the Irbil airfield without any enemy resistance. Linking up with Special Forces units that had been operating in the area, they conducted their first artillery raids on Iraqi forces on 5 and 7 April. The Special Forces had been having a hard time getting accurate fire onto forces in the open. Both the 120mm mortars of the brigade and Delta Battery, 319th Field Artillery participated in the raids across the Greater Zab river. An enemy observation post that had been directing fire onto our SF teams was knocked out by A/1-508 IN. This was the first direct fire contact since landing. Enemy fires, which had been ineffective, were totally knocked out by the counter battery fire.

On 10 April, the entire 173rd Airborne Brigade began movement to the Kirkuk area to secure the oil fields and supporting infrastructure. 2-503 IN, the main effort, attacked to seize Stabilization Plant 1 to the north of Kirkuk to prevent the destruction of key oil infrastructure, and then continued on to seize K1 airfield, west of Kirkuk. 1-508 IN attacked southeast from Irbil, destroyed enemy forces along the Kani Domlan ridge and subsequently linked up with 2-503 IN at K1 airfield. 1-63 AR was follow-on support into K1 then into Kirkuk military airfield.

On 11 April, the 173rd Airborne Brigade moved on to secure the Kirkuk military airfield. The brigade found the airfield largely abandoned and met little resistance. While the airfield was being cleared and secured, COL Mayville ordered patrols to conduct reconnaissance in Kirkuk and begin identifying local leaders. Special Forces teams and other agencies working in the area assisted with the task.

All three battalions began occupation of the city on 13-14 April. On 13 April, with looting running rampant in Kirkuk, the first meeting was held with local leaders. By 20 April, it was realized that in order to secure Kirkuk, the oil fields in the 40 kilometers outside Kirkuk had to be secured. Missions were established to occupy and secure all 19 pieces of critical infrastructure. 1-508 IN was removed from the city and tasked with securing the airfield and the infrastructure in the outlying areas. 2-503 IN and 1-63 AR remained in the city.

Checkpoints around and within the city helped to stabilize the environment and stop the looting. Although spread thin, the Sky Soldiers rose to the occasion and showed how effective squad and platoon size elements could be.

4ID Conducts RSOI in Kuwait

As the 173rd Airborne Brigade was taking the fight to the enemy in northern Iraq, the 4ID and remainder of TF Ironhorse began flowing into Kuwait. Upon arriving, their first mission was to complete reception, staging, onward movement, and integration, better known as RSOI. Reception involved meeting planes and ships to ensure that Soldiers and equipment were properly accounted for. Next came staging, which involved matching units with their assigned equipment. After that came onward movement, where units left the ports and moved forward to camps in the desert. The final phase was integration, which was comprised of numerous tasks such as uploading supplies, conducting vehicle maintenance, acclimating to the arid climate, conducting training and rehearsals, and setting up command posts. The RSOI process was scheduled to last approximately two weeks. Because of the hard work of each and every Soldier, the task force excelled at RSOI.

The advance party from Fort Hood and Fort Carson left on 27 March, arrived in Kuwait the next day, and immediately started

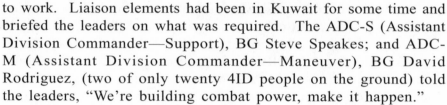

to work. Liaison elements had been in Kuwait for some time and briefed the leaders on what was required. The ADC-S (Assistant Division Commander—Support), BG Steve Speakes; and ADC-M (Assistant Division Commander—Maneuver), BG David Rodriguez, (two of only twenty 4ID people on the ground) told the leaders, "We're building combat power, make it happen."

Kuwaiti buses took the Soldiers on the long ride from the airport to temporary camps with the names of Camp New Jersey, Camp New York, Camp Virginia, Camp Udari, and Camp Pennsylvania. The camps had been built soon after Operation Desert Storm and used regularly by many units over the past decade in operations practicing for this possibility of a future war. They were simply large stretches of desert where engineers had built sand berms to mark and secure the camp perimeters. Rows upon rows of tents, vehicle parking lots, and hard-packed sand roads became their bleak new temporary homes. The rear echelons of the 3rd Infantry Division, 101st Airborne Division, Marines, and others who had recently attacked into Iraq were still in the camps. Although these camps had been built to house battalion size units, Task Force Ironhorse would soon fill them with Brigade Combat Team (BCT) strength—over four times more troops and equipment than they were designed to accommodate.

The planning and logistics for housing TF Ironhorse units, and moving their equipment from the ships to the camps consumed much of the advance parties' time. Transportation was also lacking as the transition from the comforts of stateside to the reality of a combat zone set in. Scud alerts (including two times when scuds were actually fired at the camps, but missed) added to the heightened sense of danger. Communications to Fort Hood were established to signal the advanced party of when to expect the bulk of their units—then RSOI could begin in earnest.

The TF Ironhorse orders allowed three weeks after arrival to prepare for the movement into Iraq—within ten days the movement north had begun. The intense training over the past year and a half was paying off. Executive officers, mechanics, and support personnel rose to the challenge and performed in a Herculean manner. In one case, an entire Bradley transmission was replaced in less than twelve hours to insure it was ready for the move north. It was a total team effort that prepared TF Ironhorse to begin the advance into Iraq ahead of schedule.

Between 3-5 April, the main bodies of 1-10 CAV, 1-22 IN, 1-8 IN, 1-66 AR, 3-66 AR, 299 EN, 4-42 FA, 4th FSB, 1-4 AV, 2-4 AV, and supporting troops left Fort Hood and Fort Carson. Over the next two weeks, a constant flow of units filled the skies. By mid-April, all TF Ironhorse units were in Kuwait conducting RSOI. Once units arrived, vehicle drivers and commanders went to the ports to off-load equipment. The remaining Soldiers were bused to the staging camps in the desert. The port became a flurry of round the clock activity as ships came in, vehicles were off-loaded and moved to staging areas, and the next ship came in, repeating the process. The first piece of 4ID equipment off-loaded in Iraq was an AH-64 Apache helicopter that belonged to 1-4 AV.

Fortunately, most of the vehicles were operational and rolled off under their own power. Mechanics immediately started working on those that did not run. The Soldiers who had spent the past six weeks on the ships were understandably happy to get off and see their comrades again. (On supercargo ships, units habitually assigned two to six Soldiers per ship to watch over the loaded combat vehicles and containers as the deploying unit's equipment moved to a port in a Theater of War). When vehicles were ready to roll, convoys formed and the equipment moved north to join the main body of the units.

Activity continued at a rapid pace as Soldiers acclimated to the environment. Individual and crew served weapons were test-fired and zeroed. Vehicles, radios, and digital equipment were checked to insure they were ready for the push into Iraq. Equipment and personal items were loaded onto Bradleys, tanks, and other vehicles, while leaders continued planning for the attack. Key challenges came in insuring ample supplies of ammunition and spare parts were available for each unit. GI ingenuity insured that problem was overcome and all units were properly armed.

As is common in any combat operation, the original plan did not hold, requiring last minute changes. 1-8 IN had all their equipment on one ship and were off-loaded quickly and moved to Camp Pennsylvania, while 1-22 IN had equipment scattered over three ships and off loading did not go as smoothly. When this became known, the attack plan changed: 1-8 IN became the lead unit to enter Iraq, right behind 1-10 CAV. The war had started and the 4ID was not wasting any time getting into the thick of it.

173rd ABN BDE Jumping into Bashur, Iraq - 26 March 2003

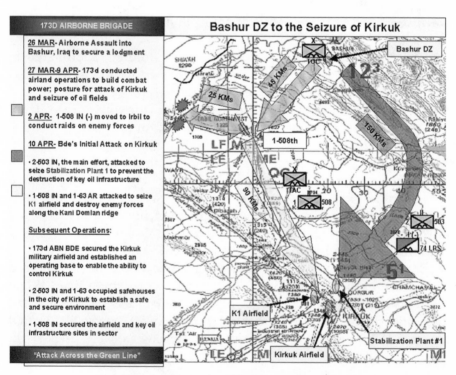

Tactical Assault Map-Bashur DZ to Kirkuk

COL William Mayville, CO, 173rd ABN BDE, addresses troops in Italy

173rd ABN BDE Machine Gunner in Bashur, Iraq

Soldiers and equipment of TF Ironhorse as they arrive in Kuwait and prepare for attack into Iraq

Ship with 4ID equipment en route to Turkey and then to Kuwait

VI

Attack to the Sunni Triangle

Movement across 500 miles of desert, Attack on Taji and Balad airfields, Initial deployment and combat actions of TF Ironhorse 15 April 2003 to 30 April 2003

1st Brigade Combat Team Leads TF Ironhorse into Iraq

AT 0200 HOURS ON 14 APRIL, THE LEAD ELEMENTS of the 1st "Raider" Brigade started rolling toward the Iraqi border, on through Baghdad, and to the Sunni Triangle in northern Iraq—a 500 mile trip. A few hours earlier, the troops had left the relative safety and comfort of the camps to a staging area in the desert. Units were lined up in order of their movement priority, waiting for Heavy Equipment Transports (HETs) to move in to load the tracked vehicles. Precisely on schedule, the lead convoy of 1-10 Cavalry (CAV), under command of LTC Ted Martin, and comprised of five march units, headed north at a speed of 25-30 miles per hour. Fuel tanker trucks from the 704th Division Support Battalion (DSB) were part of the initial convoy. Less than an hour later, the second convoy from 1-8 Infantry (IN) commanded by LTC Phil Battaglia, moved north. Alpha Company, 1-66 Armor (AR) was attached to 1-8 IN. Both 1-10 CAV and 1-8 IN were attached to 1BCT for this initial assault into Iraq. Excitement filled the Soldiers as they moved into Iraq, executing the mission for which they had long trained. The stream of vehicles moving north would continue for weeks.

In the lead elements, along with 1-10 CAV and 1-8 IN, were 1-17 Field Artillery (FA), a tank company from 1-66 AR, engineers from 299th Engineers (EN), elements of 704th DSB and 1-44 Air Defense Artillery (ADA), and other support elements. Following close behind these lead elements were the remainder of the 1st Brigade Combat Team (1BCT)—1-66 AR, 1-22 IN, 3-66 AR, 299 EN, 4th Forward Support Battalion (FSB), and 4-42 FA.

51

Over the objections of some HET commanders who didn't think it was safe, the Abrams and Bradley crews, including dismounted infantry, were loaded onto their tanks and Bradleys, with engines running and turrets traversing. The gunners and track commanders were in their fighting positions, ready to fire on any threat. Rear troop doors and top hatches were left open to allow fresh air into the Bradley troop compartments for the long trip. The Brigade recon troop, G Troop 10th Cavalry Regiment, went ahead of the first convoy to scout the route and establish control points. Other scout elements brought up the rear while still others were interspersed within the convoys. Wheeled vehicles carrying fuel, troops, ammunition, engineering materials, communications, medical equipment, and other supplies filled out the convoys. It was a formidable force snaking across the Iraqi countryside. Helicopter gunships were on call to provide fire support if needed.

The lead convoy stopped only to refuel, choosing to continue to move forward with minimal delay. Later convoys stopped every three to four hours for fuel and for a brief rest stop for the troops. Fifteen to twenty minutes later, they were continuing the movement north. Congestion and alert status increased as the convoys moved through small Iraqi towns but tension eased somewhat as they moved back into the open countryside. Destroyed Iraqi armored vehicles and still smoldering buildings along the highway were visible displays of the fighting that had gone on as the 3rd Infantry Division fought through this area only a few days before. When abandoned enemy equipment was found, high explosive rounds were fired from tanks or Bradleys to destroy it. Occasionally, convoys had to stop as hundreds of Iraqi pilgrims, waving green and black flags, crossed the highway on their pilgrimage to the holy site of Najaf in southern Iraq. Soldiers trained their weapons on the people but there were no incidents— the pilgrims ignored them.

Thirty-five to forty hours later, on the afternoon of 15 April, the lead convoys pulled into the desert assembly area ten-kilometers south of Baghdad known as Tactical Assembly Area (TAA) Ironhorse. Bradleys and tanks roared down the ramps of the HETs and prepared for the onward journey through Baghdad points north. Vehicles were fueled, weapons were checked, ammunition was resupplied, and some of the troops got a few minutes of much needed sleep as they waited for the continuation of their movement to combat. After a quick briefing by the 101st Airborne ADC (in charge of the passing of TF Ironhorse through their lines), 1-10 CAV headed into Baghdad at 1700 hours. Lead elements were moving out before the tail end of the squadron had closed into TAA Ironhorse.

Passing through the center of Baghdad, they were met by sporadic but ineffective small arms fire. By 2000 hours, 1-10 CAV reached their assembly area on the north side of Baghdad, near a canal south of their first objective, the Taji airfield. The lead elements, C Troop, G Troop, A Troop (-), and HQ Troop established their defensive perimeter, settling in for the night. It was nearly 0500 hours the next morning, 16 April, before the final elements of the squadron closed into the assembly area.

As dusk settled over TAA Ironhorse, LTC Phil Battaglia, CO of the 1-8 IN, was approached by his old company commander with whom he had served many years before. The officer, Ben Freakly, now a Brigadier General with the 101st Airborne, was responsible for the safe passage of TF Ironhorse through their lines. BG Freakly gave Battaglia a bear hug, a few lessons learned, and quickly briefed him on how to go through Baghdad. In less than an hour, under cover of darkness, 1-8 IN continued moving north through Baghdad.

Moving in blackout conditions and using night optical devices (NODs), the first company of 1-8 IN, reinforced with mortars and parts of the scout platoon, moved through Baghdad. Around midnight, they had passed through the lines of both the 101st Airborne and 3rd Infantry Divisions and then pulled off to the side of the road on the north side of Baghdad, only two to three kilometers from the objective they shared with 1-10 CAV—the Taji airfield. Like in times past, they circled their wagons (Bradley fighting vehicles in this case,) and waited for the rest of the battalion to join them. It was 0400 hours when the last unit, including fuel trucks, ammunition resupply vehicles, and other logistics support elements closed into the defensive perimeter.

The Attack on Taji and Balad Airfields

At 0600 hours, COL Don Campbell, CO of 1BCT, brought LTC Battaglia and LTC Martin together and laid out his attack plan on the hood of his Humvee. A small river had to be crossed, but the bridge was intact. 1-10 CAV was to move around the airfield to provide perimeter security on the west and north sides. 1-8 IN was to move along the road skirting the south side of the airfield and move on line to attack across the airfield, south to north. 1-10 CAV crossed the bridge at H-Hour, precisely 0900 hours, and sped along the west side of the airfield to establish their blocking positions to the north and west. 1-8 IN followed and veered right to the southern edge of the airfield. Soon, 44 Bradleys from 1-8 IN were on line, moving north, shooting at any target they saw as they swept across the field. Rate of movement was controlled and troops were limited to narrow fields of fire (from 11:00 o'clock to 1:00 o'clock to their front) to avoid friendly fire incidents. The plan was simple and it worked. Less than an hour later, the airfield had been swept and the Soldiers returned and methodically worked through every room of each building to insure there were no stragglers left behind. A Bradley from C/1-8 fired a TOW missile into a Russian made T55 tank. It exploded in spectacular fashion—no match for the TOW missile. LTC Battaglia moved his Bradley to the airfield control tower so he could be easily located by his troops.

After COL Campbell had arrived at the Taji airport complex (soon after it was taken), MG Ray Odierno landed in his helicopter and said: "Don, did you know that you just led the first combat for the 4th Infantry Division since they left Vietnam in December 1970?" The historic significance of the event was not lost on COL Campbell, but he was too busy to spend much time reflecting on it. After Taji, the next objective was the Balad airfield.

Around noon, COL Campbell brought LTC Battaglia and LTC Martin to his mobile command post (CP—his Humvee). Again, he spread his map out on the hood to give them the attack order for their next objectives. Balad airfield was the target of 1-8 IN. 1-10 CAV's objectives were the Iraqi National Military Control Center and the road junction north of the airfield. Once they had their orders, LTC Martin and LTC Battaglia passed the order on to the subordinate leaders over the digital command system, the first combat use of their new digital capability.

The battalions assembled their Soldiers, refueled vehicles, resupplied ammunition, and began the move north to the Balad airfield by 1700 hours. With the troops in need of rest, the attack was delayed until daylight on 17 April. Bradleys were circled

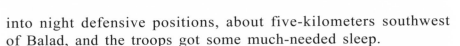

into night defensive positions, about five-kilometers southwest of Balad, and the troops got some much-needed sleep.

Before the advance toward Balad, the Unmanned Aerial Vehicle (UAV) flying over the Balad airfield beamed back live TV pictures of the activity it saw. Enemy soldiers were moving ammunition and equipment out of the airfield. Civilians mixed with the enemy combatants as they looted whatever they could use. COL Campbell had a decision to make: *Do I fire artillery onto the base to stop the looting, and risk many civilian casualties, or do I let the ammunition be carried away to be captured on another day.* Not wanting to risk civilian casualties, COL Campbell held off the fires of 1-17 FA.

An hour and a half before attacking Balad, COL Campbell was joined by COL Mike Moody, 4BCT commander and LTC Jim Muskopf, 1-4 Attack Aviation battalion commander to plan the air/ground integration of the attack. Once again COL Campbell spread his map out on the hood of his Humvee and the aviators discussed with him how they could help soften up the target and support his attack. After the brief discussion, COL Campbell agreed that the Apache Longbow helicopters would fire on the airfield to soften it up and then fly over the 1-8 IN and 1-10 CAV attack forces to provide added security as they moved up Highway 1 to Balad. The fluid nature of the battlefield did not allow for more precise planning—the simple plan made sense, so it was implemented.

There was a canal to cross, but again, the bridge was intact. The line of departure (LD) was crossed at 0600 hours with the attack on the Balad airfield scheduled for 0700 hours. As 1-8 IN again fanned out with four companies on line to sweep across the long expanse of the airfield, 1-10 CAV bypassed Balad and moved north to secure Saddam's national command bunker complex and the road junction.

Balad was a bigger and more strategic objective than Taji had been. With a larger physical space, an ammunition storage area, and airfield buildings, it was destined to become a major strategic supply area for Combined Joint Task Force 7 in Iraq, soon to become known as FOB Anaconda.

Still with 44 Bradleys and 12 tanks, 1-8 IN used the same simple attack plan on Balad that had been successfully used the day before on Taji. Results were equally successful—no American casualties and the entire airfield was in American hands very quickly. After sweeping the length and width of the airfield, the troops returned to methodically clear the buildings, room by room.

"We're Going to Tikrit."
Colonel Campbell's next command was, "We're going to Tikrit." Although Tikrit was originally planned to be the objective of the 3BCT coming up behind 1BCT, there was no reason to slow down after the success that 1BCT had. After spending the night in Balad and leaving a platoon of tanks, a platoon of Bradleys, and a platoon of Engineers to secure the Balad airfield, the remainder of 1-8 IN began the 70-80 kilometer movement toward Tikrit, short only by the four Bradleys and four tanks left in Balad. 1-10 CAV had already led the way up Highway 1 to Tikrit. They had linked up with elements of a Marine light armored battalion around Samarra before moving on to make contact with another Marine unit at the presidential palace complex in Tikrit.

Ten kilometers south of Tikrit, 1-8 IN again pulled into a night defensive perimeter. Their objective the morning of 18 April was to do a relief in place with the Marine 1st Light Armored Battalion. At a small airfield south of Tikrit, often used by Saddam Hussein, they linked up with the Marine colonel and started discussing the relief plan. 1-10 CAV had moved north and was securing an airfield on the northern side of the city in what was to become a major TF Ironhorse supply base. Its name became FOB Speicher, named after CPT Scott Speicher, an Air Force pilot who was shot down and was missing in action from Operation Desert Storm.

The Marines had bypassed Baghdad and moved into Tikrit from east to west. They occupied strong points at a UN food complex, the Saddam palace complex, and a few other strategic locations. COL Campbell and LTC Martin met with BG John Kelly, USMC commander, at the palace complex to plan the relief in place. Interestingly, COL Campbell and BG Kelly had worked together in Europe when both were in SHAPE headquarters in 1999-2001. Over the next two days the Soldiers of 1-8 IN moved in to relieve the Marines as they moved to the south airfield assembly area and then headed west toward the Syrian border for their next mission.

The first impression of the extensive palace complex built by Saddam Hussein was one of pure opulence, like Las Vegas.

56

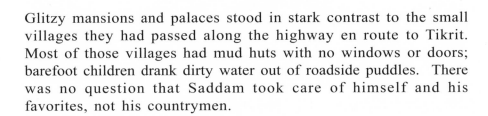

Glitzy mansions and palaces stood in stark contrast to the small villages they had passed along the highway en route to Tikrit. Most of those villages had mud huts with no windows or doors; barefoot children drank dirty water out of roadside puddles. There was no question that Saddam took care of himself and his favorites, not his countrymen.

More Troops Move Into the Fight

Close behind 1-10 CAV and 1-8 IN was the remainder of 1BCT. 1-66 AR temporarily took on the mission of securing the south side of Tikrit. 3-66 AR, with B/1-22 IN attached, moved through Tikrit and on to occupy the important oil town of Bayji. 1-22 IN, with C/3-66 AR attached, moved in to take responsibility for the north side of Tikrit.

Soon, 1-22 IN had the entire responsibility for Tikrit after 1-8 IN moved toward Tuz to return to the 3 BCT on 30 April. On 22 April, 1-66 AR, with A/1-22 IN attached, moved to Mosul with the 1st Brigade, 101st Airborne Division, to secure the airfield. TF 1-66 AR occupied the former Iraqi V Corps Headquarters with the mission of destroying enemy forces, consolidating abandoned munitions, destroying unexploded ordnance, and assisting in the distribution of fuel to Iraqis.

On 20 April the Division's Tactical Operations Center arrived in Tikrit, and on 23 April DMAIN (the Main 4ID HQ organization and equipment) was settling into the palace compound. This was now the headquarters for Task Force Ironhorse, ready to execute whatever mission came its way.

Elements of Division Support Command (DISCOM— Wrangler) had been moving north with all units. Once in the Tikrit area, they established their headquarters at FOB Speicher, the Tikrit north airfield, with operations spread around the TF Ironhorse AO.

Moving along the eastern side of the Tigris River was the 3rd Brigade Combat Team (Striker Brigade), under command of COL Fred Rudesheim and consisting of 1-12 IN, 1-68 AR, 4th EN, 64th FSB plus supporting elements. After leaving Kuwait via HET on 17 April and moving through Baghdad at night, they passed through Taji and Balad to their objective of Samarra. 1BCT had bypassed Samarra in their movement to Tikrit, so 3BCT was the first unit into Samarra.

Last in the movement north, leaving Kuwait on 24 April 2003, was the 2nd Brigade Combat Team (Warhorse Brigade), under command of COL Dennis Rogers. For the next 72 hours the brigade convoyed north towards their assigned objectives in the Diyala Province. Task Force 1-67 AR attacked along Highway 2 and seized the airfield in Baqubah, which would become FOB Warhorse. Behind TF 1-67 AR came 588th EN, 3-67 AR, 3-16 FA, and 204th FSB. Meanwhile, TF 2-8 IN executed a tactical road march, without HETs, from Camp Udari, Kuwait, to Baqubah.

The 4th Brigade Combat Team (Iron Eagle Brigade), the aviation brigade, under command of COL Michael Moody, consisting of 1-4 AVN, 2-4 AVN, and their support units flew and drove to FOB Speicher to establish their base of operations.

TF Gunner, the Division Artillery (DIVARTY—Iron Gunners), under command of COL Kevin Stramara, took control of the Taji airfield, establishing their headquarters in a former Republican Guard command center. Although it was not normal for an artillery unit to be assigned their own Area of Operations (AO) (they usually supported combat arms units who owned the AO), COL Stramara was assigned an AO and owned terrain that he, his artillerymen, and one infantry company from 179th Infantry Regiment of the Oklahoma National Guard were responsible to defend and patrol. This was an early indication that Soldiers of TF Ironhorse would be called upon to do missions that did not normally fall into their area of expertise—but they stepped up to the challenge and handled them in stride.

By the end of April, all major units of TF Ironhorse were at work in the Sunni Triangle—from Taji in the southwest to north of Bayji in the northwest to Kirkuk in the northeast to Baqubah in the southeast. Soon the area would expand further east to the Iranian border and further west to Buhayrat ath Tharthar Lake— an area of operations the size of West Virginia.

Offensive Operations Continue

No time was lost as 4ID and TF Ironhorse Soldiers established themselves in their new Forward Operating Bases (FOBs). Day and night patrols, security checkpoints, getting to know the AO and key people in it, while building up their new FOBs became the norm for all TF Ironhorse Soldiers.

Enemy weapons and ammunition caches were everywhere. Warehouses, schools, bunkers, military complexes, buried or scattered in temporary locations along the highways and in farm fields—all were filled with weapons and ammunition. All who were interviewed said, "I've never seen so much ammunition in my life." It was obvious where Saddam Hussein had spent his money. Arms dealers and insurgents were rapidly looting these stockpiles. It became a key priority to stop the looting before the weapons and munitions could be used against coalition forces.

During the night of 21 April, a firefight erupted between 1-22 IN and Iraqi arms dealers at the Iraqi military installation north of Tikrit. Sixteen arms dealers were killed in this engagement, the first of many to be waged over the next several days. Nighttime action continued in the north of Tikrit as arms dealers started moving ammunition across the Tigris River after the highways had been sealed off. Between 0200 hours and 0330 hours on 26 April, a major firefight occurred between 1-22 IN and arms dealers around two farmhouses near the Tigris River. Five large caches of ammunition were captured that had been hidden in the fields for movement across the Tigris in canoes. It was during this fight that 1LT Osbaldo Orosco, platoon leader of the Quick Reaction Force (QRF) of C/1-22 IN, became the first KIA of the 4ID in Iraq. (Thirty-eight years earlier, on 5 September 1966, PFC Albert Collins, also of C/1-22 IN, became the first KIA of the 4ID in the Vietnam War).

In Samarra, 1-68 AR and 1-12 IN made their presence felt in and around the city. On 26 April, 1-12 IN entered the city, seizing control of the walled compound that housed the Ministry of Pharmaceuticals. B/1-12 occupied the Baath party headquarters. The next day, with 3BCT HQ taking over the ministry, 1-12 IN and 1-68 AR moved north and occupied another walled compound that housed an electronics plant. Bunkers were filled with top secret Iraqi documents, ammunition, and 55-gallon drums of unknown chemicals. 1-68 AR took out an Iraqi armed with an RPG as he ran from the compound. Hundreds of tools, and crates of brand new Russian radios, complete with manuals printed in February 2003, were found in the compound. Much of the heavy manufacturing equipment was hidden in bunkers outside the buildings in anticipation of their being bombed by coalition air forces. The tools and heavy equipment were used to make parts

that were in short supply—another example of GI ingenuity.

On 29 April, based on intelligence input, a 1-12 IN mission captured a high-ranking Fedayeen general. On 30 April, the scout platoon conducted a recon mission to Ad Dawr, the village where Saddam Hussein was captured almost eight months later. Day and night patrols and checkpoints were manned as the 4ID presence became stronger in Samarra. In Baqubah, 2BCT was similarly making their presence felt.

The Mississippi Six

In late April, 4ID HQ asked the 223rd Engineer Battalion out of West Point, MS to send a team to Tikrit to do an assessment of a blown up palace building. They wanted it as the 4ID/TF Ironhorse HQ. Four Soldiers from Company B arrived by helicopter to evaluate the damage. CSM Charles Fuss, the TF Ironhorse Command Sergeant Major, met the engineers, told them where they'd be staying, and what was needed. They had no tools or transportation to get around the massive base, consequently they walked everywhere. The blown out palace was too damaged to do anything with, so the Soldiers began turning on the power to the different buildings on the compound. After the remainder of the 223rd arrived at the Tikrit North airstrip, two more Soldiers were added—and the group was dubbed, "The Mississippi Six".

Every morning they would hold a meeting at the Water Palace with all the SGMs on post to determine what needed to be done to make it better for the Soldiers. SGM Cooley, CSM of 1-44 ADA, appreciatively known as the Mayor of FOB Ironhorse, would prioritize the needs and send the Mississippi Six out to do their job for the day. Initially the job was getting power and water to all the buildings. Everything was trial and error in the early days. The Iraqi electrical system was totally different from the United States—there were no electrical codes to go by. Tracking down which lines went where was long, tedious, and tiring work.

Eventually, TF Ironhorse hired several local Iraqi people who had worked on the palace complex before the war. One was an electrical engineer; one was an air conditioning/heating engineer; and the rest were workers who had specialties in different areas. These men were hard workers and helped the Mississippi Six immensely by knowing all the complexities of the palace compound's infrastructure. Friendships developed, and the Iraqi workers took great joy in explaining their way of life and customs while asking the Mississippi Six about life in the United States. After the basic electrical work was completed, they began work on the air conditioning systems allowing many Ironhorse Soldiers to sleep a little better each night.

When the Mississippi Six left FOB Ironhorse in mid February 2004, they left behind group of Iraqi friends and took with them memories of their time with TF Ironhorse that they will always be proud of.

Ironhorse Desert News

Ironhorse Desert News, the official weekly newsletter of TF Ironhorse, reported on the initial movement into Iraq:

Ironhorse Enters Iraq

Lead elements of the 4th Infantry Division (M) entered Iraq on the morning of April 14th before sunrise. The powerful formation was built around M1A2 Main Battle Tanks, M2A3 Bradley Fighting Vehicles, M270A1 MLRS Launchers, M109A6 Paladin Howitzers, OH-58D Kiowa Warrior helicopters, and AH-64D Longbow Apache helicopters. Also included were combat support and combat service support units to provide sustainment. The deep penetration into Iraq was made with Heavy Equipment Transports (HETs) hauling the tanks and other heavy combat equipment in order to save time and fuel. Although reconnaissance and coordination teams from the task force had been operating in Iraq since April 2nd, the recent movement marked the first introduction of significant combat power. The welcome entry of Task Force Ironhorse came on the heels of the fastest deployment and integration of a heavy division in history. The rapid, complex, and well-organized movement provides the coalition with flexibility to terminate hostilities and stabilize the country. Morale remains very high, and the task force is on track.

Ironhorse Secures Large Area of Operations (AO)

After rapidly and successfully completing reception, staging, onward movement, and integration (RSOI), Task Force Ironhorse has moved into Iraq and secured a large area of operations (AO) north of Baghdad. The AO includes three Iraqi provinces and is about the size of Louisiana. In most cases, our Ironhorse troopers were the first coalition troops that local citizens have come in contact with. Our Soldiers have performed spectacularly in a wide range of operations including the destruction of Iraqi military remnants, removing the shadow of the former regime, securing sensitive sites, and starting the reconstruction process in order to build a safe environment for Iraqis to raise their families. In a little over a month on the ground, the 4th Infantry Division has already had a significant impact improving the overall security and quality of life in Iraq by removing oppressive members of the former regime, opening schools, restoring electricity and power, and allowing basic freedoms for all people. Mail has made its way to our Soldiers... Unlike the blistering temperatures in Kuwait, the weather is a bit more mild and tolerable in northern Iraq. There are also some trees and vegetation...

President Bush's Speech on 1 May
On 1 May, from the aircraft carrier USS Abraham Lincoln in the Pacific Ocean off the California coast, President Bush spoke to the assembled sailors, airmen, Marines, and a worldwide TV audience. As far as the troops were concerned, it was a perfect summation of their mission, the military's in securing and reconstructing that country.

"In this battle, we have fought for the cause of liberty and for the peace of the world. Our nation and our coalition are proud of this accomplishment, yet it is you, the members of the United States military, who achieved it. Your courage, your willingness to face danger for your country and for each other made this day possible. Because of you our nation is more secure. Because of you the tyrant has fallen and Iraq is free...

"Operation Iraqi Freedom was carried out with a combination of precision and speed and boldness the enemy did not expect and the world had not seen before... You have shown the world the skill and the might of the American armed forces...

"Our mission continues. Al Qaida is wounded, not destroyed. The scattered cells of the terrorist network still operate in many nations and we know from daily intelligence that they continue to plot against free people. The proliferation of deadly weapons remains a serious danger.

"The enemies of freedom are not idle, and neither are we. Our government has taken unprecedented measures to defend the homeland and we will continue to hunt down the enemy before he can strike.

"The war on terror is not over, yet it is not endless. We do not know the day of final victory, but we have seen the turning of the tide. No act of the terrorists will change our purpose, or weaken our resolve, or alter their fate. Their cause is lost; free nations will press on to victory…"

As President Bush stated—even though the major combat operations against large Iraqi units was over, the Global War on Terror was not. The work of TF Ironhorse had just begun. During the coming weeks and months, the Soldiers of TF Ironhorse and other coalition forces would continue to be heavily engaged with our enemies in Iraq.

Not too long after the colors were cased at Fort Hood, 4ID Soldiers were displaying captured Iraqi flags as they entered the fight in Iraq

Two Soldiers from 1-8 IN with Bradley aboard HET, ready for convoy to Baghdad - April 2003

1st combat use of Shadow Unmanned Aerial Vehicle (UAV) - April 2003

Soldiers of 1-8 IN take control tower at Balad airfield - 17 April 2003

One of many buildings in palace complex of Saddam Hussein, Tikrit-became DMAIN of FOB Ironhorse

One of many ammunition storage areas captured by TF Ironhorse Soldiers

TF Ironhorse Soldier fabricating fighting position

VII

Getting Established, the First Weeks

Disarming the MEK, Elections in Kirkuk, Early missions, Engineer operations, Frustration on the home front, Operation Peninsula Strike, Final set

1 May 2003 to 15 June 2003

T ASK FORCE IRONHORSE SOLDIERS CONTINUED AT their feverish pace as April became May. All maneuver elements were engaged and support units worked around the clock to meet the new mission of the TF. Offensive and civil-military operations were based on the four pillars of the campaign plan: military, governance, infrastructure, and economy. Over the weeks and months ahead, TF Ironhorse would relentlessly pursue those objectives.

On April 29, in a late night mission in Samarra, a raiding party from 1-12 IN and the 3BCT scout troop snatched a high ranking Fedayeen Saddam leader in an attempt to quell mounting opposition among the local population. The raiding party consisted not of Bradleys and tanks, but of Ranger qualified Soldiers who performed the "snatch and grab" mission without a shot being fired. In Tikrit the next night, a raiding party from the 1-8 IN, heavily armed with five Bradley Fighting Vehicles surrounded a two-story villa in a neighborhood formerly reserved for Baath Party members. One of the Bradleys slammed through a 10-foot wall surrounding the compound. Forty infantrymen followed, swarmed the compound, and broke down the wooden door to the house. The result, according to COL Don Campbell, CO of 1BCT was: "The capture of a prominent Baath Party member who we suspect of trying to run a shadow regime. We're continuing to target locations for people that were associated with the regime who could provide us information on the top 55 most wanted list." Raids similar to these two would become commonplace as the strong offensive focus of TF Ironhorse adapted to the reality of Iraqi resistance becoming harder to find.

As they had done in Balad during the initial attack into the Sunni Triangle, the UAV Shadow's deployed by TF Ironhorse continued to provide valuable intelligence from the air. On 2 May, Soldiers killed three suspected Iraqi paramilitary fighters after a Shadow UAV spotted them taking mortar rounds from an ammunition cache. Two Apache attack helicopters from 4BCT, after firing warning shots at the vehicle, destroyed the truck. Secondary explosions from the burning vehicle indicated it was filled with ammunition. At another ammunition cache a few miles away, the Shadow spotted a group of pickup trucks being loaded with munitions. When Apaches fired warning shots, the men abandoned the vehicles. To insure the munitions didn't fall into the wrong hands, the trucks were destroyed by the Apaches with more secondary explosions indicating stolen ammunition was aboard. COL Campbell said, "We just sent them a message that we're not going to tolerate people trying to upload or steal ammunition." This, too, was to become common practice as TF Ironhorse started to make their presence felt.

Disarming the MEK

Starting in early May, TF Ironhorse conducted a political-military operation that included a series of delicate diplomatic talks with the leaders of the Mujahedeen-e Khalq (MEK). Reputed as the trainers of the Republican Guard, the MEK was a highly disciplined Iranian terrorist organization that had previously operated in central Iraq. The MEK consisted of an armored Division's worth of tanks, artillery, and armored personnel carriers concentrated at several camps in northeast Iraq. Working with Special Forces, the MEK leaders had agreed to a cease-fire when the war began. They were allowed to keep their weapons and moved to four camps northeast of Baqubah near Hamrin Lake where they would be safe from bombing by coalition warplanes. The camps, named in honor of their female leaders, were Camp Alevi, Camp Ashraf, Camp Zora, and Camp Zekari.

U.S. commanders had a challenge with the MEK's presence. They could not allow an organization that operated freely under Saddam Hussein and that was identified by the State Department as a terrorist organization to continue to operate in Iraq. The MEK commanders had an equally difficult task at hand. COL Fred Rudesheim, commander of 3BCT, recalls one of the female commanders telling him, "She said she had fought with them for twenty years, had seen a lot of her friends martyred, and this was the toughest thing she had done in her life." They also feared that turning over their weapons to coalition forces would leave them vulnerable to attack. The Badr Corps, an Iranian-backed Shiite militia, had been their adversary for years and was still moving freely in the area.

On Thursday, 8 May, before negotiations began, COL Rudesheim told the MEK commanders that his brigade would take control of the four areas occupied by their Soldiers before the end of the day. "We pressed to take control of those areas as soon as possible," said Rudesheim. "They asked if we could wait until Friday, and then I told them we would take over their areas in one hour. They looked surprised, but we did it." 1-8 IN (now back under command of 3BCT), 1-12 IN, and 1-68 AR moved quickly to locate the MEK positions, took control, and moved the MEK soldiers and equipment back into the camps. By evening, TF Ironhorse Soldiers manned the checkpoints vacated by the MEK. The takeover went smoothly as US and MEK troops mingled together without incident.

MG Odierno, on behalf of coalition forces, negotiated the MEK's disarmament and movement to protected locations. The agreement called for the MEK to move all their personnel to one of the military-controlled camps and to move their military vehicles to another camp. MG Odierno put the terms to the MEK simply, "Throw down your arms or be destroyed." The word "surrender" did not sit well with the MEK leaders. LTC Bill McDonald, PAO of TF Ironhorse said, "They agreed to come under our control, but the term surrender implies a fight, and they are saying there has not been a fight with the MEK." The question still remained unanswered as to what would happen to MEK members once they turned over their weapons.

Tense negotiations went on for three days. MG Odierno and his team maintained their firm, unwavering stance—disarm or be destroyed. Not knowing how things would go, MG Odierno had devised a signal to the troops surrounding the building where the meeting was held. If he came out, took off his Kevlar helmet and lit a cigar, it meant the talks had broken down and the 3BCT, with supporting gunship helicopters from 4BCT, were to destroy the MEK units. Fortunately, that signal was not required. After the

MEK leaders had the terminology in the document changed to something they could live with, they agreed to turn over their heavy equipment, move it to one camp, and then move their personnel to another camp. TF Ironhorse personnel would guard both camps.

3BCT Soldiers immediately began the disarming process. All MEK vehicles were inspected to insure no ammunition was left in the tanks and other armored vehicles. The troops, over 4,000 strong, kept their personal weapons and began the movement to Camp Ashraf, north of Baqubah. 1-8 IN escorted the vehicles and equipment toward Camp Alevi. Along the way, responsibility was turned over to 2-8 IN and 2BCT. Task Force 3-67 AR secured Camp Ashraf. A/3-67 AR maintained security of the camp perimeter during the rest of the time TF Ironhorse was in Iraq. 2-8 IN took command and control of the vehicles and moved them to Camp Alevi, soon to be renamed FOB Normandy. Over 2,100 MEK tanks, armored personnel carriers, artillery pieces, air defense artillery guns, and miscellaneous vehicles were soon lined up inside FOB Normandy, and the MEK munitions were destroyed.

When the MEK agreed to disarm, agreements were made to allow them to continue contact outside of their camps. Gradually, however, coalition forces limited their ability to talk outside of the walls of Camp Ashraf. First, the logistical support the MEK was continuing for itself was cut off and replaced by US logistics. Later, the MEK radio tower that transmitted propaganda across the border to Iran was shutdown. The blackout of the MEK radio tower was a time of high tension for the leadership of 2BCT. It was feared the MEK would see this as the last straw and resist the shutdown. The responsibility to quell any opposition from the MEK was placed on the shoulders of the Warhorse Brigade.

After much preparation and intelligence gathering, 2BCT Soldiers surrounded Camp Ashraf. With an overwhelming show of force, the message of the shutdown was delivered. Immediately after the MEK leadership was informed of the shutdown, Soldiers of 2BCT dismantled the radio transmitter. Due to professionalism of the Soldiers of the Warhorse Brigade, the operation was completed without incident—no shots were fired.

173rd Airborne Operations in Kirkuk
Kirkuk is in the At Tamin province, part of the northern third of

70

the Sunni Triangle. These 25,000 square miles of battle space was what the 173rd Airborne Brigade called home for one year. It is the most ethnically and religiously diverse region in Iraq. Turkomen, Kurds, Assyrians, and Arabs all call this area home; claim that they are the majority, and that they have been discriminated against at some point in time during their history. Christians and Sunni and Shia Muslims all claim religiously significant places, martyrs, and prophets from this area. In short, the task to convince all parties, with very divergent goals, to work together—with and for one another—to establish functional and effective democratic governments and institutions fell squarely upon the shoulders of the Sky Soldiers.

Kirkuk and its outlying cities and villages were one of the first in Iraq to hold provincial elections. The Brigade initially worked in Kirkuk to establish fully functioning institutions and then quickly and deliberately moved out into the hinterlands of the battle space to bring democracy, stability, and security to the other cities and villages.

Establishing an elective government in Kirkuk was not an easy task. Bitter infighting among the ethnic groups marred the election process. Former Baath party leaders were excluded from the group of selected council members. COL Mayville and MG Odierno were personally involved to insure the process worked. Despite street fighting caused by ethnic tensions in Kirkuk and the nearby village of Huwayjah, the elections were held and a Kurd was elected as mayor in late May.

To reinforce the 173rd Airborne Brigade during this tense period, the 3BCT moved up to provide their armored strength around the outskirts of Kirkuk. When the 3BCT moved south in early June to conduct Operation Peninsula Strike, 1-12 IN (-) and C/1-68 AR stayed in the Kirkuk area for the remainder of the deployment as part of the 173rd Airborne TF.

1st Brigade Combat Team Operations in Salah Ad Din Province
With the end of major combat operations, 1BCT entered a phase of the war where the enemy was defined as trying to maintain low-grade resistance in order to break U.S. resolve. They made efforts to do so by using guerilla-type tactics, conducting attacks by fire, in the form of improvised explosive devices (IEDs), mines, mortars, rockets, RPGs, and drive-by shootings. They also

conducted anti-coalition and anti-American demonstrations and heavily influenced locals with coercion and propaganda. These enemy tactics and strategies forced 1BCT to alter traditional doctrine and initiate the analysis of conducting linkages of individuals responsible for conducting the attacks, those funding the attacks, and those coordinating the attacks.

Over the course of the remainder of Operation Iraqi Freedom I, 1BCT conducted a number of raids and offensives in order to defeat the resistance, and to kill or capture those leading operations against coalition forces. The only way to defeat this enemy was to conduct a thorough linkage of key players, conduct raids and operations, and remain on the offensive.

On 6 May, TF Regulars (1-22 IN) relieved 1-8 IN of its tactical requirements within the city of Tikrit, two additional ammunition supply points, and towns and villages south in the AOR. It tripled its area of operations and assumed responsibility for Tikrit proper, the heart of Saddam's loyalists. The TF immediately began to develop valuable intelligence information and to conduct raids against Fedayeen members, High Value Targets (HVT), bodyguards, and other anti-coalition forces.

On 15 May, TF Regulars, the 1BCT main effort for "Operation Planet X", conducted a brigade level cordon and search as the assault force and raided multiple targets within Ad Dawr, capturing #52 on the "Top 55" most wanted list. It executed the operation with its full complement of infantrymen, as all organic infantry companies comprised the task organization. May's rollup included three additional blacklisted individuals and one enemy killed in action with no task force casualties.

On the night of 7 June, TF Regulars aggressively repulsed a coordinated enemy RPG, automatic weapons, and small arms fire attack against its Civil Military Integration Cell (CMIC). The Regulars repulsed the attack, wounding two and later capturing four assailants. Its defense was not without cost as one Regular lost his life and four others were wounded in action.

Further north, TF Lancer (3-66 AR) rapidly secured all key sites and infrastructure in the Bayji area of operations to prevent their use by paramilitary and noncompliant forces. These sites included a former regime Presidential Palace and VIP facilities, a Special Republican Guard barracks, a fertilizer plant, an oil refinery, a thermal power plant, and a water treatment facility.

The oil refinery is the second largest in Iraq and provided oil for Kirkuk, Tikrit, Mosul, and Baghdad. The power plant provided power to most of the Salah Ad Din province and Baghdad. Frequent patrols, raids, and checkpoints conducted by the infantry, armor, engineer, and MP elements of TF Lancer kept the enemy off balance and away from these critical resources.

Earlier, TF Lancer had secured a 32 square kilometer ammunition storage depot near Bayji known as Objective Arlington and prevented its use by noncompliant forces. TF Lancer continued security of Objective Arlington until relieved by 14 EN BN.

TF Iron Knight (1-66 AR), after operating for three weeks with 101st Airmobile Division in the Mosul area with the mission of destroying enemy forces; consolidating and destroying abandoned ammunition; and assisting in the distribution of benzene and propane, returned to control of 1BCT and established itself in Samarra on 6 May. C/1-66 AR, with an attached infantry platoon from 1-22 IN, remained in Mosul with the 101st for the remainder of the deployment. The mission in Samarra was to destroy enemy forces, disrupt illegal arms markets, protect a hydroelectric dam and petroleum pumping stations, and conduct civil military operations. On 18 May, enemy attacks increased and armored patrols in the city and surrounding area drastically increased to locate the insurgent forces. Numerous weapons were captured and destroyed.

In response to increased coalition presence in the area, enemy forces began increasing and improving guerilla operations against coalition forces in Tikrit. The enemy's tactics of choice solidified into mortar attacks on fixed sites and armed ambushes on friendly convoys. The enemy soon selected east Tikrit as one of its primary operating areas for mortar attacks because it allowed for a clear line of sight to direct mortar and rocket fire into concentrated American forces on the DMAIN complex. The Tigris River provided a significant boundary that American armored forces could not cross to respond to these attacks. Additionally, the terrain on the east side provided orchards and wooded terrain for the enemy to hide in; an urban area and population to blend into; and a significant road network that facilitated rapid movement into and out of the area. In response to this threat, the Brigade Reconnaissance Troop, G/10 CAV, assumed an AOR east of Tikrit and across the Tigris River. The mission was to gain and maintain contact with the enemy, kill or capture him, destroy his weapons and ammunition caches, and conduct aggressive patrols to reduce or stop the enemy attacks.

2nd Brigade Operations in Diyala Province

The Warhorse Brigade served in an area roughly the size of New Jersey and also one of the most diverse provinces in Iraq. In Diyala, there was a healthy mix of Shia as well as Sunni Arabs. In northern Diyala, TF 2-8 IN had to deal with the added issue of the Kurdish presence as well. Essentially, the elements of the Warhorse Brigade sat on several religious, ethnic, and tribal "fault lines." As a result, the region was fraught with tension that spans back for generations. Motives were not always as they appeared. Every coalition action had far-reaching social, political, religious, tribal, and ethnic implications. That served to significantly complicate conducting operations in Diyala.

The terrain of Diyala was diverse as well. There were river valleys that were thick with palm groves so that only foot traffic was possible. In the intense heat of Iraq, searching and clearing the palm groves of weapons caches proved a daunting task, as these became a favored hiding spot for insurgents. Another key item in the terrain of Iraq was canal systems. They ran all over Iraq to deliver water to an agriculturally based economy. They also served as an obstacle since most of the bridges over these canals could not support the Brigade's vehicles. Elsewhere in Diyala were wide-open desert areas and mountainous ridges, all with a variety of villages and a poorly maintained road system to negotiate. These villages and cities constituted the "key terrain" and the center of gravity to be dealt with by 2BCT.

For the Soldiers of TF Warhorse, major combat operations did not end when the regime collapsed—they were just beginning. The initial phases of the war in March and April, characterized by deep penetrations north by US mechanized brigades, were replaced by constant skirmishes with an insurgent force that refused the decisive fight. Former regime loyalists, criminals, and fundamentalists relying on guerilla tactics characterized the emerging threat in Iraq. Improvised Explosive Devices (IEDs) planted along roadways, hasty ambushes of logistical convoys, and standoff attacks by mortars and rockets soon became the norm in the region. The Soldiers of TF Warhorse conducted numerous operations in the form of raids, cordon and searches, combat patrols and show-of-force patrols.

Patrols worked in and around the city of Baqubah as MG Ray Odierno and COL Dennis Rogers, 2BCT commander, met with sheiks to discuss the future of the city and surrounding area. A committee of ten local sheiks, nominated by their peers, became the direct line of communication to Rogers. A curfew, from 2300 hours to 0400 hours, to keep people who would do wrong away from those who wanted to obey the laws was enacted. Gun permits were required to carry firearms. Anyone carrying a weapon without a permit was arrested and the weapon confiscated. Missions continued to locate and eliminate enemy weapons and ammunition caches throughout the Diyala Province.

Soon after the Warhorse Brigade established its foothold in the Diyala province, the insurgent forces discovered that attacking Warhorse Soldiers by direct fire was not often survivable. The trend then shifted to firing mortars and, later, rockets from a distance where they were not under direct observation and believed they could escape after firing. FOB Warhorse, home to the Brigade Headquarters and 204th FSB, received the brunt of the enemy's mortars followed closely by FOB Normandy, the home of 2-8 IN in Muqdadiyah. However that is not to say that other FOBs were spared these attacks, as all FOBs were at different times attacked by these methods. All TF Warhorse elements had to implement a plan to mitigate these threats.

The model for the counter-mortar fight developed through predictive analysis of when and from where the enemy would shoot. Discovering their firing positions at first glance was seemingly impossible due to the open terrain and numerous escape routes into villages. A mortar firer could shoot and then blend into the populace of a village before Soldiers could react. Then it was a practice in denying key terrain, while watching over other territory. All electronic surveillance sensors available, along with maximum use of the Brigade's Unmanned Aerial Vehicles (UAV) conducted overwatch. On occasion, by having the UAV in the air at the right time and place, the Brigade Commander and staff were actually able to observe terrorists preparing to set up and fire mortars at FOB Warhorse and successfully engaged and destroyed them before they could launch a single round.

Terrain could be denied by firing harassment and interdictory (H&I) fires into a point of origin of a past mortar attack or by providing visible presence patrols in the area. Efforts were made to work with the populace as well. Iraqi farmers certainly did not want their fields to be torn up by U.S. artillery, which was the certain result of their fields being used as a firing point for insurgents. These farmers, as well as the Sheiks who claimed responsibility for the areas, were held accountable for any attacks originating from their properties. Bravo Battery, 3-16 FA provided the counter-battery fire along with battalion mortars. Through keeping a "hot gun" ready during the peak hours for mortar activity, they were able to put steel on target. Insurgents soon realized that they had very limited time to fire mortars before they would be the recipients of like treatment from TF Warhorse. The terrorists then tried to drop a few rounds and egress back into the safety of the villages, but found that egress routes from their firing points were also the targets of TF Warhorse artillery, leaving no escape. The Warhorse Brigade became very successful in the counter-mortar fight, resulting in drastically reducing the number and effectiveness of enemy mortar attacks.

Engineers at Work
Each of the three maneuver BCTs had its own organic Engineer unit—299th Engineers in 1BCT, 588th Engineers in 2BCT, and 4th Engineers in 3BCT. These organic units were deployed with each battalion within the BCT and provided the immediate engineer support in neutralizing, securing, or demolition of captured ammunition. They also participated in raids, road security, construction projects, and river patrols.

TF Ironhorse was augmented by the 555th Engineer Group (TF Able) headquartered in Fort Lewis, Washington and composed of active duty, National Guard and Reserve units from around the United States and Germany.

Bridging became a high priority mission throughout northern Iraq to allow freedom of movement for military operations. As TF Ironhorse moved into Tikrit, the 565th Engineer Battalion immediately began emplacing an Assault Float Bridge (AFB) across the Tigris to replace the fixed bridge that was damaged during combat operations. This AFB was the longest float bridge ever emplaced during combat operations in military history.

In late May, when the Tigris River was at its peak height, the bridge required 18 bridge erection boats to hold it in place against the swift current. The 14th Engineer Battalion was given the very challenging mission of constructing and maintaining the causeways that allowed vehicles to access the bridge. They designed the causeways using culverts and material to combat the erosion effects of the river. Soon after the AFB was emplaced, the 565th Engineer Battalion constructed two Mabey-Johnson Compact 200 bridges to span the 40-meter and 80-meter gaps in the damaged fixed bridge allowing both civilian and military traffic to cross.

Force protection upgrades at FOB Speicher soon became a TF Able priority as more units arrived and began to set up living and operations areas. The 223rd and 14th Engineer Battalions built a perimeter berm, constructed bunkers, fighting positions, guard towers, and a front gate with vehicle inspection area. Additionally, they repaired the existing perimeter fence. Buildings and structures along the perimeter that could be used as enemy hiding positions were destroyed.

The 244th, 223rd, and 14th Engineer Battalions all conducted road construction and repair work, ranging from patching of potholes to surveying an area for the construction of a new road network. The maintenance of Main Supply Routes (MSR) and Alternate Supply Routes (ASR) was a high priority. This assured the mobility of military convoys, as well as an avenue of movement for Iraqi civilians. Construction teams were formed to conduct major repairs to Route 1, the lifeline of Iraq, and the creation of new roads in desolate areas.

TF Able made the largest impact by constructing Forward Operating Bases (FOBs) for units in TF Ironhorse. FOBs, where US Army units live, are used as a staging area to launch operations. Their size ranged from company to battalion to brigade task force, holding from 150 to over 2,000 Soldiers. These FOBs were built in proximity of where the unit had responsibility to maintain peace and order. If a unit needed to respond to a situation or conduct operations such as raids or ambushes in a given area, the FOB provided a protected area in remote and dangerous locations to prepare for and launch missions.

Early during Operation Iraqi Freedom I, these FOBs started off as simple camps with tents, protected by berms that encircled

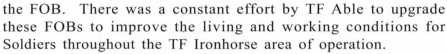
the FOB. There was a constant effort by TF Able to upgrade these FOBs to improve the living and working conditions for Soldiers throughout the TF Ironhorse area of operation.

The force protection of the TF Ironhorse Soldiers was a top priority in every mission that TF Able executed. One of the first missions TF Able received from the division was the destruction of an enemy mortar position in the Tikrit Hotel, used to target the TF Ironhorse headquarters. On 1 May, the 14th Engineer Battalion brought down the hotel that was formerly used as the headquarters for Saddam Hussein's Special Security Organization (SSO), an internal secret police organization under the direction of Hussein's son Uday. The demolition plan, requiring over 3,000 pounds of C-4, was developed by the 14th Engineer Battalion and verified by the Forward Engineer Support Team.

The force protection at FOBs was implemented during every phase of construction. The perimeter berm and fence prevented the access of enemy vehicles and personnel. Guard towers, fighting positions, and bunkers protected Soldiers from both direct and indirect fire. Living areas were protected from direct and indirect fires by HESCO bastions, concrete barrier walls, and sandbag walls. Even small details like the taping of windows to prevent injury from glass shards were not overlooked.

As TF Ironhorse pushed north into Bayji in late April, two large ammo depots were discovered. These sites, later named OBJ Tinderbox and OBJ Arlington, contained literally millions of pounds of enemy munitions that had to be secured and kept out of the hands of the Saddam loyalists. 1-10 CAV and 3-66 AR occupied both sites, approximately 30 kilometers from each other, until the 14th Engineer Battalion moved north to relieve them of the crucial security mission. During their occupation of OBJ Arlington and Tinderbox, the 14th Engineer Battalion made many improvements in both the life support area and the security posture. The Soldiers went from living next to their vehicles out of their rucksacks, to tents, and finally to refurbished buildings or containerized housing units. Security improvements included a perimeter fence, perimeter lighting, and guard towers. After all the munitions were carefully inventoried, the 14th Engineer Battalion began to sytematically destroy selected munitions at both sites. At OBJ Tinderbox, B Co. 5th Engineer Battalion screened, hired, and trained an Iraqi EOD team that made a great contribution to the mission with the destruction of tens of thousands of pounds of munitions.

The 5th Engineer Battalion, task organized under TF Gunner, also played a crucial role in the security of the Taji ammunition holding area located just north of Baghdad. This holding area served as the collection site for all captured enemy ammunition found in the southern sectors of the TF Ironhorse AO. The engineers served in a security role and provided demolition expertise in the destruction of ammunition.

Frustration on the Home Front

Mail and electronic communications from TF Ironhorse Soldiers were very spotty during the first two months after they left Kuwait. Loved ones at home became frustrated at the lack of mail and the absence of email. Although email was limited while they were in Kuwait, there was enough access that the rear detachment and Family Readiness Groups (FRG) could keep the families informed of what was happening. With the move into Iraq, communications virtually ceased.

The mail pipelines could not keep up with the great influx of American troops into Iraq. Well meaning Americans sent unsolicited mail and packages, which added to the problem. Mail to and from loved ones was seriously delayed in the system. TF Ironhorse Soldiers were equally frustrated with the slowness of regular mail and the absence of email and phones to call home. Technological breakthroughs over the past several years had spoiled both Soldiers and family members to almost instantaneous communications with loved ones.

Rear detachment personnel and FRG leaders caught the brunt of the frustration from those left at home. Whenever they heard any word from Iraq, they quickly passed it on to those on their electronic distribution lists and on their phone calling lists. On 18 May, this author saw many notes of anguish from TF Ironhorse family members on the guest book of the National 4th Infantry Division Association web site. (www.4thinfantry.org).

On that day, I began an electronic newsletter, "4ID Update From Iraq," where I passed on all information I could find from internet searches, from family members who had heard from their Soldier, and from various other sources to family members. This grew until it became a key communications link for family and friends, and Soldiers, for the remainder of the deployment. The mantra that started then was, "No news is good news, because bad news travels fast." And that was essentially true—casualty information did make it through the system without delay.

Embedded Media

The war in Iraq was an information based war as much as it was direct action against an armed enemy. The perception of people around the world about what was happening in Iraq was tempered by the perception that the press provided. Leaders and Soldiers learned quickly to understand the impacts of instant reporting and communications. Media and enemy propaganda were conditions of the battlefield.

By early May, most of the media personnel who had accompanied TF Ironhorse units from the US had either voluntarily returned home or were called home by their employers. It became obvious that the training done for the media at Fort Hood had been a worthwhile effort. No major incidents had occurred with the media who had been trained and were embedded from the States through the early stages of the deployment. When the embedded media left, their void was filled by a new set of media. Many of these were "drop by" media who stopped in for a day or so and then moved on. International media from friend and foe parts of the world became a part of the daily routine of TF Ironhorse.

MG Odierno fully understood the power and value of information. He insured that his staff and unit commanders all continued to provide strong and positive support to the media for the duration of the deployment. Daily press updates became the norm for the PAO team of TF Ironhorse. Press conferences were held frequently. Attempts were made to honor as many of the requests for interviews with specific people as was possible. Video teleconference updates with the Pentagon press were held when the situation warranted it.

The final embedded reporter to return home, in mid June, was Ed Timms of the Dallas Morning News. He lived, worked, and reported daily on the actions of G Troop, 10th Cavalry—the 1BCT Reconnaissance Troop. Often when there were no other daily reports available, Ed was reporting positively on his favorite cavalry troop.

3BCT in Operation Peninsula Strike – 9-12 June 2003

During the early morning hours of 9 June, TF Ironhorse Soldiers conducted raids to eradicate Baath Party loyalists, paramilitary groups and other subversive elements located on a peninsula along the Tigris River, northeast of Balad. The raids signaled the start of Operation Peninsula Strike.

The operation took place in two major stages. The first stage of the operation involved moving Soldiers and equipment into strike positions, intelligence gathering, and coordination with local police. During the second stage, raids were conducted within the area of operation via land, air and water to capture or destroy subversive elements. Air assault teams, ground attack squads, raid teams, river patrol boats and local security combined forces to block escape routes and operate checkpoints to ensure success.

Operation Peninsula Strike incorporated a variety of units, utilizing the overwhelming firepower and effects of a joint and combined arms team. Army infantry, armor, artillery, aviation, and engineers, along with Air Force elements worked together to accomplish the mission. Thousands of Soldiers from 3BCT, 173rd Airborne Brigade and 3rd Squadron, 7th Cavalry Regiment, 3rd Infantry Division were involved in the operation.

When it ended on 12 June, Operation Peninsula Strike had captured 377 detainees and seized numerous weapon systems and ammunition. The seizure of illegal weapons was in support of the National Weapons Policy implemented on 1 June. Four Soldiers and two hostile civilians were wounded during the operation.

Specially trained Soldiers screened the detainees to determine who would be released or who would be retained for questioning. The Soldiers also collected information which might lead to the apprehension of hostile groups who continued to commit acts of violence against coalition forces and the Iraqi people. The information also assisted coalition forces in providing a safe and secure environment for the Iraqi people. Two former Iraqi generals turned themselves in during the raids. MG Abul Ali Jasmin, Secretary of Defense Ministry and BG Abdullah Ali Jasmin, Head of the Iraqi Military Academy were detained.

Operation Peninsula Strike's success was a significant step forward in the ongoing journey of TF Ironhorse toward a safe, secure, and free Iraq.

Final Set

By the middle of June, TF Ironhorse units had become settled into what would, for the most part, be their permanent locations for the remainder of the deployment. Locations that were only unknown spots on a map a few weeks earlier were now the home and place of work for over 32,000 TF Ironhorse Soldiers. This permanence enabled the Soldiers to become familiar with the terrain, the enemy situation, the local citizens, and the rebuilding challenges. Each commander and Soldier knew the focus that was required in their AOR on the four pillars of the campaign plan: military, governance, infrastructure, and economy.

The largest concentration of forces was in the northeast section of the TF Ironhorse AOR. 1BCT (known as TF Raider) was responsible for Salah Ad Din province with its major population centers of Tikrit, Bayji, and Samarra. 1-22 IN, with C/3-66 AR attached, had responsibility for Saddam's hometown of Tikrit and the surrounding area. 4-42 FA secured an AO to the east side of the Tigris River around Tikrit. 3-66 AR, with B/1-22 IN attached, worked in and around the key oil center of Bayji. Samarra was home for 1-66 AR. In July, when 3BCT assumed responsibility for Samarra, 1-66 AR was attached to them for the remainder of the deployment. 299 EN and 4 FSB operated as key components of the combat teams.

DMAIN, consisting of 4ID/TF Ironhorse headquarters and supporting elements, was located in the Saddam Palace Complex, now called FOB Ironhorse, along the Tigris River on the south side of Tikrit. 1BCT HQ was located adjacent to FOB Ironhorse in FOB Raider.

FOB Speicher, on the north side of Tikrit, became a major supply, engineer, and aviation base. It was the home for 4BCT's (known as TF Iron Eagles) aviation units, 1-4 AVN, 2-4 AVN, and 204 FSB. 4ID Support Command or DISCOM (known as TF Wranglers), also called FOB Speicher home, as did 64 CSG and 555 EN GRP (known as TF Able). Units of these commands worked throughout the TF Ironhorse AO. Many Soldiers lived with the BCT they supported unless they were on one of their frequent trips to provide supplies and support to the TF.

Diyala province, to the southeast, was the responsibility of 2BCT (TF Warhorse). Major population centers were Baqubah, Muqdadiyah, Jalula, and Kifri. 1-67 AR, with B/2-8 IN attached, and 3-67 AR (-) had responsibility for the major city of Baqubah and its surrounding villages. FOB Warhorse, in Baqubah, was also home for 2BCT HQ. 2-8 IN, with A/1-67 AR attached established FOB Normandy in Muqdadiya, 45-kilometers northeast of Baqubah. They had responsibility for over 4,000 square kilometers of countryside in addition to providing security for the MEK equipment at FOB Normandy. C/2-8 IN moved 60 kilometers further north and established FOB Cobra in the town of Jalula. 3-16 FA established FOB Thunder in Rashidiyah, a Shia city that was essentially the doorway between Baghdad and the Diyala province. 588 EN had engineering responsibility for Baqubah as well as supporting 2-8 IN with a company in Muqdadiya. 204 FSB provided support all across the province. 1-10 CAV spent much of the year screening the border between Iran and Iraq, in the eastern part of Diyala province.

Taji and the surrounding area, on the southwestern corner of the TF Ironhorse AO, became the responsibility of TF Gunner, commanded by COL Kevin Stramara, Division Artillery (DIVARTY) commander. This major Iraqi air base, military complex, and ammunition storage point was the entry point from Baghdad into the TF Ironhorse AO. In addition to 2-20 FA and B/1-44 ADA, TF Gunner was comprised of 5th Engineers, B/1-171 IN from the Oklahoma National Guard, two chemical companies, an explosive ordnance demolition company, a Special Forces platoon from Macedonia, and various other units that flowed in and out of the TF.

In At Tamim province, in the oil rich and ethnically diverse northeast part of the TF Ironhorse AO, was the 173rd Airborne Brigade (known as TF Bayonet). Major cities included Kirkuk, Huwayjah, and Tuz. TF Bayonet consisted of 2-503 IN, 1-508 IN, TF 1-63 AR, and supporting units. 1-12 IN (-) along with C/1-68 AR were permanently attached from 3BCT to become key components of TF Bayonet from mid May forward.

Although it was July before they permanently settled into place, the 3BCT took on the critical area around the major support and air base of Balad, known as FOB Anaconda, and the key city of Samarra along the main supply route to Tikrit and points north. The 3BCT was headquartered, along with the 1-8 IN and the 1-68 AR, at FOB Anaconda. The 1-66 AR, in Samarra, was attached to 3BCT from 1BCT.

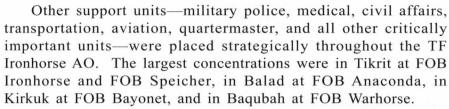

Other support units—military police, medical, civil affairs, transportation, aviation, quartermaster, and all other critically important units—were placed strategically throughout the TF Ironhorse AO. The largest concentrations were in Tikrit at FOB Ironhorse and FOB Speicher, in Balad at FOB Anaconda, in Kirkuk at FOB Bayonet, and in Baqubah at FOB Warhorse.

As the heat soared in June, the Soldiers of TF Ironhorse were settling in and making their presence felt. In an interview with MSG Debra Bingham of the Task Force Ironhorse public affairs office, COL James Barclay, TF Ironhorse Chief of Staff, said: "While the major fighting of the war appears to be over, combat operations continue. Our mission also includes civil affairs operations.

"The BCTs also continue to find, secure and consolidate or destroy weapons caches they are locating on a daily basis across the countryside. We still have a huge paramilitary presence that we're working to make sure we have under control. Every night we're having small engagements with anywhere from five to ten to fifteen man groups who are setting up ambushes and making sniper attacks on convoys.

"Every BCT has a Civilian Affairs (CA) support team, which they direct on day-to-day operations. The teams go into the communities to see what is working and what needs to be repaired. As we move into stability operations and begin working the larger civil affairs projects, we've got to work within the population centers. This means aligning the BCTs so they accomplish their civil affairs objectives.

"We also have support teams aligned around functional areas; agriculture, medical, education, and commerce. We move them around to do assessments and give us direction of where we need to go. The teams focus on public safety, city government, water, sewage, and power sources. In many cases they have also provided guidance and resources to help re-open banks, schools and hospitals.

"Members of the 555th Combat Engineer Group restored water and electricity at the Tikrit Hospital and plan more repairs in the future. The engineers also repaired a water treatment plant and continue to work with locals to maintain it. The Task Force has also donated supplies to hospitals and fuel to run generators and they've rebuilt bridges and repaired roads damaged during the war.

"In Tikrit, we have joint patrols with 1-22 Infantry and the MPs (Military Police) and local police force working together. We have several different levels of operations going on at the same time: patrolling in countryside, in towns.

"The information the CA teams gather is relayed on to higher headquarters at V Corps and to the Office of Reconstruction and Humanitarian Assistance (ORHA,) where a needs assessment is done, then projects are prioritized and funded. Jobs are created for local citizens who are hired on to do the work, which in turn helps stimulate the economy.

"There are still lots of tasks to be done and a long way to go, but once a permissive (safe) environment is established, outside agencies and teams will come in and work with the Iraqis to rebuild the country."

FOB Normandy

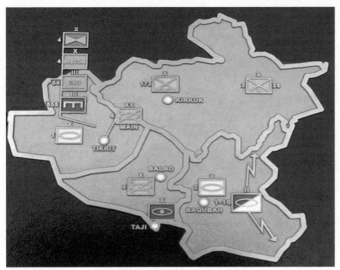

**Final set of
TF Ironhorse in
Sunni Triangle**

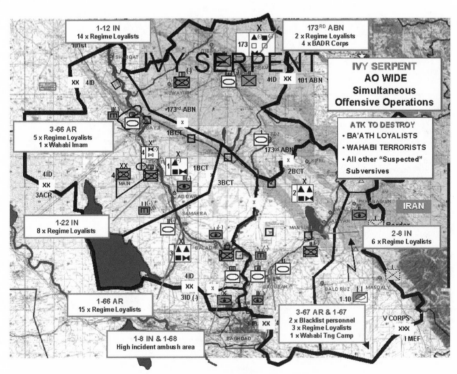

Map - Operation Ivy Serpent

3BCT escorting MEK vehicles to Camp Alevi - later called FOB Normandy

4ID Band in Colors uncasing ceremony at FOB Ironhorse in Tikrit - May 2003

Palletized Load System (PLS) helped TF Ironhorse get established

TF Ironhorse engineers building bridge across Tigris River at Tikrit

TF Ironhorse Soldiers patrolling on the Tigris River

VIII

Making Our Presence Felt

Taking the fight to the enemy, Operation Desert Scorpion, Operation
Sidewinder, Civil military operations
15 June 2003 to 5 July 2003

O FFENSIVE MILITARY ACTIONS, COUPLED WITH
meaningful work to help the Iraqi people rebuild their
country became a standard that TF Ironhorse lived by.
Day and night raids, constant patrols, roadside checkpoints, and
intelligence gathering kept the pressure on non-compliant forces.
At the same time, all units within TF Ironhorse did whatever was
required to help the Iraqi people begin overcoming the decades
of repression under Saddam Hussein.

Operation Desert Scorpion – 15-29 June
Early on the morning of 15 June, TF Ironhorse units launched
Operation Desert Scorpion in support of Combined Joint Task
Force Seven's nationwide offensive. The operation was designed
to continue to isolate and defeat remaining pockets of resistance
that were delaying the transition to a peaceful and stable Iraq.
Over twenty simultaneous raids were conducted to remove
terrorists, Baath Party loyalists, and other subversive elements
from selected areas in Tikrit, Bayji, Kirkuk, Samarra, Baqubah,
and several other locations in central and northern Iraq. Rotary
and fixed wing aircraft, patrol boats, M1 Abrams tanks, Bradley
Fighting Vehicles, and combat Soldiers combined their efforts in
brigade and battalion level strikes.

Although Coalition Forces had defeated Saddam's regime,
criminals and terrorist groups vying for power in the new Iraq
continued to attempt to undermine coalition efforts by attacking
Soldiers and innocent civilians throughout the region. The groups
consisted of the leadership of the defeated Iraqi Army, who were
paying criminals and foreign terrorists to attack coalition forces.
The remaining Fedayeen, former Baath Party hardliners and

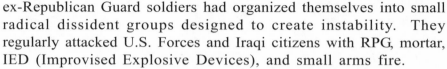

ex-Republican Guard soldiers had organized themselves into small radical dissident groups designed to create instability. They regularly attacked U.S. Forces and Iraqi citizens with RPG, mortar, IED (Improvised Explosive Devices), and small arms fire.

The goals of the operation were to neutralize subversive elements in designated cities in central and northern Iraq while simultaneously conducting actions to improve the quality of life for Iraqi citizens. TF Ironhorse programs were designed to encourage economic growth and job development, vital to helping Iraq rebuild. Unit commanders used dedicated funds to hire local labor and provide furniture and supplies to schools, hospitals, government administration offices and police stations. These projects put money back into the local economy and moved toward establishing a permissive and secure environment.

Forty-seven raids over the first three days of the operation netted numerous weapons caches, including AK-47s, hand grenades, night vision goggles, flares, C4 explosives, 90mm guns, 60mm mortars and assorted ammunition. Over 320 detainees were taken into custody. The raids were carefully planned on the basis of information obtained by intelligence sources and were directed at specific individuals who were suspected of being terrorists, Fedayeen members, and former Baath Party hardliners suspected of attacking Soldiers and innocent civilians.

Projects aimed at repairing infrastructure were conducted as part of Operation Desert Scorpion. These projects included: updates to the Huwayiah Sewage Cleaning Project; repairs and upgrades at Bayji Hospital; new furniture for the Balad Police Department; repairs to the Taji City Council Building and the Kirkuk Agricultural Bank; and upgrades to the Gahadayah Public Well Water site.

An early morning raid on 18 June delivered a major financial defeat to the enemy. Soldiers from 1-22 IN conducted two raids on separate farmhouses outside of Tikrit, seizing over eight million US dollars, millions of Iraqi Dinar, a large sum of British pounds, and Euros. Other items seized in the raid were expensive jewels and gems. Russian-made night vision goggles, a sniper rifle, and uniforms and equipment of Saddam's personal guard rounded out this significant accomplishment. They also detained 15-20 individuals associated with Saddam's Special Security Forces.

LTC Steve Russell, CO of 1-22 IN, described the raid and

previous successes in Tikrit in his email journal to family and friends: "... The curfew was strictly enforced in Tikrit—a city of approximately 75,000. Those caught out after the curfew were rounded up in the local soccer stadium where we employed them as a trash detail the next morning to help keep Tikrit beautiful (an optimistic task at best). The effect was immediate as the locals had no desire for such work and the streets were eerily empty during subsequent nights. We then focused our efforts to grab the initiative like a stick and beat the enemy with it. For the last week we have had great cooperation from the local government and police.

"Our own efforts have focused on hostile activities. Using multiple simultaneous raids, we have captured a number of important individuals that led us to bigger fish. By now you all have heard that #4 was captured here in Tikrit on the night of 16 June. Our men performed superbly and worked in cooperation with special operations forces. We also spoiled an attack on our market and our flash checkpoints from C Company captured fourteen armed men with AK-47s in the space of an hour and a half. Information from raids and pressure on people we detained led us to the info for #4's capture and culminated this week with the raids on the Hadooshi farm on the night of the 17th.

"The Hadooshi's were believed to be personal bodyguards of Saddam Hussein. It was here TF 1-22 IN seized AK-47s, night vision and surveillance equipment, sniper weapons, global position equipment and large amounts of ammunition—not your typical farm implements. But the biggest catch of all at the farm was $8,303,000 in US cash and another $1 million worth of Iraqi currency. We also found an estimated $2 million worth of jewelry belonging to the wife of Saddam Hussein.

"I had never seen such cash or treasure in my life. It simply boggles the mind. Our men preformed magnificently and our recon platoon leader, 1LT Chris Morris, ensured our great success with his quick actions at the farm. He decided to take the farm with his scouts even though we intended to maneuver additional force there. The activity at the farm called for immediate action. The element of surprise and the discipline of our men carried the day. CPT Mark Stouffer's A Company struck gold with a captured top-ranking Republican Guard officer and also one of Saddam's bodyguards. The noose is tightening; the enemy is on the run.

The morning after these operations, our men captured a man at a checkpoint attempting to flee with $800,000 US cash in a gym bag. C Company, 3-66 AR has been a big help as well with our flash checkpoints.

"Local authorities report we have hurt the subversive elements severely. Even the Muslim Imams have expressed an appreciation for our efforts. But our work is far from being over. The hostile elements remain and attempt to strike back with indirect fire attacks or attacks on our convoys. We remain vigilant. Keep us in your prayers. Know your young men are taken care of and are doing superb work.

"The men have good morale and are flushed with the recent successes. We are living well for the most part, billeted as we are in former palace compounds. The weather remains oppressive and all we generally do is soak our uniforms with our own sweat in the 115-degree heat. But we are eating well and have generally good hygiene. Our equipment is holding up relatively well given the operations and environment. The robust Bradleys and body armor have earned the absolute respect of our men as they have repeatedly shown that they will save lives."

TF Warhorse (2BCT) similarly kept the pressure on the enemy in Baqubah. Operation Strait Jacket was actually the model for a series of operations conducted by TF Warhorse in order to effectively shut down Baqubah. Whenever the Brigade received credible reports of a disturbance in Baqubah, such as a demonstration with violent intentions; reports of terrorists attempting to transit weapons, car bombs or large amounts of money through Baqubah; or terrorist fighters attempting to transit Baqubah, Operation Strait Jacket would be implemented. The Warhorse Brigade would establish checkpoints on key road networks; snipers overwatched sites normally targeted by such events; and combat camera filmed everything, providing a documentary of any disturbance. TF Warhorse would provide news releases to the populace telling them that these steps were being taken for their safety. Operation Strait Jacket II and subsequent operations utilized maximum participation of Iraqi Civil Defense Corps (ICDC) and Iraqi Police Force (IPF) as they picked up the bulk of the checkpoints and patrolled key areas.

The Warhorse Brigade worked with many Iraqi citizens,

Special Operations Forces (SOF), and Other Government Agencies (OGA) who provided information concerning anti-coalition activities in the Diyala province. Further intelligence was gained through Iraqi Security Forces such as the Iraqi Police Force, the Iraqi Border Guards and the Iraqi Civil Defense Corps. Based on the information from these and other sources, the Brigade was able to conduct numerous raids and cordon and searches in order to remove terrorists from the local populace.

An innumerable amount of weapons caches were discovered and destroyed to include RPGs, shoulder-fired surface to air missiles, small arms, and explosives.

Operation Sidewinder – 29 June to 5 July
Operation Sidewinder was launched early in the morning of 29 June, the same day that Operation Desert Scorpion ended. The operation was the third in a series of operations in the coalition force's relentless pursuit of terrorists and paramilitary forces. The operation focused on sweeping through the area of operations to root out elements attempting to undermine coalition efforts and to restore basic infrastructure and stability in the region. Over twenty simultaneous raids involving attack aviation, armor and infantry forces continued to target former Baath Party loyalists, terrorists suspected of perpetrating attacks against US forces and former Iraqi military leaders, and to locate weapons and ammunition caches. During the first few hours of the operation, over sixty suspected terrorists were detained for questioning. Multiple illegal weapons along with various military documents were seized.

Iraqi civilians and policemen grew in confidence with the American presence and added to the power of the TF Ironhorse Soldiers. In Baqubah, on 1 July, a civilian told Soldiers about a possible grenade attack on coalition forces near an ice factory and advised them to be on alert. The next day, a civilian worker at the ice factory notified Soldiers that a person carrying a grenade was in the area. The Soldiers took immediate action and were able to locate, detain and disarm the suspect. Armed with advanced information from friendly civilians, Soldiers were able to prevent a threat to Soldiers and innocent civilians before it could occur.

Similarly, Iraqi policemen helped apprehend an attacker

suspected of firing two RPG's onto the grounds of Forward Operating Base (FOB) Ironhorse in Tikrit. Elements of 1-22 IN responded to the attack and centered their search near a possible launch site where they found two Iraqi policemen detaining a suspected attacker. The policemen identified the Iraqi male as the individual responsible for firing the RPG into the compound. During an initial search of the suspect, the Iraqi Police discovered he was carrying an RPG nose cap in his pocket. The Iraqi policemen told the Soldiers that the Iraqi man in custody claimed innocence and gave them the names of three individuals he claimed were responsible for the attack. The Soldiers thanked the policemen for their cooperation and took the suspect in for questioning. Teamwork was beginning to build between TF Ironhorse and the Iraqis.

Operation Sidewinder was not without American casualties. A total of 16 Soldiers were wounded in a mortar attack against a logistics base near Balad on 3 July. A vehicle from B/1-22 IN, attached to TF 3-66 AR, struck a land mine or IED while patrolling on Highway 1 near K2 airfield near Bayji early on the morning of 4 July. The explosion injured five U.S. Soldiers who were evacuated for treatment. On 5 July, C/1-67 AR, along with a dismounted squad from B/2-8 IN, conducted a raid on a reported mortar-training site near Baqubah. These units quickly established an outer cordon and began clearing the four objective houses. While clearing the area north of the houses, a cache of two hundred mortar rounds was discovered. Elements of B/204 FSB secured the rounds and transport them for destruction.

Over the course of the seven days of Operation Sidewinder, TF Ironhorse conducted 78 raids. During the raids and other supporting operations, 282 individuals were detained and a variety of weapons were seized including 96 AK-47 rifles, three heavy machine guns, 217 RPGs, 33 grenades, 200 mortar rounds, and other military equipment, documents, weapons and ammunition. In addition, $5,000 U.S. cash and approximately 11 million Iraqi Dinar (about $6,000 U.S.) were seized. There were thirty casualties in non-compliant forces and 28 coalition forces injured. No coalition force Soldiers were killed during the operation.

173rd Airborne Operations
173rd Airborne platoons and companies, along with 1-12 IN and

1-63 AR, established a commanding presence on the streets of Kirkuk and the surrounding area. They soon earned the reputation in the province for being fair, unbiased, and resolute in their mission. Understanding that the key to stability for the province eclipsed mere military power, COL Mayville instituted a massive initiative to develop civic institutions and improve existing infrastructure. Under his auspices, the 173rd Airborne Brigade established a new police force and an independent civic government, the first free institutions to be established in the nation after the fall of the regime. Infrastructure improvements encompassed millions of dollars and resulted in Kirkuk being the first major city in Iraq to witness the complete return of basic services and the establishment of a free and functioning media. The province led the way in the nation for business development, medical facilities, local associations and guilds, civic institutions, and quality of life.

Task Force Gunner Operations
Raids and offensive actions were conducted not only by infantry and armor units, but also by artillery and their attached units. The long-established role of using artillery in support of maneuver forces was modified for these raid operations. TF 2-20 FA transitioned to conducting mounted and dismounted combat reconnaissance patrols, with the help of an attached battery of ADA Linebackers and Bradleys. TF 2-20 FA was the main planning headquarters for numerous raid missions to increase the security of the Taji Military Complex area.

During June and July, TF 2-20 FA planned and successfully executed three major operations that resulted in the detention of high-ranking enemy in the area and the confiscation of numerous illegal weapons. The raids conducted by TF 2-20 FA were missions that would usually be performed by infantry Soldiers. Mission by mission, TF 2-20 FA made it safer for the people who lived and worked in the Taji region.

Included in the TF were: HHS/B/C/2-20 FA; B/3-16 FA; A/3-29 FA; B/4-42 FA; and A/B/1-44 ADA. A/D/2-20 FA provided support to their respective BCT.

TF 2-20 FA also conducted missions focused on support and stability operations as well as humanitarian relief. The TF provided security at a local gas station, integrating gasoline rationing and stabilizing local fuel prices. Previously, Iraqis had to wait hours just to fill their tank, not to mention the attempted robberies of the local gas stations. The TF provided a place where customers could drive up, feel safe and know they were being charged a fair price for the gasoline.

In addition to gas station operations, TF 2-20 FA provided security to a local UN food warehouse until final inspections could be completed in order to provide food to the local population. The Soldiers also made the Taji area a safer environment with what they referred to as Task Force Wrecker and Task Force Haul. The operations included Soldiers ridding the local area of abandoned Iraqi military equipment and then identifying unexploded ordnance for proper disposal. These missions provided security and established stability throughout the area while greatly increasing the quality of life for the Iraqi people.

3BCT Operations

3BCT was the exception among TF Ironhorse units. It was constantly on the move during the first three months in Iraq as they responded to the hot spots in the AOR. Duties included raiding former military bases in Samarra, disarming the MEK, reinforcing the 173rd Airborne in the Kirkuk area, and clearing out non-compliant forces, weapons and ammunition caches wherever they were. Raids, helping restore basic services for the Iraqi people, dealing with local political figures, and destroying enemy ammunition caches were all in a typical day's work. In July, the brigade made its final move—to take responsibility for Balad and Samarra. The many moves caused mail and supplies to take longer to reach Soldiers. They never seemed to be able to settle into a routine or to establish any comforts of home. Their bases included an airfield, an electronics plant, a railroad station, and a house owned by "Chemical Ali", one of Saddam Hussein's key generals. Most places they occupied had been heavily looted with all electrical, plumbing, and other conveniences taken. From July forward, 3BCT had its own permanent AOR to call home. They became established and began work in the critically important area around Balad and Samarra.

This Stuff Really Works!

CPT Bryan Miller, HHB DIVARTY, described the protective

equipment available to all TF Ironhorse Soldiers in the following article printed in the Gunner Gazette, the weekly newsletter of TF Gunner: "The 4th Infantry Division Mechanized is the Army's "digital division" with the most advanced equipment and the latest technology. The most important piece of gear for the Soldiers of Task Force Gunner has not been a computer or a laser gun but new advancements on standard Soldier equipment. The helmet and body armor have been Soldier uniform standards for many years. Previously, helmets and body armor were just behind the latest weapons and provided minimal protection to the wearer. Today, the ballistic helmet known to Soldiers as the "KEVLAR" and the Interceptor Body Armor System (IBAS), or flak jacket, have recently proved their worth under fire to the Soldiers of TF Gunner.

"On two separate occasions these pieces of equipment have saved the lives of Soldiers from TF 2-20 FA. While on patrol, Soldiers came under enemy small arms fire and a sergeant was struck in the helmet. Knocked to the ground, the bullet ricocheted off his ballistic helmet. He had a headache but was just fine thanks to advancements in bullet resistant technologies. In the past, the Soldier would have been gravely injured.

"In another incident, Soldiers were preparing to conduct a raid mission, when four Iraqis fired upon them from a moving truck. The US Soldiers returned fire and subsequently killed their attackers. When the gunfire ended, one of the Soldiers was wounded in the arm, or so the unit thought. Later, after the Soldier was evacuated for treatment of his wound, his chain of command examined the Soldier's equipment. It was found that the bullet hit the small arms protective insert (SAPI) inside his IBAS protective vest. The bullet struck the Soldier in the upper chest and was deflected by the SAPI plate. Once again, because of advanced technology, a Soldier's life was saved. Disciplined Soldiers, such as those in TF 2-20, wore the right equipment the right way and lived to fight another day."

The above story is representative of stories that many Soldiers and units within TF Ironhorse could have told during their deployment. Even though it was unbearably hot, the standard of excellence in TF Ironhorse was for all Soldiers to wear their Kevlar and IBAS any time they were outside their own compound—and many times while inside their compounds.

97

Psychological Operations
This story from a TF Ironhorse news release described the beginning of psychological operations that continued throughout the deployment: "The big white truck parked near a radio tower on the University of Tikrit didn't attract much attention. What was inside that truck spoke volumes. Inside the truck was a radio station—1377 on the AM dial. Soldiers from the TF Ironhorse G-6 section and the 362nd Psychological Operations Company (PSYOP) worked together to develop the station. The radio station was one of the ways TF Ironhorse communicated with local citizens in the Tikrit area. The station began operating on 4 June and broadcast command information messages in Arabic to Iraqis."

"Soldiers from the G-6 section had the mission of finding a suitable location with an AM antennae. They found what they were looking for at the university. Soldiers combined their talents to put the station together. After initially being limited to a range of 200 meters, the broadcast range was boosted to cover the entire city of Tikrit.

"The PSYOP Soldiers broadcast hour-long command messages in the morning and evening. The messages covered a variety of topics from avoiding land mines to curfews to food distribution—all designed to keep the local citizens informed and to give TF Ironhorse a means of getting its message out. Music and news from a commercial source played the rest of the day, all from a lone truck parked in an empty field."

River Patrols
With the Tigris River running the length of the TF Ironhorse AOR, virtually all the TF engineer units had a boat patrol mission in addition to their normal engineer duties of building things and blowing things up. Day and night the engineers patrolled the river. Among the missions was the security of the east side of FOB Ironhorse. With binoculars in hand, the engineers constantly scanned the river and banks looking for anything out of the ordinary. Night vision devices went into use when the sun went down. Providing blocking positions to stop non-compliant forces from escaping across the river was a nightly job as raids were made on riverfront objectives. Searching Iraqi boats for contraband was also a routine part of the missions.

Changes of Command

As operations continued, many changes of command took place in the ranks of TF Ironhorse during June and early July. New brigade commanders came in to 1BCT, 2BCT, DISCOM, and 555 EN GRP. Many battalion and company commanders in all brigades also changed command. Some of the commanders returned to the US or other locations around the world to take on new responsibilities while others moved to new positions within TF Ironhorse. In keeping with Army tradition, MG Odierno and the 4ID Band attended as many change of command ceremonies as possible. Change was sometimes difficult, but the needs of the Army dictated the actions.

More changes were scheduled, including a change of command for the Commanding General. In early July, the decision was made to keep all commanders in place through the end of the deployment. The Pentagon decision was well received—TF Ironhorse would continue under the leadership of MG Odierno and the course that he had set.

Morale, Welfare, and Recreation

Soldiers have always started to improve their living conditions the minute they arrived in a new location. TF Ironhorse Soldiers in Iraq were no exception. The opening of the Soldiers' Inn in a palace at FOB Ironhorse, the improvement of mail and laundry facilities, and the constant improvement in living facilities are just a few examples of how Morale, Welfare, and Recreation (MWR) efforts improved in all TF Ironhorse locations.

For Soldiers living and working on FOB Ironhorse, the Soldiers' Inn was a unique gathering place. The large palace offered an assortment of activities and services for local Soldiers, and was a place where other Soldiers went for a few days of R&R. The first permanent PX facilities were established at FOB Speicher and FOB Ironhorse by AAFES.

The 4ID band was a key part of MWR operations. Force protection around FOB Ironhorse was one of their responsibilities but that did not interfere with their primary job of helping with troop morale. "Prime Mover", the 4ID show band, moved around the TF AOR providing music "by Soldiers for Soldiers." "Ironhorse Brass", the brass quintet; "Seven Ironhorsemen", the Dixie band; and "Moment's Notice", the jazz band, all provided musical programs for the entertainment of the troops. At the 4th of July party at FOB Ironhorse, Prime Mover performed for 1,800 TF Ironhorse Soldiers. During the months of June and July, the 4ID band participated in 23 change of command ceremonies to insure the proper pomp and ceremony was included in those key events, including a ceremony on the Iran border for 1-10 CAV.

An article from the Gunner Gazette gave an interesting view of how Soldiers handled their laundry duties:

"When not on operations as part of the nation's first digital division, TF Gunner had the opportunity to use important tactical lessons learned from our nation's past. One of the most important lessons learned from past wars was how to do the laundry in a non-digital world. Many would think that Soldiers of the most advanced Army in the world would have a mobile clothes washing vehicle to wash, spin, dry and fold uniforms. In reality, that capability did not exist. Soldiers reverted to systems that our ancestors used since the dawn of time—a bucket and some water. Clothes were hung from lines strung up all throughout the base camp as they harnessed the power of the sun to aid in the drying process.

"At Taji airfield, this historical system was further improved with the purchase of two washing machines. Since the plumbing was still unserviceable, Soldiers could be seen hauling five gallon buckets of water and filling the machines by hand. Water pressure was finally restored to the buildings in Taji and laundry re-entered the 20th century. In the short span of two months, TF Gunner Soldiers were able to re-live the complete history of washing clothes."

Mail delivery improved in May and early June. The 449th Postal Company, an Army Reserve unit from Brevard, North Carolina operated the mailroom at FOB Ironhorse in Tikrit. On an average day, TF Ironhorse received four 20-foot military vans of mail. FOB Ironhorse alone got a two and a half ton truck packed full of letters and packages. Sorting and distributing the mail was a monumental task but one that the postal unit and mail clerks in the individual TF Ironhorse units performed exceptionally well.

Civil Military Operations
Civil Military Operations (CMO) was equally as important to TF Ironhorse as was offensive military operations. In each location

within the TF AOR, individual units continually performed missions to improve the well being of the Iraqi population. Ten civil affairs teams from the 418th Civil Affairs (CA) Battalion, a reserve unit headquartered in Belton, MO were assigned to battalions and brigades. Civil Military Operations Centers (CMOC) were established in storefront locations in major population centers with the mission of helping to meet the moral and legal obligations to the Iraqi people. Each CA team, consisting of six people at full strength, worked with the local civilian leadership to determine the specific needs of the people in their AOR. The teams worked with the unit they were attached to for implementation of programs to meet the needs.

On 17 June, the opening of a bridge spanning the Tigris River marked the completion of one of the first joint projects undertaken by members of the 14th Engineer Battalion and local Iraqis. The structure, called Buffalo Soldier Bridge, is located approximately one hour north of Bayji. The causeway to the bridge was heavily damaged by erosion. The military engineers worked with an Iraqi contractor to repair the causeway and make it safe for military and civilian traffic. COL Christopher Toomey, commander of the 555 EN GRP, local sheiks, and other Iraqi officials attended the ribbon cutting ceremony. The cooperative project represents the first of dozens aimed at helping Iraqis rebuild and stabilize their country.

This article, extracted from the Gunner Gazette, describes one of the many operations conducted in June:

"In Iraq, medical care is one of the most important public services and has been hard to come by in many areas. On 21 June 2003, 3-29 FA along with Iraqi Health Officials brought some needed medical care to the village of Zanker. Zanker was chosen because it has not received any public medical services from the government in more than 12 years.

"The medical team consisted of the 3-29 FA Physicians Assistant, four Medics, and a seven Soldiers security and communication team. The team from the Iraqi government contained a Dentist, Pediatrician, two General Physicians, two Pharmacy Technicians and two Immunization Technicians. All the medical supplies for the mission were obtained through the Iraqi government in Kirkuk at no cost to the Coalition Forces or the village of Zanker. The medical supplies used concentrated on pediatric care and immunizations. The team treated 198 people including 128 children who received immunizations. The mission was a complete success and villagers were truly touched by the compassion and medical skill of the Coalition Soldiers."

A PAO press release on 11 July summarized the CA operations:
"Soldiers of 4ID and TF Ironhorse continue to play an important role in re-building Iraq. Projects directed at improving facilities are also providing jobs for Iraqis in the provinces of Salah Ad Din, Diyala and At Tamin, which fall within the task force area of operation. 4ID created a dedicated Project Coordination Cell to manage reconstruction projects covering a spectrum of areas, including government, public works, communications, justice, security, education, transportation, commerce and health and human services. Current and future projects will provide much needed improvements to the country's infrastructure and are generating jobs to help the economy.

"In Salah Ad Din province, over 150 projects are underway to improve the quality of life for residents. The Tikrit Model School will receive a fresh coat of paint along with improvements in its mechanical, electrical, and plumbing systems. The project also means needed jobs for Iraqis involved in the repairs. The goal is to have a model school in every city, which includes new furnishings inside classrooms and new playground equipment outside. This represents hundreds of schools across all three provinces and jobs for workers involved in the projects. At the Samarra Health Clinic and Hospital, equipment damaged or looted during the war is being purchased and installed to meet the health needs of citizens.

"Over 300 jobs have been generated in the Diyala province to complete a wide range of initiatives. The city of Baqubah's water treatment plant will soon provide clean, safe water for residents, thanks to new equipment being installed.

"Residents of At Tamim province will soon have a police force with 76 new officers thanks to the Kirkuk Police Academy. The academy is an important cooperative effort between U.S. and Iraqi police instructors. In Kirkuk, repairs and improvements are being made in the Communications Office. These changes will help the ministry re-establish vital communications in northern Iraq.

It is one of hundreds of projects aimed at providing security, improving facilities and enhancing the quality of life for residents.

"Soldiers of the 4ID and TF Ironhorse are committed to rebuilding efforts and will continue to assist in community projects benefiting the free Iraqi people. Hundreds of projects are going on now and more are projected for the future."

2-4 AVN Blackhawk taking off on a mission

TF Ironhorse Soldiers and press members admiring $8.2M captured by 1-22 IN

Part of Saddam Hussein's wife's jewelry captured by 1-22 IN on 18 June 2003

A M109A6, 155mm Paladin howitzer from A/2-29 FA - firing in support of 3BCT

TF Ironhorse Soldiers of 555th EN GRP blow down a statue of Saddam Hussein in Tikrit. Metal from this statue was used to create a monument to fallen TF Ironhorse Soldiers

One of many change of command ceremonies conducted in June and July 2003

E/1-10 CAV OH-58 Kiowa flying border reconnaissance in a mountainous area southeast of Khaniqin on the Iran-Iraq border - July 2003

IX

A Long Hot Summer

Working in unbearable heat, IEDs become a major factor, Ongoing missions, Operation Ivy Serpent, Operation Ivy Needle, Civil action successes, Development of Iraqi Border Police, Full year deployment announced, Critical role of rear detachment and FRGs
6 July 2003 to 9 September 2003

Operation Ivy Serpent – 12-17 July 2003

OPERATION SIDEWINDER ENDED ON 5 JULY BUT TF Ironhorse Soldiers did not let up the heavy pressure on non-compliant forces. On 7 July, elements from the Scouts and B/2-8 IN of the Warhorse Brigade raided a suspected Baath blacklist meeting house to capture high value targets. The units secured and cleared two complexes resulting in the capture of 19 personnel, two AK-47 rifles, one pistol, one mortar sight, and 99 mortar base plates, 91 mortar bipods, two 82mm mortar tubes, two 60mm mortar tubes, and Al Qaida paraphernalia. This was only one example of the continued aggressive pressure that TF Ironhorse applied in their AOR, both day and night.

On 12 July, TF Ironhorse launched Operation Ivy Serpent, the fourth in a series of operations focused on neutralizing Baath Party loyalists and other subversive elements in the AOR. The operation, part of CJTF-7's overall offensive in Iraq, was a preemptive strike to focus aggressively on non-compliant forces and former regime leaders who were planning attacks against coalition forces. Much of the effort was concentrated in a region along Highway1 between the cities of Bayji, Huwayiah, and Samarra.

The month of July had two days that were particularly significant to former regime loyalists. A coup d'etat on 14 July 1958 removed King Faisal, marked the end of the Hashmemite monarchy in Iraq, and is referred to as "Republic Day" or

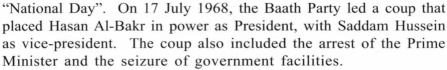

"National Day". On 17 July 1968, the Baath Party led a coup that placed Hasan Al-Bakr in power as President, with Saddam Hussein as vice-president. The coup also included the arrest of the Prime Minister and the seizure of government facilities.

Intelligence reports gathered from a variety of sources indicated former regime leaders planned attacks against coalition targets to mark the anniversary of those events. Ivy Serpent, like previous operations Peninsula Strike, Desert Scorpion, and Sidewinder, was designed to sweep the TF AOR to root out elements that were attempting to undermine coalition efforts to restore basic infrastructure and stability in the region.

In an early morning raid near Baqubah on 12 July, Soldiers of 2BCT captured two brothers—one was listed as the second in charge of the Baath party for Diyala province and the other was a Lieutenant General in the Iraqi Air Force. A Fedayeen general was also detained. Overall, TF Ironhorse detained over eighty Baath Party, Fedayeen, and other subversive elements on the first day of operation. During the course of the raids, hundreds of weapons were confiscated, including AK-47s, pistols, mortars, and items used to make explosive devices. All elements of TF Ironhorse were engaged. The 173rd Airborne Brigade detained several senior Baath Party and Fedayeen leaders on the third day of the operation. By the fourth day, over 400 individuals had been detained and more caches of weapons and ammunition were captured.

On 16 July, TF Ironhorse dealt Saddam Hussein loyalists a major blow as Operation Ivy Serpent located several major weapons caches. Soldiers from 1-22 IN, 1BCT conducted a raid near Tikrit and uncovered a large quantity of weapons and other contraband items. Soldiers found a total of 54 fifty-pound boxes of C4 plastic explosive and 25,000 blasting caps for detonating the C4. In addition, approximately 250 AK-47s, over 500 RPGs and two T-55 tanks were confiscated. In a separate raid, Soldiers with 1BCT found another cache of weapons and explosives in Tikrit. Near Kirkuk, members of the 173 Airborne Brigade received fire from looters and returned the fire, killing one attacker and wounding another. Soldiers detained three of the looters.

Two of the most visible remnants of the old regime in Tikrit sat high atop a gate leading into the palace complex. The two bronze statues of Saddam on horseback were taken down with explosive charges by the 555 EN GRP on 14 and 18 July. With the destruction of the last statue, Operation Ivy Serpent came to an end. The operation produced strong results, with the detainment of numerous personnel who were functioning in leadership roles for the subversive elements.

Overall, fifty high-value targets were captured and 549 other Iraqi aggressors were detained. Large amounts of weapons were confiscated from former regime loyalists, effectively decreasing their ability to harm coalition Soldiers and the Iraqi populace. A total of 394 AK-47s, 57 rocket-propelled grenades, 507 standard grenades, 1,736 mortar rounds, 54 fifty-pound crates of C4 plastic explosive, and a variety of other illegal arms and contraband items were seized. Twelve hostile forces were killed in combat and ten wounded. Ten coalition Soldiers were injured. Operation Ivy Serpent successfully accomplished the objective of finding and weakening those individuals that remained loyal to the ousted regime.

Offensive operations continued all across the AOR. In a late night raid on 18 July, a patrol from 588 EN BN captured two high-ranking Saddam Fedayeen generals, along with ten other loyalists. In other raids within the TF area, Soldiers confiscated 366 mortars, 12 small arms weapons, 3 RPGs, explosive devices and other contraband items.

Qusay and Uday Hussein Killed
Saddam Hussein's sons, Qusay and Uday were killed on 22 July in a "fierce gun battle," as described by LTG Ricardo Sanchez, commander of ground forces in Iraq. Based on a "walk-in tip," elements of the 101st Airborne Division, Special Forces and Air Force assets raided a residence in Mosul, Iraq. "An Iraqi source informed the 101st Airborne Division that several suspects, including Qusay and Uday—Numbers 2 and 3 on the U.S. Central Command's most wanted list—were hiding in a residence at the northern edge of Mosul. When the division's 2nd Brigade Combat Team approached the house, the Soldiers received small arms fire. The combat team employed multiple weapons systems to subdue the suspects who had barricaded themselves inside the house and continued fiercely to resist detention. Saddam's sons died when they resisted detention and the efforts of the coalition forces to go in there and apprehend them," LTG Sanchez said. "They were

killed in the ensuing gunfight and the attacks that we conducted on the residence. A total of four persons were killed during the six-hour operation; their bodies were removed from the building."

General Sanchez said, "This will prove to the Iraqi people that at least these two members of the regime will not be coming back into power, which is what we've stated over and over again. And we remain totally committed to the Hussein regime never returning to power and tormenting the Iraqi people."

The news was immediately broadcast around the world. As the news hit TF Ironhorse, they knew the remnants of Saddam's regime would act and they would have to tighten their alertness and security. It was unknown how the area around Saddam's hometown of Tikrit would react to the news.

The reaction in Tikrit was covered in detail in an email that LTC Steve Russell, CO of 1-22 IN, sent to family and friends on 26 July: "On the evening of 22 July, a strange mood descended over the city. Every eye was glued to television sets as the breaking news of Uday and Qusay Hussein's deaths jolted like an electric shock. The city was eerily quiet but not without danger. At approximately 2250 hours, another familiar 'dumpster crash' was heard, signaling an RPG attack, as we headed south in our command group convoy. We headed back north along the main highway that bisects the town and saw a pall of smoke. Local men gestured from balconies with general directions. A quick patrol from our men looped around the block but nothing was found. The target was a photo shop wedged into a corner. Maybe the assailant didn't get his film on time.

"On the 23rd we saw the enemy become very active. Perhaps the news of Uday and Qusay's deaths ignited hatred and anger. Regardless of what sparked the evening events, the enemy would soon pay dearly. At about 2130 hours, C/1-22 IN reported stopping a car that had sped at a high rate of speed with 25 million dinar (about $15,000 dollars). Being an unusual sum, the men called to ask what to do. We took my translator to the scene to decipher the situation and learned that the Iraqi males in the car had made a legitimate business transaction on the sale of some property and were afraid of being robbed, so they hurried to their house. Deducing this after verifying it with documents, we let them go and proceeded south in the city. The patrol then collapsed their checkpoint and prepared to leave.

110

"As they left the T-intersection, a crash of RPG rounds, accompanied with small arms fire, thundered about them. No damage was caused to our men in the Bradleys. The attackers fled to points south as quick as they had fired. Hearing the explosions near the location we had just left, my convoy cut to the east a couple of blocks down and then headed north in complete blackout with our night vision toward where we thought the attack might have come from.

"A white Nissan pickup fishtailed around a corner. My safety instinctively flipped to fire on my M-4 carbine. My driver veered left to block the pickup. Weapons were visible—four men in the truck. Looks of surprise flashed from underneath all black Arab headdresses. My driver rammed the vehicle. The enemy was startled by the impact. I'm on my feet charging the vehicle, shattering the windshield with rifle fire. The second vehicle in my group rounded the corner, saw enemy fire sail through the air but it was unnoticed by the two of us. My driver cut down the man exiting the passenger side of the truck. The enemy driver never made it out after my opening burst. I shifted to the two men in the back. My driver and I had them in an 'L' with no place for them to go—blurs of clothing, AK-47s and earsplitting sound. I squeezed my tactical flashlight on my weapon and fired heavily into the man in the back and then at the other man as he attempted to take cover on the other side of the vehicle. My driver denied him refuge with his rifle and he became still in a wadded up heap by the right rear wheel—AK-47 nearby. Our other Soldiers in the trail vehicles came up to support, but the enemy lay in heaps. A Fedayeen cell was destroyed.

"Simultaneously, rifle fire erupted to the east along the main street of the city. A blue car and an ambulance moved cautiously down the road. Two men exited the ambulance with AK-47s and got into the car. We had waited a long time for this one. Snipers engaged. The blue car raced as glass shards flew from its rear windshield. The ambulance driver could not maneuver. Spider-webbed circles the size of half-dollars sequentially dotted the driver's side of the windshield. The vehicle stopped. A man struggled out of the vehicle, badly injured and collapsed on the street. Unidentified fire arced toward the Soldiers. A confused 'friendly' force from a completely different unit on the main street—also a main supply route—mistook our men for the enemy.

Our men kept their heads and attempted to gain their attention, shouting that they are American forces. No avail. Our three men remained disciplined despite the automatic grenades that impacted their location. Our recon element rocketed toward the location and forcefully disengaged the confused element. Three Regulars were wounded but, thankfully, they were shrapnel flesh wounds only. Two were returned to duty, another would return shortly.

"Pumped with adrenaline as we searched the four men from the pick up, I took this latest development hard. Our ambushes had been extremely successful, now darkened by the careless actions of well-meaning but non-Infantry Soldiers. We continued the search and found Indian currency and French cigarettes. What did it mean? Three AK-47s, two RPG launchers with rounds prepped and ready, two hand grenades, an M-79 40mm grenade launcher with six rounds, and several magazines of small arms ammunition were pulled from the truck and the dead. Armed to the teeth, the enemy clearly intended on more attempts to kill Americans. Three points of the city were secured. The enemy's attack was defeated at each point with a heavy price exacted from him. We learned later that the four in the truck were the sons of bodyguards of Saddam Hussein or sons of his relatives. The sins of the fathers were visited to the next generation.

"The next day, another cell attempted a daylight attack on the C/1-22 IN compound from an open field abutting to the east. The engagement began with sporadic rifle fire. Perhaps the enemy had attempted to draw us out. He was obliged but not in the manner he expected. Bradleys in overwatch fired on a now ubiquitous Nissan white truck. A man struggled and fled the burning vehicle, only to be shot by a Soldier's rifle fire. RPGs launched and crashed from a northern side street. Additional C/1-22 IN force was brought to bear and was engaged from the south. Small arms, 25mm chain guns and machine guns cracked and thumped in swift reply. The contest ended. Another cell was destroyed with one enemy killed, two wounded and one surrendered. C/1-22 IN Soldiers were unscathed.

"The damage to the enemy was manifest. His anger and carelessness continued to cost him in deficits he cannot repay. The city took on an apprehensive calm—so continued the gurgling gasps of a dying regime. Their lifeblood now draining, it was only a matter of time. Meanwhile a new Iraq is being born."

One Year Tour Announced

Although they were told prior to departure that the deployment might be for a year, the Soldiers and their families did not know exactly how long 4ID and TF Ironhorse would remain in Iraq. From the alert in January through the deployment in April and the first months in Iraq, rumors ran wild among the family members and the Soldiers on when they would come home. Some were positive they would be home by September, others thought it would be by Christmas, and some thought they would remain for a year or more. On 22 July, the announcement was made by the Army's acting Chief of Staff that Army units sent to Iraq would serve one-year deployments. The announcement stated, "The 4th Infantry Division (Mechanized), based at Fort Hood, Texas, will rotate home next March and April (2004). It will be replaced by the 1st Infantry Division, based in Germany, plus an enhanced Army National Guard brigade yet to be named."

The news was both a relief and a disappointment to the Soldiers and their families. The families handled it with dignity and grace and were proud to support their Soldier and unit. A one-year deployment was longer than they had hoped for but it was good to know a precise date. The Family Readiness Groups pulled together and showed great strength. This was not a first for the 4ID. 4ID Soldiers in WWI were overseas from April 1918 to August 1919 (17 months), WWII 4ID Soldiers were overseas from January 1944 to July 1945 (19 months—and had been drafted for the duration of the war). Cold War 4ID Soldiers in Germany in the early 1950's served 24 month tours, and 4ID Soldiers in Vietnam had the same 12-month tour as our Soldiers in Iraq.

The Family Readiness Group (FRG) leaders renewed their commitment to support the Soldiers and family members. They overcame their personal disappointment with the news and passed the information to the family members in their unit. Assuming a 1 April 2004 return, that meant there were now "251 days and a wake-up" until TF Ironhorse returned home.

Within hours after the redeployment date was announced, MG Ray Odierno sent the following letter to the FRG leaders for distribution to all family members:

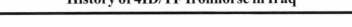

"To the Ironhorse Family,

Your husbands and wives are working tirelessly every day to improve the lives of Iraqi citizens and set the conditions that will allow us and other U.S. forces to redeploy. They have fought fiercely against the remaining Saddam loyalists, while at the same time compassionately helping the Iraqi people move to a free, democratic society. I am impressed daily by the magnificent performance and attitude of every Ironhorse Soldier. I know some of our Soldiers and their families have already sacrificed much and we will never forget them.

As the CENTCOM Commander, General Abizaid said recently while visiting Task Force Ironhorse, our mission is critical to fighting the Global War on Terror and we must defeat terrorists here so that we don't have to defeat them in the U.S. We will complete our mission no matter how long it takes.

Undoing 35 years of repression and tyranny will not be quick or easy; our Soldiers have performed brilliantly and will continue to do so. The United States will leave Iraq only after the mission is complete and free Iraqi people enjoy a safe, secure, healthy, and prosperous society.

As we said prior to deployment, we are committed to completing the mission the President has given us, and we are proud to see this task through to completion. It is the right thing to do.

In support of this long term effort, I believe the Division will be here about a year; if conditions are met that allow withdrawal of forces sooner it may not be that long, but we need to plan for a year. Our Soldiers are professionals; they will persevere and complete this continuing mission with the same motivation and dedication they've displayed from the beginning of this operation.

Our Soldiers are focused on the mission at hand. But, I have personally been proud of the unwavering support we have received from all the friends and family members of Task Force Ironhorse. You are true heroes and your continuing support allows us to maintain this focus. The exceptional way that the Ironhorse family has rallied from the moment we deployed is as important to the Division's success as the combat performance of our units. Our Soldiers will not let up the relentless pressure on the enemy; we need the same level of effort from the Ironhorse Family.

The challenges of combat will continue; the challenges at home caused by separation and anxiety will endure as well. Through your continuing support we will complete the mission and return to celebrate our success in Iraq, as well as the success of each family member who sacrifices daily as loved ones are deployed. We all look forward to being reunited with our families again.

Your mission is difficult and I greatly appreciate all you do for your Soldiers and for each other. Thank you all for your kindness, prayers and sacrifices, while you continue to support us. God bless all the Ironhorse families, and God bless our Soldiers. We will get through this together showing everyone what I already know—We have the best Soldiers and families in the Army.
Steadfast and loyal,
Ray T. Odierno
MG, Commanding

The Critically Important Role of FRGs and Rear Detachment

It was during Operation Desert Storm in 1991 that the value of Family Readiness Groups (FRG) and a strong rear detachment became understood. With multiple deployments to the National Training Center at Fort Irwin, California and occasional deployments of six months or less to other locations around the world, FRGs and the rear detachment unit grew in structure and importance through the 1990s. When the alert came for Iraq, the FRGs and rear detachments were to show their true value to the TF Ironhorse Soldiers and families.

MG Odierno's intent was vivid with his instructions to his brigade commanders: "Leave one of your best majors and master sergeants, ones you can't afford to do without, as your brigade rear detachment commander. Have each battalion do the same with a captain and a sergeant first class." As the overall rear detachment commander, MG Odierno named COL Jim Moore to take that responsibility initially. SGM David Brown was the Sergeant Major working with him. When COL Moore went to Iraq in early June to assume command of DISCOM, an equally able Colonel, COL Dan Shanahan, who had just returned to the 4ID and had previously served in many roles within the division, replaced him.

Linda Odierno, MG Odierno's wife, was the Division FRG Leader who was the senior advisor for the Division to Ft. Hood, FORSCOM and Department of the Army Family Readiness activities and the Senior Advisor to the Senior FRG Leaders in the Division. Like her husband, Linda Odierno had been through multiple deployments and knew the key roles that those left behind had to play. Valuable leadership support to Linda was offered by the wives of the 4ID Chiefs of Staff, first Debbie Barclay, and then Ann Campbell, and the spouses of the Taskforce Ironhorse Executive Steering Committee, and the Spouses of Ivy League.

The delay caused by Turkey not allowing the TF to go through their country gave the FRGs and rear detachments additional time to plan and be prepared to implement their responsibilities. Rosters, phone trees, and family information sheets were scrubbed one more time to insure their accuracy (an ongoing process that continued throughout the deployment). Volunteers stepped forward from all locations where TF Ironhorse Soldiers deployed. Critical FRG leadership roles were filled by the spouses of unit commanders, junior officers, NCOs and enlisted personnel. They learned from each other and used their own creativeness to meet the needs of their specific unit. In many cases, the FRGs went over and above what was expected of them and often tried to do too much to look out for their families and Soldiers. Army families are a special breed of people. The Army is about people, and the TF Ironhorse leaders, both in and out of uniform, showed how the Army looks out for its own. The leadership shown before, during, and after the deployment became the model that the Army is now trying to duplicate across all units.

The summer transition was a very critical time. The "stop loss" order was lifted and the rear detachments became responsible for a steady stream of Soldiers returning for new assignments or processing out of the Army, while other Soldiers were processed to take their places in Iraq. With a skeleton crew of 85 rear detachment personnel to handle the work, the numbers of incoming and outgoing personnel rose from 700 to 4,000 to be processed, housed, and moved in a timely manner either into or out of Iraq. Casualties mounted and the casualty notification process became a painful but very important role played by the rear detachments, for both those killed and those wounded. 4ID rear detachment leadership and ceremonial honor guards were provided for those killed in Iraq. A small legal staff handled the growing legal needs of Soldiers and families. Medical evaluation boards were put into place with help from other Fort Hood assets. A small chaplain group, led by reservist LTC DeWayne Brewer, provided religious leadership. Routine or totally unexpected or unplanned tasks became the norm for the rear detachment Soldiers to deal with in a professional and timely manner. Rear detachment personnel became unsung heroes of the deployment.

FRG leaders were other unsung heroes. Family issues and needs covered a wide span. The FRG leaders and volunteers stepped up to each challenge and opportunity and handled it. New babies, deaths, illnesses, family issues, loneliness, a shoulder to lean on, untold other issues—all were challenges the FRG handled on a daily basis. For some families, this was another in a long string of deployments over a career. For others, it was their first deployment. Some family members were new to the Army and did not understand how it operates. The FRGs patiently helped them with their questions and concerns. On a daily basis, the

FRGs made sure that information was passed along from all the sources available to them.

What had started as an immediate family support group for those within the locale of the unit grew to include extended family members (parents, brothers, sisters, grandparents, friends, and girl friends of deployed Soldiers) from all across the country. Communications were a critical part of the FRG mission. Many provided monthly newsletters, daily email updates, and regular phone calls to keep family members informed. Most forwarded the "4ID Update from Iraq" electronic newsletter to their members to keep them informed on a daily basis as well as the "Ironhorse Desert News" that came from Iraq each week, and their own Brigade, Battalion, and Company/Battery Level Newsletters.

The "4ID Update from Iraq" daily electronic newsletter became a great source of information for TF Ironhorse family members and friends. The service that Bob Babcock started providing on 18 May continued to grow until it was going to an estimated 50,000 people each day until the end of the deployment. The positive, yet factual, content and tone of the information, different from much that was reported in the media, became a daily source of strength, information, and encouragement for those reading it. The updates were forwarded to many Soldiers in Iraq to give them more information than they got within their own operational world. "The 4ID Update from Iraq" was unique to TF Ironhorse families and friends and became a part of the deployment history.

Working as a team, the FRGs and rear detachments provided an invaluable lifeline to the Soldiers and their extended families. Many lessons were learned, many unforeseen challenges were solved, and lifelong friendships were built within the FRGs and rear detachments. As the deployment continued, these important support elements became even stronger and more essential to the mission. A special bond of teamwork and friendship developed among the spouses and family members that will never be forgotten.

The Heat Intensifies
The extreme Iraqi heat had a profound effect on TF Ironhorse Soldiers, but did not deter them from pursuing their duties. Although official weather service records show the afternoon heat

was regularly in the 120-130 degree range, some Soldiers reported spot readings of 140-150 degrees. In LTC Steve Russell's 26 July email, he described it well: "The men are very proud of their service here. They are not despondent or feeling sorry for themselves, but rather they know they are taking away the enemy's will and that we will win. All the reasons that sent us here are just as valid today as they were when we came. We cannot lose sight of just how abominable this country and its regime was. To do so is to overlook a multitude of evil. While the enemy is small and he does engage us, he becomes weaker and we continue to drive into him. It is better to fight him here than in our American cities as he plots his cowardly attacks. He will surely fail.

"Long hot days have greeted us but not necessarily in the morning. Our men conduct operations at all hours and the average Soldier is active 16-20 hours a day. Sometimes we get more rest but nothing can be scheduled. Our operations drive our activities and Soldiers get snatches of rest when they can. They need not be told.

"The sun bores into our vehicles, our clothing, and eventually us, compensated by our profuse sweating that soaks our uniforms literally from shoulder blades to kneecaps. Our equipment absorbs even more sweat as it pinches and encases us like an exoskeleton, transforming us into stinky, sour, salty, and drenched creatures of combat. We have gotten accustomed to it now but we are comforted by the hope that we are now past the summer solstice and daily lose seven minutes of daylight, which will gradually result in cooler temperatures. When we shed our equipment, we attempt to dry out. While this is being accomplished, our uniforms take on the appearance of stiff and badly starched fatigues, with a map of salt stains lining the shores of where the sweat had advanced in our clothing.

"The sun also bores into the metal of our weapons and sometimes our rifles are so hot to the touch that we must wear gloves to remain comfortable. But the sun does not penetrate or lessen our morale or our ability. We are able to fight under these conditions as our enemy has learned to his own detriment."

In another email, written on 26 August, LTC Russell further described the incredibly hot weather that they worked in: "Hot! That's what it is. The heat sears our hands as we hold our weapons, pick up tools and handle parts. When we travel in vehicles, the

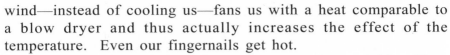
wind—instead of cooling us—fans us with a heat comparable to a blow dryer and thus actually increases the effect of the temperature. Even our fingernails get hot.

"Even so, we endure. The Iraqis are suspect of this. They cannot imagine that we can operate in our battle gear and armored vehicles in the August sun and therefore another explanation must be given other than our toughness and willpower.

Since we are Americans, we must have made some technology that allows us this freedom of movement. Iraqis ask us about our air-conditioned helmets and how they are powered. They talk on the street of our cooling vests and air-conditioned underwear. Despite all our efforts we cannot find these for purchase.

"The markets in Tikrit do offer items for relief from the heat. We have traded greenbacks for underpowered, Chinese made air conditioners and fans—with small benefit. Like most things in Iraq, they put up an initial impressive facade. Given the appearance of functionality, they soon give out or work with marginal effectiveness. We still welcome them and the fact that we have the means to attempt to use them is far better than what the average Infantryman expected when we arrived here.

"Since my last note of July 26th, we have been extremely busy. The time seems to fly, but time also seems surreal to many of us at this point in the mission. Each day becomes just another one. Days of the week blur and were it not for our watches and the incremental changes in the moon we would have scant idea of time at all. We count the days because they promise initial relief from the heat and subsequent hope of seeing our loved ones once more.

"We finally won the battle to get email. It took a lot of effort but now the Soldiers can at least drop a note every few days with better turnaround on news to their families. We set up three terminals in the battalion headquarters for the Soldiers to use... We will keep improving the communication as we can.

"We continued to thin the ranks of those attacking our men. The last week of July, we received detailed information as to the location of an important bodyguard of Saddam Hussein. This particular man was often seen in photos with Saddam and his family. The locals also knew him as a vicious murderer. In a lightning raid, the Recon Platoon and A/1-22 IN secured three houses in residential Tikrit. We were looking specifically for three men; two were bodyguards and one an organizer for the former regime. Within 45 minutes, we had all three men. The raid made national news and the men were extremely valuable to our efforts. The main target—Saddam's personal bodyguard—didn't give up without a fight. Our scouts found him upstairs, emboldened with liquor, attempting to grab a Sterling Submachine Gun. Butt strokes and quick action prevented his death. He swung at the men, but soon found himself being dragged down the stairs, his head hitting each step. Subdued and in his courtyard, with slight bleeding to the forehead, bulbs flashed from the several media present. The news quickly spread in Tikrit to the elation of all, who now saw this former cutthroat of Saddam brought into our custody."

Recruiting and Training of Iraqi Civil Defense Corps and Iraqi Police

Recruiting and training Iraqi citizens to serve in the Iraqi Civil Defense Corps (ICDC) and local police forces was another mission taken on by TF Ironhorse. A total of four battalions of ICDC were to be recruited and trained by TF Ironhorse and would have an active role in providing a safe and secure environment within Iraq. The ICDC's job was to facilitate the transition to a new Iraqi government and foster a sense of national pride. The jobs generated by the corps would also help stimulate economic recovery and provide security options for the new government. The ICDC would perform low threat tasks such as fixed site security, significantly reducing coalition force structure requirements for internal security missions. Members of the ICDC would serve as linguists, provide humanitarian and natural disaster assistance, serve as drivers for contractor vehicles and perform a variety of other tasks. Recruits were screened and had to meet certain criteria before they would be accepted into the ICDC. The program began in August.

In all the cities where TF Ironhorse worked, they also recruited and trained local police officers. That included selecting a reliable police chief, replacing those key police personnel who turned out to be disloyal or had ties to non-compliant forces, and training and equipping those who were selected for the local police forces. A PAO press release on 17 August described the training of police officers in Tikrit. Other cities used much the same training method:

"Citizens of Tikrit will soon have a police force trained on how to be true servants of the people of Iraq, thanks to the efforts of Soldiers from the 720th Military Police Battalion and the Iraqi Police Transition and Integration Program (IPTIP.) A total of 69 Iraqi Police Officers are beginning their second week of instruction in the IPTIP in Tikrit.

"The IPTIP is a three-week course developed by the U.S. led Coalition Provisional Authority. Members of 720 MP BN are conducting classes on topics such as: crime prevention, assisting crime victims; protecting human rights; and modern criminal investigation techniques.

"The goal of the program is to introduce Iraqi police officers to the principles and techniques of policing in a democratic and free society. The course is not intended to be the end of their instruction, but rather the first step in the right direction towards serving all citizens of Iraq.

"The course also focuses on a police code of conduct, freedom of religion, use of force, firearms safety and patrol procedures. Classes are held at the main Tikrit Police HQs and include lectures, small group discussions and activities, and hands-on training.

"Police stations are also being repaired and refurnished so the Iraqi police can have adequate facilities. New furniture, office supplies and communications equipment are among the items being added to police stations.

"The IPTIP is part of a broader Iraqi Police reform program being led by 720 MP BN across the Salah Ad Din province. The police reform program includes interviewing and screening all potential Iraqi Police officers, issuing new uniforms to Iraqi Police officers, as well as providing equipment such as radios, weapons and vehicles to city police forces.

"All these changes are part of a larger goal—to make the Iraqi Police force a strong, independent organization that protects and serves all citizens. It will be their job to make Iraq a safe and secure country in which to live.

"Iraqi police are currently conducting joint patrols and raids in Tikrit and surrounding villages with Soldiers of 720 MP BN."

Training and working closely with the ICDC and local police forces was an integral part of TF Ironhorse's mission for the remainder of their deployment.

Offensive Operations Continue – IED Attacks Increase

Patrols, raids, and checkpoints continued around the clock. On 24 July, Soldiers from 3BCT seized a large weapons cache near Samarra. The weapons and ammunition were found in a house and three adjacent bunkers. Weapons confiscated in the house and one of the bunkers included: ten AK-47 rifles, 42 SKS rifles, 21 submachine guns, seven machine guns, 42 RPG launchers, 152 RPG rounds, 45,000 sticks of TNT, and other ammunition. Additional weapons and ammunition were found in the other two bunkers.

Soldiers from 2BCT guarding a vehicle near the Jalula police station were attacked on 24 July. The attackers threw a grenade underneath the vehicle, wounding one Soldier. Soldiers returned fire, killing one hostile. In a separate incident, a convoy traveling south of Balad hit an improvised explosive device (IED) and encountered small arms fire, wounding one Soldier. Another convoy received small arms fire sixty miles west of Tikrit that night. Soldiers returned fire killing one hostile. No Soldiers were injured in the attack.

The enemy was learning that to try to stand and fight against TF Ironhorse was the same as a death wish. As the summer progressed, the enemy changed his tactics to more extensive use of IEDs. An IED was simple to make and could be very disruptive and deadly. IEDs ranged from a blasting cap with explosives and scraps of metal inside the carcass of a dead dog to massive explosives made from artillery shells or bombs that were rigged along roadsides and detonated as coalition patrols passed by. No unit was immune to IED attacks. It was as common for a logistics convoy to be hit as it was for a combat patrol to be the target.

With the increase in IED use, TF Ironhorse tactics changed. Single vehicle movement was no longer an option. Whenever Soldiers left a FOB, the minimum convoy allowed outside the gate was three vehicles. Work began to add armor plating to Humvees to protect the occupants. Creative talents of mechanics provided the initial armor protection until contracts could be developed for armor upgrading from the local Iraqi economy. Clearing the roads of trash and likely places for hiding IEDs became standard practice, as did firing into places where IEDs were thought to be. The problem continued throughout the deployment but defenses got better as time progressed.

Three TF Ironhorse Soldiers were killed and four wounded in an attack on 26 July in Baqubah. The Soldiers were guarding the Baqubah Children's Hospital when hostiles threw a grenade from an adjacent building.

1BCT patrols continued in and around Tikrit. LTC Steve Russell described the actions of 1-22 IN on 2 and 3 August in an email: "We learned from a frantic local sheik that the bodies of Uday and Qusay Hussein were to be delivered to his village on 2 August and then buried in the local cemetery. Not pleased at the news—as this village also has our men in it—we worked all evening to confirm this. We were told to do nothing. The corpses were to be turned over to the Red Crescent after being flown to our city. We were instructed to provide no escort or involvement. We watched at a distance as three corpses (the third being Mustafa—Qusay's 14 year old son killed while firing an AK-47 from under a bed) were laid into the dirt. Arrogant men, some veiled, surrounded the graves in pathetic prayerful worship over these murdering lifeless forms. They piled dirt mounds above their sunken corpses and then secured an Iraqi flag to each mound with dirt clods along the edges. The funeral passed uneventfully. But a candy box in the middle of the main highway in town would shatter the quiet of the previous two days.

"The enemy launched an attack in the early evening using IEDs (improvised explosive devices). The first was nearly identical to the second except in result. Each bomb appeared to be a box (one candy, the other Kleenex) packed with C-4 explosives and nuts and bolts serving as projectiles. How they were detonated remains unknown.

"Our Recon platoon traveled up the main highway through the city center. Congestion by the telephone exchange offices narrowed the lanes to one. A median, elevated with planters, served as a directional backstop for the candy box concealed among so much other trash in this unsanitary country. The first scout passed by but the second seemed to disappear in a concussive mass of flame and smoke. Glass flew everywhere from the telephone exchange building. Policemen inside were knocked off their feet. Windows from a taxi full of kids blew into the youth as the pavement took on an appearance of an unfinished mosaic of glass.

"Our Soldiers in the third HUMVEE quickly dismounted to

see if they could assist, but the truck was not there. Its driver, his eye bleeding and his arm filled with fragmentation, threw the vehicle into low gear and nursed the HUMVEE with four flat tires out of the blast zone. The Soldier in the back seat took searing heat and fragmentation to the neck and left arm. His left eardrum would register no sound. Men yelled to each other as the staff sergeant—unscathed in the front right seat—assessed his men in the vehicle. The gunner up top could be seen bleeding from the face and neck. But all were moving and so was the vehicle. The scouts continued their wobbly ride toward our compound. The perforated vehicle went through the gate. The men cleared their weapons with bloody hands and then made their way with assistance to the aid station. Two have returned to duty and the third will need more time for his ear to heal but will recover. We remain—Regulars, by God.

"The second bomb detonated approximately twenty minutes later and about two miles north along the same road. Military Police vehicles, similar in appearance to our scout vehicles, became the unintended target. No major damage occurred in the mistimed blast except a few headlamps and cosmetic damage to the fiberglass hood of a single vehicle."

After talking to my wounded scouts and seeing that they were going to be OK, we continued on with our combat patrols. That night I headed south along the highway to the burial village and located the new graves of Saddam's sons. Flushed with the emotion of having three more of my men wounded I took comfort in knowing I was standing over the graves of Uday and Qusay Hussein.

"We spent the day of 3 August planning for a simultaneous raid on each side of the river. We were looking for two individuals that have been organizing attacks on our Soldiers. Our intelligence was good and we found the locations of the farms and a house in the northern suburb. The targeted men were not there, although their families were. We found important photos, information and documents. The raid proved successful, however, as the next morning one of the two men sought came to the civil-military relations office to complain about the raid on his undamaged house. We took him to our complaint department where he has remained ever since."

Operation Ivy Needle – 11 Aug to 9 Sept 2003

Operation Ivy Needle was the sixth in a series of offensive operations conducted by TF Ironhorse. Its name gave a clue to its intent—to stitch up the gaps in the AOR where non-compliant forces remained. Operation Ivy Needle employed surgical strikes to target those areas where there had not been a large or sustained military presence within Salah Ad Din, Diyala and At Tamin provinces. In the first 36 hours, TF Ironhorse Soldiers conducted 270 patrols, 7 raids, and detained 51 individuals. Of the 51 detained, 22 were detained during a raid in the city of Khalis in Diyala Province suspected of conducting anti-coalition and criminal activities. Three were targeted former regime loyalists and 11 were arrested for keeping weapons caches. A total of 39 patrols were joint patrols conducted with Coalition forces and Iraqi police.

During a raid in Ad Dawr, Soldiers from 4-42 FA discovered a large cache of weapons, dinar and IED-making material buried in the yard of a house targeted as a location for storing weapons. Soldiers confiscated a wide variety of munitions and small arms weapons, one jewelry box with gold jewelry, and 20 million Iraqi dinar. Two former regime loyalists were captured.

In another raid near Tikrit, Soldiers discovered another weapons cache including thirteen RPG launchers, two SA-7 missiles, one 60mm mortar, one 82mm mortar round, fifteen 60mm illumination rounds, twenty RPG boosters, 130 sticks of TNT, 23 blocks of PE4A plastic explosive, 30 blasting caps, eight 36M-MK1 grenades, 28 RPG-7 grenades, 100 smoke grenades, four protective masks, four AK-47's, 25 AK-47 magazines, and 4,500 .30 cal. rounds. Additional raids and patrols throughout the TF AOR netted more weapons and equipment.

During a patrol in Abu Rajash, Soldiers from 555 EN GRP discovered a large cache of weapons including two hundred 120mm mortar rounds and one-hundred fifty-seven 155mm mortar rounds.

As part of Operation Ivy Needle, 2BCT conducted Operation Warhorse Cliffhanger on 11 August. It was the first of six brigade air assault missions and was one of the largest air assaults since the Vietnam War. TF 3-67 AR, TF 2-8 IN, and 1-10 CAV air assaulted into Ain Lalin and Qara Tapa in order to capture key terrorist leadership reported to be hiding in the area. The Brigade simultaneously inserted air assault forces and an armored ground force into the objective area. A civil-military assessment was made of both villages and contact with the village leadership was established. Though not ordinarily the strength of mechanized units, the brigade rehearsed and conducted a flawless night air assault. This mission provided the model for five additional brigade air assault missions as well as numerous battalion air assault missions. Given the terrain in Iraq and early warning systems established by key terrorist leadership, the capability to air assault TF Warhorse combat power greatly mitigated the enemy's advantage of knowledge of the terrain. Air assaults provided TF Warhorse with an element of surprise that the enemy could not counter. Weapons and equipment seized in Operation Cliffhanger included: one-hundred eighty 155mm artillery rounds; five 90mm tank rounds; three 120mm mortar rounds and fuses; two 81mm mortar rounds; and one Dishka 12.7mm heavy machine gun.

Later in the month, on 26 August, 2BCT conducted Operation Warhorse Needle, another brigade air assault. Four battalions of TF Warhorse took part—3-67 AR, 1-67 AR, 2-8 IN, and 588 EN. Prior to the onset of war, Saddam Hussein had released prisoners from his jails in order to create chaos and confusion for U.S. forces entering Iraq. A particularly nasty group of criminals had essentially established control of the town of Khalis, between Baqubah and Balad. The crime family had become powerful enough to bully the local police and create a state of fear and lawlessness within the village of Khalis and the surrounding area. These criminals further crossed the line by conducting attacks on TF Warhorse patrols. Operation Warhorse Needle removed this crime family from power and reestablished civil authority in Khalis. Integral to this mission was working with both uniformed and undercover Iraqi Police in order to build the target set. The undercover Iraqi Police nominated the targets to U.S. forces after discovering the objective was too large for them to handle alone. The leader of the crime family was approached on several occasions by Iraqi Police and was repeatedly successful in avoiding arrest; usually through intimidation. Following the completion of Warhorse Needle, the Iraqi Police were once again able to handle the town of Khalis.

Concurrent with the above operations, 2BCT made enormous

progress with the establishment of local governments and infrastructure. After generations of dictatorship, the Warhorse Brigade made critical steps in steering the Iraqis towards self-government. After careful study of the demographics and personalities in each region, TF Warhorse was able to strike a delicate balance between equal representation and freedom of choice. Every component of the government in Diyala had an Iraqi, who had a Warhorse Soldier as an advisor. Company commanders directly worked with local leaders to ensure their needs were being met and that they had available the tools needed to govern. TF Warhorse planned, resourced, and executed selection and elections in the population centers in their AOR. In contrast to the lawlessness found when the BCT arrived, Diyala province had come a long way in reestablishing the sanctity of law. The Iraqi people were beginning to solve problems through peaceful mediation rather than at gunpoint.

On 4 September, elements of TF 1-67 AR conducted a deliberate raid in order to detain high value targets suspected of selling arms. The operation called for a synchronized air insertion and ground movement to allow the TF to quickly seize the initiative and prevent any egress of anti-coalition forces. The TF simultaneously raided both objective houses resulting in the capture of six detainees, two AK-47 rifles, one rocket propelled grenade sight and round, and seven grain sacks containing various improvised explosive device components.

Morale, Welfare, and Recreation

Each month, living conditions improved. A report in The Gunner Gazette described improvements in Taji, home of TF Gunner:

"TF Ironhorse and TF Gunner are closing in on the end of their third month in Iraq. In the past few weeks, TF Gunner has made vast improvements to the quality of life for Soldiers on Taji Military Complex.

"The most improved area on Taji is the dining facility. The quality of the facility has directly affected the quality of service to the Soldiers. It was not the skill of the TF Gunner cooks that was in question, just the tools they had to work with. The building improvements, to include new window glass and ceiling fans, have made the dining facility a cooler place to eat and relax. Also, the new windows have cut down on the dust, making the dining facility easier to keep clean, which has made for a healthier eating environment. The introduction of a refrigerated tractor-trailer or 'reefer van' as they are referred to, has given the cooks the ability to have cold storage for fresh food items. Prior to the arrival of the reefer van, all of the meals were prepackaged and preserved for a long shelf life. The introduction of fresh foods has really improved the taste of the meals, which has directly improved Soldier's morale. It has also given the cooks the ability to serve cold drinks with every meal. Additionally, before installation of the ceiling fans, the dining facility (DFAC) was very hot. The building was hot because of the outside temperature and the heat from the stoves made it almost unbearable. Most Soldiers would rush through and eat fast to escape the heat. It is now nice and cool, everybody eats slower, takes the time to enjoy the meal at hand, and relax a little from their day. Dinner is served in the DFAC every day starting at 1630 hours. Breakfast is at 0630 hours on Saturday and brunch is served on Sunday at 1000 hours.

"Another of the big improvements is the opening of the Morale, Welfare and Recreation (MWR) Center located next door to the DFAC.. This facility gives the Soldiers a place to relax and hang out with their friends. The facility has a 55-inch television screen, stereo system, ping pong tables, a library, and lots of tables and chairs to play cards. The MWR facility also has new windows and ceiling fans which provide a clean and cool place to relax. In the coming weeks there are plans to add a hamburger and soda stand to the MWR facility.

"Improvements continue on Soldier housing as well. The TF has worked to restore running water in many of the buildings being used for housing. The command continues working to purchase prefabricated buildings for those units that are still living in tents on Taji. In addition to running water, generators have been brought in to supply electricity for lighting and air-conditioners. Laundry has also evolved from the use of a rock at the creek to washing machines."

One of the greatest impacts TF Able (555 EN GRP) had was in improving the living conditions of Soldiers by getting them out of tents and into containerized housing units (CHUs). The CHUs are similar to the large shipping containers you might see on a cargo ship. They are basically large rectangular boxes with lights, electrical outlets, heat, and air conditioners. The greatest advantage of these housing containers over tents is that they are clean, sturdy, and provide a weather proof, environmentally controlled living area. The temperatures in Iraq ranged from the 140s Fahrenheit in the summer to the just above freezing in the winter. As we expected our Soldiers to operate in an environment with temperatures this drastic, CHUs gave them a place to relax and sleep in relative comfort.

FOBs are meant to be temporary base camps. As the situation and missions changed, units must be mobile and follow the missions. Since CHUs can be picked up and moved, they provided a good solution to provide a mobile, yet sturdy environmentally controlled living area. Not all TF Ironhorse Soldiers lived in CHUs but those who did had much improved living conditions over the early months of the deployment.

Although CHUs were one of the most appreciated parts of a FOB for our Soldiers, the most important aspect of a FOB was protecting Soldiers by providing them a safe area to live and work. The primary element in providing this protection was pushing a seven-foot berm around the camp to conceal the location and activity of Soldiers and equipment on the base camp and to protect Soldiers from direct enemy fire. However, enemy mortar and rocket fire into the FOBs created a threat that the berm cannot protect against. To mitigate the lethality of these mortars and rockets the engineers emplaced HESCO bastion or concrete barrier walls around the CHUs and helped units sandbag the sides of the CHUs, protecting Soldiers sleeping in the containers.

TF Able constructed 46 FOBs for TF Ironhorse, spread over the entire AOR. These FOBs provided our Soldiers a relatively safe, convenient, and comfortable environment where they lived, worked, and prepared for missions.

Phones and email became more available as the summer progressed. From one satellite phone available per company, banks of phones were installed in each FOB and made available in all units. As has always been the case, availability was better for some units than others, but overall, the availability of phones greatly improved during the summer months. Similarly, email access opened another almost instant means of communications from Iraq back to the US. Mail delivery likewise improved and the early frustrations of soradic communications started to ease.

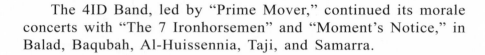

The 4ID Band, led by "Prime Mover," continued its morale concerts with "The 7 Ironhorsemen" and "Moment's Notice," in Balad, Baqubah, Al-Huissennia, Taji, and Samarra.

Civil Affairs Operations

Civil affairs operations were as important a part of TF Ironhorse operations as were their offensive military actions. Not typically reported by the media, the accomplishments were critical to helping the Iraqi people rebuild their country that had suffered so long from the neglect of the Saddam Hussein regime. With elements of the 418 CA BN working in each BCT AO, virtually all TF Ironhorse Soldiers spent a portion of their efforts working to improve the lives of the Iraqi citizens. The following press releases from the TF Ironhorse PAO show a few examples of successes during the long hot summer:

The 418 CA BN and 4 EN BN finished repairs to two water pumps in Shayke Gassim Eldori, a village five kilometers south of Ad Dawr. The water treatment facility there could again provide the normal water supply to the Ad Dawr populace and surrounding communities.

The 5 EN BN made a difference in the small town of Al Asriya. The engineers adopted the poor rural village located about 15 km northwest of Baghdad in early July and completed a variety of projects to improve conditions for locals. After meeting with village leaders and elders, the Soldiers of C/5 EN rolled into town with bulldozers, dump trucks and a bucket loader to tackle the massive amounts of trash and waste strewn throughout the village. The trash posed a serious health risk for families living in the town. The dozers moved huge mounds of trash, dirt, and debris into impromptu landfills and a burn pit. The cleanup effort helped Al Asriya move one step closer to living up to its name, which means "model town." During Saddam Hussein's regime the town was renamed Al Faris, which means 'of the family of Saddam.' Soldiers helped erect two new signs along Highway 1 to show the village had restored its original name.

After touring three rundown schools, with no running water and frayed electrical wires dangling from the walls, 5 EN BN drew up a contract to begin repairs. Projects also were undertaken to modernize the sewage system since raw sewage flowed out of the homes into shallow trenches lining the roads and courtyards, posing a health risk. In addition to improving the health situation, the improvements provided much need jobs for the residents, since approximately 90% of the men were unemployed. A spirit of mutual cooperation developed between the residents of Al Asriya and 5 EN BN. Under Saddam's reign, towns like Al Asriya across Iraq were allowed to deteriorate as he built his own luxurious palaces and stockpiled weapons.

The Soldiers of HQ Company, 4BCT "Iron Eagles" completed many projects to improve the lives of the local citizens living in the village of Al Seccor. In early August they held the reopening ceremony of the Al Seccor health clinic, which had been closed since before the war. The unit provided funding and a lot of good old fashioned elbow grease to refurbish the building, which suffered from years of neglect and damage during the war. The village and the Iron Eagle brigade had worked closely together since April. Goodwill abounded in the Al Seccor community as parents, smiling children and health care workers welcomed members of the brigade at the ceremony. With the refurbishing of the health clinic complete, and other projects in the works in Al Seccor, the Iron Eagles were committed to helping rebuild the village's infrastructure.

Soldiers from 3-16 FA, along with hospital workers and community leaders, took part in an opening ceremony for the Ar Rashidiya Hospital on 2 August. The hospital is located in the Ar Rashidiya community north of Baghdad. The facility was once the biggest and best-equipped hospital in Baghdad until it was ravaged and gutted by looters during the war. Initially, 3-16 FA set up its headquarters in the destroyed hospital, but after meeting with doctors and community leaders who emphasized the critical need for health care in the area, they decided to help restore the hospital. Soldiers began rehabilitating the hospital by reconnecting its power and water systems. Using battalion money, Soldiers also bought and installed generators for the site. With the help of a hospital surgeon, they hired engineers to fix the first floor of the hospital. Workers repaired windows, walls, ceilings, and doors and painted the hallways. The project represents three months of work and was a combined effort of Soldiers and 65 employees and eight separate contractors. A portion of the hospital was capable of treating patients. The entire hospital reconstruction effort cost approximately three million dollars of coalition funds.

Soldiers working with local Iraqis helped complete a building renovation project in Tikrit. Over a five-week period, Soldiers from 418 CA BN played a role in helping refurbish the Agriculture Ministry Building. Work on the six-story building was completed on 8 August, with workers eagerly returning to work in their new office space. The facility had been run down after years of neglect and from looting during the war. Repairs included exterior cleaning and painting, replacement of window glass, and old electrical systems. In addition, new desks, copy machines, computers and fans were installed in the building. Approximately 50 Iraqis work in the Agriculture Ministry Building. The renovation project cost approximately $85,000, with an additional $10,000 spent on office furniture. The project employed 100 local Iraqi workers and helped to stimulate the local economy.

The 244th Engineer Combat Battalion (Heavy) out of Denver, Colorado reached out to help residents of the village of Al Saquor located northwest of Tikrit. The village of 1,244 was scattered with rubble and shards of glass. Many of the town's children did not have shoes to wear. Electricity and fresh water were limited. Most of the village men were unemployed, since many locals worked at the Iraqi Air Force Academy, which is now occupied by US forces and known as Forward Operating Base Speicher.

Soldiers from 244 EN BN embraced the idea of adopting and helping the village by volunteering their time and talents and helping hands. They began by bringing heavy construction equipment into town to clean up the rubble, hauling nearly 200 loads away in their 20-ton dump trucks. They installed a new generator purchased by the US military to supplement the unreliable power grid in town. Contracts were solicited to replace the irrigation well and pump to return the areas vegetation to its former lush green state.

The village children enjoyed a new soccer field leveled by the battalion's road grader. A team of carpenters also designed and built playground equipment that was installed. A Soldier brought a welding trailer to the village and repaired old bicycles used by the children and adults to get around the village. The Battalion's Physician Assistant spent time with villagers who recognized the international symbol of the Red Cross on the sides of his ambulance. He performed an array of medical tasks, from applying bandages to children's feet to cleaning up after a

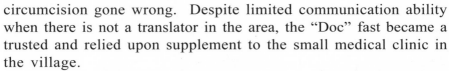

circumcision gone wrong. Despite limited communication ability when there is not a translator in the area, the "Doc" fast became a trusted and relied upon supplement to the small medical clinic in the village.

Farmers in the greater Tikrit area have a place to take their wheat crops to be processed, thanks to the efforts of 1-22 IN. During the war, the province's only flour distribution center was looted, vandalized and gutted by fire. The center had been vital to agricultural commerce in the area, since it was where farmers brought their wheat crops to be milled and sold. Members of 1-22 IN realized the importance of the facility and set about plans to repair it. Using $37,000 in unit discretionary funds, they hired a local Iraqi contractor to renovate the site. A 12-man crew worked three weeks making structural repairs to the warehouse and office areas of the building. They also fixed a faulty electrical system and brought in new office furniture and equipment. The flour distribution center reopened in early August, providing jobs for its workers, generating a source of cash for the area's farmers, and food for Iraqis.

The men, women and children of the village of Ash Sharqat were all smiles on 9 August, as once again, running water flowed into their community, thanks to the dedicated efforts of TF Ironhorse engineers. Ash Sharqat, a small town on the dusty plains of northern Iraq, had been without running water since 1982, when Saddam Hussein ordered the town's water supply to be re-routed to an Iraqi Army base being built in the area. During the engineer's initial assessment of the town's infrastructure, they discovered Ash Sharqat's critical need for water and quickly went into action. Using $40,000 of commander's emergency response funds, they established work contracts and purchased 7,000 meters of PVC pipe and five water pumps. Iraqi contractors were hired, installed pump stations, running the new pipe to the village from an existing government water line. In two weeks, engineers were able to fix twenty-years of neglect and provide running water to 300 homes.

Working with local education officials, 1BCT identified schools in critical need of refurbishment, allocating discretionary funds for repairs. On 16 August, the doors of the 'Model School' in Tikrit opened, welcoming visitors for a look at the future of Iraqi education. Two schools are housed in the remodeled facility; the Al Shaab Boys Intermediate School and the Al Nithal

Boys Secondary School. Education officials hope to bring all schools up to the 'Model School' standard over the next few years. 1BCT committed over $80,000 and employed more than 65 local Iraqi citizens in the refurbishment project. Work began on 28 June, with workers repairing major structural damage to walls and ceilings. Structural damage to the back section and second floor of the school meant only 12 of 36 classrooms could be used— now they are all operational. Litter and debris was removed from the school grounds. The interior and exterior walls of the school received a new coat of paint. Workers repaired windows, installed new doors, lights, and ceiling fans throughout the facility. Repairs were also made on eight toilet facilities. The school also received 200 new student desks.

The refurbished school will be able to accommodate up to 700 students, twice as many as before. Because of the lack of space, the intermediate school had met in the mornings and the secondary school met in the afternoons. Now both schools have the space they need and can meet at the same time and can extend school hours. The project is just one of many being conducted within the TF Ironhorse AOR. A total of 19 schools have already been repaired at a cost of $500,000. Work is planned or in progress on 132 more schools at a price of four million dollars.

Kirkuk, a city in northern Iraq with a diverse population of Arabs, Kurds, Turkmen, and Asyrians, has always been a city ripe for development. That was only a dream under the brutal dictatorship of the former regime. With its rich reserves of oil, thriving agriculture, and its strategic location, Kirkuk is capable of becoming a major transportation hub and leading metropolitan and commercial center for Iraq.

In mid-August, a group of approximately 100 political and business leaders, and senior leaders from TF Ironhorse and coalition forces, met in Sulaimanya. The meeting was a first of its kind business symposium focused on developing economic growth for the city. During the event, organized in part by the 173d Airborne Brigade, participants covered a variety of topics.

A local political leader spoke to the group about strategic city planning, current city layout, future city layout and zoning.

COL William Mayville, 173d Airborne Brigade commander, focused on Kirkuk's suitability as a major transportation hub.

"There is so much unrealized potential here, from its airport

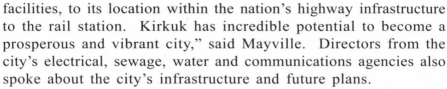

facilities, to its location within the nation's highway infrastructure to the rail station. Kirkuk has incredible potential to become a prosperous and vibrant city," said Mayville. Directors from the city's electrical, sewage, water and communications agencies also spoke about the city's infrastructure and future plans.

"From a proposal to turn the dusty, muddy, garbage strewn river area into a modern and investment attracting river walk, to a number of presentations that showcased the work completed inside the city since its liberation April 10, the symposium showcased the city's potential for growth and profit. All who attended were very pleased with the spirit of cooperation and common goal of developing Kirkuk's vast potential.

"Countries all over the world are competing with each other in a world dominated by unions and fierce competition," said Mr. Abbas Abdul Razik, Adv., vice president of the Arab Bar Association. "It's through meetings and symposiums like this that we here in Iraq and in Kirkuk will be able to better develop our city and our nation."

Farmers in the countryside south of Balad have a lot shorter distance to travel to get to town thanks to the efforts of 864 EN BN. The Engineers installed a new bridge for the residents, shortening their daily five-mile commute. Using a dump truck and crane, the Soldiers emplaced a new bridge on 16 August. The previous structure was made of mud and wood and was unable to support much weight. The new bridge has increased weight capacity and will be used by hundreds of residents each day.

The 3rd Brigade Combat Team, working with 308 CA BDE, built wells for Iraqis in their area. The wells brought much needed clean water to people in the local villages. Three wells have been completed in the Jurezrat-Hardinia area at a cost of $23,000 and provide water for approximately 10,000 people. Plans are underway to build four more wells in Neyrab, Al-Khathra, Mawakib and Al-Aleea Primary Schools in Yathrib.

Community leaders, and Soldiers from TF Ironhorse, 173rd Airborne Brigade, have joined forces to repair the neglected sewage system in Kirkuk. This extensive project was designed to rid the streets of disease-laden sewage that families have had to live, bathe, and wash dishes in for over two decades. Under the former regime, Kirkuk's sewage system had been ignored for the past 25 years, leaving it in shambles. Before the sewage repair project was began, 30% of the city's sewage was dumped in the streets, 50% was taken by vacuum trucks to a non-operational sewage plant where it quickly seeped back into the city's water system, and the other 20% was stowed in containers, then dumped outside the city.

With the help of Coalition forces, the city worked to repair this key piece of infrastructure. Currently, six projects are under construction, already having a significant impact on improving the living conditions and cleaning the sewage from the streets. To date, over $280,000 has been spent on repairs toward this ambitious project. The goal is to replace the dilapidated system throughout the entire city of Kirkuk. The project, so far, has employed over 1,200 local nationals. The project manager has hired local Kirkuk contractors to complete the much-needed improvements to the city. He has ensured that each project is multi-ethnic and is helping the entire city. When completed, the new sewer system will service the entire city, improving the health and standard of living for approximately 900,000 citizens. Raw sewage running in the streets has been replaced by children running soccer balls and enjoying clean, healthy neighborhoods.

Task Force Ironhorse Soldiers in 3-66 AR approved funds for work to be done to improve the secondary school for boys in the town of Siyniah. Leaders of the town, which has about 14,000 citizens, approached the 3-66 AR's CMIC (Civil Military Information Center) requesting assistance to get the school repaired and operational again. The school had not received any funds since 1981. 14 EN BN conducted the assessment and found that numerous repairs were required and electrical wiring would have to be installed. A request was submitted and a contract was put up for bid. Local Iraqi laborers started working on the improvements a few days later. The following repairs were made: new doors and frames installed; rooms rewired; lights and fans installed; new glass for windows installed; repainting rooms due to water and structural damage; and replaced floors and tile. The exterior fence and basketball court were also repaired. There had been some anti-U.S. sentiment in this area, and repairing the school produced positive relations with coalition Soldiers. The local citizens now know the coalition forces are there to help the Iraqi people.

TF Ironhorse Soldiers from B Detachment of the 230th Finance Battalion and 418 CA BN, in support of 1-66 AR, assessed Al Rasheed banks in the Samarra region to determine suitability for their use as exchange banks for the new Iraqi Dinar, set to begin 15 October 2003. The 230th Finance Battalion completed its assessment of one branch and a project was submitted by the 418th to make it operational. By making the banks operational again in the Iraqi communities, and supporting the exchange of the new Iraqi currency, a positive step for rebuilding Iraq's infrastructure has been demonstrated. It also is openly showing the Iraqi citizens that coalition forces are turning over the running of their country back to the Iraqi people.

Sadly, the civil affairs accomplishments noted in this section were not reported by the press. By reporting them here, these significant steps taken by TF Ironhorse throughout their AOR during the long hot summer of 2003 will be preserved.

From the arrival of TF Ironhorse in Iraq in April through the end of Operation Ivy Needle on 9 September, twenty-two TF Ironhorse Soldiers gave their lives supporting the liberation of Iraq from the Saddam Hussein regime. Unfortunately, many more would lose their lives in the months ahead.

TF Ironhorse Soldiers on patrol

BEFORE (24 JUL)

**Raw Sewage Running
In the Streets**

AFTER (11 AUG)

**Over $80,000 Worth Of
Vehicles and Equipment
and Employing over
1,500 workers**

One of many projects by TF Ironhorse Soldiers to improve the infrastructure and economy in Iraq. This is the work of 173rd ABN BDE in Kirkuk

A Band of Brothers - A/1-22 IN Soldiers in the Sunni Triangle

Abrams tank of B/1-67 AR crushes captured RPGs

3BCT Soldiers move captured ammunition so it can be destroyed

Soldiers of C/1-22 IN stopping Iraqis attacking the Saddam Birthday Palace on 24 July 2003

B/1-10 CAV tank on the Iran-Iraq border near Mandeli. The marker is a warning sign that you are approaching the border and to keep away. The troops converted it with a 4ID patch on one side and a CAV guidon on the other—July 2003

A TF Ironhorse engineer disarms a roadside IED

Soldiers of 1-22 IN questioning Iraqis in Tikrit

The American Soldier

4ID - TF Ironhorse Infantryman defending America

X

Continuing The Mission, in Cooler Weather

Continued success with missions, Operation Focus, Operations Typhoon I and II, Operation Ivy Cyclone, Combat operations, Technology unique to TF Ironhorse, Military police operations, Civil action and rebuilding

19 September 2003 to 12 December 2003

S EPTEMBER WAS STILL UNBEARABLY HOT, BUT RE-lief from the sweltering heat was in sight. TF Ironhorse Soldiers could feel the slight cooling, from the 120-130 degree range in July and August to the 100-110 range in September. They also knew that October highs were expected to be in the low 90's and by November the weather would cool into the low 80's during the days.

Operational tempo remained high. Operation Focus began on 10 September, one day after completion of Operation Ivy Needle. This operation, as its name implied, focused on killing or capturing remaining non-compliant cells and key figures leading attacks against coalition forces.

Operation Ivy Focus – 10 September to 5 November

Units conducted a series of successful raids and patrols throughout the TF AOR targeting specific former regime loyalists suspected of selling weapons and building IEDs to be used against coalition forces. In the first 24 hours of the operation, they conducted 240 patrols and seven raids, including 56 joint patrols conducted with the Iraqi police, Iraqi Civil Defense Corps, and Border Guards. Forty-eight individuals were detained over the period—six were targeted individuals.

In Tikrit, Soldiers from 1-22 IN conducted a raid on several buildings which local informants reported as housing subversive elements and workshops used to build IEDs. The raid resulted in

143

uncovering two IED workshops and the detention of five Iraqis suspected of building IEDs. Confiscated materials included batteries, electrical wire, remote control devices, one IED, chemicals, dynamite, plastic explosives, mortar rounds, smoke grenade canisters, plastic grenade casings, blasting caps, fuses, small arms ammunition, two pistols, two AK-47s with magazines, one shotgun, walkie-talkies, military uniforms, several military training manuals and six million Iraqi dinar. In other raids across the AOR, TF Ironhorse Soldiers seized a wide array of weapons and bomb making materials. Day and night raids, patrols, checkpoints, and other actions marked the continuing offensive spirit of TF Ironhorse as they worked through September, October, and November.

Newly trained Iraqi police began to take part in raids while US troops watched from a distance, ready to react if required. "We want the Iraqi police to take the initiative and be as independent as possible, so that we can go home when our job is done here,'" said LTC David Poirier, CO of 720 MP BN.

In one raid near Tikrit, a large cache of buried weapons and ammunition was found in a farm field. This was not uncommon as each day more and more lethal ammunition dumps were uncovered all across the AOR.

Ammunition and weapons were everywhere, or so it seemed. The entire country appeared to be a massive arms and ammunition dump. Mounds of earth and sand disguised huge concrete cellars full of arms. Small arms and large missiles were strewn across the desert. Craters showed where explosions—some controlled, some accidental—had taken place. The death toll from the ammunition sites rose rapidly. Many Iraqis died while looting former storage sites of Saddam's army. At a massive ammunition dump outside Bayji, guarded around the clock by 3-66 AR, two blasts in late August and early September killed 27 Iraqi looters. It was a constant challenge for the Soldiers to keep the Iraqis away from the site. In one night, they captured almost 50 Iraqis who were looting the dump. It was unknown whether they were taking the munitions to be used against the coalition forces or just for the value of the components in the ammunition. Regardless of the reason, it was a dangerous practice, both for the Iraqis and for the Americans who had to stop the looting.

On the second anniversary of the attacks on the World Trade

Center and the Pentagon, TF Ironhorse Soldiers paused to remember how 11 September 2001 had changed the world. MG Odierno, in a ceremony conducted in front of one of Saddam's palaces in Tikrit, said, "We must remember why we are here today, why we are standing on the steps of a palace in Saddam Hussein's hometown of Tikrit, why we are here. We're here to liberate a country from a brutal dictator who does not allow his people to have those freedoms, we're here to build a bright and better future for Iraq, one where its children can grow, one where they can be free, one where they can choose their own path, one where they can choose what they want to do in the future."

Raids and patrols continued through September. On 21 September, Soldiers with 3-66 AR discovered a large cache of 82mm mortar systems southeast of Bayji. Information obtained from the site assisted the Iraqi Police and 3-66 AR in the discovery of a second cache site consisting of over 100 mortar rounds.

On 27 September, troops of 1-22 IN uncovered one of their biggest weapons caches to date at a farm near Saddam Hussein's birthplace, including anti-aircraft missiles and a huge quantity of explosives used to make the homemade bombs that had killed numerous American Soldiers. In the raid on a farm near the village of Owja, where Saddam was born, troops dug through the soft dirt near a riverbank and found the cache underneath a covering of reeds and straw. The cache turned up 23 Russian-made surface to air missiles, 1,000 pounds of plastic explosives, four rocket propelled grenade launchers with 115 rockets, a mortar and 40 mortar rounds, 1,300 blasting caps and 423 hand grenades. The most significant part of the capture were the surface-to-air missiles and explosives. The SA-7 shoulder-fired missiles could pose a significant threat to the helicopters used by the U.S. military in and around Tikrit.

Also on 27 September, the U.S. Army gave Iraq's provisional government responsibilities for patrolling a stretch of the desert border between Iraq and Iran. The transfer was significant as border security was crucial. The fear was always present that al-Qaida or other terrorists could sneak through with illegal Iranian pilgrims en route to Shiite holy sites in Iraq. It was the first time since the fall of Saddam Hussein that Iraqis were given complete authority over a border area. American forces continued in an advisory role. "This is a great example of new Iraqi security forces

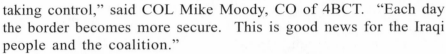

taking control," said COL Mike Moody, CO of 4BCT. "Each day the border becomes more secure. This is good news for the Iraqi people and the coalition."

The frontier included some of the most treacherous terrain in Iraq. It ran from the edges of Kurdish-controlled territory in northern Iraq to a point just southeast of Baghdad, encompassing nearly all of Diyala province. Troops of 1-10 CAV started training the Iraqi border police in May. Training included human rights of detainees as well as searches for Islamic militants or suicide bombers trying to blend in with pilgrims. LTC Reggie Allen, CO of 1-10 CAV, reported that his Soldiers, equipped with Bradleys and scout helicopters, had stopped more than 14,000 illegal pilgrims since the end of August. When caught, the Iranians were held in a collection facility, screened, and returned home.

Conditions for 1-10 CAV and other coalition troops along the border were especially harsh. Temperatures soared—there was no access to air conditioning, and Soldiers often slept on cots in the open desert to cool down at night. There was no running water and latrines, made of 55-gallon drums cut in half, were cleaned by pouring diesel fuel into them to burn (a common practice in much of the TF Ironhorse AOR). Sand fleas were everywhere. Bites from sand fleas soon caused another problem for 1-10 CAV. A parasite, leischmaniasis, carried by the sand fleas infected many of the Soldiers. Rather than risk the long recovery and scarring caused by leischmaniasis if not aggressively treated, several Soldiers were evacuated back to Walter Reed Army Hospital for thirty days of treatment. 1-10 CAV was dealing with the same level of hardship that their forefathers, the famous "Buffalo Soldiers," had dealt with on the American frontier in the late 1800's—and they did it without complaint, just as their forefathers did.

In the less remote parts of Diyala province, each of the 2BCT battalions recruited, trained, equipped, and fielded an Iraqi Civil Defense Corps (ICDC) battalion and Iraqi Police Forces (IPF). The ICDC and IPF were vital in returning control of the region to the Iraqi people and allowed them to establish their own legitimacy. The 2BCT battalions trained these forces while maintaining offensive pressure on the enemy threat. Once recruited, trained, and outfitted, the ICDC secured key infrastructure—banks, hospitals, utility stations, and check points.

This freed the 2BCT battalions to focus on offensive operations. 2BCT elements conducted countless joint operations with the ICDC and IPF in an effort to establish their confidence and legitimize their roles in the eyes of the Iraqi people. Joint operations were particularly effective in putting an Iraqi face on Iraqi security. One benefit of working with the IPF and ICDC was when culturally sensitive areas or structures, such as mosques, were required to be searched for weapons or terrorists. Insurgent propagandists would attempt to incite demonstrations and riots and promote anti-U.S. sentiment, but the IPF and ICDC robbed them of the opportunity by conducting the searches themselves.

While the number of attacks against coalition troops in Iraq remained fairly constant, the tactics enemy forces used changed. Enemy forces moved away from small-unit infantry attacks and resorted to more hit-and-run attacks, using IEDs, mortars, or rocket-propelled grenades. They had learned that if they stayed and fought, they would die. Roughly half of the attacks against coalition forces were small, with fewer than six people ambushing coalition convoys or patrols. The other half was a mixture of IEDs, remotely fired rockets, or mortar attacks. Targets were often Iraqis rather than coalition personnel as they tried to discourage the population from cooperating with the coalition. The new tactics increased the casualties among our Soldiers. After losing 22 TF Ironhorse Soldiers in the April through August period, another six were killed in September, 15 in October, and 11 in November—many the result of roadside IED explosions. Renewed focus was required to eliminate that threat to our forces.

Mid Tour Leave Announced

A rumor that had been circulating for several weeks was confirmed on 23 September. Many TF Ironhorse and other US Soldiers would be eligible to return to the US or their European base on a two-week leave. MG Odierno confirmed the announcement with a letter that day:

September 23, 2003

Families and Soldiers of Task Force Ironhorse,

We have an opportunity for many Task Force Ironhorse Soldiers to spend some time with their families in the middle of our deployment. The Secretary of Defense has approved a CENTCOM program that will allow Soldiers serving a 365-day tour of duty to take two weeks of mid-tour leave. Soldiers are eligible to take leave between their fourth and tenth month of deployment.

This is an expensive, complex undertaking by the Department of Defense; our leadership is making this investment in the morale of troops and families to lessen the hardship endured by families every day we are deployed. We will begin sending Soldiers on leave immediately and will continue the program through January; we will begin preparing units for redeployment in February.

We are in a battle daily throughout Iraq; ongoing missions and the program's enormous logistical requirements mean that we must limit the number of Soldiers away from their units. Therefore, not all Soldiers will be able to take leave prior to redeployment. Commanders will prioritize participation based primarily on the length of Soldiers' deployment; those that left home first will be the first to go on leave.

The mid-tour program is designed to be executed over a seven-month period. Since we are nearing the seventh month of deployment, we have only a four-month window to get as many Soldiers home as possible. Approximately 21,000 of the 27,000 Soldiers assigned to Task Force Ironhorse are with us for the full one-year tour and are eligible to take leave.

Despite only having four months to work with, we estimate that 60% of all Soldiers who deployed in April or before will be able to take advantage of this program.

Commanders must balance the mission with Soldiers' welfare, and will select participants fairly and equitably taking into consideration all mission and personal factors.

All flights from theater will be routed through Frankfurt, Germany, for Europe-based Soldiers, and will terminate in Baltimore-Washington International airport (BWI).

Soldiers will pay for round trip transportation from BWI to their leave location. Soldiers will purchase their tickets prior to departure from Kuwait to provide as much notice as possible to families preparing for the arrival.

This is a tremendous opportunity for our Soldiers. It is unfortunate that not everyone will be able to participate, but I am confident that leaders will take care of their Soldiers and manage the program fairly. I have tremendous faith in the Soldiers and families of Task Force Ironhorse, and I trust this program will run as smoothly as possible. Like all other missions, our Soldiers will complete this one in exceptional fashion.

Steadfast and Loyal,

Raymond T. Odierno

MG, Commanding

Mid Tour Leave was music to the ears of some Soldiers and families—a cause of concern for others. Questions quickly arose—"Will my Soldier be one of the 60% who get to come home, or will my Soldier be part of the 40% who do not get to take mid tour leave? Will my Soldier be treated fairly in the selection process? Will Reservists and National Guard Soldiers Will my Soldier make it home for our special day (anniversary, birthday, Christmas, birth of a child, etc.)? Will my Soldier be at greater risk while others are away from the unit on leave? Can we afford the expenses for my Soldier to come home? Will the second farewell, when my Soldier goes back to Iraq, be harder than the first one was?"

These and many other questions were dealt with by TF Ironhorse leadership as the program rolled out. Never in history had such a program been implemented. R&R within the theater was common in previous wars. To come back to the USA from a combat zone, and then to have to return, was unprecedented on this scale. The rules and guidelines had to be written and adjusted based on experience as the program moved forward. Some Soldiers opted not to go home. In their own personal way, they preferred to not go through the second separation, or they had other reasons for taking themselves out of the leave pool.

Overall, the mid tour leave program was a resounding success and continued with Operation Iraqi Freedom II. Additional entry points, in Atlanta and Dallas, were added to Baltimore. The decision was made for the military to pay for airfare all the way to the final destination for each Soldier. Soldiers got much needed rest and relaxation from their daily grind in Iraq, and great mid tour leave memories were made for the Soldiers and their families.

Operation ICE (Iraqi Currency Exchange)
The 230th Finance Battalion (230 FN BN) had the responsibility to insure that Operation ICE was successful in the TF Ironhorse AOR. Since their April arrival in Iraq, the 230 FN BN had provided financial support for TF Ironhorse. They were spread across the AOR—FOB Speicher, FOB Ironhorse, FOB Anaconda, FOB Warhorse, and FOB Warrior. Typical tasks included providing disbursement support, active duty and reserve component military pay support, and giving technical advice and policy guidance to commanders—much the same job as they had

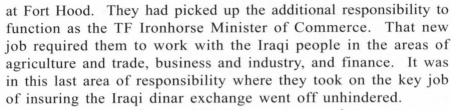

at Fort Hood. They had picked up the additional responsibility to function as the TF Ironhorse Minister of Commerce. That new job required them to work with the Iraqi people in the areas of agriculture and trade, business and industry, and finance. It was in this last area of responsibility where they took on the key job of insuring the Iraqi dinar exchange went off unhindered.

A major step in moving Iraq to a new democracy was replacing the old currency, dinar, (which had Saddam Hussein's face prominently pictured on each bill) with a new dinar, similar in appearance to Iraqi currency issued prior to 1990 known as "Swiss" dinar. The Ministry of Finance of the Coalition Provisional Authority (CPA) had ultimate responsibility for the currency exchange. Contractors were hired to lead the operation, with minimum coalition involvement desired. The plan was to maximize the use of ICDC and Iraqi Police Forces in providing security, but it was known that each BCT would have a key security role to insure nothing went wrong. Leading the entire effort for TF Ironhorse was 230 FN BN.

The plan was in three phases. The first phase, scheduled for 5-14 October, was the delivery of new dinar, printed in Europe, to selected banks and the simultaneous collection of old dinar. Phase two was the actual exchange of dinar at banks from 15 October 2003 to 15 January 2004. There was no limit to the amount of dinar that could be exchanged. Old dinar was to be defaced immediately to render it worthless. The marked dinar was then collected and moved to destruction points within each region and burned. Phase three was resupplying banks with new dinar, as necessary, during the exchange period.

Exchange banks were identified in each province to receive the new dinar. Salah Ad Din province had 12 exchange banks named, ranging from Bayji in the north, Tikrit and Ad Dawr in the central part of the province, through Samarra and Balad in the south. At Tamim province had 9 exchange banks, primarily in the Kirkuk area. Diyala province had 16 exchange banks scattered throughout the province. In late September, liaison officers from each BCT were briefed on their responsibilities. Between 29 September and 2 October, bank managers were trained by the CPA and contractors on how to perform the exchange.

Contractors built storage and sorting facilities, including life support systems, at distribution hubs. They provided local security for the distribution hubs, fixed and rotary wing transport for distribution, ground transport vehicles, convoy escort, facilities for destruction and security of the old dinar, and security/ID passes for their personnel.

TF Ironhorse provided point security at exchange points, using ICDC, Iraqi police, and TF Ironhorse Soldiers, if required. It was also their responsibility to maintain communications/liaison with contractors in their sector, develop a contingency plan to assume the contractor task as required, provide for casualty evacuation, provide a quick reaction force (QRF), and be prepared to get involved in any situation where the mission might be at risk of failure.

The contractor had limited resources and reserves to conduct the dinar exchange activities. It was the responsibility of 230 FN BN to assume the lead in identifying contractor shortfalls and to respond in a timely manner with appropriate TF Ironhorse resources. Each BCT had responsibility to secure banks on days designated for dinar delivery—starting from one hour before opening until one hour after closing time. This required a minimum of two armored vehicles with six Soldiers for each exchange bank. Additionally, they were to provide an armed escort to the convoy while traveling through their AOR. A QRF was positioned within 30 minutes of each bank during delivery and within 30 minutes of a moving convoy. A QRF consisted of an armored or mechanized infantry platoon and a section of AH-64 Apache helicopters. The TF Ironhorse resource requirement was significant.

TF Ironhorse also had the responsibility to execute an information operations plan in support of the exchange. Information had to be aggressively conveyed to the Iraqi people to insure the success of Operation ICE. This included written materials (posters and fact sheets), newspaper advertisements, radio advertisements, and working with local leaders to insure they were familiar with the specifics of the exchange program.

The extensive planning, preparation, and execution allowed Operation ICE to be successful in the TF Ironhorse AOR. Between 5-14 October, 110 ICE convoys moved through hostile areas to 34 banks. Delivery of over two trillion new Iraqi dinars was accomplished and over 25,000 one-hundred pound bags of "Saddam" dinar were collected for destruction. No Soldier or contractors were killed during the operation, despite three engagements with non-compliant forces in Samarra.

The Samarra attacks were reported in a TF Ironhorse press release as follows: "4ID and TF Ironhorse Soldiers repelled multiple ambush attempts on two separate logistic support convoys in the afternoon of 30 November, killing 46, wounding at least 18 and capturing eight in the city of Samarra. Many of the dead attackers were found wearing Fedayeen uniforms. Five Soldiers were wounded; two sustained minor injuries and will return to duty. None were life threatening, although three Soldiers did require additional treatment and were evacuated to a nearby medical facility. A civilian in the convoy was also wounded and was evacuated to the same location. The convoys were carrying new Iraqi currency for deposit at Samarra banks as part of the dinar exchange program.

"Both convoys were moving into Samarra when they were attacked with IEDs, small arms, mortars and rocket propelled grenades. The attackers attempted to block one of the convoy's route with a crude makeshift barricade. The barricade was immediately breached.

"The logistic support convoys were moving to two separate locations in Samarra. The coordinated simultaneous attacks occurred at approximately 1:30 p.m. One attack occurred on the east side of the city and one on the west. Soldiers fought the attackers at numerous locations in both ambushes. The exchanges lasted for many minutes as the convoy vehicles moved through the city.

"At each location, Soldiers from 1-66 AR and military police returned fire with small arms, 120mm tank rounds and 25mm cannon fire from Bradley Fighting Vehicles. In all of the clashes, coalition firepower overwhelmed the attackers, resulting in significant enemy losses.

"The attackers fired rocket propelled grenades and automatic weapons at the convoys from the rooftops of buildings and from alleyways. Three of the buildings the attackers used for cover during the ambush were destroyed by coalition fire.

"At approximately 2:25 p.m., in a separate attack, in another section of Samarra, 244 EN BN Soldiers were traveling in a convoy when four men using automatic weapons, riding in a black BMW, ambushed them. The Soldiers returned fire, wounding all four.

The attackers were eventually captured. The Soldiers searched the vehicle and discovered three AK-47 assault rifles and two rocket propelled grenade launchers."

Operations Ivy Typhoon I, II – 1 October to 5 November
Ivy Typhoon was another in the continuing series of offensive operations conducted by TF Ironhorse. Ivy Typhoon was timed to counter the expected increase in enemy actions during the Muslim holy month of Ramadan. It was also designed to counter the increasing threat of IEDs along the roads and supply routes. Freedom of maneuver on roads was critical to TF Ironhorse and the Iraqi people. As more ICDC personnel were trained, they manned many of the AOR checkpoints. Aviation patrols along supply routes increased to seek out those individuals who were planting the IEDs along the roads. Orders were to eliminate any suspicious persons found along the roads after curfew hours.

More than 1.2 billion Muslims worldwide celebrated the start of Ramadan, Islam's holy month of fasting, on October 26 or 27. The start and end dates for Ramadan varied because the beginning of Islamic lunar months depends on the actual sighting of the new moon. During the month of Ramadan, Muslims eat a small meal prior to each morning's dawn. They then abstain from food, drink and other physical pleasures during the daylight hours. Believers end their fast just after sunset. Often this meal is taken at a cheerful gathering of family, friends or other community members. The last ten days of the month are considered among the most blessed. Those who can will retreat to their local mosque for the duration and spend their time in prayer and reflection. Among this last ten days is Lailat ul-Qadr, the Night of Power. On this night, Muslims believe Allah sent the Quran to humanity. At the month's conclusion Eid-ul-Fitr, the three-day Feast of the Fast-Breaking, begins. This holiday began on 24 or 25 November.

In a video telephone interview from Iraq with reporters in Fort Hood, Texas and Washington, DC on 27 October, MG Odierno reported that American troops were supporting Iraq's first freely celebrated Ramadan by facilitating religious observances and honoring local customs. That included allowing freedom of travel during the fasting period, showing greater sensitivity to local traditions and working with community leaders to reduce coalition presence within urban areas. U.S. forces had

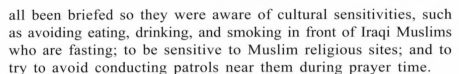

all been briefed so they were aware of cultural sensitivities, such as avoiding eating, drinking, and smoking in front of Iraqi Muslims who are fasting; to be sensitive to Muslim religious sites; and to try to avoid conducting patrols near them during prayer time.

In recognition of the charitable part of Ramadan, MG Odierno pointed out that TF Ironhorse units were continuing to pursue projects to benefit children at orphanages and schools. He said, "We agree with the charity piece of Ramadan as it goes forward and that we want to support them as they move forward with their celebration." He also highlighted some recent quality-of-life improvements carried out by TF Ironhorse Soldiers. "We have completed 883 projects," he said, "with another 505 in progress." Projects included renovating or rebuilding 480 public schools, repairing 96% of the hospitals and clinics, fixing 25 water treatment plants, and boosting electrical power generation by some 300% since the beginning of Operation Iraqi Freedom. Stability and support operations sought to improve basic municipal services such as repairing banks, courts, and telecommunications sites.

Responding to other questions from reporters, MG Odierno said the cost of finding willing attackers had gone up. "When TF Ironhorse first entered Iraq," he said, "the resistance was paying $100 for attacks and as much as $500 if the attacks succeeded. We now believe it's somewhere between $1,000 and $2,000 if you conduct an attack and $3,000 to $5,000 if you're successful." He also said everyone is working to turn public security over to the Iraqis. "Every day we train and equip more local police, who join our Soldiers in patrolling their cities," he said. "Right now there are nearly 8,000 Iraqi police officers, 1,800 Iraqi Civil Defense Corps members, and over 1,200 border police working and training alongside our Soldiers to protect and build a better future for their country," he added. He also said that the number and quality of tips coming into the coalition was growing significantly. He acknowledged that some Iraqis who did come forward with solid information faced intimidation. "There are threats to Iraqis, there is intimidation," he said. "Former Iraqi regime loyalists don't care what they do to their people. They don't care about the Iraqi people. All they care about is coming back into power."

It was unknown what violence Ramadan might bring from the non-compliant forces, but TF Ironhorse was prepared for anything that came its way. An article written on 20 October by Michael Hedges, an embedded reporter from the Houston Chronicle, described some of the show of force:

Tikrit, Iraq - The post-midnight stillness here was shattered Sunday by U.S. cannon fire that blasted fist-size chunks from Iraqi armored personnel carriers on an air base a half mile away. The Iraqis had abandoned the vehicles long ago. The purpose of the "show of force" firing by the Bradley Fighting Vehicle of the 4ID was not to kill guerrilla fighters, but to make a lasting impression on all of Saddam Hussein's loyalists who have been targeting American Soldiers. The explosive impacts of the Bradley's rounds jazzed the troops patrolling the darkness around Tikrit in thin-skinned Humvees. "And that is why the Iraqi army laid down their weapons and ran away," an officer quipped to general laughter. But while the shooting was good for the Americans' morale, it was intended to weaken the spirits of their enemies.

"What we are doing is sending a signal," said COL Don Campbell, the division's chief of staff. Sometimes, the gunners aim their fire at former Iraqi military bases. Other times, they target potential ambush sites, where loyalists to the old regime have fired mortars or rocket-propelled grenades at Soldiers.

Elsewhere in Iraq, U.S. troops, including those of the 4ID, have worked at winning the hearts and minds of the local population. But in Saddam's hometown, the objective is to force a small but determined percentage of the population still fighting to lay down their arms.

"We continue to conduct very aggressive combat operations to keep the enemy off balance," said COL James Hickey, commander of 1BCT. "It is a fight every day..."

The violence directed at the division's Soldiers seemed to culminate on Sept. 18, when coordinated attacks killed three Soldiers that routinely run nighttime patrols. Since then, the GIs have sought to break the will of the leftover Republican Guard officers, Fedayeen fighters, and others who had gathered in the Baathist Party's traditional stronghold after Baghdad fell. More than 1,300 suspected loyalists have been detained by the 1BCT alone... Campbell, the chief of staff, said the division has been successful. "It is not a fair fight," he said. "We do our homework,

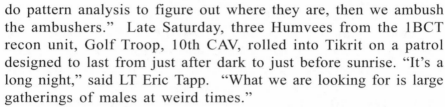

do pattern analysis to figure out where they are, then we ambush the ambushers." Late Saturday, three Humvees from the 1BCT recon unit, Golf Troop, 10th CAV, rolled into Tikrit on a patrol designed to last from just after dark to just before sunrise. "It's a long night," said LT Eric Tapp. "What we are looking for is large gatherings of males at weird times."

Earlier that day, a Humvee in a nearby unit was fired upon by a RPG, but no GI was injured. While the number of attacks has dropped since their peak in July, Soldiers still are shot at by snipers nearly every day. Tapp said his troops have an edge: night-vision optics that allow them to speed on a moonless night without headlights. "We can make our presence known in one area, but be observing the Iraqis from another," Tapp said. And heavier armor, like M1A2 tanks and the Bradleys, are nearby if a firefight erupts. Still, Tapp added, "Ambush is always a possibility."

The September 18 ambush resulted in a month long counteroffensive of raids, ambushes against suspected Iraqi guerrilla fighters, and nightly shows of force. Hickey said the operation is succeeding. "Before Sept. 18, we were being shot at from that area two or three times a day," he said. "Golf Troop was ambushed many times there. Now, it is rare for an attack to come from there."

But even a month later, the Soldiers still talk about the Sept. 18 attack. Tapp said he was just across the river and watched part of the attack through a long-range night gun sight. He told of one fluke shot, an Iraqi rocket-propelled grenade that burrowed into the cab of a U.S. vehicle and killed two Soldiers. Golf Troop and the rest of the brigade responded to that bushwhacking aggressively, rounding up about 60 Iraqis suspected of taking part. So far, U.S. officers said, four men have admitted shooting at the GIs, and they are expected to stand trial as guerrilla combatants.

Talk of ambushes and counter-ambushes created a sobering mood as patrolling Humvees rolled through back roads just outside Tikrit late Saturday. For passengers without night-vision goggles, the darkness seemed to envelop the troops. The countryside was smelled, not seen. Pungent sheep and cattle aromas floated from the fields, mixed with musky, vegetable tangs from small irrigation canals. Snarling dogs lunged at the vehicles, drawing remarks from the GIs that even the hounds are Fedayeen.

The armored show of force usually occurs after an 11 p.m. curfew, though on Saturday, several rounds exploded before then.

Soldiers using long-range, night-vision scopes checked the areas thoroughly before firing, making sure civilians were not passing through. Early in the patrol, Tapp's Humvee linked up with a Bradley carrying six Golf Troop Soldiers who were dismounts— Soldiers who fight on foot. The 4ID came to Iraq as the Army's most technologically advanced division. Its troops planned to use computer, laser and satellite technology to locate and crush Iraqi armored formations. But now, the division nightly dispatches foot patrols through the back streets of Tikrit in an attempt to surprise and disrupt small cells of Iraqis who might be manning ambushes. The Soldiers on foot looped through alleys and down dirt roads. Through night-vision goggles that greatly exaggerate any ambient light, they appeared to observers as iridescent green ghosts under glittery stars. On this night, they encountered no armed Iraqis.

Early Sunday was quiet in Tikrit, brigade officers said:

"Our intelligence suggests there are less and less of them out there," said MAJ Troy Smith, executive officer for the 1BCT. "The money to pay young gunmen to attack the Soldiers appears to be drying up," Smith said, "and some families associated with the old regime have left the area. This is just an assessment on our part. Someone could prove me wrong next week."

On 25 October, at approximately 1600 hours, one of two UH-60 Black Hawk helicopters assigned to 3-158 AVN, 12th AVN BDE, while performing a reconnaissance mission in the vicinity of Tikrit, was hit in one of its engines by a rocket propelled grenade. The crew was able to perform a controlled emergency landing. Once on the ground, the helicopter caught fire and was destroyed. All five members of the crew were able to exit the aircraft and move to safety. One of the crew suffered minor leg injuries due to shrapnel. The second UH-60 landed and picked up the crew and flew them to an aid station. Two AH-64D Apache helicopters in the area were given the location where the engagement took place. Upon their arrival, they observed two vehicles appearing to flee the area. The vehicles were forced to stop, and 1-22 IN personnel took an unknown number of suspects into custody.

Facing an increasing number of attacks, Soldiers of 1-22 IN on 31 October cordoned off the village of Owja where Saddam Hussein was born, suspecting this dusty farming community of being a secret base for funding and planning assaults against coalition forces.

LTC Steve Russell, CO of 1-22 IN, described the operation in an email to family and friends: "As Halloween approached we were nearly ready to implement a plan we had worked on for some time. Prior to my emergency leave, I told my staff I wanted to solve the problem with Owja—Saddam Hussein's birthplace. This town of about 3,500 people continued to be a thorn in the side. Every time we broke up a former regime cell or captured a funder or planner, they all seemed to have ties to this town. Ultimately, we hoped they would still have ties to Saddam. I thought through the problem of how to keep the insurgents from 'swimming' in the population at large, finding safe harbor to plot their evil deeds. I wanted to scoop up the insurgents into a 'fishbowl' to view them better. I remembered studying Napoleon's actions with a census in the Rhineland to root out insurgents and took note of techniques used by the French in Algeria. While not the same, there were certainly aspects of those operations that we could use for ourselves.

"I told my staff I wanted to fence the entire town and conduct a census. They wondered if I had somehow lost my mind. But without a complete cordon, only the fairly honest people would show up. If the town was locked down, then the only way they could get out was to register. It was a monumental undertaking but one I felt we could do and still carry out our other missions. The benefits would be several—if the criminal elements stayed, their movements would be known; if they left, they would have to give up their operational support base and would be much more visible and vulnerable to being fingered living in their mud huts on their farms; and if they stayed and changed their ways, that would still have desired affects.

"We began the effort at midnight on the 30th. I went to the tribal head sheik in the village and informed him of our actions and what would be required: All males over the age of 15 must be registered and receive a pass to enter or to leave the town. To get the badge, they had to report to the police station and fill out the information form. Once badged, they could come and go as before but were subject to search at a single entry point into and out of town. He was shocked but complied fully.

"By morning, rolls of concertina could be seen scattered along the bordering streets like tossed rings. Soldiers unraveled the wire. The scratch of the serrated steel wire on the concrete signaled the end to normal life in Owja. Soon the scratch gave way to pounding sledges for the reinforcing pickets. We buttressed the effort with about 50 Iraqi men from the local 'rent-a-worker' group in town, complete with a paid contractor. Simultaneously, the intelligence and signal staff readied the computer and camera databases to begin the issuing of badges. Scores of Iraqi men showed up at the police station by 0900 hours. They waited for their badge and once in hand, were allowed to exit the one remaining open avenue leading to Highway 1. By 3 November, we had badged 1,200 Owjite males.

"The operation amazed not only the Owjites but the international press as well. They all seemed to be fascinated at the audacity of the move. Many drew comparisons to Gaza or Jerusalem, but in reality, it never entered our minds. Nor was it a fair comparison. For one, we had an entire rifle company inside the wire with them. Second, we were not trying to separate one culture from another. Third, the town was not sealed but controlled—they could still come and go provided they had their identification. We did prevent the departure of about three-dozen individuals and informed the sheik and tribal town elders that we would question them at a later time—which we did.

"The impacts of the fencing of Owja have been outstanding. We have disrupted the enemy's command and control structure. If he fled, we were able to spot him in the villages. If he stayed, we could monitor his movements. The result had been that over the next several weeks we began to get intelligence and people we had been looking for since June and July. A momentum and sense of excitement restored our belief that we could knock the supports out of Saddam's protective circle. While we did not know the extent that the cordon would have on the terrorist infrastructure or Saddam, we knew it had to have some kind of impact.

"November finally clicked onto the calendar. It opened with a combination of raids that netted some important cell leadership and also with patrols that intercepted several roadside bombs. We began to see many varieties of explosive devices. Doorbell switches became a favorite, followed by keyless locks, toy cars and in one case a pressure switch.

"In Owja, the enemy attempted harassing fire and mortar

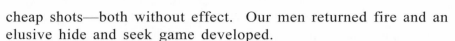

cheap shots—both without effect. Our men returned fire and an elusive hide and seek game developed.

"In Tikrit, a black Opel or Toyota sped by and lobbed an RPG at a C/1-22 IN patrol. The men returned fire but as they did, a large Mercedes truck inadvertently pulled into the line of fire and the attackers escaped down a back alley. Other patrols netted eight mortars with some ammunition while the scouts raided the northern suburbs again—and pulled the last of a set of brothers we had been pursuing for some time.

"By 4 November, the Owjites seemed resigned to their new fenced routine. I met with the tribal sheik and the town elders. We had a series of frank and honest discussions about the need for the Bayjat tribe to reconcile with the rest of Iraq. They were concerned about this, feeling that without some reconciliation, they could have no future. They would be forced to fight or die. I told them that one would surely lead to the other and that the reconciliation should be pursued. I took it up as a topic with the Monday morning sheik council meeting and it provided for some lively discussion. They admitted it was needed but they would not welcome them back simply because they said, 'I'm sorry.' They asserted that this was not their way. Reconciliation had to come from blood compensation. As I listened to all these men weave their tribal and feudalistic discussions, I was so thankful that I was an American.

"That evening, the discussions did not seem to deter a band of thugs who engaged A/1-22 IN. Firing from the vicinity of an old air defense bunker, the cutthroats launched an RPG at one of our patrols. They also followed it with rifle fire. Undaunted, the Soldiers gave back in spades. The "thump, thump, thump" of a Bradley chain gun preceded the "crack, crack, crack" of 25mm shells impacting the bunker. The Soldiers cordoned the area but the thugs were able to beat a retreat before the cordon was set.

"The next night, this cat and mouse game continued in Owja. Our Soldiers remained alert as usual. Suddenly the power cut out and the village became black. This preceded a clattering of small arms fire fired wildly but apparently within the wired village. The Soldiers searched the town but the attackers blended into the village population. The next day, CPT Stouffer shut the only gate into and out of town. The attackers were not found.

"6 November did net one attacker. On the 'Chevron' in the

northwest part of Tikrit, a C/1-22 IN ambush observed a man setting up what appeared to be a roadside bomb. He began by tying wire to a lamppost and then proceeded to run it to a location across the road. He did not accomplish this immediately. Each time he saw military vehicles in the distance he would back off and then sit passively on the side of the road to appear as one of so many Iraqi men who squat on the side of the road. Watching the pattern, C/1-22 IN clearly viewed his activities and confirmed he was emplacing a roadside bomb. What followed next was a given. Soldiers placed him in their sights, rifles popped, and the man dropped on top of his own device. Another Fedayeen dies."

Operation Ivy Cyclone – 6 November to 30 November
The 4ID and TF Ironhorse launched Operation Ivy Cyclone on 6 November. The operation focused on the Tikrit area and was designed to locate and detain or eliminate persons seeking to harm coalition forces or Iraqi civilians. Its hallmark was aggressive offensive operations including patrols, ambushes, cordon and searches, and raids. The operation was a concentrated, uncompromising effort to locate and detain or eliminate any person and/or undertaking that sought to harm coalition forces or innocent Iraqis as they worked together to bring stability and security to a free Iraq. In the first 24 hours of the operation, TF Ironhorse conducted 228 patrols, four raids and detained 16 individuals. Nineteen of the patrols were joint operations conducted with the Iraqi police, the ICDC, and the Border Guard in order to improve continually the safety and standard of living for the Iraqi people. The Navy reported on 9 November that F-16 fighter-bombers and Abrams tanks destroyed several farmhouses and buildings suspected of being used by non-compliant forces.

In one of many actions, TF Ironhorse Soldiers observed an attacker stringing monofilament wire across a road in an area near Tikrit. The individual was placing the wire at a height meant to kill a coalition Soldier riding as the gunner in a Humvee. The Soldiers gave the aggressor verbal warnings to stop. The aggressor fired on the position and Soldiers responded by firing back. The aggressor was killed as a result of the altercation.

An indication that enemy forces were taking desperate measures to avoid detection was demonstrated when TF Ironhorse Soldiers discovered a weapons cache in a cemetery near Samarra

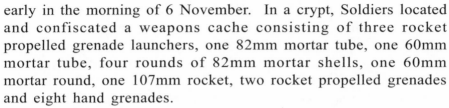
early in the morning of 6 November. In a crypt, Soldiers located and confiscated a weapons cache consisting of three rocket propelled grenade launchers, one 82mm mortar tube, one 60mm mortar tube, four rounds of 82mm mortar shells, one 60mm mortar round, one 107mm rocket, two rocket propelled grenades and eight hand grenades.

A 1-12 IN position was attacked with ten rockets at 2310 hours on 7 November. Soldiers identified the location from which the rockets came and returned fire, employing small arms and mortar rounds. Simultaneously, a patrol moved on the position in order to eliminate or detain the attackers. When the Soldiers approached, three attackers ran out from a tree line and attempted to flee. The Soldiers fired at the fleeing aggressors, killing all three. Also on 7 November, an Army helicopter was hit by hostile fire and crashed into a riverbank as it approached the Saddam palace compound, FOB Ironhorse. All six Soldiers from the 101st Airborne Division were killed.

In three separate incidents on 9 November, TF Ironhorse Soldiers located large weapons caches that had the potential to be used against innocent Iraqis and coalition forces. 3-66 AR Soldiers received a report from an AH-64 helicopter that identified a location south of Bayji as a possible weapons cache site. They went to the site and discovered storage structures that contained approximately 800 BM 21 rockets. The site was secured and the rockets were scheduled for destruction.

In another find, approximately 150 rockets were confiscated from a cache located north of Tikrit. An additional weapons cache of 1,500 rounds of 155mm artillery shells was located north of Balad. That discovery was the result of an observation made by crewmen in a 1-10 CAV helicopter. The munitions were destroyed in place.

On 11 November, TF Ironhorse Soldiers paused briefly to observe Veterans Day. In a message printed in the Ironhorse Desert news, MG Odierno said, "As we honor the veterans of past conflicts and the current Global War on Terror, I would like to thank you, the Soldiers of TF Ironhorse. And as importantly, I would like to thank your families for the sacrifices and contributions you both have made to this war. You face danger and hardship every day as you conduct combat operations to defeat the enemies of democracy in Iraq. Just as the WWI veterans of the 4ID did in the Meuse-Argonne, we are making a stand against forces that would like to see the liberties we enjoy destroyed. Our fathers and grandfathers made history on Utah Beach and in the Central Highlands of Vietnam; the spirit of these heroes is alive in TF Ironhorse and you continue the tradition of the Ivy Division in every mission you perform... On this Veterans' Day we need to reflect on the legacy of our predecessors and remember those who gave their hearts and their lives to our nation's defense. Many have made that sacrifice here; we will never forget our brethren from this or past wars. Their loss is a loss to all of us, but their contribution to preserving the lives and liberties of America will be remembered and appreciated by our nation and all of us who fight together in TF Ironhorse. We will continue to fight for our families, for our country, and for each other. God bless the Soldiers and families of TF Ironhorse and God bless America."

Operation Ivy Cyclone II, started on 16 November, was the second phase of Operation Ivy Cyclone. The second phase was marked by the use of overwhelming artillery and air strikes as well as the expansion of targets to include areas of Baqubah, Kirkuk and Balad. This operation also utilized satellite guided missiles for the first time since the end of major combat operations on 1 May. The 4ID and TF Ironhorse saw air support from Carrier Air Wing 1 of the USS Enterprise, the Navy's only aircraft carrier deployed in the 5th fleet area. Like previous operations, this operation utilized actionable intelligence combined with overwhelming combat power and precision strikes intended to isolate and capture non-compliant forces and foreign insurgents planning attacks against coalition forces.

The ongoing operation was conducted with an appropriate mix of combined arms power using close air support, Army aviation, armor, artillery, mechanized infantry and air assault operations to rapidly deploy dismounted infantry to secure their objectives. Coalition forces continued to deploy sizable resources in specific areas that had been identified as platforms for coordination and control of enemy operations. Extremist and insurgents continued to commit violent acts against innocent Iraqi and coalition Soldiers in an effort to weaken the resolve and strong relationship these partners in democracy shared. Showing that the coalition and the citizens of Iraq will not succumb to these

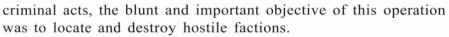

criminal acts, the blunt and important objective of this operation was to locate and destroy hostile factions.

Intelligence reports gathered from a variety of sources indicated former regime leaders, criminals and other subversive groups were operating in the areas of Tikrit, Baqubah, Kirkuk, and Balad. This operation directly targeted those operations. The intention was to permanently disrupt their capability to plan attacks against coalition targets. Coalition members encouraged the local Iraqi leadership to take the initiative and aid in the capture of subversive elements attempting to hinder the rebuilding of Iraq.

On 19 November, the 4ID and TF Ironhorse conducted 42 planned attacks as part of Operation Ivy Cyclone. Utilizing 155mm artillery, 120mm mortars, AH-64 Apache attack helicopters, and direct fire from Bradley Fighting Vehicles and M1A1 Abrams tanks, 4ID Soldiers destroyed 12 anti-coalition safe houses and buildings and suppressed 14 mortar-firing locations, as well as four ambush sites. Additionally, in six separate coordinated raids 4ID Soldiers captured 36 individuals suspected of anti-Coalition activities. During several specific missions, TF Ironhorse Soldiers diminished the capabilities of anti-coalition forces by targeting specific locations known to be used as platforms for coordination and control of enemy operations.

4ID AH-64 Apache attack helicopters targeted an athletic field in Samarra that was a known mortar firing point. Three other locations in the same area were also targeted because of their proximity to coalition positions and the fact that the locations had been used to launch mortars against the coalition in the past. As a part of the AH-64's standard armament, 30mm cannons were used to hit enemy targets, as well as two 500 pound bombs from Air Force F16 Falcons. Additionally, an artillery battery working with 1-66 AR fired numerous 155mm artillery rounds at specific targets in the same area.

On 25 November, SFC Todd Oliver, in the 173rd Airborne Brigade PAO office, wrote the following about 173rd operations around Kirkuk: "Soldiers of 2-503 IN (ABN)—better known as 'The Rock'—haven't had it easy in Iraq. But then, no one, or no unit at least, has had it easy. The Rock's problem is that its enemy is silent until it strikes, and unpredictable. Maybe most frustrating of all, is that the Rock's enemy is unseen, invisible until it strikes. The enemy in Kirkuk strikes from the roadside. It strikes from piles of garbage, it strikes from discarded soda cans. Once, it even struck from the body of a dead dog. It strikes without warning, and it strikes without mercy. An estimated 60 percent of the Rock's more than 40 wounded in action are a result of this enemy—the Improvised Explosive Device.

"Usually placed along a well-traveled road and detonated by remote control, IEDs can have a devastating effect against even the most vigilant of convoys. Made from abandoned mortar rounds or artillery shells, IEDs rip through the strongest materials, shredding vehicle and body alike. Even the mention of having driven past a suspected IED gives one cause to stop and think. When the dust has settled after an IED strikes, there's no one to take the blame. Those who detonate the devices fade away in the confusion.

"But The Rock isn't crippled, far from it. They're a battalion of paratroopers and if the fight won't come to them, well then, they'll just have to take the fight to the enemy. In the early hours of a cold, yet sunny, Monday morning the Rock did just that. They fought first. The Rock, along with a few cannons, courtesy of 173 ABN BDE's D/314 FA, and two A-10 aircraft from the U.S. Air Force, set out with a vengeance against those that would harm them. Operation Ivy Cyclone, a 4ID-wide attack, was in full effect for The Rock.

"It was a three-pronged approach," said 2-503 IN (ABN) commander, LTC Dominic Caraccilo, a day after the attacks. "The first thing we wanted to do was to deter enemy and anti-coalition forces from using the open areas surrounding Kirkuk and the airbase. Second, we wanted to show our capabilities, shooting from inside the sectors where we think the enemy was operating. Using mortars and artillery in the area the enemy was operating from, hitting their sanctuaries. Finally, we wanted to seize the IED makers and their supporters.

"We knew that there was a lot of activity in the southwestern parts of the city of Kirkuk," said Caraccilo. "We knew that activity was in the form of emplaced 107mm rockets aimed at targets which included our Soldier's safe houses and the airbase itself.

"We were fairly successful," he continued. "We captured one guy who had 12 different remote controls (taken from toy remote control cars)—that was important. They take them (the remote control portion) out of the car and use it to detonate the IED.

"Caraccilo and his men think there might be one key former regime loyalist in the city who puts the whole thing together. They think this man or, more likely, a small group of men, pay someone to provide them with the remote control devices, they pay another person to supply the ammunition, and still others to place the actual IED. Operation Ivy Cyclone netted 13 suspects for The Rock. While some of them are certain to be found innocent and will subsequently be released, some of them are most definitely 'persons of interest.'

"The guy with the 12 remotes was a fairly significant catch. We actually caught 13 guys and four are known Fedayeen members. The jury is still out on the rest. They're being interrogated and we'll figure that out, but I think this is going to have a significant effect on things.

"In addition to the raids, the Rock also did something that might seem kind of odd. They cleared the streets. It may be hard to describe to anyone from a westernized country the amount of just plain filth that lines the streets in some neighborhoods of Kirkuk. The city has only recently had its fleet of garbage trucks replaced, but many neighborhoods still dump their trash in the streets to burn at night. It's these piles of trash that are an attractive hiding place for those intent on placing IEDs.

"We actually cleared roads where there had been a significant amount of IEDs found," Caraccilo said. "We just brought bulldozers out and pushed the trash out of the way. While this doesn't prevent them from hiding IEDs, it deters them as it makes it harder. We're now going to start burning the excess vegetation in the medians of the street—which is another hiding spot for IEDs. We're going to make this problem die on the vine by killing the guys who provide the money and supplies and by making it difficult to emplace the IEDs.

"Back in Kirkuk, artillery, mortars and A-10 aircraft pound targets on the outskirts of the city, laying waste to the buildings the attackers were believed to have used. Explosion after explosion from the artillery rocks the still morning air and the distinctive sound of the A-10s chain-gun punctuates each aircraft's approach. It's an awesome sight and sound. The area they are hitting so relentlessly, three small hilltops and a small building, are empty. Empty or not though, the message is clear, you can be hit anywhere, anytime.

"As the pounding continued, the men of The Rock fan out inside the city, raiding the houses where the people responsible for the attacks were believed to have lived. It was a huge, coordinated effort, meant to send a clear message to those that meant them harm. "We're looking for anything suspicious," said SFC Sean Dohr, B/2-503 IN (ABN), as he and the members of his platoon finished searching yet another house. "We're looking for anything that could be used to make IEDs—wires, explosives, remote control devices, even photos of individuals, anything that will give us more information about who these guys are, their names, patterns, anything.

"Dohr and his platoon methodically go from house to house. They don't raid every house, just houses they have intelligence on. Houses that are believed to be hiding anyone or anything suspect. "These people work in small cells," he said. "They are usually trained by individuals who live outside the city of Kirkuk. They (the trainers) come here and train people on putting these things together. That's who we're looking for, the guy who's been trained to do it and is now being paid to do it."

"It's here at Dohr's level that the success is most plainly apparent. It's also here that success will most likely be felt—eight Soldiers in his company alone have been injured by IEDs. "This has been a great success," he said. "We have pictures of these guys now and this kind of information is priceless. We now have a face to match the people we are looking for and we can give these photos to other units, to guys manning traffic control points."

Dohr's company commander, CPT Bill Bundy, echoes those thoughts. "Today's mission was basically a cordon and search," said Bundy. "We've experienced a lot of IEDs and rocket attacks in these areas, so we've gone through looking for any kind of material that could be associated with those things.

"IEDs, their construction, use and financing are a complicated affair. The matter is further confused by the fact that each step of the process is handled in separate areas by different people. "You have a guy who makes the initiators and another guy who assembles those to the explosive devices. Then they hire a third guy to emplace the bomb and another guy throws the switch. We hope that some of those we got today know who the others are." Sadly, they aren't quick to give each other up to the Americans.

"Success or no, Bundy and his men actually live inside the

area they're searching. Besides trying to ensure that no Soldier or resident of the neighborhood is hurt in an IED attack—and IEDs do maim and kill innocent civilians almost daily—they have the added burden of trying to be good neighbors, even as they are rifling through someone's bedroom dresser. The days of kicking in doors, or more dramatically blowing them into a million small pieces with plastic explosives, are all but gone now in Kirkuk. That tactic is reserved for only the direst of cases. Rock Soldiers routinely knock first now and speak briefly to the homeowners before they begin to search.

"It doesn't matter if we go to the wrong house," Bundy said. "It doesn't matter, as long as you don't break down the door to the house. Most of the homes we go up to, we knock first. Generally, if we do go to the wrong house, and that does happen, the people inside understand. The Saddam regime was so tyrannical that people are used to getting smacked down and bouncing back from it. So they are pretty understanding of it, they know we're looking for bad people."

"The simple fact of the matter is that no matter how much the mainstream media cannot see it—things are better in many parts of Iraq, or at least in Kirkuk. A simple leisurely stroll through a market place turns up a wide assortment of goods either forbidden under Saddam's rule or unobtainable because of sanctions. Prices too are showing signs of normality and while the dinar has surely been beaten back and forth over the past years it is becoming stable and the jobs in the city pay living wages. When standing on a rooftop, you could count dozens and dozens of satellite dishes. While satellite dishes by no means describe normality and stability they are a sign that things are changing for the better. Even owning a dish a year ago was a surefire trip to prison.

"Every time we change our profile it has an immediate effect on the IED attackers. A few months ago we changed our profile by not driving during the hours they were hitting us and it had a huge impact," Bundy continued. "Now we're going to change that profile again by changing the geography of the city, cleaning up the trash, clearing up the roads, burning the vegetation in the medians and then hitting hard at where we think their sanctuaries are. The jury is out, I don't know if it will have an effect, but you've got to think that if you are going after them hard like this, you're going to make an impact."

In another incident, TF Ironhorse Soldiers saw two individuals searching for a rocket propelled grenade launcher cache already confiscated earlier by the coalition. It was suspected that a rocket propelled grenade launcher within the cache was used in an attack against the civil-military operations center in Balad the previous morning. The Soldiers saw that at least one of the persons involved was carrying an AK-47, and that person attempted to flee when given verbal warnings to stop. The attackers then fired automatic weapons at the Soldiers. In response, the Soldiers fired on them and moved to detain them. One person within the enemy faction was killed as a result of the altercation. Three others were detained for questioning.

TF Ironhorse paused for the celebration of Thanksgiving but did not stop its aggressive actions. In his Thanksgiving message to the Soldiers, MG Odierno wrote, "Years from now, when we reflect back on this Thanksgiving, we will remember celebrating this great American tradition in a country that is just beginning to develop some of the freedoms we enjoy. Every Soldier in TF Ironhorse should be proud of their tremendous contribution to Operation Iraqi Freedom and the positive impact they are having on this nation and this part of the world." He went on to say, "We give thanks today for the tremendous support we receive daily from our families and friends across the United States and the world. We would rather be with them enjoying our own unique family traditions today, but we understand our mission and will see it through. As you celebrate Thanksgiving, I ask you to consider three things: First, remember those who have given their lives for their country and their families. Next, reflect upon the freedom we cherish and the liberty we enjoy; this is what all nations strive to achieve. Finally, and most importantly, think about the vital role you are playing to ensure this country never returns to a horribly cruel dictatorship of the past."

President Bush made a surprise visit to Iraq on Thanksgiving. A few TF Ironhorse Soldiers had the honor of going to Baghdad to have Thanksgiving dinner with the Commander in Chief. Most, however, ate their Thanksgiving dinner and returned to duty helping rid Iraq of bad guys and rebuilding the country.

As November turned into December and Operation Ivy Cyclone came to a close, it was replaced on 2 December in the 173rd Airborne Brigade area with Operation Bayonet Lightning.

This was a quick, cooperative brigade-wide operation, capitalizing on the successful joint patrols conducted by 173rd Soldiers, ICDC, and the Iraqi Police. All of the forces worked together and employed raids to capture targeted regime elements that were working against the Iraqi people, attempting to destabilize the Kirkuk area. Twenty-six individuals were captured, including three targeted individuals. All of the captured were suspected of being members of Fedayeen Saddam. In addition, Soldiers located and confiscated 62 AK-47 assault rifles with ammunition, one rocket propelled grenade launcher, and two IED making kits.

Draining the Swamp
LTC Steve Russell, CO of 1-22 IN addressed the continuing hunt for Saddam Hussein and actions around Tikrit in his email sent to family and friends: "Reporters had asked me many times about the status of the hunt for Saddam. I told them he was still a priority but that we would accomplish our other missions whether we caught him or not. Frequently they would ask whether or not I thought he was in the area. I told them I believed he surely could be because his support base was clearly in Tikrit. But rarely would we get a sighting that was timely. Usually it would be third or fifth-hand information such as, 'He was here four days ago.'

"We were, however, starting to gather momentum. We knew the four controlling families that we believed surrounded Saddam. The problem was how to get them and once we got them, how to get the big guy. We had some incredible good fortune with a series of raids. The 720 MP BN, under LTC Dave Poirier, snagged a key member of a set of brothers we had been pursuing all summer. He was not the major player but we believed he would lead to his other brothers who were major players. We were right.

"In the early part of November, this brother began to sing. He gave us key information about his older brothers. One thing led to another. Soon, special operations forces found the key brother we had been seeking since late June. No Iraqi knew it at the time. They found him in a sparse, mud-brick farm well west of Tikrit. When they got him, he dropped his head in resignation. His war was now over as well.

"We were once again on the trail. We had been broadly around it in September and October but the increase of trigger pulling activity among the enemy necessitated our division of labor

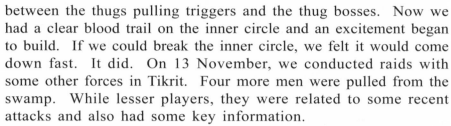

between the thugs pulling triggers and the thug bosses. Now we had a clear blood trail on the inner circle and an excitement began to build. If we could break the inner circle, we felt it would come down fast. It did. On 13 November, we conducted raids with some other forces in Tikrit. Four more men were pulled from the swamp. While lesser players, they were related to some recent attacks and also had some key information.

"The locals seemed to reach a peak in discontent—not that they ever loved us. We had oft been criticized in our efforts to win hearts and minds. But how can you win a black heart and a closed mind? The people we were dealing with could not be swayed. Handing out lollipops meant nothing to them. They understood power and respected that. Anything else would be a chance to strike back at us. November continued to have numerous roadside bomb attacks but providentially, we had been spared casualties. Even so, we came back at them with a powerful display of our weaponry. On 17 November, our battalion rolled tanks, Bradleys, Infantry, scouts, and ICDC Soldiers into town. I wanted to remind them that our Army was more than just Humvees. We had teeth and claws and would use them...

"While developing more information, we continued an indirect war with the trigger pulling thugs. Mortars impacted Owja, narrowly missing Soldiers of A/1-22 IN. An SS-30 rocket missed C/1-22 IN as it fell short, making a bomb-sized crater in town and blowing gates off of walled compounds. 1-10 CAV found the launch area on their side of the river and engaged several individuals, killing five. They were from Fallujah.

"Indirect attacks were not the only threat. The roadside bombs continued to be the favorite. On 24 November, the CO of C/3-66 AR was leaving the battalion command post when he made a right turn onto Highway 1. As he did, a powerful blast showered the convoy. But for some reason, the effects were small. The bomb, detonated by a wireless doorbell, had been placed in the opposite lanes, consequently, the blast blew away from him instead of on him. We were thankful...

"As the Muslim holiday of Ramadan approached, leaders throughout Iraq urged a lifting of curfews in the cities on the condition that no violence would occur or they would be reinstated. Our good will lasted about five minutes. Shortly after what would have been curfew, automatic weapons fire erupted near the division main gate. No one was hurt and we were never able to determine from the unit there what had happened. On 25 November, we found more roadside bombs. A big one had an 82mm mortar round with plastic explosives packed around it. They set it in the median of the main highway down town. We found it and shot it without incident. Also that evening, some thugs fired an RPG that went skipping down the front road near one of our towers. It failed to explode and no one was harmed.

"The next several days were calm. We used the lull to continue our swamp draining by refining some of our intelligence with observation and human sources. In the meantime, we also began to find evidence of weapons caches being brought in for future use. On 28 November we found another SA-7 anti-aircraft missile as well as 35 boxes of mortar fuses. We swept the same locations the next day and found over five hundred 120mm mortar rounds still in the boxes. All of these munitions were hidden in the city trash dump on the west side of Tikrit.

"December arrived with the gentle rains that, no matter how hard they tried, failed to wash away the dust and filth of this land. The nastier weather also made for a reduction in attacks on our forces but they did not cease. A roadside bomb on the main street in downtown Tikrit heralded the start of December. An alert but unarmed security guard watched as a man pulled up in a sedan and waddled to the median carrying a heavy 5-liter vegetable tin. The car sped off and the man ran into a back alley. The guard called the police who in turn called our forces. They flagged down the CO of C/1-22 IN who was out on patrol. His men shot up the bomb that exploded powerfully in the center of town. No one was harmed and no major damage was done except to the brickwork on the median.

"By 2 December, information continued to flow. A hot tip produced some HOT Missiles—missiles manufactured jointly by the French and Germans. They are wire-guided and are similar to our TOW missiles. The cache contained 20 of these, and, it was a relief to find them. Then, the next night we conducted a joint raid in downtown Tikrit. The inner circle network of brothers protecting Saddam was further exposed. Our raid captured another of these brothers. Three down. More information would follow...

"As the swamp continued to abate, there was no shortage of unusual happenings. One of our battle captains in the command post, summed it best, 'Every day in Iraq is the strangest day of my life...'"

"The next several days produced positive results all around. A couple of raids disrupted enemy activity in Owja, Tikrit and Cadaseeah. We continued to find roadside bombs and disarm or detonate them. In the midst of this, we gave pause on 6 December to light a Christmas tree in our headquarters. We sang carols and had a generally good time. We ended by singing 'Feliz Navidad' since nearly half of our battalion is Hispanic.

"We had another breakthrough on the trigger pullers on December 8. We raided four targets in Cadaseeah that netted eight thugs and explosive making materials, to include several radio-controlled cars. The next day we sucked more water from the swamp. An important tip netted a man long associated with Saddam as A/1-22 IN raided a remote western desert farmhouse. Simultaneously, special operations forces pulled his brother out of a city to the south. These two men provided additional information to add to the steady stream of intelligence already flowing from the swamp.

"As this intelligence was analyzed, we did not sit idle. We found an important link to mid-level guys and ran it down very quickly. The evening of 10 December ended with two brothers and a variety of nasty weapons. At the time I described it as a 'Fedayeen Candy Shop.' Any type of attack could have been planned with the variety of weapons found buried in the front yard of a filthy house on the outskirts of Tikrit. We captured roadside bombs, Pepsi can bombs, RPG launchers with rockets, two different and complete mortar systems (one in the outhouse!), small arms, ammunition, grenades, explosives and radio-controlled devices for bombs. The upshot of it all was that the occupants denied all knowledge of the find. They said that the Army must have put it there...

"On 11 December, A/1-22 IN raided a farm based on a tip of a Fedayeen meeting. They captured six men along with small arms, grenades and ammunition. One case of submachine gun ammunition was actually under the bedding of a baby crib— complete with baby! They left the baby but took the ammunition and the nice PPSH-41 Russian submachine gun to which it belonged. It was dated 1943 and was in museum-quality condition. It now hangs on our wall with other nice finds.

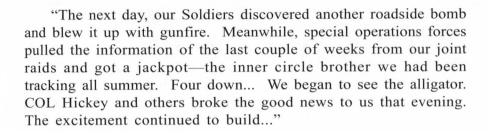
"The next day, our Soldiers discovered another roadside bomb and blew it up with gunfire. Meanwhile, special operations forces pulled the information of the last couple of weeks from our joint raids and got a jackpot—the inner circle brother we had been tracking all summer. Four down... We began to see the alligator. COL Hickey and others broke the good news to us that evening. The excitement continued to build..."

Technology Unique to TF Ironhorse

Iraq was the first combat test of the "digital division" concept that the 4ID had been testing since 1995. The technology, originally designed to be used against large armored forces, was quickly adapted to the situation in the Sunni Triangle. The 4ID combined the low-tech skills of traditional Soldiering with high-tech equipment in its daily quest to accomplish its missions.

Among the many hardware and software systems and subsystems available to the 4ID, two of the most critical components that made the "digital division" unique was the FBCB2 (Force XXI Battle Command Brigade and Below) systems in their vehicles and headquarters locations and the Unmanned Aerial Vehicles (UAV—sometimes called TUAV for Tactical Unmanned Aerial Vehicles) flying overhead. A massive room in one of Saddam's palaces, filled with computer terminals, was the HQ hub for operations. Similar rooms, on a smaller scale, were in each Brigade headquarters.

FBCB2, while very complex in all that went into it, can be described as giving real-time situational awareness to the commanders, staff, and Soldiers of 4ID that was never before known in a war. Each vehicle was equipped with a computer link so that their location could be immediately known to everyone using the FBCB2 system. Digital communications capabilities and a shared common view of the battle space greatly enhanced the command and control for commanders. Over 1,000 computers in each maneuver brigade were tied together in a seamless network, with the brigades all tied to the 4ID HQ.

COL Don Campbell, Chief of Staff of the 4ID and TF Ironhorse, described the capability in an interview. From his command and control center, Campbell could see every Bradley, tank, and Humvee in the division on extremely accurate digital maps. In addition to the location of the friendly vehicles, images sent back by UAVs gave a real-time view of the enemy vehicles and personnel. "If five bad guys were on the rooftop of a house, I could see them and shoot them," said Campbell. Literally billions of pieces of raw information were beamed into the command center via aerial antennae, analyzed, and then beamed back providing a precise picture of tactical operations to Soldiers in the field. The technology allowed Soldiers traveling in fighting vehicles to link to the command center using an array of aerial antennae. Using the same sort of antennae, a Blackhawk helicopter became a mobile command unit, or a medevac chopper could zoom right in on a wounded Soldier. On day or night patrols, Soldiers could pinpoint exactly where their friendly troops were positioned. Overhead, satellites recorded movement along the Iraqi terrain, airplanes and helicopters scoured hiding spots with thermal scans, and UAVs fed live video streams to brigade and division headquarters.

UAV "Shadows" showed their value from the first day they were used in combat. The 104 Military Intelligence Battalion (MI) received the first experimental Shadows in late 2000 and tested them extensively at Fort Hood, Texas. After the testing, the first production Shadow systems were added to the 4ID inventory in the latter part of 2002, just in time to be deployed to Iraq. The Shadow is a small, lightweight, tactical UAV with a wingspan of 12 feet, 3 inches and a length of 11 feet, 2 inches. Power is provided by a commercial 38-horsepower rotary engine. Aboard each Shadow is a commercially available electro-optic and infrared camera and communications equipment for command and control and imagery dissemination. Onboard global positioning system instrumentation provides navigation information. It is launched from a portable pneumatic launcher and is recovered by a tactical automatic landing system, without pilot intervention, on the runway. The Shadow is intended to provide coverage of a brigade area of interest for up to four hours, at 50 kilometers from the launch and recovery site. Operations were generally conducted from 8,000 to 10,000 feet above ground level during the day and 6,000 to 8,000 feet above ground level at night.

Each of the two platoons had a launch and recovery section, consisting of eleven personnel, and an operations section, also with eleven personnel. Once the UAV was launched, the operations section took control and flew the mission, which lasted an average of just over four hours. Near real-time streaming video and digital pictures were fed to the DTOC and Brigade TOC for analysis and decision making. The mission commander/pilot, frequently an E-4, sat next to the brigade commander and communicated direct to him. Cameras had a 360 degree viewing capability and could work effectively at night as well as during daylight hours and so were extremely valuable to commanders at all levels. By the end of TF Ironhorse's year in Iraq, UAVs had flown over 4,000 hours in support of missions. No planes were lost to enemy fire although some were lost (but always recovered) due to mechanical problems.

UAVs, along with FBCB2 systems, were critical to the success of the "digital division". These and other digital capabilities, both major and minor in scope, gave TF Ironhorse a real-time situational awareness of the battlefield never before available to commanders and Soldiers. This did not happen without hard work. The G-6 section in TF Ironhorse HQ was responsible to insure all systems remained operational 24 hours per day. Installation of satellite communications systems, providing secure video and audio conferencing within the AOR and back to the US, fixing computer systems that were broken, and doing the hundreds of other tasks required to maintain connectivity between TF Ironhorse HQ main command post, the 4ID tactical command post, all the brigades and separate battalions and with higher headquarters was the daily job of the G-6 section.

The digital division concept, started when 4ID began the Force XXI test in 1995, proved to be even more valuable in combat than expected. TF Ironhorse introduced a new capability that insured the 4ID lived up to its reputation as being the most lethal division ever to fight on a battlefield.

Military Police (MP) Operations
As was the case in WWI, WWII, and Vietnam, Military Police (MP) played a key role in the actions of the 4ID and TF Ironhorse. In addition to the organic 4th Military Police Company, one of the longest serving MP units in the Army, TF Ironhorse was augmented by other MP units in Iraq. They were the 720th MP BN, the 64th MP Company, the 401st MP Company, the 411th MP Company, the 978th MP Company, the 323rd MP Company,

the 649th MP Company, and the 3rd platoon of the 554th MP Company (supporting 173rd ABN BDE)—27 platoons, seven company HQs, and one battalion, all supporting TF Ironhorse.

The 4th Military Police Company was spread across the breadth of the entire TF Ironhorse AOR. The 4th and 5th platoons ran the Central Collection Point for prisoners at FOB Ironhorse. Prisoners were transferred from the BCTs to FOB Ironhorse and then moved on to a prison in Baghdad as required. The 1st platoon served with 3-66 AR in Bayji and provided pipeline security, route security, and worked to train the Bayji police force. The 2nd platoon worked with 2BCT in the Baqubah area and provided route and convoy security. The 3rd platoon, at FOB Anaconda, provided route security and for specified high value convoys.

The 978th MP Company had one platoon which worked with the 4th MP Company with detainee security and provided VIP escorts for visiting Congressmen, Generals, and other dignitaries. Two platoons provided security and escort service for prisoners at the MEK site of Camp Ashcroft. One platoon ran the 2BCT prisoner collection point at FOB Warhorse.

The 649th MP Company, made up of only two platoons, worked closely with the Baqubah police department. They trained the police and were responsible for the jail facility. Additionally, they conducted border patrols on the Iran border.

The 323rd MP Company provided route and compound security on the Iraq-Iran border. They also provided security for the Kirkush barracks where many of the ICDC and new Iraqi Army Soldiers were trained.

The 3rd platoon of the 554th MP Company provided internal escort and route security in the 173rd ABN BDE AOR.

The 720th MP Battalion was the first TF Ironhorse unit to leave Fort Hood for Kuwait, arriving there on 18-19 March 2003. During the initial attack into Iraq, they provided security for Main Supply Route (MSR) Tampa, and followed the attack of the 3ID and 101st Airmobile Division. They provided security for LSA Bushmaster, main support base for the western corridor of the attack to Baghdad. Working with both the 3ID and 101st, they provided detainee and route security on the south side of Baghdad. In late April, augmented by a Bradley company, they formed TF Gauntlet and spent a week in Fallujah calming the situation there.

In early May, the 720th MP BN, with its 64th, 401st and 411th

MP Companies, joined TF Ironhorse. Initially they were attached to 1BCT and worked around Tikrit and Bayji providing MSR security, VIP security, and worked to train and establish a functional police force in Tikrit. In August, the 720th MP BN was given the mission of operating the police training academy. That mission was done by the 64th and 401st MP Companies while the 411th MP Company stayed in Tikrit and continued the mission there. During Operation Ivy Blizzard in December 2003, the 720th MP BN established a cordon around the operational area, fired the known corrupt police, trained new police and provided funding and equipment for them. The 720th virtually built the police operations in Salah Ad Din province from nothing, conducted joint patrols with them, and built an actionable intelligence gathering capability in the Iraqi police force. During the attempted robbery of the dinar currency exchange in Samarra, the 401st MP Company was a key element in stopping the attempt and inflicting heavy casualties on the enemy.

TF Ironhorse MPs processed approximately 7,000 detainees during 11 months of operations, provided security operations of all kinds, trained and worked with the Iraqi police force, and participated in civil actions on a daily basis—a great record of accomplishments.

Civil Military Operations
TF Ironhorse work to improve the lives and infrastructure of Iraq never slowed down. Some examples of Civil Military Operations during the September to early December timeframe included:

Soldiers from 4 EN BN and 864 EN BN, part of 3BCT, coordinated Operation Soccer Sweep. The operation was a joint project between the engineers and locals Iraqis in the town of Ad Dujayl. Local Iraqi laborers worked to clear unexploded ordnance and removed hazardous material from the selected project site area under coalition forces' auspices. TF Ironhorse Soldiers managed and conducted clearing/line haul missions to support the project. They also disposed of all hazardous materials that were found. The result was four new soccer fields for the youth of the community.

Soldiers from the 555 EN GRP handed out food and water supplies to a small Iraqi town on September 14. The operation was created to ensure that provisions were supplied to some of

178

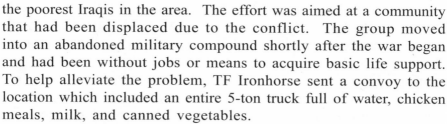
the poorest Iraqis in the area. The effort was aimed at a community that had been displaced due to the conflict. The group moved into an abandoned military compound shortly after the war began and had been without jobs or means to acquire basic life support. To help alleviate the problem, TF Ironhorse sent a convoy to the location which included an entire 5-ton truck full of water, chicken meals, milk, and canned vegetables.

2BCT Soldiers along with local Iraqi healthcare workers provided immunizations for Iraqi children during the monthly Immunization Day in Baqubah in September. Immunization Day, occurring each month on the 22nd, allowed children to receive vaccines for such health problems as diarrhea-induced illnesses and upper respiratory infections. Mobile inoculation teams, working with the five clinics in Baqubah, provided immunizations to more than 750 children a month on Immunization Day.

Operation Pencil Box was a major support project for TF Ironhorse. In a letter to the Family Readiness Groups, MG Odierno described the program, "One of our top priorities is the rehabilitation of the Iraq Public Education system. Under Saddam Hussein, Iraqi schools suffered severe neglect and stagnation. All of the schools require some level of repair and renovation, and many lack desks, chalkboards and school supplies for effective teaching. In order to address these needs, TF Ironhorse has initiated renovations on over 180 schools within our area. We are also purchasing over $250,000 worth of chalkboards and desks for distribution to local schools.

"As part of this effort, we will conduct a Division operation in late September and October called "Operation Pencil Box". TF Ironhorse Battalions will adopt local schools to assist them in preparing for the new school year. TF Ironhorse Soldiers will work alongside the parents and teachers of these schools to remove debris, install furnishings and make minor repairs. These adopted relationships will continue into the upcoming school year with frequent interaction to deliver supplies.

"The Fort Hood Family Resource Group is currently holding a school supplies drive to receive donated supplies and forward them to TF Ironhorse for distribution to our adopted schools. For those family and friends who are interested, we welcome your participation in this important program. Please feel free to share this letter with those who may be interested in contributing and ask them to forward donated supplies to the following address..."

Operation Pencil Box was successful beyond all expectations. School supplies from all over the country flowed into Fort Hood and were forwarded to Iraq. Pencils, erasers, writing tablets, writing paper, notebooks, pocket folders, rulers, scissors, glue, construction paper, crayons, chalk, chalk erasers—all the school supplies that are taken for granted in the US were donated and given to the Iraqi schools in the TF Ironhorse AOR.

Rebuilding schools was a key focus of TF Ironhorse. Soldiers from 3BCT and 308th Civil Affairs Brigade rebuilt schools in the town of Ad Duluiyah. Six sites that housed 14 separate schools and more than 4,700 students were identified as being badly in need of repair. The plumbing, plastering, and electrical systems needed complete overhauls. Minor structural repairs were required, too. Local contractors were hired and began work on the decaying structures. Over $100,000 in TF Ironhorse money was allocated to pay for the project, which was completed in time to begin the school year.

In July 2003, the 5 EN BN, operating as TF Fighter, began a project that would shape the future of a village named Al Asriya. With funds seized from ousted dictator Saddam Hussein's accumulated wealth, TF Fighter began to rebuild the local Iraqi infrastructure and helped to establish positive civil-military relationships. Following the battalion's significant work on the village sewage system and assistance rebuilding the village mosque, TF Fighter began work on one of its most important tasks—the rebuilding of the Al Asriya schools.

TF Fighter's first school project was a small primary school in an extremely rundown condition. TF Fighter began work by choosing a qualified local contractor and, by working together, slowly transformed the school into a place of which the villagers could be proud. With this transformation came a renewed hope and confidence within the people of the village. Interest as well as support slowly increased from locals. TF Fighter found themselves provided with cold water, tea, and security information that helped secure the local area of operations. The newly renovated buildings of the school grounds served a dual purpose. They became the meeting place for city hall sessions and key village events. It was in this school that the village selected its first democratic city council and drafted the first village constitution. This new forum became the voice of the villagers where they were allowed to express their concerns and ideas to the council members. In time, as support grew even more, meetings between outlying villages took place at the school.

The 5 EN BN took a great deal of pride in all missions, from combat to stability operations, but this project was a special one for TF Fighter. On 9 September, the hard work and dedication of both the Iraqi people and the Soldiers of TF Fighter were rewarded with a ceremony to commemorate the grand opening of the Al Asriya primary school. The battalion was greeted by hundreds of cheering children as they entered the village for the ceremony. Local dignitaries, families, and teachers were waiting in their best clothes at the front of the school, eager to begin the ceremony and start a new chapter in the village's history. The ceremony to celebrate the opening of the new school and the solid relations built between the Iraqi and American cultures did not happen overnight. The ceremony was by no means the culmination of TF Fighter's efforts in Iraq, merely the beginning. In the shadow of combat operations, the 5 EN BN was able to reach out and help in the rebuilding of Iraq. The Army provided TF Fighter with sufficient combat power to accomplish all missions, but the battalion found what was really needed in this case came from within—a genuine interest in the needs of people, engineering ingenuity, and the willingness to help.

TF Ironhorse band plays for first New Iraqi Army graduates in Kirkush

TF Ironhorse engineers built playground equipment as part of Model School Program

MG Odierno and other TF Ironhorse leaders in a working session with Iraqi leaders in Kirkuk

4ID combat vehicles were equipped with FBCB2 computer systems

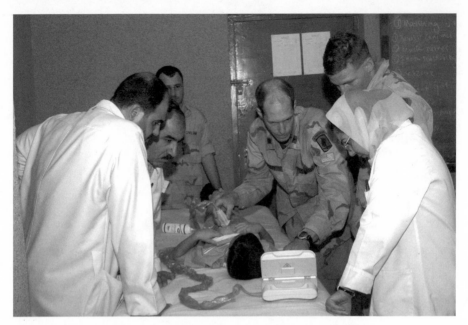

173rd Airborne Brigade doctor helping an Iraqi child while teaching Iraqi doctors in the use of advanced techniques and equipment

TF Ironhorse patrol surrounds a house before searching it for weapons and contraband

XI

"We Got Him,"
The Capture of Saddam Hussein
13-14 December 2003

THE CAPTURE OF SADDAM HUSSEIN WAS NOT happenstance or luck. It was the result of hard work and excellent intelligence gathering by TF Ironhorse. From its arrival in Iraq in mid April, TF Ironhorse had been developing intelligence designed to find not only the top 55 most wanted individuals, but to locate and kill or capture those providing the funding, coordinating opposition, and encouraging operations against coalition forces. Each day another piece of the puzzle fell into place, which led to more of the key players, both highly visible ones like Saddam Hussein and lesser ones who did the daily work against coalition forces.

In early July 2003, 1BCT conducted a raid that unearthed a veritable treasure trove of pictures, documents, uniforms, and other items that showed the close connection between the owner of the house and Saddam Hussein. The owner was not there, only women and others who proclaimed their innocence. Three weeks later, another raid was conducted on the same house. It was empty. Everything—furniture, animals, clothing, and personal effects— had been moved out. This further confirmed that this was one of the key families that would play a big part in putting the puzzle pieces together. These experiences would dramatically impact 1BCT's intelligence estimate. This individual, code named Source 1, would move to the top of the list of most wanted men. Further, the Brigade's intelligence staff under MAJ Stan Murphy would begin to build highly visual "link diagrams" that showed the structure of Saddam Hussein's personal security apparatus and the relationships among the persons identified. The estimate highlighted five key families from the Tikrit area. 1LT Angela

185

Santana and CW2 Bryan Grey were the officers who personally oversaw the development of these diagrams that proved vital to many of the decisions of the BCT Commander and the operations executed over the ensuing months. These evolving estimates were shared with TF Ironhorse and Tikrit based Special Operations Forces (SOF) commanders and staff on a daily basis. This intelligence teamwork built strong ties, a shared view of the challenge and, most importantly, trust.

As TF Ironhorse progressed through the raids of the summer and fall, it focused on these key extended families. Financiers, fighters, couriers, and others who were part of the infrastructure of unrest were killed or captured—but the key players continued to elude the raids. Many successful missions resulted in key captures, especially in the violent month of November 2003. In the course of these activities, several unsuccessful raids to kill or capture Saddam Hussein were executed in Tikrit, Bayji, and in many hamlets and farms along the Tigris River flood plains. Though unsuccessful, each resulted in additional information that further developed existing intelligence estimates. The greatest benefit, however, was tactical knowledge. Speed and flexible combined-arms tactics were identified as essential components to successful raids aimed at capturing specific individuals. Surprise was an absolute requirement.

Operation Red Dawn
What follows is the summary of the capture of Saddam Hussein as included in the 1BCT after action report and from interviews with key participants. 1BCT, in conjunction with SOF, planned and conducted the mission to capture Saddam Hussein, named Operation Red Dawn. It was an operation that included the integration of cavalry, engineers, field artillery, attack aviation, and Special Operations Forces. The mission was to attack, to kill/capture HVT #1 (High Value Target #1) in the vicinity of Ad Dawr, and to defeat enemy forces in the area of operations. For security reasons, the name of the informant is not used—he is referred to as Source 1:

On 12 December, Special Operations Forces working in Baghdad detained the key figure who had been identified back in early July. That started the ball rolling on what would, less than eighteen hours later, result in the capture of Saddam Hussein.

At 1015 hours on 13 December, SOF contacted COL James Hickey, 1BCT Commander (Raider 6), and informed him that SOF had captured Source 1, a close associate of HVT #1, the night of 12 December in Baghdad. Source 1 had been identified by 1BCT as a key security officer for Saddam Hussein as early as July 2003. He had become the focus of a specific series of raids in early December 2003 conducted by the Brigade and SOF in Tikrit, Bayji and Samarra. He was not captured but information revealed Source 1 might have fled to Baghdad. It was there that SOF found him on 12 December 2003 during the course of multiple raids.

Indicative of the teamwork and mutual support that had become routine between the 1BCT and SOF, the object of the most recent raids, Source 1, was rapidly flown to Tikrit for interrogation. This was vital—experience had shown that time was of the essence. Initial reports revealed HVT #1's possible location as being "west of Tikrit." Upon receiving this information, COL Hickey issued a warning order to TF 1-22 IN and TF 3-66 AR to be prepared to conduct operations in conjunction with SOF in order to kill/capture HVT #1. He also ordered Golf Troop, 10th Cavalry—the Brigade Reconnaissance Troop (BRT)—to begin movement south from Bayji and link up at FOB Raider. (Golf Troop had been on constant reconnaissance west of Bayji for five days and nights prior to receipt of this order, with very little rest. COL Hickey knew they were tired but he wanted them close at hand for this mission). All other scheduled missions across the BCT were either cancelled or delayed.

The terrain west of Tikrit out to Lake Thar Thar was open and arid. It was lightly populated but was well-traversed using improved and paved roads. It contained many hamlets and single structures in which sanctuary could be found. It also allowed for long fields of view. Conducting a raid in this environment would require special tactics if surprise was to be achieved.

At approximately 1300 hours, MAJ Brian Reed, 1BCT Operations Officer, met with members of SOF at their CP. COL Hickey attended a previously scheduled meeting with the governor of Salah ad Din Province and a key sheik from Owja, Saddam's hometown (he did not want to cancel and give a signal that something big was going on). MAJ Reed knew the commander's intent and had long worked with the SOF team. He was therefore

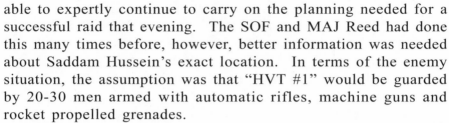

able to expertly continue to carry on the planning needed for a successful raid that evening. The SOF and MAJ Reed had done this many times before, however, better information was needed about Saddam Hussein's exact location. In terms of the enemy situation, the assumption was that "HVT #1" would be guarded by 20-30 men armed with automatic rifles, machine guns and rocket propelled grenades.

Upon completion of his meeting, COL Hickey arrived at 1500 hours at FOB Ironhorse to personally report the situation to MG Odierno; this was not news to deliver over the radio. In MG Odierno's office, Raider 6 first reported that Source 1 had been captured in Baghdad the night before and was in the Tikrit area being questioned. Secondly, Raider 6 stated that he intended to conduct a raid to kill or capture Saddam Hussein that evening and it might happen west of Tikrit. Regardless, the entire BCT was on alert, as was the SOF. Being completely familiar with 1BCT's intelligence estimates, MG Odierno knew the significance of Source 1's capture. He also knew this was the 12th or 13th raid on HVT #1 conducted by the Raiders and the SOF. He did, however, ask Raider 6 his assessment of the chances of success. Raider 6 responded that they were as good, if not better, than any previous mission. Raider 6 knew that if Source 1 could not provide accurate information, only one other man could, and he was still at large. 1BCT had done much to reduce the Saddam security network over the preceding months. However, the true basis of Raider 6's confidence was the hard won combat expertise of his Soldiers and level of cooperation achieved with the SOF. Both were at their peak of effectiveness. Besides that, it was great to be on the offense.

In the meantime, the situation had developed. Between the initial interrogation and the time MAJ Reed arrived, Source 1 changed his story and claimed that HVT #1 was now in hiding east of Tikrit and that he had not seen him in almost four months. In the course of these interrogations, he finally admitted to knowing three possible locations in which Saddam Hussein might be hiding in the farms northwest of Ad Dawr (the home of Al Duri, "HVT #6"). This information would change not only the task organization for the intended raid but also the tactics. The ground east of Tikrit and the Tigris River was characterized by vegetated palm groves, fruit orchards, and irrigated farmlands.

This reality affected the mobility of ground forces and visual observation. This would impact any tactical scheme. The approach to a raid on this ground would be fundamentally different than one west of Tikrit in the open desert.

With this information and estimate, SOF decided to conduct a close tactical reconnaissance with Source 1 in an attempt to refine the actual location. The initial assessment was that the target location was Ad Dawr, about 15 kilometers southeast of Tikrit. MAJ Reed notified 4-42 FA that the close tactical reconnaissance would occur in their AOR and issued them a warning order to be prepared to provide an outer cordon in support of potential operations in Ad Dawr. He issued a similar order to G/10 CAV to provide an inner cordon and alerted the entire BCT to stand by for whatever was required. Simultaneously, the SOF HQ element and a second assault team from SOF began movement north to Tikrit.

COL Hickey arrived at the SOF CP at approximately 1600 hours in order to continue coordination. By 1700 hours, the results of the interrogation of Source 1 and the stealthy reconnaissance of Ad Dawr indicated two objective areas, and a possible third. The ground was well known to Raider 6 and especially to LTC Pompelia's 4-42 FA who had spent over seven months patrolling and fighting in that sector. The reports made sense. Ad Dawr, situated halfway between Tikrit and Samarra, astride Highway 24, was estimated to be an enemy command and control area. Troubling, however, was the amount of direct fire contacts both 4-42 FA and 299 EN, on the west bank of the Tigris, experienced in the weeks leading up to mid-December. Further, there was only one improved trail that led to the objective area. Both the northern suburb of Ad Dawr to the northeast, and palm groves to the southwest surrounded that route; it was perfect for an enemy ambush. The raid, to be successful, had to have both the element of surprise as well as strength. There was not much time.

In conjunction with the SOF Commander, Raider 6 quickly drafted a concept. The target area included two objectives, OBJ WOLVERINE 1 and OBJ WOLVERINE 2. These represented two buildings. A third target was estimated to be an underground facility in a palm grove immediately adjacent to the east bank of the Tigris. A boat landing was apparent. 4-42 FA would provide the outer cordon to prevent enemy reinforcements from infiltrating the objective areas or HVT #1 from leaving. The 299 EN BN would establish observation posts and screen along the west bank of the Tigris River in order to deny entry or exit into or out of the objective areas via boat. A section of attack helicopters from A/1-4 AVN also screened west along Highway 1 in order to identify possible reinforcements into the objective areas. The SOF assault teams would clear the objectives to kill or capture Saddam Hussein. G Troop, 10th CAV would provide direct support to the SOF teams with a close inner cordon. A Troop, 1-10 Cavalry would be the armored reserve that would be committed to destroy any enemy defense or counter attack. 4-42 FA would have two howitzer sections in position and ready to fire in direct support.

The assault force would approach Ad Dawr at a high rate of speed moving south on Highway 24. One SOF team would be the lead assault team, followed by a BRT scout platoon (OBJ WOLVERINE 2). COL Hickey and the SOF commander were next in the order of march, followed by the second SOF team and a BRT scout platoon (OBJ WOLVERINE 1). The brigade TAC with MAJ Reed and two Bradleys would trail and provide direct-fire overwatch in the objective area. It was to be a simultaneous operation with the codeword "JACKPOT" indicating Saddam Hussein had been located. SOF attack helicopters would also support the mission from overwatch positions in the vicinity of the objective areas. They would insert Soldiers from the assault teams north and west of the objectives. 2000 hours would be the time for the assault and action on the objectives.

Within fifteen minutes, the plan of attack was finalized. The SOF commander and his key leaders received and acknowledged the concept immediately. They would linkup with G Troop and the BCT command post east of Tikrit in a granary at 1900 hours. This finalized plan was then transmitted to the remainder of the force by voice radio and digital communications. All forces were to be in position at 1930 hours. No significant movement was to be done until last light.

Time and surprise was vital. Experience taught that rapid exploitation of information about the enemy was important. The raiding force could not allow the enemy the opportunity to reposition. On an earlier raid, COL Hickey believed that they had missed Saddam by less than three hours—he was not going to let that happen again. Risks must be accepted. Surprise could be achieved by quiet, fast moving wheeled forces supported by close support aviation in a window of "zero illumination." The assault forces would use no visible light whatsoever. The assault force would physically clear all three objectives under the cover of complete darkness. Last light would be after 1800 hours. The full moon would rise just after 2100 hours. They would have a three-hour window to complete the mission.

After a quick visit to FOB Raider, the 1BCT command group departed at 1800 hours en route to the attack position in a walled corn granary, about four miles from FOB Ironhorse. A platoon from the BRT secured the attack position prior to their arrival. Shortly after the arrival of the command group, the second BRT platoon arrived.

At approximately 1845 hours, the assault teams and HQ elements from SOF arrived at the assault position. The assault team leaders conducted final coordination with the BRT platoon leaders. The NCOs put all in order by 1930 hours. Final checks and last minute inspections were complete. A/1-10 CAV could be heard not two kilometers from the granary moving into its start position, as all BCT units reported "set" via radio to Raider 3, MAJ Reed. At 1935 hours, the assault force began movement to the objectives. Radio silence was maintained. There was not much to be said.

At approximately 1945 hours, the power in Ad Dawr failed. With moonrise not until later, the city was completely dark, which aided in concealing the task force's movement as they entered the city. There was no civilian traffic along Highway 24. The force entered the objective area at 1955 hours and had forces on OBJs WOLVERINE 1 and WOLVERINE 2 by 2000 hours. G Troop was set with the inner cordon and 4-42 FA established checkpoints along Highway 24, both north and south, in order to stop all traffic from entering or leaving the city. Upon the establishment of the inner cordon, SOF began to search and exploit both objectives. The combined BCT and SOF command post was positioned south of OBJ WOLVERINE 2 with observation of the Soldiers on both objectives as well as the palm groves southwest of OBJ WOLVERINE 2.

On OBJ WOLVERINE 1, there was nothing significant to report, as was the case at OBJ WOLVERINE 2. The lead SOF assault team, as well as CPT Bailey with 1st Platoon, G Troop moved directly to the palm groves to search for a reported underground hiding place.

Source 1 led the assault team to a mud hut. One of the occupants at the location attempted to flee, but was detained. Another occupant vehemently denied knowing anything about Saddam Hussein and attempted to lead the assault team away from the objective. Before he could do so, Source 1 identified and pointed out the location of a potential hiding position near the edge of the orchard. The assault team cleared the entrance to the hole of dirt, debris, and mats, and removed the Styrofoam insert. The person inside of the hole put his hands in the air and responded to the question, "Who are you?" with "I am Saddam Hussein, the President of Iraq, and I am willing to negotiate." With that, a Soldier from the assault team responded with, "President Bush sends his regards," and Saddam Hussein was pulled from the hole. After a search of the area, a helicopter landed and evacuated Saddam Hussein. By 2015 hours, initial reports of a "JACKPOT" were sent to Raider 6. At 2026 hours "JACKPOT" was confirmed.

COL Hickey and the SOF commander were less than 200 meters away from Saddam's location when the word, "Jackpot" came to them. Both leaders shared a smile, and a quick hug acknowledging the historic event, and then their total focus was on preparing for the rapid evacuation of "HVT #1" and the expected enemy response, which never came. COL Hickey was able to quietly inform CSM Wilson of the capture. Raider 7 responded with his signature smile. In the meantime, A/1-10 CAV had successfully moved into the area north of Ad Dawr, significantly increasing the security of the assault elements. With that, the 1BCT command group moved up to the objective area. After congratulating the Soldiers, Raider 6 and his command team secured $750,000 discovered on the objective. The SOF detained the remaining two occupants of the mud hut.

The operation demonstrated the BCT's ability to act swiftly on intelligence and to plan, coordinate, and execute on a moment's notice. Effective battle drills and battle-hardened Soldiers and leaders operating on instinct were the keys to success. Cooperation between a flexible and heavily armed armored brigade and superbly skilled SOF Soldiers proved to be a combined force that the enemy could not resist. That night the enemy was caught off

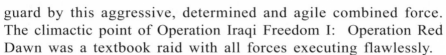

guard by this aggressive, determined and agile combined force. The climactic point of Operation Iraqi Freedom I: Operation Red Dawn was a textbook raid with all forces executing flawlessly.

With the capture accomplished, much excitement and many challenges lay ahead. The 4ID/TF Ironhorse team, along with SOF, had accomplished a feat that would forever be a part of world history. The challenge now was to keep it secret until it was ready to be announced to the world. They knew this would be a major worldwide media event and it was critically important that the announcement be handled properly.

COL Hickey reported the results via secure, mobile telephone to MG Odierno who was sitting with his key staff members in the TF Ironhorse TOC. "Sir, this is Jim Hickey, we've captured Number 1... and I have about a million dollars in the back of my Humvee to give you. I will be at your headquarters in about 20 to 30 minutes." After confirming what he had heard, MG Odierno whispered the message to COL Don Campbell, Chief of Staff; LTC Todd Megill, G-2; LTC Ted Martin, G-3; and others sitting with him. A roar went up from the group but quickly stopped as they realized that news reporters were working in the room next to them. The information about the capture was not ready to be released. MG Odierno's next call was to his signal officer, telling him to cut off all telephone and internet access from FOB Ironhorse to the outside world.

With similar thinking, COL Hickey radioed LTC Troy Smith, his XO at 1BCT HQ telling him to cut off all telephone and internet communications from Raider base. There would be no leaks coming out of his HQ before the official announcement was made.

After instructing CPT Desmond Bailey, CO of G Troop to secure the site until they were relieved by 4-42 FA, COL Hickey and his command group drove back to FOB Raider. A CNN cameraman watched them drive through the gate. It was not normal for a unit to return to base at that time of night. He immediately sensed something big was up and started asking questions, but no one would tell him anything. COL Hickey assembled his troops for a picture in front of a Bradley and told them the significance of what they had just accomplished. He instructed them to not breathe a word about it to anyone until it was officially announced. The CNN cameraman watched from afar, but could not find out what had happened.

The Media Role after Operation Red Dawn

MAJ Josslyn Aberle, deputy PAO, had returned to her quarters when a runner came to give her the message, "MG Odierno wants you at the CP, right now!" She hurriedly made her way to HQ, wondering what was so important. As she walked in, MG Odierno told her, "We got him! Black List #1."

She had long known that it was not a matter of "if" they caught Saddam; it was just a matter of "when", so she had already put together a capture announcement plan. She knew the whole world would go into a media frenzy when the news was announced. In an interview with MAJ Aberle, she said, "My mind raced as I pictured what the next few days would hold in dealing with the world's media. I knew this was going to be a very stressful and memorable experience."

COL Hickey soon arrived at DMAIN with the suitcase full of $750,000 in US one-hundred dollar bills. In celebration, they smoked cigars as he reviewed the raid and capture to MG Odierno and his staff. From this, the structured announcement plan was completed—but it would be eighteen hours before the news was given to the world.

Throughout the night, the announcement plan was refined, questions and answers were crafted, and MG Odierno was prepped for the press conference that he would hold after the official announcement. MAJ Aberle finally got back to her quarters to clean up and change uniform before catching a Blackhawk helicopter with COL Hickey at 0600 hours for the flight to Baghdad. Accompanying them were CPT Wagner, 1BCT Plans Officer, who was responsible for the After Action Report (AAR) and mission information brief, and SPC Joe Ghamdi, COL Hickey's fluent Arabic interpreter. They were to meet with Lieutenant General Ricardo Sanchez and Ambassador Paul Bremer. On the short flight, a beautiful red dawn bathed the landscape of the Sunni Triangle. MAJ Aberle turned to COL Hickey, smiled, and said, "How appropriate a name for this mission."

As COL Hickey and MAJ Aberle walked into Coalition HQ, few who saw them knew why they were there. The news blackout had been maintained; only those at the highest levels had been informed of the capture. As COL Hickey, MAJ Aberle, and CPT Wagner briefed General Sanchez, Ambassador Bremer, and their public relations staffs and debated the plan for the announcement; back in Tikrit, LTC Bill McDonald, TF Ironhorse PAO, and the Soldiers of the 357th Public Affairs Detachment hurriedly prepared for the press conference and media assault that would descend on FOB Ironhorse. MAJ Aberle fed the decisions made in Baghdad back to FOB Ironhorse so that MG Odierno could continue preparations for the press conference that he would preside over within four hours of the announcement in Baghdad.

When Ambassador Bremer walked to the podium and made the announcement, "We got him!" the room full of reporters, three-quarters of whom were Iraqi citizens, broke into cheers of sheer, unadulterated joy. For years they had dreamed of this, now it was reality. At 0615 EDT, as Americans at home were waking up on Sunday morning, the news flashed across the nation. Similar elation gripped both the United States and Iraq.

As the announcement unfolded and the 4ID role in the capture was revealed, the reporters turned their attention to COL Hickey and MAJ Aberle—wearing two of only four 4ID patches visible in the room. To avoid preempting the press conference to follow in Tikrit, they hurriedly moved out a side door, finalized what had to be done in Baghdad, boarded the Blackhawk, and headed back to Tikrit. Twenty minutes before MG Odierno's press conference, broadcast live around the world, MAJ Aberle and COL Hickey arrived back at FOB Ironhorse.

By the end of the day, 73 media representatives were in the TF Ironhorse headquarters area. The next day, three Blackhawk helicopters shuttled media to the capture site. On that first day, 45 different news organizations visited the site, and each reporter and camera person physically got into the hole. MG Odierno understood the historical significance of handling this with sensitivity to the media. COL Hickey, CPT Bailey, and several of the G/10 CAV Soldiers made themselves available at the site to discuss the operation. (In keeping with their style, the SOF troops moved on to their next mission—media exposure was not a part of their job).

Over the next ten days, over 600 press representatives visited the site, 56 TV show interviews were held, and the press inquiries count stopped when it reached 1,280.

Saddam had been captured and 4ID/TF Ironhorse received the well-deserved credit. In World War I, World War II, the Cold

War, and Vietnam, the 4ID accomplishments had gone virtually unreported—now the TF Ironhorse Soldiers were making up for the past and bringing the proud Ivy Leaf patch into the view of the world. They couldn't, however, rest on their laurels; they steeled themselves for unknown challenges as the Iraqi people reacted to this news.

Some of key 1BCT players in the capture of Saddam Hussein: CW2 Bryan Gray, CSM Lawrence Wilson, COL James Hickey, and SPC Joe Ghamdi (holding box of money)

COL James B. Hickey, 1BCT Commander

Soldier at Saddam capture site

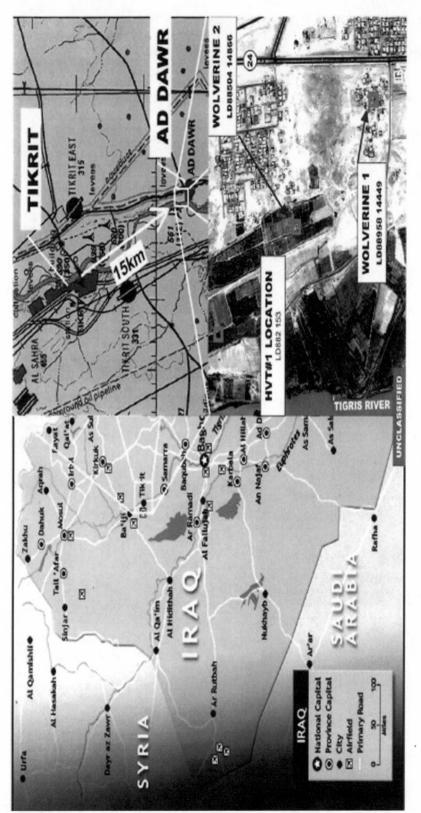

Maps showing where Saddam Hussein was captured outside Ad Dawr

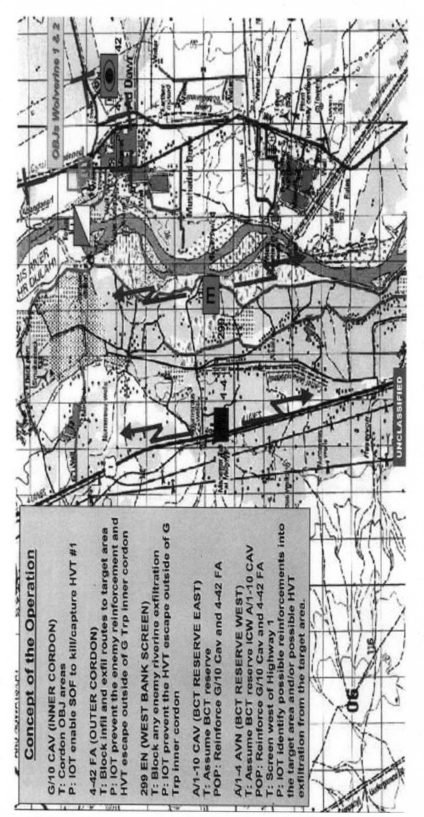

Concept of Operation

UNCLASSIFIED

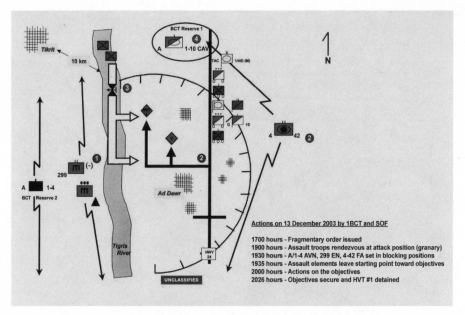

Schematic of Concept of Operations

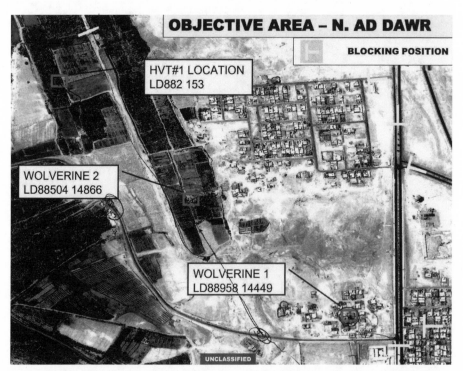

Surveillance picture taken from UAV showing objective area where Saddam Hussein was captured

Photo taken from helicopter of immediate capture site of Saddam Hussein, taken the day after the capture

Small farmhouse where Saddam Hussein was captured on 13 December 2003, outside Ad Dawr

Four views of the entrance to the underground hideout where Saddam Hussein was found - 13 December 2003

Picture taken of Saddam Hussein after he was moved from hideout to TF Ironhorse headquarters in Tikrit

MG Ray Odierno, CG of 4ID/TF Ironhorse, giving press briefing on capture of Saddam Hussein - 14 December 2003

TF Ironhorse Soldiers show off the $750,000 in US cash captured with Saddam Hussein

The briefing room in Saddam's palace complex was filled with reporters as MG Odierno explained the capture of Saddam Hussein

Some of the 1BCT Soldiers who participated in the raid that captured Saddam Hussein - taken at night, shortly after returning from the raid

XII

Winter in Iraq, and More Missions

Reaction to the capture of Saddam Hussein, Intelligence gathering, Ongoing civil actions and combat missions, Operation Ivy Blizzard, Medical operations, Aviation operations, Information operations
15 December 2003 to 31 January 2004

EMOTIONS AND ELATION RAN HIGH AMONG TF Ironhorse Soldiers and their families as they celebrated the capture of Saddam Hussein. A great sense of pride in the historic accomplishment of 4ID/TF Ironhorse permeated all who were (or ever had been) associated with the 4ID. Many Soldiers in Iraq, families at home, and veterans of the 4ID expressed their feelings in email messages sent for publication in the "4ID Update from Iraq," a daily email posting to TF Ironhorse families. The following messages have been copied verbatim and are a small sampling of what I received:

"Our son, a member of 104 MI BN wrote, 'Cigars are being smoked and hands are being shook... Well, I am not much for smoking cigars but I have had a few Cubans already today and I think there will be a few more after work. To be part of the intelligence department of the Brigade that captured him is a great feeling. I guess you guys must have been praying that I would capture him. Of course it wasn't me out there, but I worked on the intel for it and can say I had a hand in it. Not a big one but still an important part. Well, I can't say much else. The news will have everything that is important for now...'

"Our son, with C/1-10 CAV told us, 'WE GOT HIM. We just found out today and had to get called out because the whole town was shooting in the air and celebrating.'"

"My husband told me yesterday, 12 December, around 1300 hours Texas time, that he thought they had gotten him, meaning Saddam Hussein. He is an AH-64D Longbow Apache driver with

1-4 AVN BN at FOB Speicher in Tikrit. His and another aircraft were both flying during the time of capture. He said, 'All hell broke loose on the radios and everyone was excited and saying Jackpot, Jackpot.' He said being in the air, he couldn't get confirmation. He hadn't been to his briefing yet for the night, but was pretty sure that Saddam was either caught or dead. He couldn't tell me Saddam's name over the phone so he called him Elvis..."

"An electronic pawn shop sign near the home of the 4ID at Fort Hood, Texas said it all on Sunday: 'SADDAM HUSSEIN CAPTURED. THANK YOU TO ALL OUR TROOPS! THANK YOU!'"

"My husband (4-42 FA) was part of the Raider Brigade who caught Saddam. I received a phone call early this morning about the capture. Before that my husband had e-mailed me and here is a little of what he had to say, 'We got him! Here in Ad Dawr. I will one day tell my kids that I was on that mission. After a long cold night out there, it's over. Saddam Hussein is captured. I, of course, was not on the raid team but my battery provided security for Specials Ops... I'm not going to lie; when I heard that 'the package has been delivered' I wanted to come to tears, I don't really know why... Just knowing I was involved and I was part of it. Mission accomplished!"

"My son in 1st Platoon, G Troop 10th CAV wrote: '...Ok, I know you want to know. Yes, I was there when we got Saddam. There was one platoon as well as Special Ops troops on each objective. It just so happens that my platoon's objective had Saddam. Pretty cool to be able to be party to the capture of the most wanted man in the world. Unfortunately, I can't say that we did too much, the real credit goes to the Special Ops guys, but we were still right there on top of the action. Sorry, you know the deal, no specifics, but it was pretty exciting. We stayed out till noon today (we started at about 1900 hours yesterday) so I am pretty tired...'"

"Our son with 1-12 IN sent this email, 'About an hour after the broadcast was made in Iraq about the capture of Saddam, about a half dozen Iraqis came to our location. They came up to the

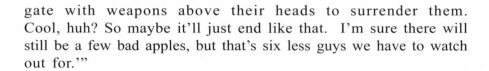
gate with weapons above their heads to surrender them.
Cool, huh? So maybe it'll just end like that. I'm sure there will
still be a few bad apples, but that's six less guys we have to watch
out for.'"

"From a 4ID WWII vet who landed on D-Day, was wounded,
came back to the unit and fought through the war: 'I am still flying
high on the news. I had just turned the radio on when the news
came. I received calls from three WWII 4ID buddies, we all acted
like kids. We all agreed that we were so fortunate that we wore
the 4ID patch. The 4ID is getting much deserved press, especially
here in Chicago as COL Hickey's parents live close to me, and he
grew up not too far from here. Maybe our prayers are finally
being answered...'"

Mike Hedges, formerly embedded with 1BCT during two
tours in Iraq wrote for the Houston Chronicle: "For the Soldiers
of the Fort Hood-based 4th Infantry Division, capturing Saddam
Hussein was sweet reward after spending nearly eight tough and
sometimes frustrating months in Iraq and validated their tactic of
tightening the noose in the former dictator's home area, senior
officers said Sunday... 'There is a lot of pride in the division and
the task force today,' said COL Don Campbell, chief of staff of
TF Ironhorse, which is composed of the 4ID and attached units,
some 34,000 troops. 'This is the culmination of a lot of hard work,'
Campbell said by phone from Tikrit, Iraq. 'We'll be emotionally
high for a little while, then we know we have to get back to work.'
    "While the division's commanders were under no illusions
that Saddam's capture would end the daily skirmishing in central
Iraq, they believed it did mark a decisive moment in the war.
'We've removed the guy who held this area in an aura of fear,'
Campbell said.
    "The information that led to Saddam's capture came from
one of dozens of loyalists rounded up for questioning in recent
weeks by Soldiers conducting so-called noose-tightening raids.
'What we realized early on in the summer is that we believe the
people that we had to get were the mid-level individuals—the
bodyguards and other people who were closely associated with
him,' the division's commander, MG Ray Odierno, said from
Baghdad. 'We tried to work through family and tribal ties that

might have been close to Saddam. As we continued to conduct raids and capture people, we got more and more information. And finally we got the ultimate information from one of these individuals...'

"With Saddam's capture, officers said they were bracing for retaliatory attacks and were continuing their own aggressive patrols. 'Since we really took the offensive in October and November, we've seen a dramatic drop off in attacks against us,' Campbell said. 'Last week, there were 42 attacks, and none were successful, none inflicted injuries upon our Soldiers or even damaged equipment.'"

SSG David Bennett of the 367th Mobile Public Affairs Detachment, part of TF Ironhorse, summarized the capture with his article entitled, "Long Search for Saddam Ends In 4th Infantry Division's Backyard". He described it as follows:

AD DAWR, Iraq, Dec. 15, 2003 – The image of a bearded and bowed Saddam Hussein, who was captured Dec. 13 in this small farming village, is now a worldwide phenomenon. However, the final chapter in the ousted dictator's apprehension has been a story of patience and persistence for members of the 4ID and TF Ironhorse.

"It feels good," said SPC Michael Tillery, a 4-42 FA Soldier who participated in the successful raid. "All the work has paid off and that one step is finally over—finding Saddam."

"The plan to capture Hussein—code-named 'Operation Red Dawn'—was an exercise in tenacious and determined planning," said COL James Hickey, commander of the 1BCT, which spearheaded the operation. "You make things happen by being on the offensive," said Hickey, a Chicago native. "That's allowed us to gather large amounts of information. We're not passive; we're very aggressive."

Confident that the ousted dictator was never too far from Hussein's hometown of Tikrit, MG Ray Odierno, commander of the 4ID, said he felt that information would finally surface that would lead to Hussein's whereabouts. "We tried to work through family and tribal ties that might have been close to Saddam Hussein," Odierno said.

It was a tip from someone inside the dictator's secret circle that eventually led a group of 600 Soldiers from various units to a rustic mud brick hut and the man-made hole in the ground, where the famous fugitive was finally discovered huddled with a pistol and $750,000 in American bills. Hussein had eluded coalition forces since the war began March 21.

Compared to the palatial complex that Hussein had constructed just 10 miles north in Tikrit, the hideaway was sparse. Soldiers discovered a one-room hut barely large enough to house a twin bed. A rickety lean-to outside had been converted into a disheveled kitchen.

COL Hickey said his brigade, as well as other units, have conducted more than 500 raids in the TF Ironhorse area during the last eight months—some even along the stretch of rural farmland in Ad Dawr where the former Iraqi leader was eventually discovered and captured.

Though he never spoke directly to the man that his brigade sought for so long, COL Hickey said he was aware of what the event meant to the coalition and the Iraqi people. "At that moment, I felt a great sense of accomplishment because I know the work the Soldiers had done," he said.

Intelligence Gathering that Led to Capture of Saddam Hussein

The previous chapter started with the statement, "The capture of Saddam Hussein was not happenstance or luck. It was the result of hard work and excellent intelligence gathering..." To explain that statement in greater detail, MAJ Stan Murphy, S-2 (Intelligence) officer of 1BCT, was asked to write about their operations:

"When I arrived at 1st BDE HQs on 1 July, the BDE had been in the area since April. Already, the amount of data in the database seemed to me to be a mountain, and we would increase that amount ten-fold prior to the capture of Saddam. Trying to figure out what the 'Bad Guys' were doing in our AO felt like an overwhelming task. The intelligence section, or S2 shop, was functioning, but seemed to lack organization of the data and/or effort to depict to COL Hickey and all the Task Force Commanders what the enemy was doing, what he looked like, and how he was fighting. My first weeks were more than a challenge. Every Brigade Commander's update meeting was an adventure.

"Prior to a brief to the CENTCOM commander in late July,

I discussed with the commander and intelligence specialist for the Special Operations Forces working out of Tikrit, a theory I had about how to track and attrite the enemy. It was just a theory, and I was not sure about what we were seeing day in and day out or the data we had from the previous three months. We all agreed that it made as much sense as anything else we were doing so we would see where it would lead us.

"Shortly after that, we received a number of interrogation reports on one of the top 55, and I noticed four names that kept coming up and seemed to be linked. I knew the names from reviewing the data the shop had compiled prior to my arrival. I told my Analytical Control Team chief, 1LT Angela Santana, and All Source Intelligence Technician, CW2 Bryan Grey, to take those names and compare what we already had and start making links out of them. In less than a week, those four names had grown to more than a hundred. In a month, the names and families filled a 36 inch by 36 inch sheet of paper and were difficult to understand at first glance. Over time, we understood how each name was connected to the next, and understood the importance of the ground we were operating on.

"We then began to track how the enemy operated. Over the days and months, we tracked the trends and patterns. We looked at the tactics the enemy employed, and started to connect the enemy tendencies with the names and groups on our tracking charts. We felt like we were on the right track, but we still needed to capture a key player in the enemy organization to confirm or deny we were on the right track. On 7 November, we captured two key figures, and through the interrogations, we learned our template was accurate and by continuing with our operations, we would eventually succeed. We made minor adjustments to our template and kept looking at all the critical data points to find what we may have missed.

"About this time, the information flow seemed to slow down. We stayed aggressive and kept looking for a golden nugget of information; no matter how big or small, which could lead to breaking the enemy's ability to continue the fight. Then about the Thanksgiving time period, information came pouring in. It was all we could do to analyze it all. This information led to a series of raids, all designed to capture key individuals/leaders of the former regime that could eventually lead to the capture of

Saddam Hussein. During each raid we gathered more information that led to the next raid. We captured a number of mid-level leaders of the former regime and worked our way into the inner circle of those most trusted by Saddam.

"Since the end of July, all the information we gathered was shared with the Special Operation Forces. The SOF also shared what they gathered with us. It was truly a team effort. The series of raids at the end of November and early December were also a team effort. Many were planned and executed jointly. This close relationship was forged in the heat of the Iraqi summer and continued after the capture of Saddam. We spoke and/or exchanged information daily, often multiple times a day. The SOF teams rotated out and the new team continued the relationship. As the pace picked up, our cooperation proved vital. The raids led to other areas of Iraq, and on the night of 12 December they captured an individual we knew was critical to Saddam and his ability to continue the resistance. He was flown to Tikrit for more interrogation. He finally gave us the information we needed to conduct the raid to capture the 'Ace of Spades'. The close relationship forged through months of hard, detailed work between us and the SOF paid off. In a matter of hours the plan was developed, issued, and troops gathered. It ended with the most wanted man being pulled out of a hole in the ground on a farm not far from an area where he once celebrated his birthdays.

"I could have gone on the raid that ended with the capture of Saddam. I gave up my seat to CW2 Grey. Chief was a workhorse and in my mind, deserved to be there if this was the raid where #1 was captured. Chief and I did not always see eye to eye, but when it came to figuring out what the enemy was doing, we always came together to present the best possible picture to COL Hickey and the rest of the Brigade. We knew all the other wanted was to find the right answer, and to present it in such a way that our aggressive operations could quickly defeat the enemy, and perhaps save the lives of Soldiers.

"I sat in the TOC listening to the radio. I was hopeful, but afraid that it had been too long between the time our key informant was captured and the raid. We had been in this very same situation a number of times over the summer and fall only to come up empty handed. As time passed, I was more convinced that we had missed him and would have to start our template over again. I got up and gave a few instructions to my crew on how we might start again and I was headed out to call my wife whom I hadn't spoken to in a couple of weeks. As I was leaving the TOC, I heard the key word we had waited for that meant Saddam had been captured. There wasn't a lot of yelling or back slapping, just a sense of disbelief, at least for me. We had worked so long and hard for this day that I wasn't sure how to feel when it finally arrived. I recommended to LTC Smith that we cut all communications by any means except to communicate with higher and our subordinate units. The next day we all watched the announcement to the rest of the world. It was great to know we had contributed to that announcement being possible."

Offensive Operations Continue – 14 through 31 December 2003
The capture of Saddam was great news but TF Ironhorse Soldiers knew there was much more work to be done and they continued to do it. Operations continued with a new enthusiasm and a heightened sense of alertness. LTC Steve Russell, CO of 1-22 IN, described the first operations in Tikrit the day after the capture: "The next day, the world was abuzz. Rumors and rumblings finally gave way to confirmations. Then the electrifying announcement came from Baghdad. Now we could finally talk about it. That evening when we patrolled the town, it was quiet as a mosque mouse. The city appeared at 2130 hours the same as if it were 0300 hours. In each flop house, apartment, and home you could see faces lit palely by the television. The regime's war was now over, too.

"We braced ourselves for the activity sure to follow— especially in Tikrit. We saw a spike in violence after Saddam's sons were killed in Mosul in July. We didn't have to wait long. While activity was low on 14 December, we did have a couple of thugs fire on a C/1-22 IN patrol south of the 'Chevron' in town. None of our men were injured although the alleyways and distance prevented maintaining contact with the attackers.

"A new type of resistance raised its head on 15 December— demonstrations. We had experienced a few attempts at them in late September and early October but broke them up as soon as they tried to assemble. This month was no different. I was meeting with the tribal council of sheiks at about 1000 hours and had gotten through the preliminaries when my operations sergeant came and interrupted our meeting. He whispered that there were several hundred students forming at the tip of the 'Chevron' and a separate group on the main street. I closed the meeting with apologies and we mounted up our Humvees and sped in the direction of the demonstrations.

"The CO of C/1-22 IN had already moved to the 'Chevron' to contain about 500 male students. They were marching south along Highway 1 and appeared to be heading toward the second reported group on the main street. The A/1-22 IN CO heard the chatter on the net and readied some of his company to support. I took the command convoy and sped north along Highway 1 where it turns into the main street. In the distance we could see a group of about 250 people, mostly women. C/1-22 IN reported that he had forces closing on the northern group. Looking ahead, I called on my guys to ready the bullhorn. I had learned in Kosovo the value of having a bullhorn that doubled as both siren and loudspeaker. We bounced up sidewalks to get nearer the crowd and then flipped on the blaring siren when we were near the back of the crowd.

"The picture that followed reminded me of that 'Blues Brothers' scene where they drive the big car into the demonstration on the bridge. Startled women and their flowing black robes scattered in all directions. Cowardly men, once at the head of the group, suddenly melted into the population at large. Our Soldiers grabbed the various Saddam posters and shouted for all of them to clear out or be arrested. Gaining the element of surprise, we bought a bit of time. I called the CO of A/1-22 IN to come to my location to take over traffic control and to keep the main highway open. He was already moving.

"Meanwhile, the CO of C/1-22 IN brought his Soldiers around the group and through careful maneuver, herded the group into a dead end. Soon, the scratch of concertina wire could be heard surrounding the trapped troublemakers. His men had already gained moral dominance by heading straight for the angry-faced thug leading the group and then proceeded to subdue him—soundly. Once accomplished, the rest of the crowd scattered but really had no place to go..."

TF Ironhorse Soldiers traveling through the city of Samarra repelled a complex ambush in the afternoon of 15 December and

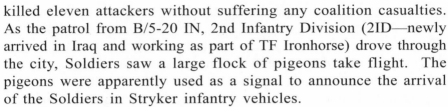
killed eleven attackers without suffering any coalition casualties. As the patrol from B/5-20 IN, 2nd Infantry Division (2ID—newly arrived in Iraq and working as part of TF Ironhorse) drove through the city, Soldiers saw a large flock of pigeons take flight. The pigeons were apparently used as a signal to announce the arrival of the Soldiers in Stryker infantry vehicles.

Moments later, two men on a motorcycle firing automatic weapons used children leaving school as cover to attack the patrol. Soldiers, in consideration of the children and a nearby mosque, employed snipers to target the attackers and successfully suppressed the enemy's ability to inflict damage. The attackers fled as the patrol continued their movement through the city.

A short distance later, the patrol was attacked again by automatic weapons fire from a group using an overgrown field for cover. In a simultaneous action, attackers detonated an IED to the south of the patrol. The patrol was then inundated by fire when, in a continuing coordinated effort, the patrol was attacked by former regime elements using rocket propelled grenades coming from the west and mortar fire that emanated from the north. The enemy's attack was ineffective, causing neither casualties nor damage to any vehicle.

Soldiers radioed a nearby patrol and requested support. A/5-20 IN, 2ID (also part of TF Ironhorse) Soldiers responded and moved toward the embattled patrol. Both U.S. elements fought through the ambush and eliminated the threat. A company commander on the scene confirmed that 11 attackers had been killed. There were no coalition casualties during the firefight.

A Fedayeen leader and anti-coalition activity financier was captured along with 72 others when Soldiers from C/1-8 IN raided a building west of Balad in the early morning of 16 December. The raid was based on information received from Iraqi citizens. The Soldiers confiscated 16 AK-47 assault rifles, 75 rolls of detonation cord, 33 full magazines of AK-47 ammunition, seven machine guns, one assault rifle, one sniper rifle, one rocket propelled grenade launcher, twelve 82mm mortar rounds, 89 detonation devices, 11 car batteries, eight 155mm artillery rounds, 135 lbs. of gun powder and numerous rounds of small arms ammunition. In light of what was found, it is believed that the location was a significant IED making facility.

Three Soldiers were wounded when a patrol from 1-22 IN

was attacked with an IED in Tikrit, the morning of 16 December.

In the town of Muqdadiyah in the evening of 16 December, Soldiers from 2-8 IN were in the vicinity of the PUK headquarters when individuals using automatic weapons fired at them from the rooftop. The Soldiers returned fire and wounded one attacker while five others fled. They confiscated two AK-47 assault rifles, still hot from being fired.

1BCT Soldiers raided three locations in the early morning hours of 17 December in south Tikrit, looking for targeted individuals. Five people, including two targets, were captured without incident.

2BCT Soldiers in Baqubah arrested five Iraqis, including one suspected of recruiting guerrillas, on 23 December. The other four were believed to be associates of al-Douri, number six on the U.S. list of 55 most wanted Iraqis. In another raid in Baqubah, troops also detained a former Iraqi army colonel suspected of recruiting ex-Iraqi soldiers to fight the U.S. military. The ex-colonel was believed to be connected to a local businessman helping to finance the insurgency. Other Soldiers in the area arrested two Iraqis who were discovered digging up a cache of one-hundred 82mm mortar rounds and 20 rockets.

An Iraqi citizen provided information to U.S. Air Force airmen concerning a large weapons cache that he said consisted of close to six hundred rockets. The Air Force in turn asked the U.S. Army for assistance. Air Force personnel and a patrol from 1-68 AR went to the identified site on the evening of 27 December to investigate. The intelligence acquired suggested the rockets could be found hidden in some undergrowth along the river next to a tree line. After a short search, the Soldiers and airmen found a berm near a tree line that was approximately 35-feet long and four feet high. Buried in the berm, covered with plastic and dirt, they found 580 enemy 57-millimeter rockets. The unit secured the perimeter of the site and coordinated with an explosive ordinance disposal team for the destruction of the weapons.

Soldiers from 1-68 AR raided a building in Shahab Almab before daybreak on 29 December. In addition to weapons and ammunition, the Soldiers captured 20 people suspected of involvement in anti-coalition activities, 10 of whom were specifically targeted.

A patrol from A/1-67 AR discovered nine surface-to-air

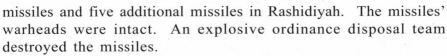

missiles and five additional missiles in Rashidiyah. The missiles' warheads were intact. An explosive ordinance disposal team destroyed the missiles.

Soldiers from 1-8 IN cordoned off an area east of Lake Thar Thar in the morning of 29 December looking for targeted individuals with suspected involvement in anti-coalition activities. The unit raided three locations and detained 68 people for questioning. The Soldiers also located and confiscated 14 AK-47 assault rifles, two shotguns and several full AK-47 ammunition magazines.

A raid during the evening of 28 December, conducted by Soldiers from 173rd ABN BDE, netted two suspected weapons dealers, weapons, and ammunition. Soldiers captured ten people, and located and confiscated four AK-47 assault rifles, two cases of artillery propellant, 14 grenade fuses, a block of C4 explosives and five AK-47 ammunition magazines.

TF Ironhorse's 3rd Stryker Brigade of 2ID, known as the Arrowhead Brigade, discovered a significant weapons cache southeast of Samarra on the morning of 29 December. Some of the items located were found in a false wall. The cache consisted of 43 rocket-propelled grenade launchers, 79 rocket-propelled grenades, 19 AK-47 assault rifles, one machine gun, one 40mm grenade launcher, six 60mm mortar tubes with base plates, 7,920 rounds of 7.62mm ammunition, more than 160 mortar rounds, thirty-four 100mm BMP rounds, six rifle grenades, forty 82mm fuses, two 40mm grenades, 25 fragmentary grenades, five pounds of artillery propellant, 16 mortar primers, a significant amount of C4 and TNT, one assembled improvised explosive device and materials to make additional devices. Al Qaida literature and videotapes were also found as well as a British made ceramic body armor plate with a bullet hole. This was an indication that the enemy faction was testing the personal protection plate's ability to withstand expended anti-personnel ammunition.

An unexpected but very well deserved honor came with the announcement by Time Magazine that the American Soldier had been named Time Magazine's "Person of the Year." Nancy Gibbs of Time Magazine wrote: "They swept across Iraq and conquered it in 21 days. They stand guard on streets pot-holed with skepticism and rancor. They caught Saddam Hussein. They are the face of America, its might and good will, in a region unused to democracy. The U.S. G.I. is TIME's Person of the Year." The honor covers all our military—those in Iraq, in Afghanistan, and in all other places around the world, including the United States. It includes all active, National Guard, and reserve military—all who are protecting our American way of life.

Operation Ivy Blizzard – 15 December 2003 to 15 January 2004
Operation Ivy Blizzard had been planned for several weeks prior to the capture of Saddam Hussein. Samarra had been identified as a city that required aggressive offensive and civil military operations. An ancient city of approximately 250,000 people, Samarra was the largest city in Salah ad Din province, located approximately 30 kilometers south of Tikrit on the Tigris River. TF Ironhorse forces had been in the city since late April but enemy activity against TF Ironhorse, ICDC, and the local political leadership remained high. By November 2003, the situation in Samarra was stagnant. Although the ICDC seemed to be making significant improvements, the police forces continued to be untrustworthy and largely ineffective. Since May, eight different police chiefs had been put in place and later relieved. The City Council was functioning and prepared to begin making decisions and implementing solutions to political problems, but the sustained enemy activity hampered all attempts to make progress.

MG Odierno stated clearly what TF Ironhorse had to accomplish. The purpose of the operation was to destroy enemy cells operating in and around Samarra. To accomplish this, 4ID would refine intelligence in order to identify enemy forces. The city would then be physically isolated and TF Ironhorse would apply overwhelming combat power on focused objectives within the city to kill or capture enemy forces. Throughout the entire operation, TF Ironhorse would utilize aggressive Information Operations and Civil-Military Operations to inform the population of coalition intentions, protect the populace from enemy forces, minimize and mitigate civil disturbance on coalition operations, and reassure the population of the coalition's commitment to developing a secure and stable Iraq. The end state for Operation Ivy Blizzard would be the destruction of the enemy forces in Samarra, coalition forces would conduct ongoing joint security operations with Iraqi forces, and Civil-Military Operations would repair damages and make improvements to the infrastructure.

Lastly, TF Ironhorse would improve the viability of the government, police force, and ICDC as well as improve the basic quality of life.

The first phase of the operation, from 30 November to 15 December, focused on gathering intelligence. The TF expanded the available Signal Intelligence (SIGINT) and Human Intelligence (HUMINT) focus and assets to develop actionable intelligence. The Civil Affairs community began to develop a detailed target list of improvement projects that totaled over $10 million dollars. The restructuring of the police force and ICDC was also begun. The developing of intelligence throughout the city and surrounding areas provided the TF with focused target areas and further developed the link diagrams for all the non-compliant forces within the AO. This process provided the TF with a threat picture of the city, allowing the development of brigade level missions to be executed in Phase II operations.

The operation was announced in a Central Command news release on 17 December after Phase II had begun: "Early this morning the 4ID and TF Ironhorse initiated Operation Ivy Blizzard, a joint operation with Iraqi security forces within Samarra at the request of local leadership. The operation is a combined effort to target, isolate and eliminate former regime elements and other anti-coalition cells that continue to try to destabilize Iraq and intimidate innocent Iraqi citizens who choose freedom over tyranny.

"Saddam Hussein's capture is one of the most significant events in Iraq's progress as the country continues to advance towards realizing its potential. However, there are still those who would deny Iraq this opportunity. Operation Ivy Blizzard will target those former regime elements that held power for decades at the expense of Iraq's future. Another goal of the operation is for TF Ironhorse to engage the Samarra community leadership, identify infrastructure repair priorities, and fund projects to improve quality of life, stimulate economic growth and further strengthen and empower the local government.

"Operation Ivy Blizzard is a comprehensive, coordinated and offensive regimen of isolation of insurgents and extremists. The purpose of this objective is to deny anti-coalition elements freedom of movement, communication, and organization while providing innocent citizens a stable environment free from reprisals and indiscriminate violence of former regime loyalists. Swift and decisive action will be taken against those who flagrantly disregard the rule of law and commit crimes against the coalition and their fellow Iraqis. Additional phases of the operation include recruiting and training Iraqi Civil Defense Corps Soldiers and local police, and empowering Iraqi governmental leadership in their efforts to successfully transition to a free and democratic society."

Operation Ivy Blizzard was conducted under command of 3BCT. 3BCT units involved were TF 1-66 AR, TF 1-68 AR, TF 2-3 IN (OPCON from 2ID), TF 1-8 IN, TF 3-29 FA, 4 EN (-), 64 FSB (-), and brigade controlled elements from B/1-12 IN, B/2-9 CAV, 720 MP BN (-), C/104 MI (+), 534 SIG (-), C/1-4 AVN, C/1-101 AVN, B DET/230 FIN, and 418 CA BN (-).

On 29 December, a TF Ironhorse press release reported that Operation Ivy Blizzard continued. The operation would transition to Phase III when the conditions were right. That included the city council's being capable of independent action and the Iraqi Police and the ICDC being ready to secure the city. It was expected that transition would require an additional two to three weeks. Task Force Ironhorse Soldiers were undertaking funding projects in the city of Samarra and the surrounding area in order to demonstrate to the citizens that the coalition "is in Samarra to stay." Working with the civic and religious leadership of Samarra, TF Ironhorse had identified projects and provided money that addressed those priorities through the Commander's Emergency Relief Fund.

More than three million dollars had been earmarked for distribution to essential government services such as ICDC and the Iraqi National Police. The police received an initial amount of just under $100,000 for equipment and furnishings for the police station in Samarra, repair of police vehicles and uniforms for the local police. ICDC also benefited from the infusion of money. They received almost 1.8 million dollars to address similar needs such as purchasing equipment, uniforms and new vehicles and repairing the ICDC headquarters building in Samarra.

Ivy Blizzard resulted in the capture of 125 detainees and 17 caches, which yielded 11 RPG launchers, seven 82mm mortars with 225 mortar rounds, and over one-hundred 57mm rockets.

Christmas in Iraq
As generations of Soldiers before them have done, TF Ironhorse Soldiers spent their Christmas away from home. Christmas was celebrated with religious services, turkey and ham dinners, carols, concerts, and a talent show. On a muddy field in front of one of Saddam Hussein's palaces, Soldiers played flag football games. Phone calls, email, and instant messaging to loved ones at home helped ease the pain of being away on Christmas. For many of the TF Ironhorse Soldiers, it was the first ever Christmas away from home.

Mail with packages from family members and complete strangers brightened the day. Officers and NCOs, some dressed as Santa Claus, delivered candy and packages to their troops. At all TF Ironhorse FOBs, attempts were made to keep the day as festive as possible. Guard duty continued, details had to be conducted, and the reality of combat was ever present. Three Soldiers were killed by an IED on Christmas Eve, one was electrocuted while working on an electrical line, and two others were killed in a mortar attack on FOB Warhorse.

Ironhorse Sheepdog and Other Chaplain Stories
Chaplain (LTC) Gil Richardson served as the Division Chaplain of 4ID/TF Ironhorse from June 2002 through June 2004. His call sign was "Ironhorse Sheepdog". To preserve this critical part of TF Ironhorse and 4ID history, Chaplain Richardson provided his, and his chaplains', reflections. This is a cross section of chaplain memories from Iraq:

From Chaplain (LTC) Gil Richardson:
"I work for the Good Shepherd (God, not MG Ray Odierno, although I always look skyward to both). I tend His flock, bark when danger approaches, round up the "sheep" that stray from the flock, and drool a lot when I fall asleep in long meetings.

"The hardest thing for me, and probably others, was attending memorials for our fallen comrades. To consider and pray for our Soldiers in grief, for the families at home who experienced the worst nightmare of any Army family, for the leaders bearing grief and anguish, yet carrying on—it was tough. For me, to go up to our battalion and brigade chaplains, to see them doing what they do best—helping Soldiers acknowledge their grief and sorrow, but pointing them to the light of hope that no darkness can overcome—gave me strength and peace, as well as pride in their work. To look into their eyes before and after, to give them a hug and say a prayer with them, and thank them was pretty much my ministry with these great chaplains and chaplain assistants who helped the command to honor our dead.

"We had the most incredibly talented Soldiers, leaders, and staffers I have ever seen. Visiting our Soldiers and young leaders humbled and excited me. Simply incredible heroes who did amazing things in combat actions, everyday duties, and humanitarian missions—that defines our Task Force Ironhorse Soldiers in Iraq.

"Humor, like prayer, kept us going. The Air Liaison Officer, LTC "Bones" Broten, used to say that 'War (for staffers) is defined as long periods of boredom interspersed with moments of sheer monotony.'

"When I approached the CG with an idea for our D-Day Observance (always a big deal for the Ivy Division), it was to read a brief message at the 6 June evening BUB (Battle Update Briefing). After I read it, MG Odierno told me to have a thought for the day to open every evening BUB. Some were humorous, some were poignant, some were religious, a few were by the seat of my pants.

"I lived to regret one of my BUB thoughts. I had prepared a one minute plus message for the 4th of July BUB. COL Don Campbell, the newly appointed Chief of Staff, sternly directed, 'This BUB will last no more than fifteen minutes. Chaplain, your part is thirty seconds, no more.' He then looked at his watch to time me. I threw my 'timeless' message on the floor, quickly muttered something about the Declaration of Independence being the birth certificate of freedom for our nation and the world. Glancing frantically at the grim time-keeper, I quickly said, "To our Soldiers, airmen, civilians, families, friends and supporters, God bless you and our nation. To all the critics and nay sayers..." here I hesitated briefly for the right phrase, and all I could think of was a saying of our Warhorse BCT Chaplain—'to those who oppose us, BITE ME! Steadfast and Loyal, Sir.' I sat down amid laughter and shock, and I have never lived that moment down. Many Soldiers I visited in following weeks would ask me, 'Chaplain, did you really say 'bite me' on the air?'"

"Our UMTs (Unit Ministry Teams—typically a chaplain and a chaplain assistant) were innovative and relentless. When the 4th (AVN) Brigade UMT at FOB Speicher (North Tikrit Airfield) tired of services in the Mess Tent, they began building an outdoor worship pavilion from scrap wood. Herb Franklin and his assistant, 1-17 FA out of Fort Sill, set up a chapel room out of concrete blocks, boards, scrap wood, and sweat at Kirkush Barracks near the Iran-Iraq border. Likewise, the 4th FSB UMT turned a dumpy, trashed building into a beautiful chapel/prayer room. Most of our battalion and brigade UMTs found ways to set up a place of sanctuary, prayer, and worship for our Soldiers.

"The Striker (3BCT) UMT had Mississippi National Guard engineers construct a chapel complete with four plywood walls, air conditioning (courtesy of the XO), and a steeple (courtesy of the HHC 1SG—all to the chagrin of visiting inspectors from Baghdad but blessed by Striker 6, COL Fred Rudesheim) in Camp Colorado—a walled "parking lot" (all asphalt)—outside Kirkuk, in May. When 3BCT moved to Balad (LSA Anaconda), the Striker UMT dismantled the chapel, and had it rebuilt next to Striker HQ. In time, they had a concrete porch laid, complete with awning and cheap lawn chairs outside the front. When they hosted local religious leaders for the pre-Ramadan brief, Terry Simmons and his NCO had water and basins for foot washing, as well as prayer rugs for their Muslim guests to observe afternoon prayers. It was always a first class ministry throughout that brigade.

"Xuan Tran, our 1-22 IN Chaplain, was a good Southern Baptist whose HHC shared our compound in Tikrit. Initially, he baptized some Soldiers in a shallow channel of the Tigris until we told him that the Tigris was off limits due to safety considerations. He moved his baptisms to the manmade lake first used by Lance Fadeley, the 124 SIG BN Chaplain, and was given the green light by the Division Surgeon, Division Safety, and Division CSM for baptisms. This lake was also the site of the famous "Water Palace," where news magazines had shown pictures of Saddam dog paddling and enjoying himself. What a difference a few months makes. A tyrant splashes at one end of the lake, and months later, young American Soldiers—the embodiment of freedom and everything good, decent, honorable, and brave about our nation—make a public profession of faith and are immersed with prayer in the name of the Trinity.

"I was told early on we would not get a rabbi. The III Corps Chaplain (COL) Chip Fowler saw otherwise. He was able to get Chaplain David Goldstrum transferred in September. I was with MSG (P) Wright (my NCOIC, battle buddy, and the best Division UMT NCO in the Army) at Camp Victory (outside Baghdad) when Chaplain (LTC) Mitch Ackerson, the senior rabbi in theater, was there with frozen Kosher foods, yarmulkes, prayer booklets, breads, and a case containing a sacred Torah on loan from the U.S.—to take back to Tikrit.

"God found a way. Mitch, MSG Wright, and I loaded it into a Humvee, and raced to a helipad. We worried that with other passengers expecting to ride to Tikrit, we would not be allowed to load all the items on the helicopter. Time was of the essence, we knew that Rosh Hashanah for our Jewish Soldiers would begin at sundown. The other Soldiers scheduled to fly with us had grabbed another helicopter ride so we had plenty of room. The magnificent crew chiefs and pilots lashed all the treasures down, smiled, and flew us to Tikrit. We arrived barely in time and more than twenty Soldiers celebrated Rosh Hashanah with Rabbi Goldstrum that evening and the following day. They were in the land of the Bible, a town forty miles south of Ashurqat (ancient city of Assur, the city-state which spawned Assyria); seventy-five miles south of Nineveh, where God sent Jonah to preach; and one hundred eighty miles north of ancient Babylon. Kudos went to our chaplain assistants who made that festive time happen.

"When we deployed, we had 56 UMTs (112 chaplains and assistants) in TF Ironhorse. We lost some of our non-divisional UMTs with their units when detached in Kuwait, but we averaged 46-48 UMTs. We had only one Catholic priest initially for our 32,000 Soldier TF. Later we got two more, one in division, and one from the Civil Affairs Brigade. These three guys, David Kirk, John Longbucco, and Mark Plausin, with their assistants, covered more miles than any other battalion-level chaplains I knew. Every week they were on the road or in the air going to a different battalion to say Mass and hear confession. Our brigade UMTs did their best to see that Soldiers were able to attend Mass at least twice per month.

"Our first worship services in Tikrit were in a ballroom in the recreation "palace" (no glass left, no power, no running water, but plenty of pigeon poop and dust). Over time, with the vision of CSM Fuss (Division CSM), this large, elegant, but gaudy (it had "Yes" and "Saddam Hussein" carved all over the ceiling panels), broken-glass strewn, dusty, dimly lit room became our movie theater/chapel/division band performance hall. In those first few Sundays, with no glass to keep the wind or dust out, with limited lighting, our worshippers—traditional Protestant, Gospel Protestant, Roman Catholic, and Latter Day Saints—felt a new breeze, a new breath, a new wind sweeping through the room. Where once Saddam's cronies lounged and plotted who-knows-what evil, now the Holy Spirit, the winds of freedom, the prayers of the faithful filled the air and swept clean the place with new hope. We prayed the same would happen throughout Iraq. Steadfast and Loyal —"Sheepdog."'

From Chaplain (MAJ) Jim Caraway, Deputy Division Chaplain TF Ironhorse/4ID:
"One keynote event for me as a Chaplain in TF Ironhorse was the Easter Sunrise Service at Camp New Jersey the day we launched for Iraq. The tension was very evident during the service, but there was a confidence that God was in our midst. It was a definite faith growing experience for all in attendance. We did not know what was ahead of us once we crossed the berm. That service was crucial as we literally experienced 'walking through the valley of the shadow of death.' That was further evidenced when my vehicle's generator and wiring harness burnt up about six hours into the road march to Tikrit. I remember keeping that "beast" running for 48 hours straight (even through fuel stops) before the HHC mechanics could scrounge up the parts from two generators to replace mine just south of Baghdad at a rest/refuel stop. I did not want to be left behind and reload our equipment. Praying without ceasing became an even bigger part of my life on that continuous road march of 72 hours.

"Another memorable experience was that of visiting one of our S-2 folks who was hit by shrapnel from an Iraqi mortar round that landed near her on FOB Ironhorse just two hours after she accepted a proposal for marriage (her fiance was also hit). Watching them walk around FOB Ironhorse was a testimony of true love and devotion to each other and to our country.

"Perhaps the crowning memory took place while traveling south to leave Iraq with DMAIN. The convoy mistakenly took a wrong turn (one exit too soon) and we got a great tour of Baghdad suburbs!

Ten minutes after we mistakenly turned off, an IED went off on the route we were supposed to be on. I got a lot of comments from the guys and gals in the convoy stating that they were glad to have the Chaplain along (as if my presence had anything to do with it!) However, the convoy leader, (who was once a minister of music in a church before entering the Army in his present capacity) certainly had his faith bolstered!"

From Chaplain (MAJ) Oscar Arauco, 1BCT Chaplain:
"A Soldier died today. It was a sandy road covering an enemy antitank mine. Later on, Soldiers would tell me it was just another day, just another detail. The commander led his men to the release point as planned. He pulled over when he got to the sand to let his armored vehicles take the lead, as planned. Ten meters later the mine exploded and the armored vehicle burned on fire.

"When I arrived, the men were in various stages of disbelief and shock. We gathered around a makeshift table and they began telling their stories. The men told me how they rushed to pull out their wounded friend, ignoring other possible mines or the burning fire. They placed him in a makeshift ambulance. One said he'd seen things like this on TV, but never for real. This was not TV anymore. Another talked about the Soldier's wife and four children living in northern Texas. Another couldn't say anything, he just cried softly. The Soldiers remembered their friend's good humor and goofy comments that cheered everyone up. They honored their friend with their pain and grief.

"Still, God was not absent in all this. We realized together that close behind the struck vehicle was a lighter Humvee carrying seven Soldiers. Seven Soldiers who would have died were spared because of the sacrifice of the one. A lieutenant had been first on the scene, his driver close behind with a fire extinguisher. They had ignored other possible mines and the fire to try and save this Soldier. They would leave no man behind. The Soldiers talked until there was a lull, then we prayed together. We prayed for our fallen Soldier and his wife who would soon receive the terrible news. We prayed for his children whose father had died keeping them safe. We prayed thanks for the Soldiers spared and their courage. We prayed God would keep us safe in the missions ahead.

"The Soldiers honored their friend who had died so others might live and died keeping his wife and children safe. Yet they knew that soon they would have to put their grief aside. The enemy was not going away and neither were they. No one, not one Soldier asked to quit and go home. They knew one more thing, that while they may have watched movies, this was not TV anymore. This is war and they are now indeed, a band of brothers. Tomorrow, there would be more sandy roads to cross. Please pray for the Soldiers and families..."

From Chaplain (MAJ) Klon Kitchen, Jr., 4BCT (AVN BDE) Chaplain:
"My philosophy has always been that 65% of my job was ministering to two people in any command. The two are the Commander and the Command Sergeant Major. Usually I was older than, or at least as old as them and was able to give them a safe place to be themselves and share anything with me. Because I modeled this with them, they in turn understood when I would not discuss Soldier's personal issues with them. I would, of course, bring to them trends or general issues that affected the command but NEVER discussed anyone's personal issues, unless given permission by the person themselves. If I was taking care of these two, I was in effect touching the lives of all the Soldiers in that command.

"When 4BCT rolled into the small airfield north of Tikrit, we were establishing what was to become an important military installation in that region. 4BCT was given the responsibility of force protection of this FOB, later to be called FOB Speicher. As this FOB developed, it became a very large operation. On average, we had seventeen Unit Ministry Teams (UMT's) on the camp. As my Commander was the "Mayor," it fell to me to be the UMT Coordinator and Representative to the overall community. At one point, there were over 58 weekly opportunities to worship within this five mile square FOB. And this was but a small part of the UMT mission in Iraq. It was not the Worship Services which defined the UMT, it was the daily living of its values and in sharing those with everyone we met.

"Unfortunately, I had the opportunity to do too many Memorial Ceremonies for the fallen comrades of our unit. It was unfortunate that they had to die. It was an honor to remember them in a way which was fitting and meaningful for their sacrifice.

"Since our FOB had a Combat Support Hospital (CSH), I also made sure their UMT was supported to the max. We made sure they were always remembered and included in UMT team meetings and at other times. Since I was the senior chaplain, and hospital trained, I filled in for the CSH chaplain when he went on leave or was away from his unit. The first day I did this a Medevac came in with four wounded Soldiers that had hit an IED. In the course of ministering to them, three of the four looked up and asked me if they were going to die. Since I had spoken with the medical staff already, and after looking to the doctor right then, I had to say "yes" to all three. The good part of this story is that I was able to ask them the hard question of were they ready to meet their God, and assist them in being ready! In one instance, I was holding the hand of a Soldier when he was ushered into the very kingdom and presence of God. There is no greater responsibility or honor than that!

"When I think of my experience in Iraq, that day especially, is what I remember. Not the constant daily dangers of war or of the fear of losing my own life but of the importance of my availability to do what God had called me, placed me, and enabled me to do! In my own strength, I would have never recovered from that day, but because of HIM, I was able to do what He wanted and carry on. I would like to say that my experience was unique and that other UMT's didn't have to do this, but the truth is, all of them had similar and equally important ministries and the key was always the same. God enabled us, and the Army and our endorsing agencies empowered us, to do the will of God in times when it was needed the most."

From Chaplain (MAJ) Steve Maglio, DIVARTY Chaplain:

"I arrived on 7 August 2003 and replaced a great young chaplain, CH (CPT) Dennis Hysom. The day I arrived, his vehicle was hit by an IED, wounding two Soldiers in the vehicle. The chaplain and assistant (SGTGrove) were unharmed. That was my introduction to Iraq. We were at FOB Gunner (Taji) until 26 February 2004 when we returned to Ft Hood, TX. The highlights for the Unit Ministry Team were projects and opportunities we were given, which enabled the UMT to work closely with our Soldiers and get into the community and work with local children.

"One of the projects was "Operation Clothes for Kids." We were able to deliver 181 boxes (over 3,500 lbs) of clothes collected from churches, schools, and civic groups from the United States to children of Iraq. We set up convoys and delivered the clothes directly into the hands of children in schools, clinics and a mosque. We felt that this was a great way to build relationships and trust with children as well as local community leaders.

"Ministry in the aid station was provided for wounded Soldiers, civilians, and enemy combatants. Chaplains were continually providing ministry to the wounded and to others involved in each incident. Ministry was provided for the medical personnel after each serious incident.

"Daily worship opportunities for Soldiers and DA civilians were ongoing. A mosque was even cleaned up and refurbished for our Muslim Soldiers. One of the freedoms our country enjoys is the freedom to worship. We provided every opportunity for Soldiers to worship regardless of their denomination or religion. Memorial Ceremonies for our fallen comrades were conducted with respect and incredible care; the memories of these will last forever. This article could go on for several more pages, but the most rewarding experience I remember is how proud I felt about the American Soldier. Our young people are people of principle and high ethics. Our young people never ducked a mission and numerous times put their lives on the line. It was a privilege and honor to serve in the TF Ironhorse's DIVARTY."

Offensive Operations Continue in the New Year

A 1BCT patrol discovered a weapons cache in the early morning of 2 January, ten kilometers south of Bayji. The cache consisted of two 120-millimeter mortar rounds, six 60-millimeter mortar rounds, two rocket-propelled grenades (RPGs) and 20 fuses. The weapons were destroyed. A 1-68 AR observation post was watching a weapons cache consisting of RPGs southwest of Tarmiyah in the afternoon of 2 January when three individuals walked up to the site. Soldiers fired on the group as they attempted to flee. One of the suspected attackers was wounded and the other two were captured. Soldiers had been watching the location since 1 January when attackers abandoned the RPG rounds to escape the U.S. forces that were pursuing them. In an early morning raid on 3 January in the town of Had Maksar, 3-67 AR Soldiers captured 15 individuals, including five persons targeted for anti-coalition activities. All were suspected of being members of a former regime cell. Soldiers confiscated five AK-47 assault rifles with magazines and 150 rounds of AK-47 ammunition.

In Dibis, 173rd ABN BDE Soldiers discovered an ammunition cache during the evening of 2 January. The cache appeared to have been at the location since before Operation Iraqi Freedom began and consisted of 163 enemy 60-millimeter mortar rounds, 17 hand grenades and 17 flares. All the munitions were secured and later destroyed.

Soldiers from 1-8 IN raided a building south of Balad in the early morning of 3 January, targeting former regime elements suspected of attacking a forward operating base with mortars. As the Soldiers approached the building, two men armed with AK-47 assault rifles aimed their weapons at the patrol. Soldiers took a defensive posture and responded to the threat by firing at the armed men, killing them both. The patrol continued with the mission and captured 11 individuals and located and confiscated 30 AK-47 assault rifles at the site.

173rd ABN BDE Soldiers killed a suspected criminal who was the target of a 3 January dawn raid in Mastul as he came at the patrol with an AK-47 assault rifle. Soldiers fired at the armed man after he attempted to fire his weapon at the Soldiers. Following the confrontation, Soldiers continued the raid, capturing five enemy individuals and locating four AK-47 assault rifles. Working with Iraqi National Police, Soldiers from the 173rd ABN BDE searched a KDP building in Kirkuk the morning of 3 January and found numerous weapons. A senior KDP official was detained. The Soldiers and police continued their search at an adjacent PUK building. They located and confiscated one AK-47 assault rifle and five RPGs. In another incident illustrating police and Soldier cooperation, Kirkuk police turned over a person targeted by the 173rd. The individual was a colonel in the former regime's military.

A former regime official was captured 15-kilometers south of Dibis on the afternoon of 7 January by 1-63 AR Soldiers. The individual was targeted for capture by the 173rd ABN BDE for killing eight Iraqi soldiers during the war and for suspected anti-coalition activity. The Soldiers captured the targeted person without incident.

A raid by 1-22 Infantry in Tikrit on 8 January resulted in the arrest of 13 Iraqis wanted for bombing and shooting at coalition forces. More than 300 Soldiers launched the series of raids on 20 houses and three shops across the city. The targeted individuals operated in a cell that was involved in attacks on coalition forces. They had also been counterfeiting identification papers, including fake police ID cards. The operation had been planned over the past two weeks and was aided by intelligence provided by local Iraqi citizens and officers from the ICDC.

A terrorist attack against innocent Iraqis was thwarted at the Tahrir Husseinia mosque in Baqubah when an observant mosque official decided to investigate a suspicious vehicle parked near the building at approximately 1400 hours on 9 January. The official asked people in the area and those at prayer if they knew who owned the unfamiliar automobile. He went to the extent of asking for information about the car over the mosque's loudspeaker. When no one claimed the vehicle he contacted the Iraqi Police. The police responded and discovered that the vehicle was in fact a potentially deadly car bomb packed with 250 pounds of plastic explosives and three 130-millimeter artillery rounds with a remote control detonator wired to the car's antenna. The Iraqi Police immediately requested assistance from 588th EN BN's explosive ordnance disposal team and evacuated people from the mosque and the surrounding area. With the assistance of the Iraqi Police bomb squad, the 588th EOD team successfully disarmed the device. The vehicle was moved to a secure location for further inspection and investigation.

On 10 January, an early morning raid in Baqubah by the 588 EN BN targeted a father and his six sons who were suspected of being involved in attacks against the coalition. The father and three of his sons were captured without incident. A woman was also detained. The detained woman was searched by a female Soldier and was found to have four hand grenades hidden within her clothing. Additionally, the Soldiers located and confiscated four AK-47 assault rifles, a U.S.-made body armor vest, and ICDC uniforms in the house.

Earlier in the evening on 10 January, 588 EN BN conducted another raid in north Baqubah and captured two people suspected of being weapons dealers. One of those captured was a local sheik. The Soldiers located and confiscated three AK-47 assault rifles, one pistol, one hand grenade and 11 million Iraqi dinar. The Soldiers also found a briefcase filled with identification cards, including one of the captured individual's Baath party cards.

Information from an Iraqi citizen about a possible weapons cache brought 5th EN BN Soldiers to a house in Taji during the afternoon of 10 January. The Soldiers searched the house and found 418 C5M rockets; 260 rocket-propelled grenades (RPGs); two-hundred fifty 82-millimeter mortars; fifty 57-millimeter mortars; sixty-five 120-millimeter artillery rounds; 15 PG7 anti-tank rounds; 13 cases of 7.62-millimeter ammunition; 30 hand grenades; 100 rounds of 7.62-millimeter armor piercing ammunition; 2,000 additional rounds of automatic weapon ammunition; and 30 grenades and four rifles. The site was also used as an IED factory. Soldiers found nine 155-millimeter artillery rounds that were configured as IEDs, as well as a bag of black powder with a time fuse attached. Additional IED-making material confiscated included five command detonation systems, four remote detonation systems, four blasting caps, several feet of time fuse cord, several feet of detonation cord, four push button switches used in the production of IEDs and 16 crates of plastic explosives. Two individuals in the house were detained.

At FOB Ironhorse, a new security guard was added—one who could sniff out trouble before others knew it was coming. Excerpts from an article by SPC Bronwyn Meyer of the 367th Mobil Public Affairs Detachment explained, "...Rocky, a German Shepherd trained as an explosive sniffing dog, is part of the base's frontline defense, searching vehicles and baggage. His handler, Navy Master of Arms 1st Class Sean Stull, is the other half of the team.

"'A lot of people think they can get stuff over on people, but it is pretty hard to fool a dog, especially a well trained explosives dog,' said Stull, a native of Kings Bay, Georgia. The arrival of Rocky, along with a second dog, has made vehicle and baggage searches faster, easier and more effective. 'It speeds up the searching process, and the dog's nose is a heck of a lot more accurate,' said Stull. 'He can search the vehicle in half the time a person can.' Before Rocky came to FOB Ironhorse, the military police methodically searched through vehicles and baggage, not knowing if they would encounter hidden explosives. Rocky can search a vehicle thoroughly, keying on explosives or other material that he has been trained to find. '(He) can sniff out anything we miss,' said PFC Jennifer Sperber, with the 411th MP Company."

Soldiers from 173rd ABN BDE discovered two weapons caches near Kirkuk in the afternoon of 12 January. The first cache consisted of 50 rounds of 120-millimeter mortar and the second cache found nearby consisted of 13 rounds of 120-millimeter mortar and one 62-millimeter rocket. The caches were destroyed.

A logistical patrol from 3-29 FA saw attackers firing automatic weapons at two dump trucks 15 kilometers southwest of Balad in the afternoon of 12 January. The patrol requested assistance and a 1-10 CAV quick reaction force responded. When they arrived they learned that the two drivers had been injured and were taken to a local hospital. The Soldiers also learned the attackers fled the scene in a four-door dark sedan. An OH-58 "Kiowa" observation helicopter responded to the request for assistance as well and located the attackers' vehicle at a house 15 kilometers from the scene of the attack. The quick reaction force went to the location, searched the house and found two AK-47 assault rifles. Six individuals in the house were detained for questioning.

ICDC Soldiers detained an Imam in Jabal during a joint raid by ICDC and 2-8 IN Soldiers the night of 12 January. According to an Iraqi police officer, who brought the information to the ICDC, the Imam invited an individual from Fallujah to speak during prayer call through the mosque's loudspeaker. The individual told the people of the town that it was their duty to attack coalition forces, ICDC and the Iraqi police. The Imam was detained without further incident.

On 14 January, Soldiers from 720 MP BN raided two houses in a neighborhood of Samarra after receiving a tip. They captured four nephews of former Iraqi Vice President Izzat Ibrahim al-Douri, who was once a right-hand man to Saddam Hussein. Al-Douri was suspected to have been orchestrating insurgent attacks on coalition forces. The former Revolutionary Command Council vice chairman was number six on the U.S. list of 55 most-wanted Iraqis. The first five on the list had already been killed or captured.

"One of these days his head will rise up above the water, and we will be able to capture him as well," said LTC David J. Poirier. "The two 'main targets' are believed to be in close touch with al-Douri and finding safe houses for him. They are his enablers and his movers. They have information they can provide to us ... that would be extremely important."

Bank notes bearing Saddam's portrait became obsolete on 15 January as a three-month period to exchange them for the new dinar ended. "More than 10,000 tons of worthless notes were destroyed," said a joint statement by the Central Bank of Iraq and the Coalition Provisional Authority.

Soldiers from the 101st Airborne Division began their movement back to the US on 16 January, which included movement through the TF Ironhorse AOR. Over 6,000 vehicles and 1,600 containers would pass through the AOR in the next weeks. TF Ironhorse assumed the mission of securing the roads for the 101st movement through the AOR and for the 1st Infantry Division as their advance elements began their movement to relieve TF Ironhorse in March.

Soldiers from C/1-8 IN searched three locations north of Balad before dawn on 17 January looking for individuals they suspected were responsible for attacks against coalition forces. Soldiers captured seven individuals and confiscated six AK-47 assault rifles, one bayonet, six AK-47 ammunition magazines, one shotgun and one bolt-action rifle.

A patrol from C/1-10 CAV saw missile fins sticking out of the ground in Kanan in the afternoon of 17 January. The Soldiers investigated and uncovered 146 enemy 57mm rockets. One person was detained for questioning. It was later determined this person was not involved with the buried cache but was wanted for his suspected actions in another incident. The rockets were taken to a nearby FOB and destroyed.

An IED detonated prematurely in an automobile in downtown Tikrit at approximately 2200 hours on 17 January, killing two individuals and wounding another in the vehicle. They were apparently transporting the IED with intentions of emplacing it. No coalition forces or Iraqi civilians were wounded in the incident.

In his State of the Union address on 20 January, President Bush praised service members around the world for their sacrifices to defend America. He said that the men and women of the American armed forces "have taken the hardest duty" in the war on terror. "We've seen their skill and their courage in armored charges, and midnight raids and lonely hours on faithful watch," Bush said at the U.S. Capitol. "We have seen the joy when they return, and felt the sorrow when one is lost."

Attending as guests of first lady Laura Bush at the State of

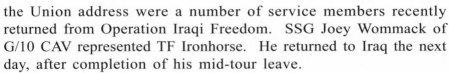

the Union address were a number of service members recently returned from Operation Iraqi Freedom. SSG Joey Wommack of G/10 CAV represented TF Ironhorse. He returned to Iraq the next day, after completion of his mid-tour leave.

Soldiers of 588 EN BN and Iraqi Police raided locations in Baqubah on the morning of 25 January and captured 46 individuals. Three were specifically targeted for suspected involvement in anti-coalition activities and 43 were held for violating weapons regulations. Soldiers and Iraqi Police confiscated 58 assault rifles, two rifles and 72 AK-47 magazines.

Soldiers on patrol from 173 ABN BDE discovered a cache 16 km west of Tuz during the evening of 29 January. The cache consisted of seventy-eight 120 mm mortar rounds; over a hundred 82 mm mortar rounds; forty-eight 60 mm rounds; 15 rocket-propelled grenades; 22 grenades, and one complete 120 mm mortar system. This cache had been buried in a sealed, water proofed bunker. The Soldiers destroyed the cache in place.

In a search of locations near Balad, Soldiers from B/1-10 CAV captured four individuals, including one person specifically targeted, in the morning of 30 January. The captured individual was suspected of involvement in IED attacks. The Soldiers confiscated two AK-47 assault rifles, one SKS automatic weapon and one rifle. Another individual targeted for suspected involvement in IED attacks was brought to a forward operating base a short time later by Iraqi citizens and was detained.

1-63 AR Soldiers, working with 173 ABN BDE, captured fifteen individuals in Bajawan, including six individuals specifically targeted for suspected involvement in attacks against the Kirkuk Air Base, in the morning of 30 January. The U.S. Air Force's Office of Special Investigations investigated the attacks and provided information that led Soldiers to the raided location. The six captured enemy were wanted for arms dealing as well. The Air Force targeted the other nine for suspected involvement in attacks and for selling Strella missiles. The 1-63 AR Soldiers located and confiscated one AK-47 assault rifle, one SMG automatic weapon and pictures of Saddam.

One person was killed when he attempted to crash through a 3-67 AR and ICDC checkpoint near the village of Abu Huraybish in the morning of 30 January. ICDC Soldiers fired at the vehicle in response to the aggressive action. They searched the vehicle and discovered one AK-47 assault rifle and 25,000 Iraqi dinar. A second vehicle eluded the Soldiers

Soldiers from 14 EN BN discovered an ammunition cache just north of Tikrit on 30 January. The cache consisted of approximately 500 tank rounds and 700 mortar rounds distributed among 12 holes. Soldiers secured the site and notified an explosive ordinance disposal team who destroyed them.

A patrol from 1-8 IN came under attack by enemy using automatic weapons south of Balad in the late evening of 30 January. The patrol returned fire, killing one of the attackers. Soldiers captured three individuals and seized three AK-47 assault rifles and three grenades.

News Conference by MG Odierno

On 22 January, MG Ray Odierno conducted a video press conference with Pentagon reporters where he discussed the accomplishments of TF Ironhorse and the current situation. Jim Garamone, reporter with American Forces Press Service, reported on the press conference as follows:

WASHINGTON, Jan. 22, 2004 – Former regime elements have been "brought to their knees" in the 4th Infantry Division area of Iraq, the division commander said in a news conference today. Speaking with Pentagon reporters here in a video conference from Tikrit, Iraq, Army Maj. Gen. Raymond T. Odierno said the capture of Saddam Hussein was a major defeat for the enemy. The most important result of the capture, he added, was the increase in intelligence coming from Iraqis on anti-coalition activities.

The general said attacks on the coalition are down, and the intensity is less than last month. The intelligence allows division Soldiers to conduct precise raids "to kill or capture financiers, IED-makers and mid-level leaders of the former regime. These groups are still a threat—but a fractured, sporadic threat with the leadership destabilized, finances interdicted and no hope of the Baathists' return to power."

Odierno said that while the overall numbers of attacks are declining, the percentage of those aimed at Iraqi civilians and Iraqi security forces has risen. He said this is having a backlash against the former regime forces, and even Sunni Iraqis—those most likely to support the former regime—are showing signs of frustration. "I believe the Iraqis feel 'Why are they doing this?'"

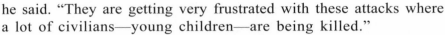

he said. "They are getting very frustrated with these attacks where a lot of civilians—young children—are being killed."

The division has set up joint operations centers in all the major cities in the area, and coalition personnel and Iraqi Civil Defense Corps personnel and police are working to gather intelligence and conduct raids.

In his [MG Odierno] area of operations alone, the coalition has recruited 5,000 members of the ICDC, 18,000 Iraqi police and 2,000 Border Police. "These forces are conducting joint patrols with coalition forces as well as independent operations to defeat anti-coalition elements," Odierno said.

Odierno said that as anti-coalition forces become more desperate, he expects a change in tactics. He said suicide bmbers could become more of a problem in the future, and that foreign fighters are trying to organize in Iraq. He also said the threat is changing. "I think the threat is moving to a somewhat nationalistic threat, and away from a former regime threat. There's still some reorganization going on as a result of how much we fractured them in the last 60 to 90 days. Not sure how many enemy are out there, but I do know the attacks have decreased significantly. It's clear they have financial problems; what they are trying to do now is attacks that are criminally related, or they are trying to forge their way to establish their place in the future government."

The coalition continues to emphasize civil-military projects. Odierno said that over 10 months, the division has completed nearly 2,000 improvement projects costing $41 million, ith another 700 projects worth $42 million in progress. Soldiers have refurbished about 600 schools, 70 mosques, and 75 medical facilities. They also have improved 500 miles of roads, and built soccer fields and youth centers.

The 4th Infantry Division is readying a transition of the area's mission to the 1st Infantry Division... Odierno said the two divisions' staffs already are working together, and he anticipates a "seamless" transition. He said he expects no drop-off in operational effectiveness, but added it will take time for 1st Infantry Division leaders to develop the personal relationships with Iraqis that are so crucial to progress in the region.

Toppled Saddam statues reborn as memorial for U.S. Soldiers
Recognizing the ultimate sacrifice made by TF Ironhorse Soldiers

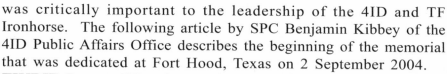

was critically important to the leadership of the 4ID and TF Ironhorse. The following article by SPC Benjamin Kibbey of the 4ID Public Affairs Office describes the beginning of the memorial that was dedicated at Fort Hood, Texas on 2 September 2004.

TIKRIT, Iraq — When he was forced to fashion statues of Saddam Hussein on horseback, the Iraqi sculptor had no idea that someday he would melt them down to create a memorial for U.S. Soldiers. The two statues, which adorned a gate at the palace complex that houses Fort Hood's 4th Infantry Division headquarters group, were removed with explosives in early July," said 1SG Mark Anderson with Headquarters and Headquarters Company. He has monitored the project's progress since the end of July (2003).

The toppled statues were cut into pieces by members of the 555 EN GRP and taken quietly to the artist, Kalat. He reshaped the chunks of bronze into a likeness of an American Soldier being comforted by a small girl as he mourns a fallen comrade. In July, 1SG Glen Simpson, the former first sergeant of headquarters' company, knelt for the picture that has been turned into a bronze," said CSM Charles Fuss, the division's command sergeant major.

The artist, who fears retaliation from former regime loyalists for his work with the coalition, spent several months sculpting and casting the statue. The sculpture is based on a scene many in Iraq have witnessed in one form or another. A Soldier kneels before a memorial of boots, rifle and helmet, his forehead resting in the hollow of his hand. Behind and to his right stands a small Iraqi girl with her hand reaching out to touch his shoulder. The little girl portrays in her eyes and presence, a sympathy mixed with gratitude. "She reminds people of why the sacrifice was made," Fuss said. "It's about freedom for this country, but it's also about children who will grow up in a free society."

Sitting in Saddam's former palace in his hometown, the statue will soon be shuttled to Fort Hood, where it will become part of a larger memorial project at the 4th Infantry Division Museum. There, plaques will be hung in memory of those TF Ironhorse Soldiers who have given their lives in Iraq... "The cost of the new statue was paid for through small donations from the Soldiers of TF Ironhorse," Anderson said. Fuss and Anderson credited the Soldiers' generosity and Simpson's vision for the memorial.

"I think this is the best way we can honor their families and their memories," Fuss said.

Civil and Military Operations

LTC Joe Martin, CO of 1-67 AR, wrote the following report, one of a long list of ongoing civic operations that TF Ironhorse Soldiers were doing to help the Iraqi people.

"Last summer, the Death Dealers (1-67 AR) made an observation that many children were playing in the streets without shoes. We noted this observation in our bi-weekly message back home and they responded in spades. Many families shipped shoes to us for distribution. Of note, relatives of LTC Joe Martin solicited support from the Westside Christian Church in Topeka, Kansas. The church conducted a drive that received local media publicity. They were able to collect in excess of 1,000 pairs of shoes and the postage to send the shoes to us in Iraq.

"During Ramadan, the Soldiers of TF 1-67 sorted the shoes by size and prepared them for distribution. On 15 November, a group of TF 1-67 Soldiers led by CPT Kris Howell moved to a small rural village south of the city of Kanaan. The shoes were downloaded and arranged by type and size so that the children and some adults could pick out any pair of shoes they desired. It touched the heart to watch, as little toddlers to teenagers to adult citizens picked a brand new pair of shoes. They received the donations just in time for the rainy season and were very appreciative of the generosity. Task Force 1-67 also collected and distributed hundreds of pounds of school supplies and other donations from home. Everyone had the goal of helping the Iraqis embrace their newly found freedom. Acts like these have demonstrated to the Iraqis and the Soldiers of TF 1-67 how we all can work together to make Iraq a better place, one child at a time."

Efforts to improve the lives of the Iraqi people continued across all provinces where TF Ironhorse Soldiers operated and did not stop until the day they returned back to the US.

Medical Support for TF Ironhorse

Medical support continues to improve with each of America's wars. The support provided to TF Ironhorse was no exception. From the aid person at the platoon and company level, the battalion aid station, the Forward Support Medevac Team (FSMT), the Forward Surgical Teams (FST), to the Combat Support Hospital (CSH), medical support was always available to meet the needs of TF Ironhorse Soldiers. As LTC Kirk Eggleston, Division Surgeon of TF Ironhorse, traveled around the area, he frequently heard from the battalion commanders, "I have the best medical section in the Army."

The first line of medical support came from the front line medics and combat lifesavers. The combat lifesavers program was lauded by commanders with constant requests to train all unit members on combat lifesaving skills. There is no telling how many lives were saved by the line medics and combat lifesavers who were always on the spot and ready to help at the time of injury. Front line medics were supported by battalion aid stations. Daily sickness, aches and pains, and combat casualties were handled with professionalism by these Soldiers. When wounds required evacuation, the Soldiers were picked up by one of the FSMT units and whisked off to the nearest FST or CSH. TF Ironhorse prescribed to the 'golden hour coverage' philosophy, no Soldier was more than an hour away by Medevac chopper from a modern medical facility—it was less than half an hour to a hospital in virtually all cases, including those on the Iranian border.

Four Forward Surgical Teams (FST) supported TF Ironhorse. One of them, the 250th FST, jumped into Iraq with the 173rd ABN BDE and stayed with them in Kirkuk; the 1982nd FST was with 2BCT in Baqubah and were replaced by 240th FST that was split with one part covering the Kirkush Military Training Base and the other at FOB Warhorse; the 915th FST supported the 3BCT as they moved around before settling in FOB Anaconda.

Two Combat Support Hospitals (CSH), the 21st CSH and 28th CSH, provided level III hospitalization for TF Ironhorse casualties. The 21st CSH, stationed at Fort Hood, Texas, is a Medical Reengineered Initiative (MRI) 248-bed hospital designed to move an 84-bed hospital with its organic movement assets far forward on the battlefield and provide resuscitative surgery, stabilization and evacuation. The 507 Soldiers (26 Medical Corps Officers, 2 Dental Corps Officers, 121 Nurse Corps Officers, 15 Medical Service Corps Officers, 3 Specialty Corps Officers, 2 Warrant Officers, and 351 Enlisted Soldiers) with their equipment did exactly that during Operation Iraqi Freedom. During Operation Iraqi Freedom I, the 21st CSH treated over 32,000 outpatients, 3,300 inpatients with an average daily census of 36 patients, and performed 1,400 surgical procedures. The 21st CSH also

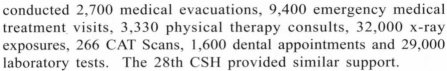

conducted 2,700 medical evacuations, 9,400 emergency medical treatment visits, 3,330 physical therapy consults, 32,000 x-ray exposures, 266 CAT Scans, 1,600 dental appointments and 29,000 laboratory tests. The 28th CSH provided similar support.

Both the CSH's conducted split-based operations. This was the first time in the history of the Army Medical Department that any CSH had conducted split-based operations during combat. The 28th CSH had a hospital facility in Baghdad and one at Camp Speicher in Tikrit. The 21st CSH operated facilities at FOB Anaconda in Balad and in Mosul, supporting the 101st Airmobile Division. Except for the Baghdad facility, which worked from a permanent facility, all hospital units operated out of the MRI facilities they brought with them. The Air Force also provided an Emergency Medical team and facility in Kirkuk, which worked well with TF Ironhorse medical teams.

Casualties that required evacuation beyond the CSH were flown from Balad or Kirkuk by Air Force evacuation teams to Landstuhl Hospital in Germany or direct to the US, via Ramstein AFB in Germany. One of the constant challenges encountered by the TF Ironhorse medical team was keeping track of the patients that had been evacuated out of Iraq and those in various facilities still in Iraq.

Key to success of the front line medics was the continual training conducted for medics. SFC Royel Johnson led the effort to set up accredited training for all medics so they could continue to train and test to become fully MOS qualified and get their National Registry of Emergency Medical Technicians (NRMET) certifications. TF Ironhorse had the first and only formal, accredited program in Iraq—a program that two other divisions were planning to emulate as TF Ironhorse left Iraq. By the time TF Ironhorse left Iraq, over 70% of the medics were full MOS qualified, against a DA goal of having 50% fully qualified by the end of FY04.

Medical support for the Iraqi civilian population was a secondary mission provided by the TF Ironhorse medical teams. Units were encouraged to get to know the local medical facilities and doctors—29 hospitals and 185 clinics were dotted around the provinces where TF Ironhorse worked. Among the services provided to the Iraqis were immediate trauma support for life, limb, and eyesight threatening injuries, including wounds, automobile accident, and burn victims brought to TF Ironhorse facilities; participation in the national immunization program held on the 20th of each month, often including going house to house to immunize children; teaching local doctors in hospitals how to use fiber optics and other equipment that was available but never taught to them; consulting with doctors, sharing information, paying to repair facilities, buying equipment, and training.

A very significant service provided to the Iraqi medical professionals was in providing current medical books and journals that were in extremely short supply. This effort was described in an Ironhorse Desert News article by SSG David Bennett:

"Soldiers from the 4ID Division Surgeon's Office, the 28th CSH and the 418th Civil Affairs Battalion began a major effort to update the medical library at Tikrit Medical College. A huge shipment of books and current medical journals was donated on September 20th (many more came in over subsequent months).

"The Division Surgeon, LTC Kirk Eggleston, headed up the operation with assistance from COL Colin Greene, 28th CSH CO and CPT Alex Garza, medical team officer with 418th CA BN. LTC Eggleston contacted each of 4ID's Brigade Surgeons, and all the doctors contacted colleagues from their alma maters and medical associations. Those individuals then contacted their contemporaries, and an educational avalanche ensued.

"Captain Garza received and donated 20 boxes of journals already," said Eggleston. "I've got 15 boxes now; more come in every day."

"The college has been upgraded considerably. The 29 hospitals in TF Ironhorse's AO are being augmented with books and journals, too. There is one medical and one nursing school in the AO as well (clinics later received donations).

"The upgrade started when Eggleston did an assessment at the Tikrit Medical College, determining that there was a bleak system in place. Doctors could not stay up to date on the latest medical technology. The college only had two, maybe three Xerox copies of a particular medical journal. Most were written in the 1980s.

"That is ancient, considering how far medical technology has advanced in the last 20 years," said Eggleston.

"According to Eggleston, doctors and pharmacists worldwide receive their education in English. Therefore, the journals received from the U.S. are put to use right away. "There is a challenge, though," said Eggleston. "Nurses and paramedics receive their education in their native language." Work is being done to translate articles into Arabic so Iraqi health care workers can benefit from all the information coming in to the college.

"Another great thing about this program," said Eggleston, "is the cost. No cost to the United States Army. The only expense is mailing the boxes from the States to Iraq."

"National media attention has contributed to the effort, too. "We've received a lot of positive media coverage," said Eggleston. "The National Organization of Medical Libraries has helped a great deal, too." The Iraqi health care system is receiving an educational injection. Journals replaced IV solution being pumped into the veins of higher education. "This is a significant upgrade to the Iraqi medical education," added Eggleston.

"With the continued efforts of Coalition forces helping Iraqis with current medical information, Iraq's hospitals, doctors and health care facilities will improve to the point that quality care is given to the citizens. This quality health care is a positive step to Iraq's taking care of its citizens and its infrastructure."

Aviation Support
Included in virtually all the actions described throughout this book is the support provided by TF Ironhorse aviation assets. While Soldiers on the ground manned the checkpoints, went on the patrols, kicked in the doors of bad guy homes, and provided humanitarian support to the Iraqi people, aviation support was always only a radio call away.

Intense preparation for the Iraq deployment began in September 2002 as the Aviation Brigade (4BCT) crammed as much as possible into their training calendar. They were aware of overhaul schedule requirements and focused on banking time on the airframes so they would be fully available once deployed. Initially available to TF Ironhorse were 18 AH-64 Apache assault helicopters, 16 UH-60 Blackhawk lift helicopters, and 16 OH-58 Kiowa scout helicopters. Ten Blackhawks from the 101st ABN DIV came under the command of 4BCT and others were added as required—at one time there were 53 Blackhawks under the control of TF Ironhorse. Flying day and night, the aviation assets were always on station ready to provide support. During the

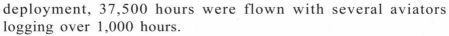
deployment, 37,500 hours were flown with several aviators logging over 1,000 hours.

The attack helicopters worked as part of a combined arms team with each BCT. Each brigade was assigned an assault helicopter company that became an integral part of the team. By working together daily, they learned the terrain, the mission requirements, and the overall plans of the brigade—much better than being called in without knowledge of the overall mission and plans.

Keeping the helicopters operational were the mechanics of 404th ASB. Apaches maintained an operational readiness level above 85% and Blackhawks and Kiowas exceeded 71%. Just as their forefathers had done in the Vietnam war, the aviation assets were always on station ready to provide the necessary support to all TF Ironhorse missions.

Information Operations in Task Force Ironhorse
Task Force Ironhorse conducted Information Operations from the outset of the war. A new function was added to the 4ID HQ staff prior to deployment to Iraq. The Information Operations officer had two major functions—developing consistent messages and talking points to get the message out to the Iraqi people, and, the development of media to deliver that message. MAJ Joe Cox, Information Operations officer for TF Ironhorse, wrote the following explanation:

"We nominated targets for attack by aircraft and cruise missiles. These targets were general command and control structures and networks that allowed the Iraqi military to control its forces in the areas in which we were going to operate. These attacks also limited the Iraqi Government's ability to communicate directly to its people. We also used Psychological Operations (PSYOP) to help reach the Iraqi soldiers and civilians with Coalition information.

"Each maneuver brigade had attached to it a tactical PSYOP detachment that helped carry the commander's message to the Iraqis living and working in the areas under our control. These teams used a variety of means to get the word out. First, they used a Humvee with a loud speaker mounted on it. It could be heard for several blocks in every city in which they operated. The loud speakers proved invaluable in controlling what few demonstrations occurred during our time in Iraq. Another method the PSYOP detachments used to reach the populace was distributing handbills and posters directly to the Iraqis. These products provided information on enlisting in the ICDC, the New Iraqi Army, updates on the infrastructure repair process, and of course, announcing the reward for information leading to the capture of Saddam Hussein. The most effective way of reaching large numbers of Iraqis was through mass media—radio, television, and newspapers.

"Prior to the war, information was controlled centrally in Baghdad. There were no independent media outlets operating in Iraq. Even satellite dishes were banned for most Iraqis. There was also no concept of a free and responsible press operating in the country. Our challenge was to promote the growth of an independent media in our AO while, at the same time, using that media to help us reach the Iraqi people. We knew we would not be successful in developing a reliable and trusted media if we controlled the media, but we could also ill afford a hostile press agency operating in our AO.

Our solution to the problem was two fold. First, we helped the Iraqi Ministry of Information employees who had not been high level Baathists rebuild their shattered radio and TV networks. In most cases this meant rebuilding radio and TV stations from the ground up since most outlets were either bombed or looted, or both, during the ground offensive into Iraq. In May there was only one operational radio or TV transmitter in our entire AO, in Kirkuk. By the time we left, we had radio and TV stations operational in Kirkuk, Tikrit, Samarra and Baqubah. The station in Baqubah would eventually become the backup transmission point for the Iraqi Media Network (IMN), which was later known as Iraqia. This allowed us to reach approximately 90% of all households in our AO with radio or TV, or both in most cases. The affiliation with IMN/Iraqia allowed us to repair transmission facilities and develop crude production facilities without having to use other infrastructure monies to repair the broadcast stations. This promoted an independent radio and media outlet in the AO.

"The second part of our solution was to foster the growth of professional newspapers in our AO. Prior to our arrival there were no newspapers in our AO. They were all written in Baghdad. By the time we left in March 2004, we had established newspapers in Samarra, Tikrit, Baqubah, and Kirkuk. All these papers were written and edited by Iraqis with little input from coalition forces. In fact, most of the stories were written by Iraqis with no direction from coalition forces. All we provided on a regular basis to the newspapers was funding and one to five stories a week that we asked them to publish. (We even left the decision to publish the article with the editorial staff of the paper). On a weekly basis we were paying $17,000 to publish four newspapers that reached every major city in our area of operations.

"The one challenge we had in promoting these media outlets was helping them maintain legitimacy in the eyes of the Iraqis. We could not afford to have the newspapers and broadcast stations being viewed simply as the mouthpiece of coalition forces. We did this by: 1) Limiting our communication to the outlet manager/ publisher. This allowed him to deal with all the aspects of running the paper. We told each publisher that we would pay a set amount for the papers—it was up to him to negotiate for production and dissemination of his paper. (IMN/Iraqia salaries and expenses were controlled centrally in Baghdad for all ministry employees). 2) We set an extremely liberal editorial policy with the outlets; they only had to meet three conditions: first, not incite violence against coalition forces; second, the story had to be true, and third, the story had to be balanced. This essentially allowed the outlets to produce whatever they wanted to put in their paper. 3) While we would provide articles to the paper, we never required the articles be printed in any paper and we allowed the editors to make changes. (to make it appear more Iraqi), so long as the intent of the article remained unchanged.

"Every paper agreed to the terms and soon began publishing. As we prepared to depart Iraq, we were supporting four newspapers. Three of them were almost capable of surviving on their own with no economic assistance from us. The region was well on its way to having independent and reliable media outlets."

TF Ironhorse Bradley on patrol

Apache Longbow attack helicopter from 1-4 AVN patrols the skies of Iraq

Soldiers from C/1-12 IN knock down mural of Saddam Hussein in Huwayjah

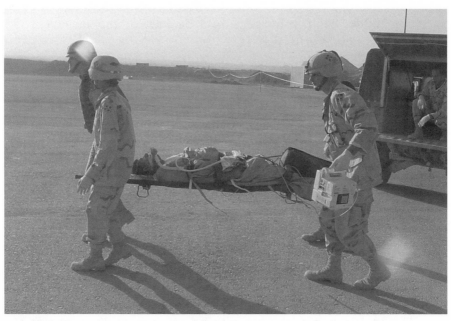

Medics move a wounded TF Ironhorse Soldier from a medevac helicopter to surgery

XIII

Redeployment—Operation Iraqi Freedom I Comes to an End

Largest movement of troops since WWII, Insuring seamless transfer of authority and responsibility, Operation Ivy Typhoon III, Combat and civil operations continue, Transfer of authority to 1ID, Movement back to the US

1 February 2004 to 1 April 2004

T HE ANNOUNCEMENT WAS MADE ON 22 JULY 2003 that the deployment to Iraq would be one year. After the initial disappointment that they wouldn't return home sooner, TF Ironhorse Soldiers continued their missions and focused on a return to the US during the March and April 2004 timeframe. Planning by the commanders and staffs began in the last months of 2003 and redeployment implementation began early in 2004. TF Ironhorse would be part of the largest troop movement since World War II.

Between late January and May 2004, the US military planned the rotation of about 250,000 troops in and out of Iraq. Air Force General Richard B. Myers, chairman of the Joint Chiefs of Staff said the rotation would be "a logistics feat that would rival any in history." Security was a concern as massive numbers of troops would be on the roads, the seas, and in the air. A Pentagon official emphasized the need for effective force protection measures "to ensure that you don't present an inviting target." Vehicle accidents during such a large movement of forces were also a concern.

Another concern expressed by Secretary of Defense Donald Rumsfeld was, "The turnover of people—you lose situational awareness, you lose relationships, you lose the experience. The people going over are ready, but the people there are experienced and really know their stuff. So what we're going to have to do is to manage that transition very carefully. There's going to have to be overlap. We're going to have to be sensitive to the fact that the

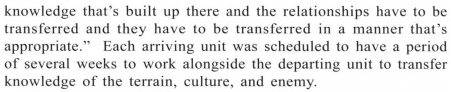
knowledge that's built up there and the relationships have to be transferred and they have to be transferred in a manner that's appropriate." Each arriving unit was scheduled to have a period of several weeks to work alongside the departing unit to transfer knowledge of the terrain, culture, and enemy.

Equipment, as well as troops, would be rotated into and out of Iraq. The replacement forces going in for Operation Iraqi Freedom II would have fewer Abrams tanks and Bradley Fighting Vehicles, but more armored Humvees to reflect the enemy situation. Departing units included elements of the 82nd ABN DIV; the 3rd AR CAV RGT; the 1st AR DIV; the 101st ABN DIV; and the 4ID (including all of TF Ironhorse who had been in Iraq for a year).

Arriving units included elements of a Marine Expeditionary Force; elements of the 25ID from Hawaii and the 10th MTN DIV from Fort Drum, New York (to Iraq and Afghanistan); the 1st CAV DIV from Fort Hood, Texas; the 1ID from Germany; and three National Guard combat brigades from Arkansas, Washington state and North Carolina. The equivalent of eight and a half of the Army's ten divisions was involved in the rotation.

The changes presented an enormous logistics challenge, not only for the Army and Marine Corps, but also for the Air Force and Navy, whose planes and ships moved the troops to and from Iraq and Afghanistan.

The incoming Marines were to operate in the area west of Baghdad, replacing Soldiers of the 82nd ABN DIV, a brigade from 1ID, and 3rd AR CAV RGT.

Two brigades of the 1ID, along with a brigade of the 25ID and the 30th IN BDE of the North Carolina National Guard, would operate in the area around Tikrit, Baqubah, Bayji, Samarra, Balad, Taji, and Kirkuk, replacing TF Ironhorse. The Stryker Brigade of the 2ID, which had been operating with TF Ironhorse since November, would move north to the Mosul area to relieve the 101st ABN DIV. The 1st CAV DIV would replace the 1AD in Baghdad. The 39th IN BDE of the Arkansas National Guard would be working with the 1st CAV DIV.

A new senior Army commander for all forces in Iraq, LTG Thomas F. Metz, CG of III Corps, based at Fort Hood, Texas would replace LTG Ricardo Sanchez, CG of V Corps, based in Germany, as III Corps assumed command responsibility from V Corps.

Just as the movement from the US to Iraq had been a logistical feat of massive proportions, the return back from Iraq would be equally as demanding and challenging. The limited availability of HETs to transport all the tracked vehicles that would be leaving and coming into Iraq was just one of many challenges. To help alleviate that problem, TF Ironhorse leadership directed that all nonessential vehicles and equipment be sent to Kuwait starting as early as November 2003. As they had done with the original deployment to Iraq, individual initiative of the leaders and Soldiers would make the redeployment a success.

Operation Ivy Typhoon III – 1 February to 16 March 2004
The final named operation of TF Ironhorse's deployment to Iraq, Operation Ivy Typhoon III, was designed to provide security for the virtually nonstop convoys passing through their AOR. Vehicles and personnel from 101st ABN DIV moving from Mosul to Kuwait passed through the AOR, as did the troops of the 1ID coming in to relieve TF Ironhorse. Masses of vehicles loaded with troops and equipment had to be protected from the constant threat of IEDs, ambushes, and other enemy actions. TF Ironhorse added the beefed up protection of the main and alternate supply routes in their AOR to their ongoing offensive and civil affairs operations.

Offensive Operations in February 2004
TF Ironhorse started offensive operations when they crossed the Line of Departure (LD) from Kuwait into Iraq on 15 April 2003 and their offensive spirit would not end until they turned over responsibility for the AOR to 1ID on 16 March 2004. Aggressive actions by all units were focused on killing or capturing the remaining non-compliant forces and making Iraq a more stable environment for its citizens.

On 4 February, Soldiers of 299 EN BN sealed the underground bunker where Saddam Hussein was captured, to prevent it from becoming a tourist attraction. A 300-pound slab of concrete was used to seal the hole. The cover could be removed if access to the hole was needed in the future.

Pilots of an OH-58D "Kiowa Warrior" were providing security while searching an area three kilometers west of FOB Anaconda near Balad during the morning of 7 February. The pilots

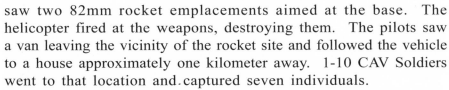
saw two 82mm rocket emplacements aimed at the base. The helicopter fired at the weapons, destroying them. The pilots saw a van leaving the vicinity of the rocket site and followed the vehicle to a house approximately one kilometer away. 1-10 CAV Soldiers went to that location and.captured seven individuals.

Iraqi police discovered and reported an IED emplacement at an east Tikrit traffic circle during the morning of 7 February. Soldiers from 1-22 IN and the ICDC were called to the scene. The IED consisted of six 82mm mortar rounds with wire attached to a blasting cap, buried in the median. The Soldiers disarmed the device and followed the wire to a nearby building. In the residence, the Soldiers found a number of rounds of 57mm anti-aircraft ammunition and captured two individuals. An explosive ordnance disposal (EOD) team destroyed the munitions.

During the late evening of 7 February, pilots of an OH-58D "Kiowa Warrior" identified two armed individuals in the village of Abayachi. The individuals were given warnings to stop, but refused to comply and attempted to flee. In response, the helicopter fired on them, killing one. Soldiers from 4th EN BN went to the scene and tried to locate the other individual, but were unsuccessful.

After seeing two explosions near a forward operating base in Kirkuk, Soldiers from the 173rd ABN BDE established a checkpoint during the evening of 7 February to stop the attackers. A truck approached the position at a high rate of speed in an attempt to avoid being halted. Soldiers fired on the vehicle to disable it, wounding the driver. The captured individual was treated for a minor wound and was held for questioning.

During an evening raid on 7 February, Soldiers of 1-66 AR located and confiscated a weapons and ammunition cache in the back yard of a Samarra dental clinic. Found, were two 82mm mortars, seven 82mm mortar fuses, one round of 57mm anti-aircraft ammunition, one 60mm mortar round, 15 explosive primers and seven sticks of dynamite. No one was in the clinic at the time of the raid.

A patrol from 1-67 AR was proceeding on the evening of 8 February to a location identified as a possible rocket launch site after FOB Warhorse was attacked. Soldiers encountered five armed individuals four kilometers south of Al Hadid who attempted to flee when the patrol approached. The Soldiers responded and fired at the armed individuals, wounding one. The Soldiers continued their pursuit and went to a nearby building and captured 13 people, including one person with a gunshot wound. Six of the men were detained.

An Iraqi citizen informed a 2-8 IN patrol about a possible weapons cache in the town of Jalula on 9 February. Soldiers went to the location and confiscated five RPGs and one 60mm mortar tube, which they destroyed.

On 10 February, a patrol from 2-8 IN saw ten Iraqis armed with automatic weapons and RPGs establishing an ambush north of the town of Muqdadiyah. The armed men did not comply with warnings and in response, the Soldiers fired, killing all ten. The Soldiers recovered five AK-47 assault rifles, four grenade launchers with five grenades, two machine guns, two hand grenades, and a pair of night vision goggles.

Soldiers from 1-10 CAV raided a location in Yathrib on 10 February and captured two individuals suspected of financing and planning rocket and IED attacks against coalition forces and innocent Iraqi citizens. Soldiers captured five other individuals and confiscated three AK-47 assault rifles, one bolt-action rifle, three AK-47 assault rifle upper receivers, one 40mm mortar round, one Iraqi field manual for rocket and artillery equipment and PVC pipes that were the same color and type used in previous attacks.

Soldiers from 1-12 IN and 1-27 IN (newly arrived as part of 25ID and OPCON to 173rd ABN BDE) fired on an automobile, wounding one individual, after the driver of the vehicle tried to avoid a checkpoint established during a search of a location east of Huwiyjah the evening of 10 February. Soldiers were in the area searching for individuals believed to be responsible for attacks against coalition forces when several individuals using automatic weapons attacked them. Soldiers returned fire and the attackers fled.

A patrol from A/1-22 IN saw a mortar round explode near Owja in the late afternoon of 10 February. The Soldiers went to where they believed the mortar was fired. There, Soldiers encountered an Iraqi who led them to a weapons and ammunition cache of one 60mm mortar tube and fifteen 60mm mortar rounds. Eight individuals found near the mortar cache were detained.

A Moldovan patrol (one of our coalition partners) working with 3-29 FA discovered a weapons and ammunition cache during the evening of 12 February. The cache consisted of 27 rocket-propelled grenades, 32 RPG propellants, two RPG launchers, three pounds of PE-4 plastic explosives, 500 rounds of 7.62mm ammunition and 10 AK-47 ammunition magazines.

Soldiers from 2-8 IN raided a location in the distant village of Juspa, 23 kilometers northwest of Jalula, during the early morning of 12 February, searching for a suspected weapons dealer. The targeted person was captured and Soldiers located and confiscated one RPG launcher, one AK-47 assault rifle with a full ammunition magazine, a tripod and mount for a machine gun, and one bolt-action rifle.

An Iraqi citizen came to the civil-military operations center in Baqubah during the evening of 12 February and told Soldiers he thought an IED was buried in his front yard. An EOD team went to the site and discovered a device consisting of eight 120mm artillery shells. The EOD team retrieved the IED and later destroyed it.

Soldiers from 2BCT raided a building eight kilometers south of Baqubah during the afternoon of 12 February. An Iraqi citizen had informed them that a person targeted for capture, because he was a suspected financier of attacks on the Baqubah radio tower, would be attending a meeting. He and twenty other individuals were captured in the raid without incident.

ICDC forces and 3-66 AR Soldiers cordoned off an area west of Bayji in the early morning of 13 February in search of suspected leaders of an anti-Coalition cell in Sulayman. Soldiers raided numerous locations and captured four individuals specifically targeted. The Soldiers also located and confiscated two AK-47 assault rifles, five pounds of PE-4 plastic explosives, 50 blasting caps, 150 feet of detonation cord, and 400 rounds of 7.62 mm ammunition.

On 15 February, Soldiers from 3-67 AR captured two individuals suspected of attacking coalition forces with rocket propelled grenades. The Soldiers located and confiscated three AK-47 assault rifles and one bolt-action rifle.

A quick-reaction force from 3-66 AR responded to a rocket attack on a FOB on 15 February. The Soldiers went to the enemy firing position and found five rocket-propelled grenades, an electrical firing mechanism, four long tubes and one 120mm rocket casing with batteries connected to the tubes. They also discovered two firing positions for tubes that were dug in with aiming stakes, using the water tower on the FOB for reference. The patrol encountered a local man who had been in the area at the time of the attack and he agreed to show them where he thought one of the attackers lived. The Soldiers did not find the attacker at the identified house, but they did discover a second firing position that had five modified brackets for firing rockets. The brackets appeared to have been recently emplaced, and, there was evidence that rockets had been fired from the position. The Soldiers destroyed all the makeshift firing equipment.

An Iraqi citizen led a patrol from 555 EN GRP to a location northwest of Duluiyah on 15 February, where it found a 107mm rocket set to detonate as an IED. The Soldiers also located three 120mm rockets, one of which was wired for detonation. Other items confiscated included 11 blasting caps, one drum of AK-47 ammunition and a small amount of artillery powder. An explosive ordinance disposal team disarmed the IEDs, destroying them later.

On 15 February, Soldiers from C/1-21 IN of 2BCT/25ID (part of TF Ironhorse) captured eight individuals, five of whom were suspected of being members of the Fedayeen, northwest of Kirkuk. The captured individuals were suspected of involvement in attacks on the airbase in Kirkuk. Soldiers located and confiscated one AK-47 assault rifle, one musket and documents from the former Baath party. In another incident nineteen kilometers west of Kirkuk, Soldiers from 1-21 IN located and confiscated a weapons cache of one-hundred 81mm mortar rounds.

In a palm grove outside of the village of Mukisa, on 15 February, Soldiers from 3-67 AR discovered and confiscated one container of artillery propellant, one roll of detonation cord, one grenade, two blasting caps and nine magazines filled with 7.62mm ammunition.

Also on 15 February, Soldiers from 2-8 IN killed an attacker after he fired an automatic weapon at them from an adjacent rooftop while they were searching a house they had just raided in Muqdadiyah. They returned fire in response to the attack. The Soldiers searched an additional two houses and detained three enemy known to be selling weapons. Soldiers confiscated four AK-47s and one shotgun in the raids.

On 15 February, an unmanned observation aircraft (UAV) identified three individuals loitering in a palm grove approximately

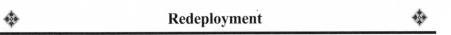
15 kilometers north of Baqubah, previously used by the enemy to fire mortars at FOB Warhorse. The three individuals were joined by seven other men and began to emplace what appeared to be a rocket or mortar. An AH-64 Apache helicopter sent to investigate at approximately 2050 hours observed the individuals attempting to flee. 2BCT artillery fired at the location, killing at least one enemy. Soldiers from 3-67 AR went to the site and found one complete 120mm mortar system, one mortar base plate and one 120mm mortar round.

Soldiers from B/1-12 IN raided three locations in Samarra just after midnight on 17 February and captured specifically targeted individuals suspected of attacking coalition forces.

Residents near Balad asked Soldiers from B/1-8 IN to remove weapons from their home on 17 February. The Soldiers removed and confiscated an improvised rocket tube, a rocket, three AK-47 assault rifles, one SKS automatic weapon and assorted electrical components similar to those used to make IEDs.

An off-duty Iraqi police officer stopped a patrol from 2-8 IN near the village of Wajihiyah and told the Soldiers about an ammunition cache. The Soldiers went to the location and found thirty rounds of 152mm artillery shells.

Iraqi police brought an explosive device made of four 155mm artillery rounds to Soldiers from the 4th MP Company. The police found the device partially buried at the side of the road near the village of Jabal Makhul.

Soldiers from A/3-66 AR were in Bayji on 17 February when they saw a pickup truck drive away at a high speed. The Soldiers were not able to stop the fleeing truck, but went to the house from which they saw the truck leave. They located and confiscated two rocket-propelled grenade launchers, two AK-47s, eight Beretta submachine guns, a recoilless rifle sight and numerous containers for missiles. The house was littered with military paraphernalia. One person was detained for questioning.

In Muqdadiyah, Soldiers from 2-8 IN conducted two raids on 17 February looking for individuals suspected of being involved in attacks against coalition forces. One person specifically targeted was among six people they captured. Soldiers confiscated two AK-47s, three bolt-action rifles, one SKS automatic weapon, a shotgun, an antiquated machine gun and six AK-47 ammunition magazines.

On 19 February, Iraqi Police led Soldiers from 2BCT/25ID to a location northwest of Kirkuk that contained a large cache of mortar rounds. The cache was buried but there were signs that someone had been digging recently. Soldiers uncovered the cache, finding 500 rounds of 120mm mortar. The Soldiers excavated the rounds and discovered a second cache that consisted of 2,000 rounds of 130mm artillery. The site was secured and an EOD team destroyed the munitions.

Four former regime extremists were captured on 19 February by Soldiers from C/1-8 IN west of Balad. Three other men not specifically targeted were also captured. At about the same time, Soldiers from B/64 EN BN of 2BCT/25ID discovered an ammunition cache consisting of 300 rounds of 57mm anti-aircraft ammunition. The engineer Soldiers destroyed the ammunition.

1-14 IN, 2BCT/25ID Soldiers discovered an ammunition cache southeast of Kirkuk on 24 February. The cache consisted of 126 enemy 60mm mortars and sixty 82mm mortar rounds. An EOD team destroyed the munitions in place.

A coalition convoy was attacked 24 February in Baqubah by anti-coalition forces using an IED. The convoy continued without sustaining any significant damage. Soldiers from 1-66 AR and ICDC saw five individuals flee from the attack site. The Soldiers pursued the men into a nearby building and captured all of them.

Individuals using an IED attacked a patrol from C/1-68 AR four kilometers west of Tarmiyah on 24 February. No one in the patrol was injured and there was no damage to equipment. Soldiers searched the area with the assistance of OH-58D Kiowa Warrior helicopters and found a second IED hidden in weeds. The patrol captured one person suspected of placing the IED.

After an attack in the village of Samir during the evening of 18 February that destroyed an ICDC vehicle, the ICDC and Iraqi police worked together to capture the person responsible, based on eyewitness identification. On 24 February, the commander of the ICDC in the area and a captain in the Duluiyah police department brought the suspected attacker to FOB Pacesetter and turned him over to coalition forces.

Soldiers from 3-67 AR on patrol discovered an IED near Khalis on 24 February. As they approached the IED, the Soldiers saw two men running from the scene. The patrol pursued and captured one of the men. The IED was partially buried and

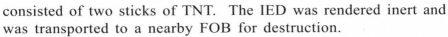

consisted of two sticks of TNT. The IED was rendered inert and was transported to a nearby FOB for destruction.

An Iraqi citizen provided information to 1-14 IN, 2BCT/25ID Soldiers about a possible weapons and ammo cache south of Kirkuk. Soldiers went to the location on 24 February and discovered one 37mm anti-aircraft gun and 100 rounds of 37mm anti-aircraft ammunition. The patrol disabled the weapon with hand grenades and an EOD team destroyed the ammunition.

Soldiers from 3BCT conducted a joint raid with ICDC forces in coordination with the Baghdad police to capture Nahdem Al Marsumi, the leader of a terrorist cell trying to operate out of Samarra. During the raid, coalition forces captured seven individuals, including Marsumi and five men known to be a part of the terrorist cell. The ICDC also captured an individual suspected of being involved in an attack at the Samarra city council building in January. Once the ICDC Soldiers received a tip from a local source on the whereabouts of Marsumi, they organized and initiated the raid and were on site within two hours of receiving initial reports.

TF Ironhorse Soldiers from 555 EN GRP located a cache of ammunition buried approximately five kilometers east of FOB Speicher on 27 February. The Soldiers found more than a thousand rounds of high explosive artillery and mortar rounds and fifty BLU-97 munitions. The site was secured and an EOD team destroyed the cache in place.

While on his way to work on 27 February, an ICDC Soldier observed some men digging near a house north of Bayji. He reported the suspicious activity to his supervisor who sent an ICDC patrol to investigate. The patrol discovered an ammunition cache. They established an overwatch position on the house and captured one individual suspected of burying the ammunition when he returned to the site later that day. The ICDC seized the cache and turned it in to 4ID Soldiers. The cache included twenty 68mm helicopter rockets, seven rocket-propelled grenades, seventeen 82mm mortar rounds and six 60mm mortar rounds.

Working together, 4ID Soldiers from 3-67 AR, the ICDC, and Iraqi police captured five individuals suspected of anti-coalition activities in a joint raid in the town of As Sadah in Diyala Province on 27 February. The individuals were suspects in the bombing of a local health clinic.

An Iraqi citizen led Soldiers from TF Ironhorse's 14 EN BN to three weapons caches approximately twenty kilometers north of Tikrit on 27 February. The caches included five 82mm rockets and 15 rocket warheads. All three caches were destroyed in place.

While on patrols to clear the highways of IEDs, Soldiers from the 14 EN BN discovered a cache consisting of two hundred 100mm tank rounds located about 150 feet off the north side of Highway 1, west of Balad. The cache was destroyed in place.

Soldiers from TF Ironhorse AVN BDE were conducting operations near the Jabal Hamrin Ridge near the Tikrit to Kirkuk highway when they discovered a cache of 100-200 artillery and mortar rounds on 29 February. They informed 2BCT/25ID who sent a quick-reaction force to investigate and secure the cache.

TF Ironhorse Soldiers from 2-11 FA, along with ICDC Soldiers, stopped two trucks carrying lumber on 29 February west of Altun Kapri. Upon inspection, the Soldiers discovered a cache of ammunition in the trucks. The cache contained one thousand 122mm rounds. It was taken to the Altun Kapri police station, where Soldiers from 2BCT/25ID destroyed the munitions. Four individuals in the trucks were detained.

4ID Soldiers from 3-66 AR conducted a raid targeting suspected weapons caches on 29 February in Ash Sharqat. The Soldiers searched three target locations and captured two individuals. They confiscated three AK-47 rifles, one 9mm Makarov pistol, 75 pounds of artillery propellant, 22 AK-47 magazines, thirty 12.7mm rounds, thirty 7.62mm rounds, two radios, one radio base station and power supply, one flare gun, five flares and assorted ammunition.

The Coalition's Man Portable Air Defense Weapons (MANPAD) buy-back program continued to have results throughout the TF Ironhorse AO. The 4ID's 2BCT purchased seven SA missiles on 29 February while conducting operations in Diyala Province.

TF Ironhorse Soldiers sought out and destroyed anti-coalition forces in February with as much enthusiasm and vigor as when they had first entered Iraq. Never did TF Ironhorse Soldiers act like "short-timers." They kept their eye on the target and maintained their offensive spirit in seeking out the enemy. Joint operations with ICDC units became more prevalent and more successful as the teamwork matured.

173rd Redeployment to Italy

The 173rd ABN BDE began redeployment to their home station in Italy on 2 February with the redeployment of the "Torch Party", led by MAJ William Ostlund. On 17 February, the first flight of 212 Sky Soldiers departed Kirkuk Army Airfield en route to Italy. That flight was followed by similar flights on 18, 19, and 20 February. The official Transfer of Authority (TOA) was conducted at Kirkuk AAF on 19 February when the 173rd ABN BDE passed the torch to 2BCT of 25ID. Concurrent with the TOA, over five days, the 173rd ABN BDE brought its remaining forces and equipment to Kuwait by ground convoy. The nearly 600 pieces of rolling stock drove 600 miles from Kirkuk, through the Sunni Triangle, to Kuwait. While en route to Kuwait, the last two Sky Soldiers to be wounded in action were wounded south of Baghdad. 1LT Lee and SFC Fatuesi were both wounded by the same IED and were both returned to duty after treatment. Once in Kuwait, MAJ Kevin Petit, the BDE XO, forcefully and efficiently pushed the Brigade from Kuwait to Italy where the Brigade completed their redeployment on 7 March. Upon redeployment, the Brigade conducted a thorough reintegration process for all Soldiers. On 12 March, the SETAF community sponsored a Welcome Home Party.

Redeployment Operations in February

Concurrent with offensive and civil action operations, TF Ironhorse had the challenge of planning and implementing its redeployment back to the US. This included preparing everything they had brought to Iraq for shipment home, first to Kuwait and then on to the US. The advance party of 1ID began to flow into the AOR to prepare for the arrival of their main body. Soldiers from 2BCT/25ID arrived in Kirkuk to begin their relief of the 173rd ABN BDE. As the main body arrived in the various locations, joint operations were conducted to allow the TF Ironhorse team to pass on its knowledge to 1ID and 2BCT/25ID.

Decisions were made on the sequence of troops and equipment leaving the AOR for the long trek to Kuwait. In most cases, units did not leave all at once but kept the required strength in place to continue the mission as they moved other parts of the unit out. Rear detachment personnel in the U.S. assumed an even more critical role as the redeployment gained momentum.

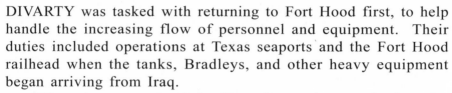

DIVARTY was tasked with returning to Fort Hood first, to help handle the increasing flow of personnel and equipment. Their duties included operations at Texas seaports and the Fort Hood railhead when the tanks, Bradleys, and other heavy equipment began arriving from Iraq.

When troops arrived in Kuwait, equipment had to be thoroughly cleaned, ammunition turned in, customs and agricultural inspections passed, and equipment loaded onto ships before Soldiers were freed for flights back to the US. Each departing ship was accompanied by a small team of TF Ironhorse Soldiers who assumed responsibility for the equipment on the trip home.

Redeployment preparation started at Fort Hood in January. At the 4ID Family Redeployment Day on 24 January, which took place on the campuses of Meadows Elementary School, Bennett Health Clinic, and the 4ID Headquarters, family members of deployed 4ID Soldiers prepared for the return of the unit. The event consisted of classes and activities provided by various Fort Hood agencies to help prepare and support families for their Soldier's return from Iraq. The classes were on topics such as nutrition and stress management, recognizing combat stress and what to expect when the Soldiers came home. Additionally, family members began creating "Welcome Home" banners, which would be prominently displayed on Fort Hood until the last 4ID Soldier returned home. Family redeployment briefings for each unit were scheduled for the last half of February. Concurrently with preparing for their Soldiers homecoming, the FRG leaders were working with 1st Cavalry Division FRG leaders to pass on their experience to them as they began their deployment.

Improvements continued at FOB Ironhorse even as TF Ironhorse Soldiers were packing to go home, paving the way for their replacements. All over FOB Ironhorse, facilities were being built or improved in an effort to provide a better environment for Soldiers stationed there. "Half of the ideas for improvements come from my head and half of them from the relief in place policies," said SGM Rodney Placzek, garrison SGM for FOB Ironhorse.

In January, more than 15,000 cubic meters of gravel had been spread, laying the foundation for many of the changes. Upgrades included four new helipads, a new wash rack, more shower

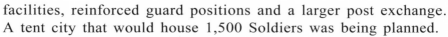

facilities, reinforced guard positions and a larger post exchange. A tent city that would house 1,500 Soldiers was being planned.

"We're using a lot of Iraqi businessmen to do the work," said 4ID CSM Charles Fuss. "Our engineers are out improving other FOBs, local infrastructure, and building things like bridges. When we hire locals, it boosts the economy and gives them jobs. If they're working, they're not attacking us."

One of the most important projects was the container yard for customs inspections. "Units will be able to get their conexes inspected here and sealed by customs before shipping them," Placzek said. "It will make things go smoothly when units prepare to leave."

On 5 February, Central Command reported the Transfer of Authority (TOA) of the 101st ABN DIV in Mosul to TF Olympia, the Stryker Brigade of 2ID, previously assigned to TF Ironhorse. The announcement stated: "MOSUL, Iraq—As hundreds of regional Iraqi leaders and coalition partners looked on, the 101st ABN DIV (Air Assault) transferred authority and operational control of Ninewa, Irbil and Dahuk provinces to TF Olympia today at the palace headquarters complex in northern Mosul.

"TF Olympia is a sub-element of I Corps headquarters based at Fort Lewis, Washington. The unit includes representatives from all three components of the United States Army (Active, Reserve and National Guard) as well as United States Marine Corps and Australian officers. TF Olympia's subordinate units include the 3BCT, 2ID (Stryker BCT) from Fort Lewis, four ICDC battalions, three Iraq Border Police battalions and several thousand members of the Iraq Facility Protection Security Forces and will soon include an Iraq Armed Forces battalion.

"The ceremony marked the culmination of several weeks of transition operations and regional handovers in Tall Afar, Qayyara and Mosul, as many units under the operational control of TF Olympia worked in conjunction with 101st ABN DIV Soldiers to ensure a seamless transition of authority. The 101st ABN DIV will redeploy to Fort Campbell, Kentucky after a yearlong deployment in support of Operation Iraqi Freedom," he said. That was good news for TF Ironhorse—they were next in line to transfer authority, scheduled for March.

Marking the beginning of the 4ID's official return from its deployment to Iraq, the entry of sixty Soldiers into Starker Gym

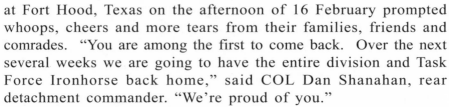

at Fort Hood, Texas on the afternoon of 16 February prompted whoops, cheers and more tears from their families, friends and comrades. "You are among the first to come back. Over the next several weeks we are going to have the entire division and Task Force Ironhorse back home," said COL Dan Shanahan, rear detachment commander. "We're proud of you."

On 19 February, Pentagon officials announced that the rotation of troops into and out of Iraq was in full swing. More than 40,000 troops scheduled to deploy to Iraq had moved into theater, and 35,000 of those scheduled to go home had already departed. They restated that the rotation was the largest troop movement since WWII. A logistics official in Kuwait said it was like the Normandy invasion "in both directions". More than 60 commercial ships were carrying more than 350,000 short tons of equipment to and from the theater. More than 90 military aircraft and 20 commercial aircraft were involved daily in the transfer of personnel and equipment. At the same time, military operations in Iraq continued with no letup.

SFC Henry Bacon, HHT/1-10 CAV was killed on 20 February, south of the town of Ad Dujayl on Highway 1 as his convoy was en route to Kuwait. The convoy had stopped to recover an unserviceable five-ton truck. During the stop, SFC Bacon got out of his vehicle and walked toward the front of the convoy when he was struck and killed by another vehicle.

In a Central Command press briefing on 23 February, BG Mark Kimmitt, deputy director of operations, CJTF-7 responded to the press in a Q&A session: "With regards to the ongoing transition, we're probably about halfway there for the coalition overall and about 40 percent there in U.S. troops. We've already rotated the commands of Multinational Division Southeast, Multinational Division Central South, and, as you know, the 101st ABN DIV. Three of the six divisions have gone through the full transfer of authority (TOA). We're now working in the 4ID sector. The 173rd ABN BDE from Italy has departed. The 2BCT/25ID has conducted TOA with them. We're continuing the transfer of authority within the 4ID region and we're going to start seeing it over in the 82nd ABN DIV region, then finishing up with the 1st AR DIV here in Baghdad.

"It's going well. The logisticians have done a brilliant job in terms of the planning. It's been a little disruptive, as you might imagine, to the civilians on the roads as hundreds and thousands of vehicles and personnel are coming in and out, but we've been talking to the civilians and we've been talking to the Iraqi press to try to manage this as well as possible. We have not seen any directed threat aimed at any of the incoming or outgoing units. It's always something that we take as a given that the most vulnerable time for a unit is around TOA. So as you can imagine, we add extra force protection measures. We're a little more vigilant. And up to this point, we have not seen in any of the transfer of authorities, either in the activities or the actual ceremonies themselves, that there has been any increased activity. But we stay vigilant.

"As relates to convoys—after the first couple of convoys started, there were a couple of IED and small arms fire attacks. Very quickly, the enemy saw how quick we were to respond, both on the ground and from the air. They also recognized that these troops were not declaring victory, holstering their weapons, and driving out drinking soda pops. Those troops, as they were going down out of the country, were treating that as a combat convoy. The enemy realized that it was not in their best interest to try to attack those convoys. That's what we've seen since then..."

On 24 February, 75 Soldiers from 3BCT arrived back at Fort Carson, the first of a steady flow scheduled to arrive over the next six weeks. Previously, on 13 February, advance party elements had arrived at Fort Carson to prepare for the return.

In Kuwait, it was reported the 4ID would require 19 of the Navy's massive "roll-on, roll-off" (Ro-Ro) ships to return all of its tanks, Bradleys, and heavy bridging equipment back to the US. On the deployment in early 2003, the 4ID had used 39 smaller vessels to transport their equipment. A spokesman at the port in Kuwait said, "They brought absolutely everything with them. The enormous multi-role bridging units needed for the planned assault through Turkey were a particular space-grabber."

The Kuwaiti port of al-Shuaiba had been the U.S. military's chief landing area for war supplies used in the invasion and occupation of Iraq. The port was now proving essential in the troop rotation, since 90 percent of the tonnage for the occupation was being shipped by sea. Kuwaiti authorities had given most of the port over to the U.S. military, which had unloaded and loaded war supplies from 428 ships since the war preparations began.

"Without them we couldn't do this operation. It's that simple,'" said MG Stephen M. Speakes, the commander in charge of the troop rotation.

By the end of February, six planeloads of approximately 200 Soldiers each had returned to Fort Hood. All of the 173rd ABN BDE had returned to their home base of Aviano, Italy. Other TF Ironhorse units had begun trickling into their home locations around the US. The flow would increase greatly in March.

Offensive Actions Continue Through 16 March

Soldiers from 3-67 AR conducted a raid 1 March southwest of Abu Sayda. The raid was to capture an individual responsible for sniper attacks against coalition forces. The Soldiers captured the individual along with two others, but discovered no weapons.

Iraqi Police discovered an IED south of Baqubah on 1 March. The IED was a series of four partially buried 152mm artillery rounds and was wired in a "daisy chain" for remote detonation. The police secured the area and an EOD team from 555 EN GRP disarmed the IED and removed it to a safe place for destruction.

TF Ironhorse Aviators from 1-10 CAV observed two individuals attempting to loot a weapons storage site on 1 March. The individuals were contained by the flight of OH-58D Kiowa Warriors until a combat patrol from 3-66 AR captured them. While on the scene, the Soldiers discovered a cache of expended mortar rounds, 50 high-explosive mortar rounds and 21 mortar fuses. The cache was destroyed in place and the captured individuals were turned over to the Iraqi police.

A 4th EN BN combat patrol discovered a weapons cache west of Abu Shakur on 1 March. The Soldiers secured two thousand 14.5mm antiaircraft rounds and transported them to a secure location where EOD personnel destroyed them.

Aviators and Soldiers from 2BCT worked together using aircraft and a tactical unmanned aerial vehicle (UAV) to observe six individuals attempting to emplace IEDs near Zaghiriyah on 1 March. An AH-64 Apache engaged the would-be attackers. Two individuals fled toward the town after the Apache broke contact. The UAV provided surveillance over the site and observed one of the individuals, who appeared to be wounded, being helped into a vehicle by two others. Later, the UAV showed several individuals attempting to recover the remains of casualties

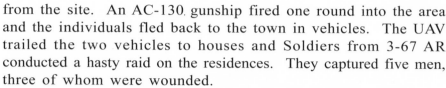

from the site. An AC-130 gunship fired one round into the area and the individuals fled back to the town in vehicles. The UAV trailed the two vehicles to houses and Soldiers from 3-67 AR conducted a hasty raid on the residences. They captured five men, three of whom were wounded.

Insurgents launched four mortar rounds at FOB Ironhorse in Tikrit on 2 March, including one that landed near a dining hall during suppertime, no one was hurt. The rounds were fired from the east side of the Tigris River. Two of the rounds were defective and EOD Soldiers defused the unexploded shells.

TF Ironhorse Soldiers from 588 EN BN conducted a raid east of Baqubah on 3 March. They captured two individuals, including one individual suspected of emplacing an IED at the Baqubah governor's building on 29 February. Iraqi Police and 4ID Soldiers apprehended Sami Ahmed in a joint raid. Ahmed is the suspected leader of a local Wahabi terrorist cell and former Iraqi Intelligence service officer. 588 EN BN Soldiers apprehended Ahmed along with 13 individuals. Nine of the 13 were specifically targeted as suspects in attacks against U.S. forces in the area.

1-68 AR Soldiers captured three suspected members of a local terrorist cell near Tarmiyah during a raid on 4 March. The primary target was not at the residence, but the Soldiers detained the other men for questioning.

The ICDC and 2-8 IN forces searched a bunker south of Muqdadiyah and discovered a cache of weapons on 3 March, during a joint raid. The coalition forces captured six individuals. Four individuals were released after initial questioning, but two individuals were detained

TF Ironhorse Soldiers assigned to 341 MP Company located a cache of twenty-five 130mm tank rounds near a destroyed tank approximately twelve kilometers south of Ad Dujayl on 4 March. Soldiers from 1-68 AR and EOD secured the cache and transported the rounds for later destruction.

TF Ironhorse Soldiers from 1-14 IN, 2BCT/25ID conducted a raid on 4 March southeast of Tuz and captured two individuals suspected in anti-coalition attacks in the towns of Hafriyah and Luqum. The Soldiers confiscated two AK-47 assault rifles, four AK-47 magazines, one machine gun and two protective masks.

4ID Soldiers and Iraqi police conducted a joint raid in Buhriz in Diyala Province on 4 March. Soldiers from 588 EN BN and

1-67 AR captured seven individuals suspected in attacks against coalition forces in Buhriz. Three of the seven individuals were the targets of the raid. The Soldiers confiscated 57 AK-47 assault rifles during the raid.

Soldiers from 2-11 FA conducted a joint raid with coalition Soldiers on 3 March in Madiawa. The raid was conducted based on information that a suspected terrorist cell leader, Sabir Ali, would be in the town. Coalition forces captured Ali and his son, both of whom were detained.

Soldiers from 1-67 AR and 3-68 AR captured seven individuals suspected of being involved in an IED attack that wounded one TF Ironhorse Soldier on 4 March near Hadid. Soldiers pursued a motorcycle and a black four-door Opel sedan following the attack. The individual on the motorcycle dismounted and attempted to flee the scene on foot but was wounded by small-arms fire. The wounded individual escaped but was captured later. Soldiers stopped the black Opel and captured three individuals. Soldiers also captured three other individuals in a building near the IED attack.

TF Ironhorse Soldiers from 1-21 IN, 2BCT/25ID conducted weapons-compliance inspections at political party headquarters throughout Kirkuk. They inspected 27 buildings and confiscated a variety of weapons, including nine AK-47s, 17 AK-47 magazines, one bayonet, one hand grenade, one pistol and one 60mm mortar base plate. Two individuals were detained for making threats against the Soldiers conducting the inspections.

Soldiers from 3-67 AR conducted a raid to capture individuals responsible for bombing a health clinic in Baqubah last month. The Soldiers captured two individuals during the raid.

4ID Soldiers from 2-8 IN conducted a raid against anti-coalition forces north of Muqdadiyah. The Soldiers captured three individuals suspected in mortar attacks in the area. Soldiers confiscated two AK-47 assault rifles, one 9mm pistol, one flare gun and 12.7mm antiaircraft ammunition. There were no injuries or damage to equipment during the raid.

A former ICDC Soldier reported a weapons cache to a combat patrol of 1-22 IN, located southeast of Owja on 5 March. The patrol discovered a cache of eighteen 82mm mortar rounds. The Soldiers secured the cache until it could be destroyed.

Iraqi police conducted a raid on 6 March near Hib Hib to

capture Shiek Amir, an individual suspected in attacks against anti-coalition forces. The police captured Sheik Amir and turned him over to Soldiers from 588 EN BN for questioning.

Iraqi police reported a cache of rocket and mortar rounds to Soldiers from 4-42 FA near Ad Dawr. Soldiers from 1-4 CAV conducted a patrol to investigate the cache and discovered four cylinders, six to eight feet long, that the police suspect were used to fire rockets. The tubes were confiscated and later destroyed.

Acting on information provided by an Iraqi citizen, 4ID Soldiers from 1-22 IN conducted a raid near Bayji on 6 March to capture individuals suspected of an RPG attack in late January. Soldiers captured two individuals and confiscated one computer, one AK-47 and one loaded AK-47 magazine. They were taken to a coalition detention center for questioning.

Members of Iraq's Governing Council signed an interim constitution on 8 March after resolving a political impasse caused by objections from the country's most powerful cleric. The twenty-five council members signed the document on an antique desk once owned by King Faisal I, Iraq's first monarch. Council president Mohammed Bahr al-Ulloum called the signing, "a historic moment, decisive in the history of Iraq."

A 4ID/TF Ironhorse Soldier was featured on the cover of Time Magazine on 8 March (magazine dated 15 March). SPC Cody Hoefer, driver for the CO of 1-22 IN, was the first person from his native Montana to ever be pictured on the cover of Time.

Soldiers with 588 EN BN captured Abu Omar, a target suspected of attacking coalition forces, during a hasty raid near Baqubah on 7 March. Omar was captured along with three others. Information obtained from the raid resulted in the capture of ten individuals during a second raid at approximately 0010 hours on 8 March. This raid also resulted in the confiscation of a light antitank weapon, four rocket-propelled-grenade launchers, 12 AK-47 assault rifles, four medium machine guns, two computers and several compact discs of valuable information.

TF Ironhorse Soldiers from C/588 EN BN captured Sheik Mohammed Moriah during a raid near Khalis on 7 March. Moriah, who preached jihad and led the Wahabi movement in Khalis, was linked to an IED attack in December. An ICDC traffic-control post discovered five 120mm and 155mm mortar rounds while searching eight trailer trucks south of Sawaat on 7 March.

The ICDC Soldiers discovered the rounds and an unknown number of mortar tubes in the trailers that were allegedly transporting scrap metal. The ICDC Soldiers seized the contraband along with eight individuals who were taken to the Khalis jail, where they remained until Soldiers from 3-67 AR transported them to FOB Warhorse for questioning.

Soldiers from 1-68 AR discovered seven IEDs during a convoy west of Tarmiyah on 8 March. Five of the devices consisted of 130mm mortar rounds and two were 155mm rounds. Firing mechanisms varied and included electronic blasting caps, daisy chains, and detonation cord. EOD personnel destroyed the IEDs.

TF Ironhorse Soldiers with 244 EN BN captured one individual and confiscated 1.7 million dinar along with 1,000 electric blasting caps during a search of a house located just north of Taji on 8 March. The individual and contraband were turned over to the 3BCT.

TF Ironhorse Soldiers from 1-27 IN, 2BCT/25ID captured two targeted individuals, Hawas Maneh Salleh and Makmed Mohammed Hussein, in a raid near Huwijah. The targets were suspected of attacking coalition forces. The 8 March midnight raid also resulted in the confiscation of two heavy machine guns, a spare barrel, nine rocket propelled grenade launchers, seven RPG rounds, six anti-armor RPG rounds and 7.62mm and .30-caliber ammunition.

TF Ironhorse Soldiers with 1-21 IN, 2BCT/25ID discovered nineteen 122mm rockets northwest of Krab on 10 March. The rockets were aimed at FOB Warrior in Kirkuk. EOD personnel destroyed the rounds.

CPL Bert E. Hoyer, 652 EN BN of the Wisconsin NG, working with 2BCT, was killed by an IED in Diyala Province on 10 March 2004. CPL Hoyer was the last TF Ironhorse Soldier killed during Operation Iraqi Freedom I.

4ID Soldiers with 1-67 AR and 3-67 AR captured nine individuals, six of whom were targets, during an air-assault operation near Khan Bani Sad on 11 March. The targeted individuals were suspected of being members of a local terrorist cell operating in the area.

A 1-67 AR patrol captured two individuals who were emplacing an IED north of Ghalibiyah on 11 March.

Three individuals attacked an ICDC patrol in Baqubah with

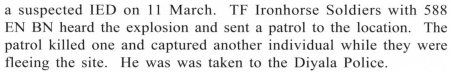

a suspected IED on 11 March. TF Ironhorse Soldiers with 588 EN BN heard the explosion and sent a patrol to the location. The patrol killed one and captured another individual while they were fleeing the site. He was was taken to the Diyala Police.

1-67 AR Soldiers captured four targeted individuals in a raid on 12 March in an area south of Kanan. The targeted individuals were suspects in attacks against coalition forces in the area.

Soldiers of 1-22 IN raided one last house on 12 March as they ended a year long deployment in Tikrit, Saddam Hussein's hometown. After months of fierce battles, Tikrit had been virtually subdued by the constant offensive actions of TF 1-22 IN. 1-22 IN was relieved by 1-18 IN of 1ID on 13 March. LTC Steve Russell, CO of TF 1-22 IN said, "The local insurgency was dealt a major blow by the capture of Saddam on 13 December and the deaths of his two sons, Uday and Qusay, on 22 July." For eleven months, Russell's TF 1-22 IN patrolled the area's meanest streets, confronting, killing, and capturing insurgents while losing nine Soldiers. Enemy actions that occurred several times daily during the summer had dwindled down to almost nothing by March. "Saddam's supporters started to realize that the old regime wasn't coming back," Russell said.

TF 1-22 IN arrested several of the 55 most wanted Iraqis and rounded up hundreds of people suspected of attacking U.S. troops and conducting other anti-coalition activities. They also helped supporters of the U.S.-led occupation form a regional government and establish Iraqi police and ICDC forces.

4ID Transfers Authority to 1ID in Sunni Triangle
On Tuesday, 16 March, outside Saddam Hussein's former presidential palace in Tikrit, MG Ray Odierno transferred authority from 4ID and TF Ironhorse to MG John Batiste with 1ID and TF Danger. Seth Robson reported the event in the European edition of Stars and Stripes on 17 March:
TIKRIT, Iraq — The U.S. Army's 1ID took control of Iraq's deadly Sunni Triangle on Tuesday when the 4ID transferred its authority to the incoming division. Soldiers from the divisions assembled at FOB Danger in Tikrit for the change of command from the 4ID's TF Ironhorse to 1ID's TF Danger. The ceremony was marked by the casing of the 4ID colors and uncasing of the Big Red One's colors in front of Saddam Hussein's former

presidential palace complex, now 1ID, TF Danger headquarters. The 1ID takes responsibility for security in north-central Iraq, an area which includes cities such as Tikrit, Samarra, Baqubah and Kirkuk, all hotbeds of anti-coalition activity.

The commander of coalition forces in Iraq, LTG Ricardo Sanchez, told those gathered that the change of command was a historic moment and an honor for "two great divisions, their Soldiers and leaders."

"4ID conducted thousands of raids, captured tons of ammunition, spent millions of dollars rebuilding Iraq and created more than 50,000 jobs," he said. The division's greatest moment in Iraq came in December when it helped capture Saddam Hussein.

1ID commander MG John Batiste praised 4ID's work in Iraq but added: "for the leaders of 1ID and TF Danger the mission continues. Terrorists, foreign fighters, former regime elements, criminals and 'anyone trying to destabilize Iraq' are the common enemies of U.S. Soldiers and Iraqi security forces." ...

Zac Sorensen reported the TOA in the Killeen Daily Herald with the following report: "Tuesday marked the official end of the 4ID's mission in Iraq. Division commander, MG Raymond Odierno, reflected on a successful mission while commenting on his hopes for the future of Iraq.

"The ceremony marked the shifting of authority of North Central Iraq to the 1ID, based out of Germany. The ceremony took place in Tikrit at 10 a.m. Iraq time as the 1ID unveiled its colors, signifying its responsibility in the multinational division in Iraq.

"LTG Ricardo S. Sanchez, the commander of Combined Joint Task Force Seven, controls all areas of Iraq. 'What a day to honor two great divisions and their leaders,' Sanchez said. 'This transfer of authority is a historic moment. Let me start out by thanking the steadfast and loyal TF Ironhorse, whose achievements are the result of a tremendous team effort,' Sanchez said. 'The Army's most technologically advanced division adapted with remarkable ease. They conducted 11 major operations, 2,500 raids, 3,100 ambushes, 111,000 patrols, seized 94,000 tons of enemy ammunition and ultimately captured Saddam Hussein. There is no doubt that Iraq is a better place today because of their sacrifices.'

"After a year of conducting a wide spectrum of missions, the

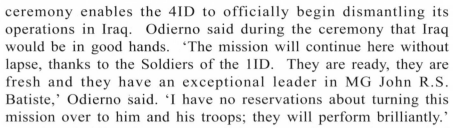
ceremony enables the 4ID to officially begin dismantling its operations in Iraq. Odierno said during the ceremony that Iraq would be in good hands. 'The mission will continue here without lapse, thanks to the Soldiers of the 1ID. They are ready, they are fresh and they have an exceptional leader in MG John R.S. Batiste,' Odierno said. 'I have no reservations about turning this mission over to him and his troops; they will perform brilliantly.'

'Our Soldiers have accomplished more in Iraq than we had the right to expect,' Odierno said.

"Offering his thanks for all that the 4ID has accomplished, Batiste said his division was ready to take control of the region. 'This transfer of authority is a symbol of America's unwavering commitment to Iraq. My Soldiers and I are honored to serve in this great and historic country,' Batiste said. 'We will conduct joint operations with the Iraqi Security to achieve a safe and secure environment.'"

Selected Highlights from OIF: The First Year
On the first anniversary of the start of the war in Iraq, Central Command reported this in a news release dated 3-18-04:
TAMPA, Fla. — Operation Iraqi Freedom Coalition Forces have successfully liberated 25 million Iraqis from the brutal dictatorship of Saddam Hussein. These highlights provide information regarding the accomplishments of the Coalition throughout the past year.

The OIF Coalition is comprised of 34 countries, including 11 NATO countries, and they have provided over 22,000 troops to support the efforts in Iraq. There are two multinational divisions in Iraq: one led by the United Kingdom in central-south Iraq, and one led by Poland in south Iraq.

The international community has pledged at least $32 billion to improve schools, health care, roads, water and electricity supplies, agriculture and other essential services. The World Bank, International Monetary Fund, the European Union, and 38 countries have pledged to extend loans and grants to Iraq. Other nations are contributing humanitarian assistance, extending export credits and reducing Iraqi debt. The UN Security Council on October 16, 2003, unanimously approved Resolution 1511 that calls on members to support the work of the multinational force.

Security: America's armed forces are taking the offensive against remnants of Saddam Hussein's regime and foreign terrorists, leading more than 1,600 patrols a day and conducting an average of 180 raids a week. Forty-five of the 55 most wanted Hussein regime members have been captured or killed, including the brutal dictator himself, whose capture sent a powerful message to the Iraqi people that the tyranny of the past will never return. The capture of Saddam Hussein provided a boost to intelligence throughout western Iraq. The quality of intelligence is cascading as a result of the Saddam capture: the intelligence is of higher quality and allows a higher level of captures. Saddam's capture is allowing the Coalition to apprehend more mid-level financiers and organizers.

More than 230,000 Iraqis now provide security for their fellow citizens, and Iraqi security forces now account for the majority of all forces in Iraq. These forces include Iraqi Police, Iraqi Civil Defense Corps, Iraqi Border Police, Iraqi Facility Protection Service and the New Iraqi Army.

Law/Governance: Since July 2003, the 25-person Iraqi Governing Council has had the authority to: name interim Ministers; exercise government oversight; prepare policy initiatives on Iraq's national security, including reform of the armed forces, police and courts; lead development of a constitution; and approve Iraq's national budget. Twenty-four Iraqi Cabinet Members contributed to the business of the government. For the first time in 13 years, an ambassador to the US was appointed to restore diplomatic relations. Ninety-percent of Iraq's districts have munincipal / government councils with more than 19 million Iraqis engaging in local political discourse. The Ministry of Justice has established a Council of Judges to oversee the judiciary and prosecutors.

Public Health: Two-hundred forty hospitals and most of Iraq's 1200 clinics have reopened, 70 private hospitals are operating. Eight-hundred tons of high protein biscuits have been delivered to 15 Governorates for malnourished children and pregnant/ nursing mothers. Over one-million humanitarian daily rations have been distributed to date. Twenty-two million children and 700,000 women have been inoculated against diseases since the war; 90% of all Iraqi children now receive routine vaccinations.

Pharmaceuticals distribution improved from 0 to 12,000 tons today, more than $210 million approved for the Iraqi Ministry of Heath for pharmaceutical supplies and equipment, basic health care services, medical equipment and generators for hospitals.

Schools: Nearly all schools are open and 5.1 million students are attending class. 25 Fulbright Scholarships were awarded for the first time in 14 years; the Fulbright Office added 2 new programs for Iraqis. There are over 13,500 school buildings in Iraq and $4.4 million has been spent to complete 2,299 school renovations. UNICEF, among other non-government organizations, are rehabilitating 105 schools. Over 183,000 desks, 57,000 chairs, 61,000 chalkboards and 25,000 metal cabinets have been distributed. More than 33,000 teachers and 3,000 supervisors were trained in instructional practices and classroom management.

Commerce and Trade: Iraqis use a single, unified currency for the first time in 15 years; 4.6 trillion new Iraqi dinars are in circulation. The Iraq Stock Exchange will open in April 2004; Iraq Central Bank is fully independent and has been opened since Sep 2003. Currently, 83% of all pre-war bank branches are open. Umm Qasr Port was turned over to Iraqi control, Jan 2004. Almost 394,000 jobs have been created. Estimated crude oil export revenues exceed $3.3 billion for Iraqi reconstruction. Telephone service continues to expand with 95% of it outside Baghdad. More than 170 newspapers are published in Iraq.

Power: The current seven-day average is 4400 megawatts per day, up from 300 megawatts per day in 2003. USAID will spend more than $250 million for infrastructure repair funds on power rehabilitation and an additional $75 million allocated to power reconstruction.

Water: Coalition programs have cleared over 16,500 kilometers of irrigation canals, helping over 10,000 farms. Water storage in most Iraqi reservoirs approached historic averages. Rehabilitated water treatment plants will treat nearly 800 million liters/day, benefiting 3.5 million people. Ninety-percent of Iraqis will have potable water by April 2005.

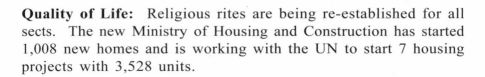

Quality of Life: Religious rites are being re-established for all sects. The new Ministry of Housing and Construction has started 1,008 new homes and is working with the UN to start 7 housing projects with 3,528 units.

Redeployment Operations in March

As March began, an ever increasing flow of TF Ironhorse Soldiers and their equipment left their AOR in Iraq and began the trek to Kuwait before flying to the US. Convoys moved with few incidents. Soldiers always maintained their alert status until they reached the relative safety of the Kuwait camps. Work began immediately to clean and prepare vehicles for loading onto ships. The Soldiers were very aware that they could not leave until their equipment had passed all inspections for return to the US.

On 4 March, the 5th EN BN, the only Missouri-based active duty combat unit to go to Iraq, returned to Fort Leonard, Missouri to a balloon-and-flag-bedecked gymnasium crowded with family members. When the 500-member battalion marched into the field house, the bleachers packed with people erupted into screams. Also on 4 March, more than a thousand people lined the streets in Calhoun City, Mississippi as 95 returning National Guardsmen from B/223 EN BN returned home after spending a year serving with TF Ironhorse. These were among the first complete units to arrive home—most units did not return all at the same time.

By 10 March, one or more flights of returning TF Ironhorse Soldiers were arriving at Fort Hood and Fort Carson each day. Each returning flight was greeted with an emotional Welcome Home ceremony, regardless of the time of day or night.

By 15 March, the trickle of returning troops was turning into a flood. Several flights returned each day. As more and more TF Ironhorse Soldiers moved from Iraq to the redeployment staging area in Kuwait, the systems improved and less time was required to prepare equipment for loading aboard ships.

On 16 March, the Transfer of Authority ceremony from 4ID to 1ID was completed, and virtually all TF Ironhorse Soldiers headed toward Kuwait. Soldiers not needed to help with the operations in Kuwait flew direct from FOB Anaconda in Balad to begin their journey home.

On 16 March, the 416th Chemical Detachment returned to their home in Greenville, South Carolina. The five members of

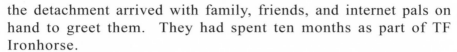

the detachment arrived with family, friends, and internet pals on hand to greet them. They had spent ten months as part of TF Ironhorse.

On 24 March, COL Dan Shanahan, TF Ironhorse Rear Detachment commander reported: "We are running over two weeks ahead on our return airflow! We have 28% still deployed, with 72% redeployed between here (Fort Hood) and Fort Carson! We expect 95% to have redeployed by 2 April 2004. Thanks to all the wonderful family members and friends who make our receptions in Starker and Abrams Gyms the events of a lifetime... We are sure enjoying all those big smiles, tears of joy, and long awaited hugs."

On 1 April, COL Shanahan reported that approximately 95% of TF Ironhorse Soldiers had safely returned to the US. More were scheduled to return over the following two weeks and virtually all Soldiers were home by 15 April. A few Soldiers, with critical wrap-up jobs, and those riding the ships with the equipment, did not arrive until late in April. TF Ironhorse had successfully completed its mission in Operation Iraqi Freedom I.

Civil Operations Continued Until the Day TOA was Completed
Just as offensive combat operations continued from the moment they crossed the LD until they turned over authority to 1ID and TF Danger, civil operations in the TF Ironhorse AOR continued without letup. Space does not permit covering all the operations; highlights are summarized in the next chapter. One example of how TF Ironhorse Soldiers helped the Iraqi people is contained in the following article written by SSG Nate Orme, Public Affairs NCO for the 3rd Personnel Command:

KIRKUK, Iraq — Field artillery officers aren't typically known for their sensitive side, but when it comes to helping kids, they can be like guardian angels. At least that's what some Iraqi kids will surely think when they receive the tons of school supplies 1LT Kyle Barden is planning to bring them, donated by Americans through the charity he and his brother started.

It all started after Barden's unit, the 173rd ABN BDE, was placed in the somewhat unfamiliar position of running a town, directed and aided in their task by thinly stretched civil affairs units. "When we first got here (in northern Iraq) the environment was such that they put us in charge of a town," Barden said. "The town is a mostly Kurdish village named Laylan with about 10,000 people. We are in charge of establishing and running the police force, electing the mayor, the city council, the utilities, and the school system. The civil affairs assets were very few and far between. There was a CMOC (Civil Military Operations Center) in downtown Kirkuk with representatives for different types of projects. Units would go to them and get contracts. The water rep helped us contract out and funded three water towers."

Barden said one of the biggest problems was that the town's eight functioning schools did not have many supplies. "I emailed my older brother in Charlotte, N.C., and asked him to send some school supplies," Barden explained. "He started by writing a letter to extended family, friends and church. Before you knew it, it was huge. The Charlotte Observer did a story on it. People from other states learned about it; the President mentioned it in his address; it's been on the news."

Barden's brother, Taylor Barden, set up a nonprofit corporation which the lieutenant bashfully said is called Kyle's Schools, adding that he wants to change the name to get the focus off him. "The intent was to square my schools away. In Laylan there are approximately 2,000 kids. We're going to saturate Laylan then start going to other towns," Barden said.

With the response so far, it shouldn't be hard. Barden said that both businesses, particularly Office Depot, and citizens have donated. "My brother told me to expect 20,000 pounds of supplies. We were having a hard time getting it here, but then a pilot from Delta Airlines, James Harper, offered to fly it over here for free."

Barden said the town has been very enthusiastic about the projects his unit has initiated. It's a primarily Kurdish town and the Kurds love Americans," Barden stated. "I've told the mayor about the school supplies, but the kids have no idea. There's every type of supply you can imagine—also toys. We're just going to show up and start handing stuff out."

All TF Ironhorse vehicles had to be thoroughly cleaned on a wash rack in Kuwait before being loaded on ships to return to the US

Shadow UAV ready to launch

Night patrol of TF Ironhorse Soldiers as seen through night vision goggles

**Soldiers transferring authority with 1st Infantry Division
16 March 2004**

XIV

Highlights — Individual Unit Accomplishments

THE FIRST THIRTEEN CHAPTERS OF THIS BOOK HAVE covered significant events in the deployment of TF Iron-horse in Operation Iraqi Freedom I, based on research and interviews conducted by the author. This chapter gives the highlights of each Brigade sized unit from the perspective of the commander of the unit. Each commander's writing style is different but they all have one common trait—a great pride in the accomplishments of their unit.

Before beginning the Brigade summaries, the following highlights the overall accomplishments of TF Ironhorse during Operation Iraqi Freedom I:

TF Ironhorse Offensive Actions - 2003-2004

Peninsula Strike	08-15 June
Desert Scorpion	15-29 June
Sidewinder	29 June-5 July
Ivy Serpent	12-17 July
Ivy Needle	11 Aug-09 Sept
Ivy Focus	10 Sept-05 Nov
Ivy Typhoon I, II	01 Oct – 05 Nov
Ivy Cyclone	06-30 Nov
Ivy Blizzard	15 Dec – 15 Jan
Ivy Typhoon III	01 Feb – 16 Mar

Battle Damage Assessment from Operations

- 10,000 (+) Detainees
- 1,000 (+) Targets
- 32 Iraqi Intel Agents
- $10.1 Million US
- 100.5 Million Dinar
- 50 Gold Bars
- 22 Financiers
- 25 IED Makers
- 6,123 Hand Grenades
- 13,817 Mortar Rds
- 254 RPG Launchers
- 4,550 RPG Rockets

- 9,654 Artillery Rds
- 52 SA-7
- 2,413 Rockets
- 813 Missiles
- 1,500 Tank Rds
- 45,080 Sticks TNT
- 80,000(+) Feet Det Cord
- 3,200(+) Lbs C4
- 3,078 Blasting Caps
- 230 ADA Rds
- 194 AT/AP Mines
- 277 IEDs

As important as combat operations were, the work TF Ironhorse did to help rebuild Iraq was of equal importance. Leading the TF Ironhorse efforts was the Effects Coordination Cell, working under the leadership of the Chief of Staff, COL Don Campbell.

Effects Coordination Cell - Working with the Iraqi Ministries (Setting the Conditions for the Brigade Combat Teams)

Many of the key accomplishments of TF Ironhorse came as a result of the work of the Effects Coordination Cell (ECC). Tested in Warfighter exercises at Fort Hood in 2002, the ECC concept proved to be sound when used in Iraq. Based on an emerging Army doctrine of integrating lethal and non-lethal effects into combat operations, the ECC evolved from the Division Deep Operations Cell. The ECC, largely manned by personnel from Division Fire Support Element (FSE), effectively synchronized information operations and civil-military operations into ongoing combat operations in support of the TF Ironhorse campaign plan. The TF Ironhorse campaign plan was based on four pillars—military, governance, infrastructure, and economy. As the BCTs conducted military operations to eliminate non-compliant forces, the ECC focused on shaping operations addressing governance, infrastructure, and the Iraqi economy.

Functionally, the 4ID plans team planned future operations (one to twelve months in the future). The ECC used a technique adapted from targeting processes known as D3A (Decide, Detect, Deliver, Assess) to conduct shaping operations targeted at settingconditions—achieving effects—one to three weeks into the future. Using this methodology, the ECC allowed the CG to decide priorities over the next one to three weeks, detect the situation that would influence operations, deliver the essential tasks to support the operations, and assess the effects to feed back into the planning process. The Command Information Center focused on executing offensive and civil affairs operations in the current week and also provided feedback into the planning process. The Project Coordination Cell coordinated and monitored ECC projects and the Civil Military Operations Center worked with local leaders and assessed results of the projects.

Within the construct of the ECC, each staff function in 4ID HQ had responsibility for an Iraqi ministry. These ministries were responsible for civil functions that were closely aligned to their staff functional responsibility. The Division communications officer, LTC John Schleiffer, the G-6, was assigned responsibility as the Minister of Communication. As such, the Minister of Communication was responsible for the local telecommunications network to include telephones, switches and relays, repair of those items, and the cell phone contract that was established. One of the key accomplishments of the Minister of communication was the repair of the Samarra switch, a multi-million dollar project that restored local telecommunications to thousands of Iraqis.

The Provost Marshall was the Minister of Security, responsible for the establishment of local police forces and the security guards at fixed site facilities. Under the aggressive leadership of the Provost Marshall, LTC Doug Ingros, TF Ironhorse hired and started training and equipping over 21,000 new policemen and 2,000 border police, significantly increasing the security of local populations. One of the key successes of the Minister of Security was the transfer of authority of the fixed site security forces to the Iraqi ministries, effectively transferring the management of Iraqi forces to Iraqis.

The Division Chaplain, LTC Gil Richardson, was the Minister of Culture and Religion. Among the responsibilities of the minister of culture was dealing with religious outreach programs, cultural sensitivity, and engagement with local religious leaders. Under the Chaplain's leadership, the BCTs of TF Ironhorse executed the Religious Site Engagement Initiative, a program of culturally sensitive donations to prominent clerics during the highly volatile period preceding Ramadan. This program served to ease tensions and break down barriers between religious leaders and TF Ironhorse Soldiers.

The Division Surgeon, LTC Kirk Eggleston, was Minister of Health and Human Services, responsible for clinics, hospitals, medical care and the distribution of medical supplies across the AOR. LTC Eggleston coordinated the execution of National Immunization and spearheaded an initiative to modernize the distribution of medical supplies within the AOR.

The Division Engineer, COL Bobby Nicholson, served as the Minister of Public Works. As the minister of public works, COL Nicholson was responsible for an extremely wide range of functions. He was responsible for water, sewage, irrigation, power, and oil. Functions included water and sewage treatment facilities and distribution; power generation, electrical distribution, and monitoring electricity; the infrastructure and distribution of oil to include pipelines and dealings with oil processing and sale. Under his leadership, power generation in the AOR increased over 300%, bringing stable and consistent power to whole cities and regions that had never received consistent power before. He also oversaw the repair and restoration of 40 water treatment facilities. Key among these was the refurbishment of the Bayji water treatment plant, a project that brought safe drinking water to thousands of Iraqi citizens.

The 230th Finance Battalion commander, LTC Scott Schmidt, was the Minister of Finance and Agriculture. As the minister of Finance, LTC Schmidt was responsible for small business initiatives, banking initiatives, small business loans, and civil servant payments. One of his key initiatives was the model bank program. Under this program, LTC Schmidt selected and supervised the reconstruction and modernization of important financial institutions in key population centers, bringing modern banking techniques and accounting procedures to an outdated industry. Perhaps the Minister of Finance's most remarkable achievement was the New Iraqi dinar exchange, an integrated operation that oversaw the replacement of the old dinar, tender bearing the image of Saddam Hussein, with new currency bearing symbols of national pride and unity.

The G-5, LTC Donald Hick, was Minister of Education, responsible for all school programs to include the Model School

Program, and Operation Pencil Box. Operation Pencil Box, a division-wide effort, made an immediate and timely impact on over 115 schools in key areas right before the opening of the school year in October 2003.

In this operation, units adopted schools and conducted low-cost refurbishments; units also distributed school supplies that were purchased and donated from around the world. Operation Pencil Box, and its sister program, the Model School program, were key in establishing the commitment of TF Ironhorse with the Iraqi people.

The TF Ironhorse Staff Judge Advocate (SJA), first LTC Flora Darpino and later LTC Tracy Barnes, was the Minister of Justice. The minister of Justice was responsible for courts to include refurbishing of decrepit courtrooms and legal facilities. The purpose of these projects was to add legitimacy to the courts after years of Saddam's corrupt judiciary process. The SJA also worked at hiring judges that were not corrupt. Perhaps most importantly for the stability of the region, they worked to solve long term legal problems caused by Saddam's Arabization policy, a policy in which Saddam Hussein encouraged Arabs to move north into Kurdistan to displace Kurds from their traditional homeland. After Saddam's overthrow, the Kurds moved back, creating nearly inconceivable ethnic tensions. One of the key pieces of this involvement was to create a workable system for handling and adjudication of land claims that would inhibit local planting seasons. Under their concerned involvement, a workable solution was developed that encouraged local farmers to plant fields that otherwise might have gone fallow.

The G-2, LTC Todd Megill, and the BCT COs were Ministers of Government. Once the governments were up and running, responsibility went from the G-2 to the BCT commander. The G-2 ran the initial establishment of the governments, the vetting process, and the voting for delegates. Kirkuk was the first government established. By the time TF Ironhorse left Iraq, governments were functioning in all provinces.

The G-3, LTC Ted Martin, was the Minister of Defense with responsibility for recruiting, training, and equipping of defense forces, specifically the ICDC and the New Iraqi Army. (The NIA was a national army, and the ICDC was more like a national guard). Under LTC Martin's direction, the ICDC grew from nothing more

283

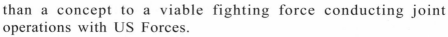

than a concept to a viable fighting force conducting joint operations with US Forces.

The G-4, LTC Terry Hermans, became the Minister of Transportation who worked hand in hand with the Division Engineer to focus on roads, bridges, and rail terminals. One of his key projects was an attempt to establish the Kirkuk airport as an international airport.

Each of the ministers, working with the BCTs and their Iraqi counterparts, brought forward recommended projects to be approved by the ECC. A working group, made up of key staff members in each HQ organization, met several times per week to prioritize the recommended projects to take forward to the Chief of Staff, Ministers, and Commanding General for approval. Each week, decisions were made for projects to be implemented. In all cases, projects used local Iraqi labor to accomplish the work. Funding, in some cases, came from the Coalition Provision Authority (CPA) but the majority of funding came from the Brigade and CG's CERP (Commander's Emergency Relief Program) funds. By February, over $46 million had been expended with another $44 million obligated for future projects.

The ECC, established under the leadership of the Deputy Fire Support Coordinator, LTC Rick Richardson and later MAJ Tim Bush, effectively established a working battle rhythm that allowed the CG to visualize the battle space, synchronize lethal and non-lethal assets (maneuver, fires, information operations, and civil-military operations), and create full-spectrum effects in order to set the conditions for the success of the BCTs. Working across all the ministries was the Information Officer, MAJ Joe Cox, who supported each ministry to insure that information operations were synchronized to deal with the local and international media coverage. He was also responsible for repairing and supporting local media—radio stations and newspapers. Instrumental throughout this process was CW4 Walter Ayer, the Division targeting officer, an expert field artilleryman who worked closely in guiding the D3A process of the ECC throughout the deployment.

Following is a more complete list of the Civil Military Initiatives accomplished by TF Ironhorse before their departure in March 2004:

TF Ironhorse Civil Military Initiatives

- **Iraqi Security Forces**
  - ICDC (5,098 operating w/TF Ironhorse)
  - New Iraqi Army
  - Municipal Police Forces (18,565)
  - Border Police (2,127)
  - Military Advisory Committee

- **Iraqi Interim Governments**
  - First Democratic Process
  - Multi-Ethnic Participation
  - Provincial governors selected
  - Provincial Councils selected
  - Local Councils established
  - Government/Sheik Engagement Program
  - Provincial Budget Process
  - Courthouse Refurbishments

- **Schools Program (640+ impacted)**
  - Model School Program (40 identified)
  - Operation Pencil Box (115 impacted)
  - Youth Centers
  - Sports Programs
  - Computer Training Centers

- **Social Services Initiatives**
  - Women's Rights Councils
  - Religious Site Engagement Initiative
  - Employment Center Initiative (30K jobs)
  - NGO Recruiting and Housing Initiative

- **Infrastructure Repair**
  - Power Generation (300% increase)
  - Sewage/Services (10)
  - Water Treatment Refurbishment (40 projects initiated)
  - Road Improvement Program
  - Fuel Distribution Initiative
  - FEST-I Teams

- **Iraqi Medical Programs**
  - Facility Refurbishment (96% Hospitals/ 95% Clinics)
  - National Immunization Day
  - Medical Text Donation Program

285

TF Ironhorse Civil Military Initiatives (Continued)

- **Economic Initiatives**
  - Model Bank Program
  - Business and Industry Surveys
  - New Iraqi Dinar Exchange
  - Harvest Payments
  - Civil Servant Payments
  - Small Business Grants

- **Kirkuk Targeted Initiatives**
  - Comprehensive Economic Development Plan
  - Business and Industry Symposium
  - Rail/Airport Initiative

- **Iraqi Media and Telecommunications Initiatives**
  - AM/FM/TV Stations (AM-2, AM Repeaters-2; FM- 4; TV- 5)
  - Regional/Governorate Newspapers (1/3)
  - Iraqi Embeds Initiative
  - Internet Cafés (3)
  - Exchange/Infrastructure Repair (82% operational)

1st Brigade Combat Team – Raider Brigade - by COL James Hickey, CO

On 16 April 2003, COL Don Campbell and the Raider Brigade, along with 1-10 CAV, attacked north out of the Baghdad area along Highway 1 toward Tikrit. The 1st Brigade Combat Team (BCT) was organized as 1-66 AR, 3-66 AR, 1-22 IN, 1-8 IN, 299th EN and supported by 4-42 FA, 1-4 AVN and 4 FSB.

This force quickly seized Taji, Balad Airfield, Samarra, Tikrit and Bayji. In so doing, the Raiders and the Troopers of 1-10 CAV engaged and destroyed several pockets of organized enemy forces. Upon arrival in Tikrit on 18 April, the Raiders linked up with and relieved in place the United States Marine Corps' Task Force Tarawa that had conducted a route reconnaissance on Highway 1 to Tikrit.

The BCT continued operations by dispatching TF 1-66 AR north to Mosul to seize the airfield allowing the 101st Airborne Division to enter the city. North of Bayji, 1-10 CAV screened along the heights of the Jabal Makuel. TF 3-66 AR secured the city and oil production facilities in and around Bayji itself. TF 1-22 IN and TF 1-8 IN secured Tikrit and its surrounding area

286

with the support of 299 EN. 4-42 FA occupied Ad Dawr on the East side of the Tigris River. This allowed the 4ID to establish its headquarters as well as the base of operation for its Aviation Brigade and Support Command in Tikrit.

TF 1-66 AR eventually repositioned south back to Samarra after detaching a company team to the 101st Airborne. TF 1-8 IN rejoined 3BCT. 1-10 CAV returned to Division control. By late May, the Raiders were patrolling an area that extended from the ancient city of Samarra in the south to Ah Shaquat on its northern boundary. To the west lay Lake Thar Thar and to the east the Jabal Hamarin ridge. It was a huge area made up of cities, desert, mountains, cultivated fields and the fast flowing Tigris River. This was the northern half of the infamous "Sunni Triangle."

Enemy activity remained low after the initial attack into the zone. In April and May, the BCT had 25 contacts with enemy forces. This would soon change. In June, there were 32 enemy contacts and 73 in July. Our enemy was a confederacy of Republican Guard groups fighting without uniforms, youths who conducted attacks for money, and former regime leaders who both directed and paid for operations. Enemy tactics centered on ambushes and attacks by fire with small arms, mortars and rocket propelled grenades. This would dramatically expand with the employment of improvised explosive devices (IEDs) and land mines by September.

On 13 June, COL James Hickey assumed command of 1BCT. On 15 June, the BCT began sector wide offensive operations as part of Operation Desert Scorpion. By the end of that same month, the Raiders executed 72 raids. In so doing, the BCT had captured High Value Target #4, forced Saddam Hussein's sons to flee to Mosul, captured tons of enemy weapons and munitions, and killed or captured hundreds of enemy terrorists. In so doing, the Raiders established a close and enduring partnership with our Special Operations Forces. Further, the Brigade's leaders developed a very accurate estimate of the enemy; an estimate that produced an intelligence effort proving to have great tactical and operational impact during the campaign. Most significantly, this period would allow the Raider Brigade to mature its operational methods. The Raiders would remain on an unwavering, unequivocal offensive footing. Continuous patrolling, constant reconnaissance, and daily raids across the zone ensured the tactical initiative.

In July, the BCT executed 100 raids—many of which were large, brigade-level operations in areas outside of our normal areas of activity. Speed and surprise became essential elements to our tactics. The troopers and leaders endured many violent ambushes as the enemy resisted our increased, ever present patrolling. Our response to these direct and indirect fire attacks was always aggressive. By August, enemy activity was reduced. Regardless, the BCT remained on the offense executing 72 raids during the month. Tactical successes, effective civil-military operations, and the detention of large numbers of senior Baathist Regime members encouraged increasing numbers of average Iraqis to provide accurate and timely information about enemy insurgents within the zone. This continued each successive month. It gave great depth to our understanding of the enemy and allowed for agile tactical operations.

The BCT initiated Operation Thunder Run in September in response to the enemy's IEDs. This operation defeated the enemy using these weapons. Between September and November 2003, the enemy attacked our forces with 173 IEDs or mines. By February and March, he could only attempt 23—of which 19 were discovered by friendly patrols prior to detonation.

Enemy activity was greatest in the months of October and November 2003 with over 273 contacts. Operation Ivy Cyclone, however, proved decisive in defeating the enemy within the 1BCT area of operation as well as across the Division. By December, all that moved after nightfall were Raiders on patrol or the hundreds of Iraqi Civil Defense Corps (ICDC) Soldiers or police that we trained and equipped.

On 13 December 2003, the Raiders, in cooperation with Special Operations Forces, executed a raid that was the product of six months of raids, reconnaissance and intelligence staff work. At 2015 local time, north of the City of Ad Dawr, this team captured Saddam Hussein in a fast paced, combined-arms offensive operation—Operation Red Dawn. This raid epitomized all that we had perfected after long, hard months of fighting. It was an operation built on teamwork, reconnaissance, quick decision-making, combined-arms, speed and surprise.

By the New Year, the Raider area of operation was secured. The enemy had been defeated. Contact was less than half of what we saw in November, and ineffectual. No Raiders were killed or wounded in our last two months in Iraq. The area remained calm for months after our relief by 2BCT, 1ID in March 2004.

Vital to this offensive effort was the BCT's continuous and robust civil-military operations. This effort ensured an elected governor and council for the Salah ad Din Province, as well as thousands of trained police and ICDC Soldiers. We secured and improved vital infrastructure. We funded the reconstruction of schools, water purification facilities and hospitals. The stable and secure environment that we established allowed for a rapid and efficient service based economy that provided all that most citizens needed to live normal lives. These efforts helped isolate our enemy and proved to the vast majority of peaceful Iraqis that our intent was to stay as long as needed and to do what was necessary to prevail.

The victory of the First Raider Brigade Combat Team was not without sacrifice. We lost 16 of our comrades on the field and 118 were wounded. These Soldiers gave all to their country, our mission, and fought and died protecting their friends. Their legacy to us and to the Iraqi People, was liberty. These Raiders will never be forgotten. They remain in our thoughts and prayers.

2nd Brigade Combat Team - Warhorse Brigade - by COL David Hogg, CO

The 2BCT arrived in Kuwait as part of the Division's Advance Party in early April with the primary mission of downloading the 4ID ships and pushing the lead elements of the Division into Iraq. On 24 April 2003, 4ID ordered the 2BCT into the Diyala Province with an initial mission to secure the airfield in the vicinity of the city of Baqubah, 35 miles north of Baghdad. At the time that 2BCT was given its mission to move into this area, little was known about Baqubah or the Diyala Province, nor was there any idea that this area would be one of the most lethal areas in the Division's sector, accounting for almost half of the Division's casualties throughout its year long deployment. The 2BCT was a supporting effort to the 4ID's initial main thrust of securing Saddam's hometown of Tikrit and would remain a supporting effort as the 4ID conducted full-spectrum offensive operations.

Shortly after arriving in Diyala, the brigade conducted several changes of command. COL Dennis Rogers relinquished command of 2BCT to COL Dave Hogg on 25 June 2003. The Brigade also conducted two battalion and multiple company level changes of commands, as well as field grade officer moves with the final team being set by the first part of July. Despite these changes of command and movement of key field grade officers, 2BCT was able to continue its mission, largely due to the training and professionalism of our Soldiers.

The Diyala Province is roughly the size of New Jersey. The terrain varied from thick, lush palm groves and fields to arid flat and rocky deserts. The main occupation of the local Iraqis was farming, to include winter wheat, date palms, rice, watermelon, Pomegranates, and grapes, to name a few of the major produce grown throughout the province. It is an agrarian based economy, with none of the lavish palaces found in other areas of Iraq. The Province starts just north of Baghdad, runs along the Iranian Border in the east, with the Tigris River along its western border and the northern border running along the Kurdish "green line". Its 2.5 million population consisted of Sunni and Shia Arabs, Kurds, Iranians, Turkish and even a small Christian population. The Diyala Province had over 600 registered Sheiks, of which only about 30 were real or hereditary Sheiks. The Diyala Province contained every flavor of bad guy including Fedayeen, hard core Baathist, terrorists from outside of Iraq, the Iranian Badar Corps, the MEK, released criminals, and everyday thugs. It was a challenging area of operations and one that the Soldiers of the Warhorse Brigade were able to adapt to and take the fight to wherever the enemy decided to operate.

The Brigade consisted of about 4,100 Soldiers, Active, Reserve and National Guard. All of the Battalions within the Warhorse Brigade fought as combat task forces, and everyone was expected to fight like infantry. Each TF in the Brigade was given specific areas of responsibilities as outlined below.

In the north, TF 2-8 IN, under the command of LTC John Miller, had responsibility for the area surrounding the major city of Muqdadiyah, which also included a Company FOB (FOB Cobra) in the town of Jalula, a key area in the Brigade's sector due to the Arab-Kurd fault line that ran through the northern portion of the Diyala Province. Muqdadiyah was the home city of the Provincial Governor, Dr. Abdullah Hassan Rasheed Al Jubouri, and a key link for the Brigade with the Al Jubouri tribe.

TF 3-67 AR, commanded by LTC Mark Young, had a variety

290

of areas they were responsible for and were split into three main areas. FOB Gator had the responsibility for security outside of the MEK camp in the vicinity of Ashraf, as well as providing a quick reaction force should the MEK decide to fight. FOB Rock was located in the town of Kahlis, home to the Deputy Governor of the Diyala Province. FOB Comanche was in the city of As Sadia and was an important area due to the large population of former regime fighters and its location along the eastern portion of the Diyala River and the thick palm groves where the enemy liked to hide, plan and attack from. The remaining elements of TF 3-67 worked out of FOB Hound and were responsible for the eastern side of the Diyala River and the east west road north of Baqubah known as 'RPG Alley". The Hounds also controlled the "canal road" that ran parallel to the Diyala River.

TF 1-67 AR, commanded by LTC Joe Martin, occupied FOB Scunion, just north of Baqubah and across from FOB Warhorse, and was responsible for the areas along the western side of the Diyala River and regularly patrolled the cities of Al Hadid, Hib Hib, Aswad and Khanan. TF 1-67 was responsible for the outside security of FOB Warhorse at the Baqubah airfield as well as counter mortar, IED and ambush operations in this former regime stronghold. The mortar platoon from TF 1-67 shot over 400 rounds of 120mm mortars in support of 2BCT operations.

LTC Bill Adamson commanded TF 588 EN and had responsibility for the contentious city of Baqubah, operating out of FOB Gabe. Along with the 588th were the 652nd NG MRBC (Multi-Role Bridge Company) from Wisconsin and the 649th MP Company. The 588th also was responsible for the training of the Provincial Iraqi Police Force. The 649th MP Company actually lived in the Provincial Police station, downtown Baqubah, and over time developed an Iraqi swat team and undercover police force that proved instrumental in collecting intelligence and taking the fight to the enemy. The relations that were developed with the Iraqi Police by 588th and the rest of 2BCT were a critical part of our operations in the Diyala Province.

TF 3-16 FA, commanded by LTC Mike Mahoney, worked out of FOB Thunder, a destroyed former military hospital and was in the southern portion of the Brigade's sector, just north of Baghdad. Working the major cities of Ar Rashidiya and Kahn Bani Said, mainly a Shia stronghold, the work of the TF 3-16

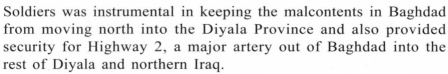

Soldiers was instrumental in keeping the malcontents in Baghdad from moving north into the Diyala Province and also provided security for Highway 2, a major artery out of Baghdad into the rest of Diyala and northern Iraq.

LTC Vince Price, commander of TF 1-17 FA, was responsible for the eastern portion of Diyala Province and they functioned as an economy of force along the Iraq-Iran border, occupying company level FOBs in the vicinity of Khanaquin, Balad Ruz, and Mandali, with the Battalion FOB located at FOB Caldwell, the training base of the New Iraqi Army. Their primary responsibility was working with and training the Iraqi Border Police and integrating the initial units of the New Iraqi Army with coalition forces.

FOB Warhorse, just to the north of Baqubah, was the location of the Brigade Headquarters as well as the 204th FSB, commanded by LTC Doug Tostrud. The 204th had the challenging mission of providing logistical support to 2BCT throughout the Diyala Province, with his Soldiers driving thousands of miles through hostile territory in order to accomplish this critical mission. In addition to the 204th, the Brigade also had the 240th and 629th Forward Surgical Teams, organizations that were worth their weight in gold and were responsible for saving the lives of countless Soldiers who were wounded in action. Along with the FSTs, we also had elements from the 57th Air Medevac and our Combat Stress Team from the 113th MED. Along with the 204th, the 200th NG MRBC from South Dakota operated out of FOB Warhorse and was responsible for bridging the Tigris River and maintaining this key logistical link between FOB Anaconda and the 2BCT AO.

Finally, the Brigade Recon Troop operated in the most southeastern portion of the sector in the vicinity of the town of Salman Pak. Salman Pak was on the eastern side of the Tigris River, directly across from Baghdad. The area was a major smuggling route of money, bad guys and arms into the Baghdad area. Operating independently, the BRT put a major dent in the enemy forces' freedom of movement and action, to the point where the enemy began to focus on trying to destroy this small unit in deliberate ambushes and direct attacks against the FOB.

A dusty, nasty area with few hardstands for the Soldiers to occupy, the living conditions for the Soldiers of 2BCT in the

Diyala Province were some of the toughest in the TF Ironhorse AOR and were given priority for upgrades by MG Odierno early on in the plan for improvements to the quality of life of the Soldiers. Priorities within the Brigade were to improve the outlying FOBs first, concentrating on Company FOBs, with FOB Warhorse last in priority. The Brigade Tactical Operations Center (TOC) operated out of its command vehicles and tents throughout the year. The Soldiers at FOB Warhorse moved out of tents and into containers in October, after living in tents since April and suffering through summer temperatures up to 160 degrees, without air conditioning. Regardless of where Soldiers were living, everyone understood the requirement for sandbags due to the large number of mortar attacks taking place during the year long deployment. Sandbagging tents, living containers, and command centers was the standard and proved that dirt was a combat multiplier, especially after a mortar attack in July hit outside the Brigade TOC, wounding several Soldiers and destroying three computers inside the TOC. Had it not been for the dirt berm surrounding the TOC, the mortar attack would have been devastating.

Throughout the year deployment, the key to success relied on maintaining offensive pressure in everything 2BCT did, to include direct action, collection of intelligence, civil-military operations and working with the local tribal leadership and the Provincial Government. Putting constant pressure on the enemy throughout the sector was successful and resulted in not only reducing the number of attacks against the Brigade, but literally pushing the enemy out of the AO and forcing them to be constantly on the defensive. The Warhorse Brigade trained over 3,400 Iraqi police, 3,900 Iraqi Civil Defense Forces, and 1,200 Iraqi Border Police. In addition to these forces, the Brigade also developed an Iraqi Intelligence section as part of the ICDC that was made up of Sunni, Shia, Kurd and others whose sole purpose was to gather intelligence on enemy forces and hand that intelligence off to the units for direct action.

There were many Iraqi heroes in this fight, but the two most important ones to the Brigade Combat Team were GEN Wahlid Al Azzawi, the Provincial Police Chief and Mohammad Al Jubouri, the interpreter for Warhorse 6. GEN Wahlid assumed his duties as the Provincial Police Chief in July of 2003 after the former Police Chief was arrested for criminal activity. At the time, Wahlid was a LTC with the investigative branch of the Iraqi Police force. He was hand picked by COL Hogg to train, develop and lead the Diyala Police force based on observations and recommendation from the Soldiers who had daily contact with him. Chief Wahlid proved to be a great leader and friend to 2BCT and was instrumental in the integration of Iraqi Police with coalition operations. Always leading from the front, GEN Wahlid was tireless in his efforts to bring security to the people of Diyala and establish the rules of law. A target of many assassination attempts, GEN Wahlid continues to do his duties in support of the New Iraqi Government.

Mohammad Al Jubori was a former member of the Iraqi Security Forces until his arrest by Saddam for anti-Saddam activities. He spent seven years in prison, with the first two years as a guest of the Iraqi Security Services, where he was tortured on a daily basis. He was released from prison shortly before the war as part of Saddam's prison release program. He originally was working with 1BCT in the Tikrit Area and came south to Diyala when MAJ Mike Silverman came to the Brigade to be the Brigade XO. Mohammad spoke seven different languages and developed contacts throughout the Diyala Province and even into Baghdad, providing targetable intelligence for 2BCT. He participated in literally hundreds of operations, at times leading the assault forces to the target areas. He was also the veteran of many air assaults, accompanying the Brigade Commander wherever he went. His insight into the culture and traditions of the Iraqi people and the tribal systems was priceless. A patriot and a friend, he was assassinated two months after 2BCT redeployed from Iraq, while conducting operations in the vicinity of Najaf, leaving behind two wives and three children. He will be missed, but never forgotten by the men and women of the Warhorse Brigade Combat Team.

One of the major challenges of conducting offensive operations was how to get to the target area without alerting your target that you were coming after him. The Brigade developed two techniques on how to do this. The first was the use of helicopters in air assault operations. Every Soldier in 2BCT was expected to be able to conduct air assaults and, with the support of COL Mike Moody and his 4BCT lift companies, we were able to take advantage of this asset. Not only did 2BCT conduct large air assault operations, but it was very common for a two or four ship operation to hit key targets in some of the more rural areas of the Province. The use of air along with linking up with heavy ground forces was a common practice and one that brought a unique capability to the heavy force. The other technique was the use of converging forces to quickly surround a target area and take it down, without tipping your hand as to your final destination. The TF commanders became experts in both of these techniques.

The Warhorse Brigade deployed the first Soldiers to Kuwait to assist with RSOI of the rest of the Division and was the last unit to leave Iraq. The last convoy out of Iraq was the Brigade Commander, COL Dave Hogg along with the Brigade Command Sergeant Major CSM Fred Johnson and two gun trucks from the Brigade Recon Troop. They crossed the Kuwaiti Berm on 22 March 2004, officially ending the Warhorse Brigade's mission in support of OIF 1.

The accomplishments of 2BCT after its yearlong deployment were as follows:

- Establishment of the Provincial Council in Iraq
- Established the first functional radio and TV station in Iraq
- Established 19 district and city councils
- Established and repaired 13 court houses
- Spent over $15 Million dollars in projects
  - o 247 schools refurbished to include school supplies
  - o Repaired and helped equip 50 medical treatment facilities
  - o 88 projects to repair/upgrade water and sewer systems
- Issued $95,000 in small business grants
- Conducted over 2,700 joint patrols and over 3,000 joint checkpoints
- Conducted over 16,000 combat patrols, over 600 raids, and over 425 ambushes
- 97 Soldiers awarded the Army Commendation Medal for Valor
- 39 Soldiers awarded the Bronze Star Medal for Valor
- 1 Soldier awarded the Silver Star
- 187 Soldiers awarded the Purple Heart

The lesson learned from our yearlong deployment was very simple: the Heavy Brigade Combat Team is a very adaptable and flexible force. Every Soldier in the Brigade, regardless of MOS could conduct dismounted operations, do a four-man stack and clear buildings and also conduct air assaults. The M1A2 SEP Tank and the M2A3 Bradley were worth their weight in gold—when they rolled, the bad guys took notice and when they fired, the enemy died. Augmented with UAV, AH64Ds, Blackhawks, 155mm artillery, 120mm Mortars, AC-130 Gunships, SOF and Iraqi Security Forces, along with Civil Affairs and Psyops personnel, the idea of simultaneous full spectrum operations was a reality and a key to the successes of the Warhorse Brigade, the 4th Infantry Division, and TF Ironhorse.

The last and the most important lesson learned was that the quality of the American Soldier is unmatchable. Our young men and women fought with bravery and with compassion and served their Nation well in a harsh and complicated environment. The mission that our Soldiers accomplished; the 27 Brigade Soldiers lost, the 187 wounded; being away from our families and loved ones; and the blood, sweat and tears were all worth it. These young kids are from a different generation, but they are tough, they are committed, they are professional and they understand what this fight is all about. Our Nation is at war and our enemy is an organized network of terrorists and thugs who will stop at nothing to achieve its goals of stopping our Nation's progress and destroying what our Nation stands for. Our Soldiers would much rather fight this war in someone else's backyard versus here in the United States in our own backyard — WARHORSE.

3rd Brigade Combat Team – Striker Brigade - by COL Fred Rudesheim, CO

The 3BCT flew out of Fort Carson and staged in Camp New Jersey, Kuwait from 4-20 April 2003. The Brigade began its journey north as lead elements crossed the berm into Iraq on 20 April. The initial TAC location was southwest of Balad Southeast Airfield from 21-23 April. TF 1-12 IN seized Samarra East Airfield on 23 April and the remainder of 3BCT closed on Samarra East Airfield on 24 April.

The BCT began clearing the eastern side of the Tigris River from Samarra to Tikrit East Airfield from 25-27 April. The TOC remained at Samarra East Airfield until 27 April, until it jumped to an abandoned electronics factory south of Ad Dawr. The BCT continued operations on the eastern bank of the Tigris, with TF 1-68 AR in Tikrit East Airfield, TF 1-12 IN operating in Samarra, and 3BCT TOC in Ad Dawr. The 64th FSB, 3-29 FA and 4 EN remained in Samarra East Airfield during this period. 4 EN conducted a relief in place with TF 1-12 Infantry in Samarra on 28 April and TF 1-12 IN moved north to co-locate with the 3BCT TOC in Ad Dawr. During this period the BCT cleared the eastern side of the Tigris and reattached 1-8 IN from 1BCT on 6 May.

On 7 May, the 3BCT began moving east to the Iranian border to secure the surrender of the Mujaheddin Al Khalq (MEK), a paramilitary group of Iranian dissidents dedicated to overthrowing the theocratic government in Iran. This move took 3BCT from Ad Dawr to Jalula. 4 EN completed a relief in place with TF 1-66 AR in Samarra and rejoined 3BCT in Jalula after we closed. TF 1-12 IN, TF 1-68 AR and 1-8 IN secured the surrender of the MEK and 3BCT prepared to move north on 15 May.

From 15-19 May, 3BCT moved north and then jumped the TOC to the south of Kifri and conducted operations in Jalula, Tuz, Kallar, Kifri and Qara Tapa. During this period 3BCT focused on civil military operations and the monitoring of Kurdish Peshmerga in the AO.

On 19 May, 3BCT moved north to the south of Kirkuk. The BCT conducted operations against former regime loyalists in Al Huwayjah and Riyadh (to the southwest of Kirkuk. The 3BCT also maintained a presence in Tuz . The focus in the Kirkuk AOR was civil military and defeating former regime loyalists. During this period the 3BCT conducted a major operation in the south to destroy former regime loyalists, vicinity Ad Dulu'iyah. This operation was named "Operation Peninsula Strike" and involved 1-8 IN, 720th MP BN, 3-7 CAV, 2-503 PIR, 12th AVN, 3-16 FA, B/1-4 AVN (ATK) and C/1-101 AVN (ATK). This was the largest operation the brigade had conducted to that point. The initial air and ground assault commenced on 9 June and the clearing of the peninsula south of the town lasted until 17 June. The operation resulted in over 300 detainees, over a third of which were identified as former regime loyalists.

On 17 June, 3BCT TAC and most of the combat elements involved in Operation Peninsula Strike moved back to Kirkuk.

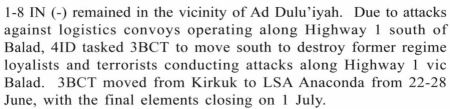

1-8 IN (-) remained in the vicinity of Ad Dulu'iyah. Due to attacks against logistics convoys operating along Highway 1 south of Balad, 4ID tasked 3BCT to move south to destroy former regime loyalists and terrorists conducting attacks along Highway 1 vic Balad. 3BCT moved from Kirkuk to LSA Anaconda from 22-28 June, with the final elements closing on 1 July.

During the initial phase of the operation, named "Operation Sidewinder", 3-7 CAV (OPCON to 3 BCT) operated vic Balad along Highway 1, 1-8 IN operated vic Ad Dulu'iyah, and TF 1-68 AR operated to the south, focused on the southern portion of Highway 1 and At Tarmiyah. TF 1-12 IN remained vic Al Huwayjah, OPCON to 173d ABN. Additionally, the 3BCT received TF 1-66 AR OPCON from 1BCT on 5 July, expanding the 3BCT AO to the northwest to include the city of Samarra. 3-7 CAV reverted to the Corps Reserve on 13 July, continuing to work with the 3BCT along Highway 1, vic Balad, until 10 August.

On 10 August, 1-8 IN conducted a RIP with 3-7 CAV, who moved south for redeployment to CONUS, and the 3BCT readjusted battalion boundaries to reflect our current set. 3-29 FA completed a RIP with 1-8 IN in Ad Dulu'iyah and operated north of the Tigris River, 1-8 IN assumed responsibility for Balad, the northern portion of Highway 1, and the area surrounding Corps Logistics Support Area (LSA) Anaconda, the largest troop concentration in Iraq. TF 1-66 AR remained in Samarra, TF 1-68 AR remained focused on At Tarmiyah and Highway 1 south, 4 EN operated in and around the town of Ad Dujayl, TF 1-12 IN remained OPCON to 173d ABN vic Kirkuk, and the 64th FSB operated out of LSA Anaconda. The 3BCT TOC, BRT and C/104 MI were also located on LSA Anaconda. 3BCT remained in this general set until relieved by 2BCT, 1ID, in March 2004.

While finally in the same location for an extended period of time, the 3BCT was tasked to protect all coalition traffic on Highway 1, restore and maintain order in all urban areas, as well as the protection of the Corps LSA (15,000 Soldiers and contractors) and the growing Air Force presence (all military air traffic was diverted from Baghdad International Airport). In December, the 3BCT received OPCON of 2-3 IN, 3BCT, 2ID (STRIKER vehicle equipped). 2-3 IN conducted a relief in place with 1-8 IN, enabling 1-8 IN to move north to Samarra to participate in the Division Operation "Ivy Blizzard."

On 17 December, the 3BCT, along with 3BDE, 2ID, began Operation "Ivy Blizzard" to kill or capture all former regime elements in and around Samarra. 1-8 IN and 4 EN participated in this Christmas offensive in the historic city (approx. 200,000 people). After completely dominating the city with multiple simultaneous attacks and aggressive military patrolling, the city's police and civilian authorities restored order with the significant infusion of reconstruction funds. By the end of January 2004, all reinforcing troops were withdrawn and Samarra reverted exclusively to 1-66 AR control.

The 3BCT began intensive relief in place coordination with elements of the 2BCT 1ID in March 2004. On 15 March, the 3BCT, along with 1BCT 4ID, conducted the formal RIP ceremony with 2BCT 1ID. The STRIKERS of the 3BCT began the long trek through Kuwait to get Soldiers and equipment home to Fort Carson, Colorado.

173rd Airborne Brigade - Sky Soldiers! - by COL William Mayville CO

Sky Soldiers of the173rd Airborne Brigade demonstrated unparalleled operational flexibility when, in seven days, it moved nearly 600 pieces of equipment by land over 200 miles from Livorno, Italy to Aviano Air Base, reconfigured that equipment from a movement-by-sea posture to a demanding airborne insertion posture.

When ordered, the Brigade conducted a combat parachute assault that initiated Operation Northern Delay, which opened the Northern Front in Operation Iraqi Freedom. The Brigade's parachute assault was the largest combat parachute assault on a single drop zone since Operation Just Cause (Panama, 1989) and the first combat parachute assault ever conducted with the C-17. Without a northern front, six Iraqi divisions arrayed in northern Iraq would have been free to move south to reinforce Baghdad and affect dramatically the balance of power around Baghdad.

Shortly after arriving in Northern Iraq, the brigade brought together a team, in combat, that consisted of the 173rd Airborne Brigade, two airborne battalions (2-503rd and 1-508th), an armored task force (1-63 AR), a mechanized task force (1-12IN), an attack helicopter battalion (1-101 AVN) and numerous separate companies. The 173rd Combat Team became a model for Army transformation—deploying units from several locations to merge into a team on a distant battlefield.

The Brigade seized four airfields en route to seize the city of Kirkuk and its surrounding oil infrastructure. The Brigade's operations in the vicinity of Kirkuk included securing and preventing the destruction of the second largest oil field in the world. After seizing Kirkuk, the Brigade conducted continuous and simultaneous combat and stability operations, unabated for 10 months, in the At Tamin and As Sulaymaniyah provinces—an area encompassing nearly 25,000 square miles.

The Brigade rapidly brought stability to the volatile and strategic region of Kirkuk, preventing the escalation of civil tensions and violence—preventing civil war—in a multi-ethnic province that was assessed by strategic planners as the potential powder keg of the nation. The Brigade quickly turned the At Tamin Province into a model of stability and development within Iraq. The success of the 173rd Airborne Brigade in securing, and subsequently controlling and then rebuilding, the At Tamin Province and later the As Sulaymaniyah Province was unmatched in theater.

The Brigade prioritized developing civic institutions and immediately improving existing infrastructure. Kirkuk was the first major city in Iraq to witness the complete restoration of basic services and the establishment of a free and functioning media. The Brigade assisted Kirkuk to establish a functioning and credible government where none had previously existed. Kirkuk, the fourth largest city in Iraq, was the second city to hold democratic elections. The Kirkuk government systems became the model in Northern Iraq and maintain their credibility today.

The Brigade organized, trained, and mentored the Kirkuk City Council, to include the Governor and Deputy Governor, ensuring the Council was both synchronized with US goals and credible in the eyes of Iraqis. This mentorship included planning and monitoring the spending of a $20 million City budget. The Brigade established, trained, and supervised the Kirkuk Province De-Baathification Office. This office became completely Iraqi operated within 60 days. The Brigade organized the Kirkuk City Planning Department that began the planning for the city. This included managing over 800 government buildings within the city. The Brigade opened the first Employment and Budget Offices in

Northern Iraq. The Brigade established the Rural City Leader's Meeting, Tribal Council, and Political Party meetings in the Province to provide forums for debate and allowed issues to be floored and solved through nonviolent means. The Brigade also began an information campaign that brought together the diverse population under the newly formed government instead of faction leaders. The above procedures were monitored by the Coalition provisional Authority and modeled throughout Iraq.

Within months of arriving in Kirkuk, the Brigade authored and then established a resettlement agreement in the two most contested land areas in Kirkuk (possibly Iraq), which stopped widespread killing between the Kurds, Arabs, and Turkmen. Additionally, the Brigade assisted in establishing the credible Kirkuk Resettlement Office, which handled property and land disputes. Resettlement was the most volatile issue in the province as Saddam had ethnically cleansed and pillaged hundreds of thousands of people from the Province in his 30 years in power. Kirkuk resettlement initiatives were studied by CPA and other military units and became the example for other units dealing with resettlement problems throughout Iraq.

The Brigade quickly understood that economic development was a main engine that contributed to securing and stabilizing the volatile At Tamin Province. The Brigade formed Team Stability, which focused on establishing basic services that would allow other businesses to flourish in Kirkuk. These services included: communications, hotels, private banking, construction materials, and establishing functional Chambers of Commerce and Contractors' Unions throughout the Province. The Brigade facilitated the opening of numerous banks that were credible and capable of conducting international banking transactions. The Brigade planned, secured, and monitored the Northern Iraq currency exchange program. The Brigade attracted Foreign Direct Investment by establishing the Kirkuk Business Center; the first of many that would follow in Iraq. The Brigade was also the catalyst for CPA's micro-loan program, affording many Iraqi entrepreneurs the opportunity to jump-start free markets in their local areas.

For long-term stability, the Brigade sought to reconcile the past. Contributing to this were the many multi-ethnic forums facilitated by leaders throughout the Brigade. The most visible and most important symbol was the establishment and opening of the Kirkuk Museum, which continuously brought together disparate members of the community for common and noble purposes.

To maintain security and facilitate long-term stability, the Brigade cleared a corps' worth of munitions from the province with its organic engineer company and minor augmentation. The Brigade recruited, equipped, trained, and monitored 5,100 police officers, 600 facility protection officers, 700 border guards, and over 2,100 members of the Iraqi Civil Defense Corps.

The Brigade experienced early and consistent success with local Iraqi security forces and routinely became the model for others to emulate. The establishment of a Military Advisory Council, which was a council of former senior Iraqi officers who had once served Saddam Hussein, was risky but proved to be a respected and positive member body in the province's security apparatus. The ICDC was equipped and employed as a highway patrol to protect the province's valuable transportation infrastructure. In addition, the ICDC formed a Kirkuk Bureau of Investigation, which professionalized the investigative functions of the ICDC, police, and other first responders. The Brigade's ICDC also formed as engineer companies to assist with the clearance of unexploded and unsecured explosives, clear improvised explosive devices, and rebuild the government infrastructure.

4th Brigade Combat Team – Aviation Brigade – by COL Michael Moody, CO

It was my goal that the 4th Infantry Division's Aviation brigade be remembered for its part in Operation Iraqi Freedom as an organization that far exceeded conventional expectations, embraced changes in the operating environment, was always there when called and lastly, caused no one else to fall short of their mission. The Soldiers, non-commissioned officers and officers of the brigade accomplished these goals and will be remembered by their peers as a vital contributor to the accomplishment of 4th Infantry Division's missions. I hope our legacy is one of teamwork and unselfishness.

The Brigade's road to war began as the first unit called to the III Corps and Ft. Hood Deployment Ready Facility (DRF).

The Brigade HHC was unit number one on the Division order of march to the DRF and we consequently became the "Captain" of the first vessel to be loaded at the Port of Beaumont. Our approach to these initial assignments was to ensure that no matter how "ugly" the process was, we would not miss the deadlines for reporting, rail loading, or ship loading. I felt that the first units had to get out of the way on time, lest the impact be felt by all those that followed. Company commanders and senior NCOs pushed hard and I am very proud to say neither train nor boat waited for the Brigade's equipment to get ready. It may not have always been pretty, but it was always on time.

I hope that attitude was observed by all of our combined arms partners. The aggressiveness of 1-10 CAV, regardless of who they worked for (and I think the Buffalo Soldiers worked for every BCT in 4ID at one time or another), the omnipresence of 1-4 AVN at every commanders request, the determination of 2-4 AVN to meet every mission, and the phenomenal support of the 404th Aviation Support Battalion, FCO 1-58 Air Traffic Services, and our Medevac brothers all demonstrated a willingness to meet every task and accomplish every mission. We were obsessed by that thought.

The Soldiers and leaders of 1-4 Aviation perhaps displayed the most agility. I recall on the day that 1BCT attacked to seize the Iraqi Army depot at Taji, the transformation of attack helicopter employment in 4ID. Over the hood of a Humvee, COL Don Campbell, LTC Ted Martin, LTC Jim Muskopf, and I coordinated for the OPCON (Operational Control) of attack helicopters to 1BCT. From that day forward, 4ID adopted a technique of OPCON of attack helicopters, employed in pairs, designed to provide maximum coverage to ground units and at the direction of the commanders at the lowest level. It set the mold for the almost 11,000+ hours that the aviators of 1-4 AVN would fly and marked the beginning of a phenomenally close relationship between 1-4 AVN and all the BCT commanders.

If the aviators of 1-4 AVN were the most agile, then the aviators of 2-4 AVN were the most determined. 2-4 AVN began flying general support missions for the division the day the aircraft were off-loaded and assembled. Twelve thousand hours later, they were still flying missions. For the first eight months, everything that could fly did fly each and every day. Only weather

303

stopped them during the winter of 2003. The Warlocks often flew to Kuwait to retrieve critical repair parts and chased UAV and radar parts all over Iraq. 2-4 AVN conducted day and NVG (Night Vision Goggles) air assaults and flew virtually every MOS in COL Dave Hogg's 2nd Brigade proving that tankers, engineers, and artillerymen readily adapt to helicopters. Lastly, I was always impressed with the way they included our Medevac partners into the Brigade and offered Soldier, operational, and maintenance support to those vital members of the Brigade team. Their sense of team also extended to elements assigned to the division from the 101st's 5-159 AVN BN and 10th Mountain Division. 2-4 AVN embraced them all and at one time had operational control of more than 50 UH-60s.

I was often reminded by MG Odierno, and always in good nature, that though I took care of the Division's Cavalry, they truly belonged to the Commanding General. 1-10 Cavalry led the Division's way out of Baghdad and then into every major division objective thereafter. The aviators of 1-10 CAV flew harder than any other in the theater. Many exceeded over 1,000 hours, most achieved more than 700 hours, and all were wanted by the BCT commanders for observation, reconnaissance, and direct close combat attack. The sophistication of the air ground coordination achieved by 1-10 CAV was the model for the Division. Cavalry commanders at all levels will do well to study their accomplishments.

The high OPTEMPO (Operational Tempo) was only possible by the ground-breaking work of the 404th Aviation Support Battalion (ASB). LTC Al Stull and then LTC Al Evans wrote aviation doctrine, as theirs was the first ASB to deploy. 404 ASB originated the concept of support for the Division Cavalry Squadron and supported their split operations for a year. F Company 1-58 AVN Air Traffic Services came to the Brigade at notification for our deployment. Led by a First Sergeant who was literally bigger than life, F Company represented the familiar voice each day the Brigades aviators returned from missions.

The contribution of our Medevac partners from the 571st and then the 57th Medevac companies cannot be overstated. I am convinced the assignment of the Medevac to the Aviation Brigade with the mission to support the BCTs was a wining combination, providing both responsiveness and supportability for the division.

The aviators in 1-4 AVN, 2-4 AVN, and 1-10 CAV flew at the highest OPTEMPO (hours per airframe per month) of any like unit in the theater during that time. I was proud to let MG Odierno know that his aviation was busting their butts for the division and whenever and wherever a BCT commander called, aviation was there. His confidence in us was embodied by the number of hours he flew (in excess of 700) on the Aviation Brigade's aircraft.

The young Lieutenants and Company Commanders of the Brigade were rewarded with the professional thanks of all whom they served. Many were personally invited to battalion and brigade changes of command and had battalion and brigade commanders show up to theirs. COL Hogg, COL Hickey, COL Rudesheim, COL Campbell and COL Rogers regularly made the effort to convey their thanks to our aviators. As a result, a whole new generation of aviators and ground commanders are now wedded to air/ground integration the way our professional fathers were in Vietnam.

555th Engineer Group - Willing and Able! – By COL Christopher Toomey, CO

Deploying in support of Operation Iraqi Freedom in April 2003, the Fort Lewis-based 555th Engineer Group (the Triple Nickel) conducted extensive operations with the 4th Infantry Division's Task Force Ironhorse by conducting full-spectrum engineer combat operations. As the brigade-level engineer headquarters with the 4th Infantry Division, the 555th conducted echelon-above-brigade operations across the entire division area of responsibility (AOR) and was often called to conduct security and infantry operations. The following briefly summarizes the task force's operations and presents some observations based on its experiences.

The 555th (designated Task Force Able) benefited from a unique variety of skills and experience. Of the six battalions eventually assigned to the group, three were active duty (the 5th Combat Engineer Battalion from Fort Leonard Wood, Missouri; the 14th Combat Engineer Battalion from Fort Lewis, Washington; and the 565th Engineer Battalion from Hanau, Germany), two were Army National Guard (the 223rd Engineer Battalion from West Point, Mississippi and the 1092nd Combat Engineer Battalion from Wheeling, West Virginia), and one was US Army

Reserve (the 244th Engineer Battalion from Fort Carson, Colorado). Similarly, the separate companies also came from all components, notably the 229th Combat Support Equipment Company from the Wisconsin National Guard; the 285th Combat Support Equipment Company (USAR) from Dallas, Texas; the 74th Bridge Company from Fort Hood, Texas and the 814th Bridge Company from Fort Polk, Louisiana. The achievements of the task force demonstrated that active Army/Reserve Component integration works. Task Force Able was also multifunctional and included combat engineers, construction engineers, and bridge builders. This diversity and agility of the units gave the task force the ability to perform just about every engineer mission imaginable while working over the entire division area and with every brigade combat team.

Within the division area, Task Force Able operated along several main lines of operation based around the most common missions. Throughout, the task force provided direct and general support to the division's brigade combat teams and conducted raids, ambushes, and performed security operations.

Forward Operating Bases (FOBs)
The 555th contributed to building more than 50 FOBs for division troops. In a harsh environment, with temperatures in excess of 140 degrees Fahrenheit in the summer, these were important to maintain the health and safety of the force. The FOBs varied in size from company outposts to battalion-sized bases. Each FOB included living areas, power, water, and accommodation for sewage (ranging from burnout to chemical latrines). Gravel was the primary material used for soil stabilization, and Task Force Able spread tons of gravel over thousands of square meters to provide a stable surface. Proper force protection was a key piece of FOB development and the task force constructed bunkers and fighting positions and emplaced numerous berms and wires to secure perimeters.

Force Protection
Aside from FOBs, Task Force Able's efforts extended to protecting all manner of US, coalition, and pro-coalition Iraqi installations. The task force constructed multiple traffic control points along major routes and emplaced protective measures for Iraqi civil infrastructure, police stations, and civil defense

installations to guard against attack—particularly against vehicle-borne IEDs.

Mobility Operations

Task Force Able improved and rebuilt thousands of kilometers of roads and trails. Additionally, the task force emplaced several military bridges over the Tigris River to provide mobility for military traffic (both the 101st Airborne Division (Air Assault) near Mosul in the north and the 4th Infantry Division called on the task force for bridging) and civilian traffic. With most significant bridges over the Tigris River destroyed during the early part of the war, it was essential to establish crossing sites. These included the longest Mabey & Johnson float bridge ever erected. Named for two Soldiers from the 14 EN BN; lost in the conflict, the Haight-Jordan Bridge was more than 320 meters long.

Tied to bridging was ensuring mobility along the waterways, principally the Tigris River that effectively bisected the division's area. In a great show of flexibility, Task Force Able assumed water patrol missions using bridge erection boats as riverine patrol craft. The efforts of the task force ensured that coalition forces controlled the river and effectively denied it to the enemy.

A major combat operation for Task Force Able was route clearance. In a noncontiguous and dispersed battlefield, security and clearance of routes connecting nodes of combat power is critical. The enemy quickly seized on coalition routes—extended, exposed, and difficult to secure—as vulnerable points to launch ambushes and attacks. To thwart these attacks, Task Force Able launched a concerted campaign of route clearance and presence to inhibit, find, and destroy IEDs and mines and those emplacing them. The task force assumed this mission with the intent to suffocate the enemy's ability to emplace IEDs or mines, while capturing or killing those who did. The operation, known as Trailblazer, lasted several months and resulted in the clearing of more than 23,000 kilometers of road and the destruction of great quantities of IEDs. Of particular help to the Trailblazer mission was the use of a new generation of mine clearing and detection devices and vehicles currently being fielded. The Buffalo—a wheeled vehicle with a camera-equipped mine-excavating arm to allow standoff—was particularly useful.

Unexploded Ordnance and Captured Enemy Ammunition

Iraq is littered with both unexploded ordnance (UXO) and

captured enemy ammunition (CEA). Task Force Able was charged with securing and destroying several large caches of enemy ammunition. In all, the task force destroyed several hundred tons of CEA and cleared thousands of square miles of terrain while managing several large fixed sites north of Bayji.

Civil Infrastructure

Task Force Able brought a wealth of talent to the civil infrastructure effort, a major step in creating a secure and stable Iraq. The task force worked across the division to orchestrate the building and repair of a myriad of water treatment facilities, power plants, civilian bridges, and schools. Working closely with local Iraqis, the task force helped facilitate the creation of local governments in some areas. The bulk of the Iraqi people with whom the units worked were appreciative, and the Soldiers saw very positive behavior in response to their efforts.

During Operation Iraqi Freedom, the diverse mixture of combat and construction engineers comprising Task Force Able provided the 4th Infantry Division and Task Force Ironhorse with versatile and effective echelon-above-brigade engineer support. Yet the true measure of Task Force Able is the courage of the more than 3,200 engineer Soldiers who fought across north central Iraq operating in all manner of terrain and weather. Despite numerous casualties, the engineers demonstrated their true mettle and that they were equal to their motto: Willing and Able.

Division Artillery (DIVARTY) - Iron Gunners - by COL Kevin Stramara, CO

Operations of Division Artillery, the Iron Gunners, fell into three categories—Combat Operations, Stability Operations, and Quality of Life.

Combat Operations:

Lethal Fires

Prior to deployment, Supporters and Cannon/MLRS crewmen of the 4th DIVARTY trained to master their mission essential tasks. More than 15,000 artillery rounds were fired in support of TF Ironhorse during Operation Iraqi Freedom.

Counter-Mortar Operations

DIVARTY effectively developed tactics, techniques and

procedures to counter non-compliant forces' indirect fire attacks. Effective sensor-to-shooter links and sensor-to-sensor cross-queuing strategies (radar to UAV and/or aerial/ground QRF) allowed for the responsive attack of enemy mortar and rocket attacks. Key to this success was the management of 13 Firefinder radars across the AOR.

Joint Fires and Effect

By developing an Effects Coordination Cell (ECC) the Ironhorse Staff led by the Division FSE was able to leverage kinetic and non-kinetic fires to meet the Commanding General's intent. Working closely with the CJTF-7 Fire Support Element (FSE), the Ironhorse FSE, and BCT FSEs, TF Ironhorse synchronized and coordinated airspace in order to attack targets using joint fires.

Harassment and Interdiction (H&I) Fire

The use of mortar, cannon and MLRS H&I Fires became a staple of TF tactics to effect enemy activity in the AOR. Enemy mortar positions, training areas, troop concentrations and command and control nodes were common targets for indirect fires.

Redlegs and Riflemen

FA Commanders owned terrain as a maneuver commander. In all cases, from DIVARTY to Battalion to Battery, commanders task organized forces to achieve mission accomplishment. DIVARTY task organized as TF Gunner in the Taji AOR; 4-42 FA as TF Arrow in Ad Dawr; 2-20 FA as TF Deep Strike in the South Taji AOR; 3-29 FA as TF Pacesetter in the Balad AOR; and 3-16 FA as TF Thunder in the Baqubah AOR. Every Soldier performed duties as an infantryman during mounted and dismounted patrols, armed reconnaissance operations, counter mortar and IED operations, raids, cordon and search operations as well as their primary duties as cannon/MLRS crewmen, mechanics, cooks, supply and administrative clerks.

Task Organization

Perhaps the most challenging and most satisfying aspect of OIF for DIVARTY was the formation of a combat force from units from multiple backgrounds, cultures and organizations. TF Gunner's ranks were composed of units organic to the 4ID, from the reserve component (USAR and National Guard), coalition forces (Macedonian Special Forces Task Force), III Corps Units (2 CHEM BN), FORSCOM (the Fighting 5th EN BN) and Iraqi Civil Defense Corps Soldiers.

Active Component/Reserve Component Integration

B/1-179 IN from the Oklahoma National Guard fought in over 22 combat missions while attached to TF Gunner. The Thunderbirds played an integral role in the capture and/or killing of non-compliant forces, training of cannoneers and MLRS crewmen in MOUT operations and the capture of countless enemy weapons and munitions. The 44th RAOC "Vampires" from the Illinois Army National Guard provided FOB Gunner security.

Coalition Forces

The Macedonian Special Forces TF was attached to TF Gunner in July 2003. The TF was highly trained small unit and counterinsurgency operations. The Macedonians conducted dismounted patrols, raids, sniper operations, and counter IED operations.

Iraqi Civil Defense Corps (ICDC)

Working closely with local tribal and governmental leaders, all DIVARTY units effectively recruited, trained, and equipped ICDC formations. In TF Gunner, the 5 EN BN and TF 2-20 FA were responsible for standing up the 211th ICDC BN, consisting of more than 400 ICDC Soldiers. Following nearly two months of preparation, the ICDC units conducted joint operations with U.S. Forces, proving to be able partners in combating non-compliant forces and establishing a safe and secure environment in the AOR.

Stability Operations:

Captured Enemy Ammunition and Material (CEA/CEM)

The TF Ironhorse AOR was riddled with numerous ammunition storage points and caches that contained literally hundreds of thousands of tons of various types of ammunition, ranging from small arms ammunition to Al Samoud Missiles. TF Gunner was tasked with the identification, consolidation, security and destruction of CEA. Working closely with other forces, DIVARTY was able to coordinate security and/or destruction of more than 120,000 tons of enemy ammunition. The AOR had thousands of Iraqi Army vehicles, weapon systems, and equipment abandoned on the battlefield. Operation Bone Yard effectively consolidated and secured CEM on the Taji Military Complex at FOB Gunner. More than 2,000 armored vehicles, artillery pieces, assorted military trucks, ADA systems and engineer equipment were contained in the Gunner Bone Yard.

Economy Restoration
Spending more than 15 million dollars, DIVARTY units contracted Iraqi companies to improve FOB force protection and build, improve and renovate roads, schools and medical treatment facilities, refurbish irrigation/drinking water systems and rebuild mosques. These initiatives aided economic recovery and served to improve Coalition-Iraqi relations as the Iraqi people appreciated steady employment and the prioritized focus on infrastructure and quality of life improvements.

Help from Home
Two significant "humanitarian" initiatives that significantly aided the Iraqi people were "Clothes for Kids" and "Operation Pencil Box". "Clothes for Kids" was a DIVARTY effort focused on providing donated clothes to orphan children in the TF Gunner AOR. Coinciding with Ramadan, the "Clothes for Kids" donations came from more than 17 states and included more than 250 boxes of clothes. "Operation Pencil Box" ran in conjunction with the opening of local schools. FRGs solicited commercial businesses and provided school supplies for Iraqi children. Soldiers not only distributed the supplies but also built soccer fields, volleyball courts, and basketball courts for the schools

Establishment of Regional Democratic Government
Understanding the concept of democracy, electing neighborhood, district and county officials and institution of democratic processes was a foreign concept to many Iraqis. After seven months of hard work, the various levels of government were able to establish meeting agendas, prioritize projects, and allocate resources while conducting elections for representatives.

Quality of Life:

Family Readiness Group (FRG) Operations
The Soldiers of DIVARTY will never know the sacrifices that our FRG members made on our behalf. Their selflessness, positive attitude, perseverance and genuine care for one another were hallmarks of their service. The Gunners will be forever indebted to our FRG members for their hard work.

Rear Detachment Operations
The DIVARTY rear detachment was the "Go To" team at Fort Hood. Not only did this team have responsibility for organic DIVARTY units but also had oversight for 124 SIG BN, 2 CHEM

BN, 104 MI BN and HHC 4ID. Throughout Operation Iraqi Freedom, the Gunner Rear Detachment successfully conducted video teleconferences with Soldiers in theater, trained and prepared Soldiers for deployment, inventoried and secured stay-behind equipment, prepared and refurbished billets for returning Soldiers, conducted legal/administrative operations for more than 1,000 Soldiers, and supported families and FRGs.

Soldier Quality of Life (QOL)

In nearly all cases, facilities formerly used by the Iraqi military were in desperate need of repair. The hard work of key NCOs made life bearable for our 4,000 troops living in those facilities. After six months in country, all units had running water, electricity, air conditioning, internet availability, chapels and gym/workout facilities. At FOB Gunner, a gymnasium was constructed, a boxing ring erected and three Taji Night Fights or Boxing Smokers were hosted on FOB Gunner. Soldiers from across TF Ironhorse competed in the boxing matches.

4ID Division Support Command (DISCOM) – Wranglers! – by COL James M. Moore, CO

The Soldiers of the mighty Wrangler team went beyond my expectation of a Division Support Command (DISCOM). Their tenacity to complete the mission is a tribute to all the young Soldiers in the Brigade. The Division Support Command, in keeping with the high standards of the 4ID, ensured that the TF Ironhorse team was supported for victory!

Our mission was to sustain the combat power of the 4ID troops while deployed in support of Operation Iraqi Freedom (OIF) with maintenance, supply, transportation, and combat health support. We were responsible for managing every aspect of logistics within the Division Task Force. Typically limited to 15,000 Soldiers, TF Ironhorse during OIF exceeded 27,000 Soldiers, with a peak of over 32,000.

As part of the only Division in the US Army organized under the Force XXI concept, DISCOM was designed to support a division composed of five brigade-sized elements across an area more than twice that of an Army of Excellence (AOE) division. During OIF, DISCOM provided support to the division task force as it expanded to nine brigades and covered an area of operations approximately eight times the doctrinal size of an AOE division.

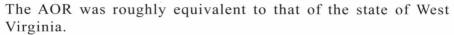

The AOR was roughly equivalent to that of the state of West Virginia.

One of the significant tasks in accomplishing this mission was developing the concept of support for the RSOI and employment of the Stryker Brigade Combat Team out of Fort Lewis, Washington. This newly designed, high profile brigade was integrated into TF Ironhorse and we enabled them to move immediately into the division's largest offensive operation, Operation Ivy Blizzard. In addition, all aspects of logistics: Arm, Fix, Fuel, Move, and Sustain were accomplished with great skill and motivation by the young men and women of DISCOM.

Arm

The Division Ammunition Office (DAO) planned, prepared and shipped over 1,704 containers of ammunition to support the division's combat operations. Due to its bulk, weight, and special handling requirements, ammunition throughout the large AOR proved initially to be one of the most significant logistical challenges. The DAO managed the downloading, prioritizing, and moving of the required ammunition for 1-10 CAV's rapid movement across the Iraqi LD and then rapidly transitioned into the task of managing the ammunition for the rest of the division, also on the verge of crossing the LD. The DAO closely managed the turn-in process of ammunition as the division transitioned its operations to the follow-on forces. Particularly difficult due to the sustained combat operations, the DAO developed a solution for a smooth transition with no loss of combat power forward.

Fix

Providing logistics support involved distributing an immense amount of newly developed major combat vehicles items throughout the division's area. The Material Management Office (MMO) achieved a combat readiness rate of over 90% for M1 Tanks and over 82% for M2/3 Bradley Fighting Vehicles. These readiness rates were vast improvements over the one-time rates of 40%. Through diligent parts management and requisition tracking, the MMO improved the combat effectiveness of the division by two-fold.

Fuel

The General Supply Office managed the accurate distribution of fuel for the nearly 10,000 vehicles of TF Ironhorse operating across the huge AOR. The volume of this management effort

313

equaled approximately 630,000 gallons per week or 26 million gallons total.

Move

The Movement Control Office (MCO) coordinated for the Heavy Equipment Transport (HET) and flatbed movement of more than 1,000 individual pieces of equipment and jointly planned with the Division Transportation Office for the road march movement of the entire division to and from the combat zone between Iraq and Kuwait. In addition, the MCO provided lift asset coordination for numerous re-supply missions across the Task Force and for the issue of all ICDC, New Iraqi Army, and Iraqi Police Force uniforms and gear.

Sustain

The Property Book Office (PBO) was primarily responsible for distributing a wide variety of items that included Up-Armored Humvees, Warlock explosive device defensive systems, thermal weapons' sites, Kevlar blankets, Outer Tactical Vests, and Small Arms Protective Inserts. The PBO further enabled the Soldiers of this large task force to perform their missions by providing them with additional sets of Desert Camouflaged Uniforms, Gortex waterproof coats, and desert boots.

The combined efforts of the Distribution Management Center (DMC) and the PBO contributed directly to the division's mission of creating a safe and stable Iraq by providing personal equipment to three Brigades of the ICDC. This equipment included over 8,900 AK-47 rifles, over 1 million rounds of ammunition, individual uniforms, flak vests, and RPGs. This equipment was the initial issue to stand up these newly trained brigades and was critical in the accomplishment of their new missions. Their combined efforts also directly supported the division's mission by receiving, storing, and managing the distribution of police gear for the 6,000 member Iraqi Police Force including Glock pistols, ammunition, and uniforms.

The DMC and PBO also assisted the division in building the good will of Iraqi citizens by managing and distributing school supplies provided by organizations in the US as part of Operation Pencil Box. These supplies were chalk boards, tables, pens and pencils, desks, paper, and notebooks. All told, this operation completely filled one twenty-foot milvan with donated supplies.

The actions of the Wranglers speak for themselves. It was a

great honor to serve with these fine men and women, officers and NCOs, leaders and subordinates. I would be remiss if we did not acknowledge the ultimate sacrifice six of our DISCOM teammates paid in support of our great country. They and their fellow Soldiers are heroes in my eyes and I take great pride in saying I served with each and every one of them. Wranglers!

(COL James M. Moore was killed, along with six other 4ID Soldiers, in a Blackhawk helicopter crash outside Fort Hood, Texas on 29 November 2004).

64th Corps Support Group (CSG)–by COL Thomas Richardson, CO

The 64th CSG deployed to Kuwait on 31 March 2003 and linked up with the advance party to begin movement to Iraq. To ensure logistical support was in place prior to the arrival of maneuver units, HHC 64th CSG crossed the Line of Departure (LD) before any Task Force Ironhorse Element. They drove over 800 miles under hostile conditions to establish support operational areas for the maneuver force.

They moved to the Tikrit North Airfield, later to be named Camp Speicher, in Tikrit and assumed command responsibility of four battalions (180th Transportation Battalion, 544th Maintenance Battalion, 553rd Corps Support Battalion, 44th Corps Support Battalion) and 31 separate units from Active, Reserve and National Guard elements. In addition to providing continual service to Task Force Ironhorse and area units, the Group also provided humanitarian aid in distribution of food and water to the families of the local village.

The Group stored, issued and transported 16 million meals, 15.2 million bottles of water, 23 million gallons of fuel, produced 32 million gallons of water, provided over 200,000 showers, cleaned over 160,000 bundles of laundry, sewed over forty-thousand patches and insignia, and processed over 8,500 air force pallets of repair parts. In addition, the Group escorted over 1,200 class A ration trucks between Kuwait and Camp Speicher and 1,500 fuel trucks between Mosul and Camp Speicher.

Support of railhead operations in Bayji was also the responsibility of 64 CSG. The Iraqi railroad system was not advanced but it did provide a way of relieving trucks from transporting items such as bottled water and other bulk items that were best transported by rail. They also performed the very important mission of providing primary HET (Heavy Equipment Transport) support to all of CJTF-7. The Group traveled over 16 million miles, experiencing over 60 enemy attacks, ranging from IEDs, mines, RPG and small arms fire. Unfortunately, the Group sustained 26 Soldiers wounded in action during these attacks but luckily, no fatalities. 64 CSG was a large unit, with an average of 4,000 Soldiers (with peak strength of 5,000 Soldiers) providing support to the TF Ironhorse mission.

The 180th Transportation Battalion headquarters deployed in support of Operation Iraqi Freedom on 26 March 2003. Upon arrival in Kuwait, the battalion was quickly formed as the theater of operation's only heavy equipment transportation battalion. Nicknamed the "Iron Horse Express," the Battalion and HETs from theater transportation units moved over 2,500 pieces of combat and support equipment with crews 325 miles into Iraq to ensure the rapid success of offensive operations. HETs were the sources of long-range movement for tracked vehicles and many other items. Over 12 million miles were traveled by the 370 HETs that were available in Iraq. In the US, a HET traveled an average of 3,000 miles per year. In Iraq, they covered over 3,000 miles per month—many of those were over IED infested roads. During the initial push into Iraq in April and May, HETs ran virtually 24-hours per day. After the 4ID had been moved into their AOR, the HETs moved the 1st Armored Division into Baghdad. Several HETs were lost to land mines, RPG attacks, and IEDs but none of the 64 CSG personnel were killed. Once that was accomplished, they went into the sustainment phase where there was an average of 116 HETs on the road each day, traveling in convoys that averaged 30 vehicles each.

In addition to the HET mission, 180 TRAN BN had medium and light truck companies that provided command and control of convoys, along with gun trucks to provide security for both military and civilian convoys traveling within Iraq and coming out of Turkey and Kuwait. Among the highlights were: transporting over 834 containers from the Bayji railhead mission to Camp Speicher, delivering over 16 million gallons of bulk water to TF Ironhorse, providing gun truck escort for over 6,000 trucks from Mosul, Iraq and Doha, Kuwait carrying critical logistic support for the V Corps. There was not a part of Iraq that was not supported by 64 CSG. Throughout the deployment, the battalion routinely had over 250 vehicles and 600 personnel on the treacherous roadways of Iraq each day, accumulating over 15 million miles. The truckers of the 180th Transportation Battalion have remained true to their motto, "King of the Road...fired up!"

The 544th Maintenance Battalion deployed on 31 March 2003 and provided continual support to TF Ironhorse. During the yearlong deployment, the 544th stored and distributed over 44,000,000 gallons of bulk fuel and issued over 1,000,000 gallons of retail fuel. Facilities for handling palletized load systems (PLS) and providing the breakpoint for rations and bottled water were also part of the 544th mission. They operated the Patriot forward logistics element (FLE) at Camp Anaconda that supported 204th FSB, TF Gunner and Kirkush with food, bottled water, repair parts distribution, and fuel. They completed over 5,764 Direct Support Work Orders and conducted over 613 successful recovery missions. They hauled supplies and fuel over two million miles. The 544th Maintenance Battalion made an invaluable contribution to the coalition's efforts during Operation Iraqi Freedom. Eleven Soldiers were injured from hostile action during the course of operations and earned Purple Hearts. Through vigorous training and preparation, no loss of life occurred during the execution of this very dangerous mission. The Battalion's efforts helped lay the groundwork for follow-on operations and improve the military and civilian environment in Iraq.

The 553rd Corps Support Battalion (CSB) deployed to Operation Iraqi Freedom on 1 April 2003. Providing a variety of support to TF Ironhorse, the Battalion executed Laundry and Shower support to Kirkush, 4th FSB, 204th FSB, 64th FSB, 296th BSB, MEK, and Camp Speicher. The Battalion transported fuel, rations and repair parts to Kirkuk, provided ammunition support, renovation support, direct support maintenance, and PLS transportation support. It also produced water at FOB Lancer, FOB Brassfield Mora, Kirkush, and FOB Gabe. Units of the 553rd CSB drove over 2.6 million miles, delivered over 9.5 million gallons of fuel, conducted the ammunition upload and download of over 48,000 short tons of ammunition, operated three Captured Enemy Ammunition (CEA) sites, cleaned over 244,000 bundles of laundry, provided over 234,000 showers, repaired over 50,000 uniforms, purified over 6.6 million gallons of water, and distributed

317

over 3.1 million gallons of water. Additionally, the 553rd was a critical link in keeping the HET Fleet operational, maintaining a 90% operational rate of the fleet they supported. Numerous battalion Soldiers distinguished themselves admirably in actions against the enemy.

The 44 CSB provided primary support to the Stryker Brigade of the 2nd Infantry Division when they arrived in Iraq to join TF Ironhorse in November 2003. They transported all required supplies, water, rations, and fuel, provided water production, operated a bulk fuel farm, provided maintenance support and handled mail for the Stryker Brigade. Once the Stryker Brigade moved to Mosul, the battalion assumed all responsibilities for flow of logistics from the north. This ensured that TF Ironhorse would have an uninterrupted flow of supplies from Turkey. This was critical to the support of the task force and units in the area

Working as a seamless team, 64 CSG and DISCOM insured that TF Ironhorse never wanted for anything in accomplishing their missions.

Rear Detachment and Family Readiness Groups– by COL Dan Shanahan, CO

The vision for the Rear Detachment was a strong cohesive unit, resourced with the personnel and equipment to complete the mission. Our Commanding General, MG Raymond T. Odierno was directly responsible for the success of the Rear Detachment. General Odierno set the template for success—a Colonel and Sergeant Major at Division level, Majors and Master Sergeants at the Brigade level, Captains and Sergeants First Class for every Battalion with staffs to enable accountability while leaders maintained standards. COL Jim Moore and Sergeant Major David Brown led from the start. COL Dan Shanahan arrived on 1 June. CSM Lloyd Coley took over Sergeant Major duties in October.

The Rear Detachment and the Family Readiness Groups were critical to the success of the 4th Infantry Division (Mech) during Operation Iraqi Freedom. Good communication was the difference between success and failure. Interaction was frequent. We believed open communications were essential to Soldiers focusing on the mission and families informed on loved ones in combat throughout Iraq. Meetings and gatherings were the staples of good communications, but we all were on the computer or the phone more than we'd all care to admit. Bi-weekly meetings hosted by the Division Rear Detachment Commander, COL Dan Shanahan and Mrs. Linda Odierno, Senior Family Readiness Group Representative with Command Group Spouses, Brigade and Separate Battalion Spouses, and key Division Staff were a central focus point for information sharing and decision making. COL Shanahan often joked that he'd prepare more for these meetings than any in his career. Tough questions were asked, decisions were sought, and information was shared by all in attendance. From these meetings and inputs from Installation Support Agencies on Ft Hood, the Brigade/Battalion Rear Detachments and Brigade/Battalion Family Readiness Leadership could provide information to their teams. No one had the same meeting schedule or information sharing protocols. All were effective in their own ways—providing vital information to Families and Soldiers.

Our notification process for Soldiers killed in action or wounded in action was important to preserve the privacy of the Family and to provide the needed support during critical periods. The procedures we started with were not the procedures we finished the deployment with. Continual improvements were made. Liaison officers were placed at critical points (hospitals) to better track and care for our Soldiers' needs and for the needs of our Families. Each Brigade task force was a little different in notifying the Rear Detachment, but the results were a timely notification for both injuries and in cases of loss of life. The media played a big part in raising anxiety for many families when a quick report on Fox News or CNN alerted families of 4ID Soldiers of injuries or deaths in Iraq. We always tried to notify long before an incident became news, but with reporters in Iraq with our Soldiers, this was not always possible. Too often (and one time is too many), families were notified long after an incident was reported on the news.

Those were very difficult days for our families, our Family Readiness Groups, and our Rear Detachments. Trained Soldiers and leaders did their very best to make these important notifications the most professional possible. In all cases, the goals were very high. In some cases, good Soldiers fell short in providing the care families thought they deserved. Leadership worked hard on all cases to preserve the most dignity in these

319

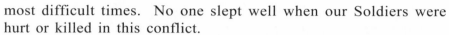

most difficult times. No one slept well when our Soldiers were hurt or killed in this conflict.

An especially important part played by our Rear Detachments and our Family Readiness Groups was assisting in preparing the III Corps Leadership and 1st Cavalry Division Leadership for their own deployments the following year. At off-sites and during preparation meetings, the 4th Infantry Division gave all the support it could muster to assist Families and Soldiers of our sister units, based on our own experiences. We all feel very good about this assistance to those who followed in the deployments to Iraq and Kuwait.

The unsung heroes of Operation Iraqi Freedom were the Brigade, Battalion, and Company level Rear Detachment leadership and Family Readiness Group leadership. Problems were identified and resolved daily by this dedicated group. History will say little of the Command Financial Specialists who helped families so their loved ones could focus on the mission, ultimately finding and capturing Saddam Hussein. Combat readiness started at home with sergeants and young company-grade officers helping families take care of themselves so our Soldiers could do their job.

We cannot thank the young wives who represented our Army, our Nation, and their Soldier with such poise and grace—taking care of each other in the time of need. Well done. We salute all our Heroes!

The highlights of this past year are varied from the perspective of our Rear Detachments and our Family Readiness Groups. We would all say that the early morning call from Ann Moody on the capture of Saddam was a highlight. The Return Ceremonies in Starker Gym were another highlight with SSG Mack leading the antics with the huge crowds welcoming home 'our Soldiers'.

Brigade and Battalion/Squadron events were a highlight for many, as well as the Christmas Party planned and led by the DIVARTY team. The daily "4ID Update from Iraq" emails from Bob Babcock, which kept us all informed with current and positive news, was a great morale booster.

The 4th Brigade Christmas Tree activity was a highlight and the Reunion Fair at Meadows School, planned by many and led by the staff of Bennett Clinic, was a highlight. The tremendous support from MG and Mrs. Peter Chiarelli to the 4th Division prior to the 1st Cavalry's deployment was an important highlight as Soldiers pitched in from across Ft Hood to make a difference for our Families. The 17th of July sticks in my head as the last vestiges of Saddam's power were destroyed and melted to form the centerpiece of the Fallen Soldier Memorial we all know well in our own hearts. The most memorable highlight perhaps was watching the 4th Division march onto the parade field in triumph on 22 April to restore the Division, Brigade, and Battalion level Colors. The follow-on celebration was a pretty good time as well, and one for the record book

MAJ Tony Garza (Left) - Dr. Hamid (Center) - LTC Kirk Eggleston, Division Surgeon, (Right) Distributing Medical Books to Iraqi Hospitals

Task Force Ironhorse Campaign Plan

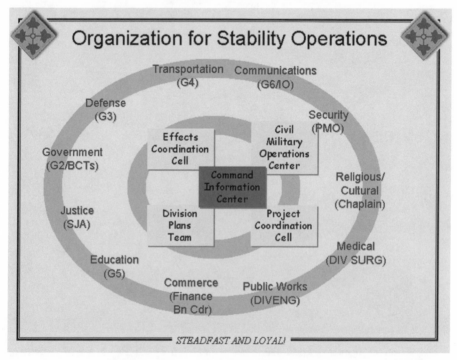

Organization for Stability Organization

Soldier from 1-22 IN clearing a house

555 EN GRP Change of Command, July 2003 - COL James Vosler, MG Ray Odierno, COL Christopher Toomey

Saint Barbara's Day Celebration, Taji Iraq: LTC Vince Price (1-17FA BN), LTC Jeff Springman (3-29 FA BN), COL Kevin Stramara (4th DIVARTY), LTC Rick French (2-20 FA BN), LTC Mike Mahoney (3-16 FA BN)

Mohammad Al Jubouri on raid with COL David Hogg (Warhorse 6) and Soldiers from 2-8 IN

COL Fred Rudesheim, CO of 3BCT; MG Ray Odierno, CG of TF Ironhorse; LTC Ryan Gonsalves, CO of 1-66 AR; and LTC Jeff Springman, CO of 3-29 FA

COL Don Campbell, TF Ironhorse Chief of Staff

TF Ironhorse Soldiers admire statue of Saddam Hussein on horse after it was blown down

Command team of 173rd Airborne Brigade, soon after parachute jump into Iraq - Left to right: LTC Randy A. George, Deputy Commander; CSM William W. Gunter, Command Sergeant Major; COL William C. Mayville, Jr., Commander

Commanders of TF Ironhorse after Transfer of Authority on 16 March 2004

Front row - left to right:
CSM Charles Henry, DISCOM
COL Jim Moore, DISCOM
COL Chris Toomey, 555 EN GRP
BG Mike Barbero, TF ADC/M
CSM Johnson, 2BCT
COL Lloyd Miles, 3BCT/25ID

Second row - left to right:
COL Bobby Nicholson, DIVENG
COL Jim Hickey, 1BCT
MG Ray Odierno, TF CG
CSM Chuck Fuss, TF CSM
COL Mike Moody, 4BCT
CSM Michael Davis, 124 SIG BN

Third row - left to right:
CSM Gregory Glen, 555 EN GRP
LTC John Baker, 124 SIG BN
CSM Lawrence Wilson, 1BCT
CSM Dennis Johnson, 3BCT
COL Dave Hogg, 2BCT
COL Fred Rudesheim, 3BCT
CSM Joseph Tainatongo, 4BCT

Commanders of 1BCT at their Tikrit HQ - February 2004

2BCT Commanders
Photo taken at FOB Warhorse vicinity of Baqubah, Iraq - Feb 04
(L-R) CPT Kevin O'Keefe, CO B Co 104th MI; LTC Joe Martin,
CO 1-67 AR; LTC Doug Tostrud, CO 204th SPT BN; LTC Mark Young,
CO 3-67 AR; LTC John Miller, CO 2-8 IN; COL Dave Hogg,
CO 2nd BCT; LTC Mike Mahoney, CO 3-16 FA; LTC Bill Adamson,
CO 588th EN; LTC Vince Price, CO 1-17th FA; CPT Chuck Thrash,
CO Brigade Recon Troop; CPT Chihung Szeto, CO HHC 2nd Bde

Commanders and CSMs of 3BCT
Rear Row (L-R): 3-29 FA: LTC Jeffrey Springman, CSM Cornilius
Speed; CSM Charles Fuss, MG Raymond Odierno; 3BCT: COL
Frederick Rudesheim, CSM Dennis Johnson; 1-8 IN: LTC Nathan
Sassaman, CSM Jessey Topasna; 1-12IN: LTC William Schafer, CSM
Eli Thomas; 1-68 AR: LTC Aubrey Garner, CSM Gary Cheesebrew
Front Row (L-R): 4EN: CSM Kimlock, LTC Laura Loftus; 64FSB:
LTC Joe Lofgren, CSM Morris

Battalion and Company Commanders of 64th Combat Support Group
44th CSB was in Mosul and not available for picture

DISCOM Command team - LTC Barry Diehl, S-3; COL Jim Moore, CO; CSM Charles Henry; LTC Jan Hooper, XO

"Patch" ceremony for 4BCT - 14 Nov 2003 Camp Speicher (Tikrit North Airfield)

XV

Welcome Home

Welcome home ceremonies, Colors uncased at Fort Hood, Ironhorse University, Lessons learned conference, Change of command of 4ID 1 March 2004 to 18 June 2004

T HE WELCOME HOME OF THE 4ID/TF IRONHORSE Soldiers came in several forms over the months of February, March, April, May, and June 2004.

As each planeload of troops arrived safely back at Fort Hood, or one of the other posts where TF Ironhorse Soldiers returned, emotional welcome home ceremonies were held for the Soldiers. At the peak of arrivals in March, there were up to four or five welcome home events in a single day, and each was a memorable life event for all who attended. The final planeload of Soldiers arrived at Fort Hood on the afternoon of April 21, only one day before the day long division wide "Welcome Home and Colors Uncasing Ceremony" held outside 4ID HQ on April 22.

Following these formal and informal Welcome Home ceremonies, the Soldiers attended a special "Ironhorse University" starting the last week of April and concluding in mid-May. Ironhorse University was designed to assist the Soldiers and their families in the transition from the combat environment of Iraq to home life in the United States.

To insure that the experience gained in Iraq was not lost, MG Odierno hosted a four-day "Lessons Learned Conference" in San Antonio for all TF Ironhorse battalion and brigade commanders and their command sergeants major. Spouses of these Soldiers were included in what was a valuable opportunity to share experiences learned both in Iraq and by the Family Readiness Groups at home. It was also a well-earned chance to relax and reflect with those who had shared the common experiences of war and separation.

After a 30 day block leave from mid-May through mid-June, the 4ID/TF Ironhorse portion of the history of "Operation Iraqi

Freedom I" came to an end with the Change of Command ceremony on June 18, 2004 when MG Ray Odierno turned over command of the 4ID to MG J.D. Thurman.

This chapter highlights the details of the Welcome Home experiences.

Welcome Home Ceremony for each Planeload of Soldiers
It was this author's good fortune to attend seven welcome home ceremonies as troops arrived in Fort Hood. I could describe the events but the notes sent by three of the 4ID wives, and an Army reporter, portray the events better than I can. These notes are unedited. In them, they express their extreme joy at having their Soldier husband safely home.

"I just wanted to send you an update on my husband getting home. He FINALLY got in on Thursday, March 11th at around 3:00 P.M. I got to the gym at around 1:00 P.M. and that last hour before we saw him was the longest hour in my whole year away from him!!! Being in the gym was like being at a high school pep rally. They had a DJ playing music for the kids to dance to and patriotic music to get us all pumped, and let me tell you what... they had us SO very pumped up!! I thought we were going to bring the walls down in that gym!! Being in there with all the other families who were also waiting to hug their Soldiers for the first time in a long time and knowing that we all had been through a very long year was just AWESOME!!

"Even though I didn't know a lot of the people in there, I still felt an overwhelming sense of comfort that we all had been through the same thing. The first call came at about 2:10 P.M. to SSG Mack who was keeping us all informed about the arrival of the airplane. WE ALL CUT LOOSE!!! The next call came in that the buses were rolling to the gym from the airfield. We all got even more excited!! When the final call came in that the buses had just rolled up outside the gym, I thought I might pass out and that all four walls of the gym were going to come tumbling down!!!!

"The Soldiers had to do a short formation outside before coming into the gym, but when they did, and that fog was rolling across the doorway, and they each ran in singing ... it was the most EXHILERATING and overwhelming sense of PRIDE I have EVER felt in my life!!! I wasn't able to spot my husband at first in the sea of DCUs but when we finally did find him there was no holding me or my 7-year-old daughter back!

"Our youngest daughter was a little reluctant to go to Daddy at first, but he offered her some Oreo cookies he had left over from his sack lunch and they quickly became reunited! We are VERY happy to have him home and I just can't wait for everyone else to be home too!!"

A second wife wrote: "I had to share with you the most unbelievable welcome home I could have imagined. Starker Gym was packed, SSG Mack said, "Welcome back, Task force Ironhorse." The crowd went crazy, screaming so loud that we couldn't hear our own voice within the sound. SSG Mack ran through the fog that was released from a fogger from the rear gym entrance and Soldiers one after another came running through after him...and there he was "OUR Soldier", arms in the air with one giant jump and a fist through the air. We knew it was him, all of our girls yelled, "Daddy!

"After every Soldier was in formation, the Commander introduced the National Anthem, then prayer. We stared at each other the entire time during the National Anthem and prayer, and all of us were crying, him included. The families had practiced saying 'dismissed' with SSG Mack all morning so we could release OUR troops. The time came and the Commander said, 'Family members, on three—1,2,3' and the crowd said, 'DISMISSED!' I ran and jumped right into his arms and our girls latched on (we have six girls). We all went to the ground. Remember 'dog pile' when you were a kid? That is what we looked like. We had a friend at the top of the bleachers that was there for the sole purpose of video taping this beautiful memory.

"We are so blessed that he is home and with us tonight. Everything to him right now is a luxury—warm water, a mattress, and being outside without a helmet or vest on.   Above all, we are a family together again and we do not take it for granted. He is sleeping now and has no worry of an attack."

Finally, the third wife wrote: "My husband's unit, (5th Platoon, 4th MP Company, 4ID) along with four other units, arrived back at Fort Hood on Tuesday morning. I just wanted to pay tribute to the wonderful Homecoming ceremony the Army had organized at the gym. All the family members were crowded on the bleachers, and when the troops finally ran in, with smoke bombs going off all around, the place went wild! I had trouble seeing my husband among the ranks, but as soon as the order to dismiss was given he came walking straight towards me with tears running down his face. I think it was the happiest moment of my life. His parents were there too, having traveled from Alabama to welcome him home from his first combat tour. We've only been married just over a year, but I've decided that no other way of life could provide such extremes of emotion—both good and bad! I must admit that morning in the gym made up for a year of worry. It was truly fantastic!"

All who attended the Fort Hood welcome home ceremonies will remember the enthusiasm and leadership of SSG Mack and the National Anthem singing of Carol Hearron. The Fort Hood Sentinel had this article on March 18:

Returning Soldiers treated to a 'Big Mack Attack'
By Staff Sgt. Robert Stephenson
444th MPAD, 4th Inf. Div. PAO

"As you leave here, remember one thing; I will be here for you when you return. That's a promise."

With those words, Staff Sgt. Terrance Mack, Personnel NCO of HHC, 1st Brigade, 4th Infantry Division helped to send off members of the Ivy Division to Iraq for Operation Iraqi Freedom. That was more than a year ago.

Mack recently stood on the basketball court of Starker Gymnasium with a microphone in his hand as the master of ceremonies during the welcome home reception for members of the 4th Forward Support Battalion.

Just as he has done for the better part of a month for every component of the 4th Inf. Div. as they return home, Mack provides a service not only to the Soldiers, but to their families as well.

"The family members are real receptive to what I do—I get a lot of people to say thank you," said Mack. "Even though they're sitting in the gym for hours on end, they appreciate it."

While family members crowd into bleachers, Mack not only provides them with entertainment, but also gives them information on where their loved ones are on the way home, all the while revving up the crowd and instructing them on how the ceremony will go and on the most important word they need to know—'dismissed,' which comes at the end of the festivities.

A 17-year Army veteran, Mack has had three tours in Germany, one in Fort Benning and one at Fort Stewart. However, he is most proud of his accomplishment while at Fort Hood, where he became the NCOIC of an all-digital Tactical Operations Center.

Although Mack would love to have accompanied his unit overseas, nature intervened.

"I had to have brain surgery, and it took me out of deployment status," he said. "Since I can't go forward, I will stay here and take care of things back home."

What has now become a full-time duty began by chance, according to Mack. "One day I walked into the Abrams Gym and there was this guy doing it (master of ceremonies), and I thought I could do a better job, so I asked if I could take the microphone and I took it over and that's where it started."

Although the job of master of ceremonies is not a true duty position yet, it might as well be as far as Mack is concerned, but that's not why he goes to the gym almost every day.

"I don't do it because the Army says so, I do it because I like doing stuff like this," Mack said.

And then there is the other reason.

"I promised every Soldier on their deployment to Iraq that I would be there for them—and I kept my promise."

Unlike in previous wars, the Army did a fantastic job in insuring the welcome home for our Soldiers and their families was what they deserved.

Bangor, Maine Troop Greeters

Equally as much a part of the homecoming ceremonies as the events in the Fort Hood, Fort Carson, and other welcoming centers, was a unique tribute to many of our returning Soldiers as they made a refueling stop in Bangor, Maine. Starting soon after the September 11, 2001 tragedy, these citizens have greeted every planeload of Soldiers returning from Iraq and Afghanistan, regardless of the time of day or night.

One of our Soldier's parents wrote describing the Bangor greeting. "My husband and I met our son coming off his flight in Bangor, on his way to Ft. Hood with the 1-67 Armor. Arriving on Monday night we met several veterans and their spouses who greet the flights; learning that there was a flight due at 12:30 A.M.

I was up for that, as our son was supposed to be in sometime the next day. I was not going to let an opportunity go by to Welcome Home our guys. It was wonderful, the Soldiers came down off the ramp, a line of Vets and just normal townspeople were there, we shook their hands and said, "welcome home." If a Soldier held out his arms, I knew a hug was in order, so we hugged those guys and told them about the free phones.

"The 82 year old WW II Vet coordinator has 40 phones available for free calls to parents, wives, or anyone the Soldier wants to call. It was great to tell the men they could use those free phones and to see their eyes light up (especially the young guys), and to hear the excitement as they woke up family.

"I remember one man at 1:00 A.M. talking into an answering machine as loud as he could until his wife woke up and took the call!!   Despite the late hour, the airport snack bar was especially opened for these guys to get burgers, etc. At 2:00 A.M. I sat around with the Vets and wives eating leftover burgers, and since the next flight was scheduled for 8:30 A.M., we felt everyone could get a good night's sleep. At 6:30 the next morning I saw Soldiers out my hotel window and raced over to the airport, in case my son was with that group. This was the 8:30 flight, two hours ahead of schedule. But our faithful coordinator, Bill Knight, had gotten the call sometime after 2:00 A.M. to alert him of the men coming in, and he was there with some of those hearty souls who left at 2:00 A.M. My son came in on the next flight, and we could see him coming down the ramp, I jumped into his arms, his Dad had tears in his eyes, it was terrific.

"You cannot say enough about what those local "Maine Troop Greeters" have organized and their dedication—70,000 troops greeted so far, 377 flights, and some of the volunteers leaving at 2:00 A.M., and back there by 5:30 A.M. to greet again. Some days they greet as many as nine flights, averaging around 200 or more men and women per flight. Our Soldiers were surprised and very happy to have those Vets shake their hands and thank them. This is truly a dedicated group, from the 70ish widow whose husband was not a Veteran and had no children, to the Vets from all the Wars and conflicts, to the grandmother who has a grandson in Iraq, to the regular folks who show up to help, it is amazing."

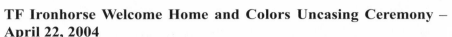

TF Ironhorse Welcome Home and Colors Uncasing Ceremony – April 22, 2004

In June 2003, MG Ray Odierno took his aide, CPT Charles Armstrong, aside and told him his initial thoughts about the welcome home ceremony he wanted to have for the Soldiers of TF Ironhorse. His commander's intent, reflecting the high esteem he had for his Soldiers, was simply, "Do it first class."

In September, MG Odierno sent CPT Armstrong back to Fort Hood to start working on the welcome home ceremony. From that simple commander's intent, CPT Armstrong embarked on developing a welcome home ceremony like no military post had ever done before. He enlisted help from the Morale, Welfare, and Recreation (MWR) organization at Fort Hood and soon had Tracy Thomas working on sponsorships and Daphne Avila working on contracts and signing up entertainers. Others soon joined in the monumental effort.

The scope of the event continued to grow and as January came around it was obvious that this was a major production that would be second to none ever conducted when American Soldiers returned from a combat zone. The communities surrounding Fort Hood rallied around the opportunity to support the Soldiers who meant so much to them. April 22, 2004 was announced as the date for the Welcome Home event.

The list of entertainers grew in both quantity and quality. Before it was completed, it turned out to be the largest show that the USO had ever put on in the continental United States. Entertainers, performing on the main stage erected in front of 4ID HQ or on other stages scattered around the HQ area, included: Randy Travis, Tracy Byrd, John Michael Montgomery, Stone Cold Steve Austin, the Undertake, Lynyrd Skynyrd, Eddie Griffin, Bruce Bruce, the Dallas Cowboys Cheerleaders, Mercy Me, Wayne Newton, Drew Carey, Jessica Simpson, Ludacris and many more.

The children of our Soldiers were not ignored at this family event. In addition to a carnival that had been set up close to 4ID HQ, a Kids Stage was erected with entertainers that appealed to the younger set.

A few statistics will show the scope of the Welcome Home ceremony. The event had 120,000 people in attendance during the course of the day and night. 70,000 servings of food, 135,000 donuts, 100,000 cold drinks, and 300 kegs of beer were consumed. It is estimated that the value of the entertainment exceeded $3,000,000—yet the total cost of the event to the 4ID and TF Ironhorse was only $150,000. (Thanks again to all the sponsors, the communities, the unpaid volunteers, and the leadership who made this a "first class event" for our deserving Soldiers).

The following day, the Army Press Service released the following:

Fort Hood Hosts Texas-Size Homecoming Celebration
By Tam Cummings
Special to American Forces Press Service
FORT HOOD, Texas, April 23, 2004 – The flag of the Army's 4th Infantry Division was uncased here April 22 in ceremonies marking the official return of Task Force Ironhorse to the nation's largest military base.

Division commander Maj. Gen. Ray Odierno and Les Brownlee, acting secretary of the Army, oversaw the event held before an estimated crowd of 60,000 Soldiers, family members and national, state and community leaders. Some 700 Soldiers took part in the uncasing, representing the various units that made up the task force in Operation Iraqi Freedom.

The division colors had been cased one month ago in Iraq as the division prepared to redeploy and Soldiers from the 1st Infantry Division took their place.

"Thirteen months ago, in March 2003, Task Force Ironhorse was deployed to destroy a corrupt and dangerous regime," Brownlee said. Iraqis found the 'veil of oppression lifted' because of the success of the Soldiers' mission, he continued. "They overcame all difficulties and succeeded in typical Ironhorse fashion. They established their headquarters in Tikrit, Saddam Hussein's hometown."

Odierno praised the Soldiers, saying the "capture of Saddam symbolized an end to the psychological, political and military terror the dictator represented to the people of Iraq. Task Force Ironhorse Soldiers and other members of the team never let up," he said. "Never before has a theater of operations been more complex," the general told them. "You are as bright and innovative as you are lethal. No doubt our enemy would attempt to defeat us here. But we will destroy them in their own nest. The 4th Infantry Division and the nation will never forget your sacrifice."

Odierno thanked family members representing division Soldiers who died in service. "It is a debt we can never repay," he said, turning right to address the seated families. "Eighty-one Soldiers of Ironhorse made the ultimate sacrifice. We in the nation are in awe of the families of these Soldiers. Your loss is not in vain." The general told the group, "The fight continues in Iraq and around the world today," and that "small bands of heartless, murderous criminals" will be punished

Odierno also thanked families attending the uncasing for their support of the troops during the deployment. "This is a celebration of the return of heroes," he said. "For an Army spouse, there is uncertainty, worrying whether your Soldier is in harm's way. One who provides strength today needs to cry tomorrow."

Before the pass in review, four sets of balloons were released into the cloudy sky. Red, white and blue balloons represented the Soldiers, yellow balloons served as a reminder of Soldiers still at their posts, purple balloons honored the wounded, and black balloons marked memories for the slain Soldiers.

Tam Cummings is assigned to Fort Hood public affairs.

4ID/TF Ironhorse Monument

A separate effort, running concurrently with the planning for the Welcome Home ceremony, was the building of a monument to the fallen Soldiers of TF Ironhorse. In Iraq, the 4ID had contracted with an Iraqi artist to build a statue from the bronze in two monuments of Saddam on a horse. Engineers of the 555th Engineer Group had blown down the monuments in Tikrit on July 7, 2003. The new monument is of a Soldier kneeling in front of a rifle, boots, and helmet, the symbol of a fallen Soldier. A small girl stands behind him with her hand on his shoulder. The statue was paid for by the Soldiers of TF Ironhorse. It was delivered to their HQ in Tikrit in December 2003. Brought home in a wooden crate on one of the returning flights, the challenge was to raise the money to build the monument where the statue would permanently remain and to do it before the April 22 ceremony.

Retired COL Ted Kostich, former 2nd Brigade commander and Chief of Staff of the 4ID, and president of the Ironhorse Chapter of the National 4th Infantry Division Association, took on the challenge of raising funds and getting the support of the local community. With the Homebuilders Association of Central

Texas donating most of the labor and much of the materials, in little more than a month the required money to start construction of the Monument was in hand. In late March, work began on the site between the 4ID parade field and the 4ID museum, only 60-feet from the existing Wall of Honor dedicated to 4ID Medal of Honor recipients. Working feverishly, the statue was put into place late in the afternoon of April 20, the stained glass 4ID patch was installed and sod was put on the ground on April 21, and the Monument with statue were ready for the Welcome Home ceremony on April 22. It was truly a monumental effort that was made possible through the leadership of COL Ted Kostich and the many volunteers who devoted their time and money to the effort. (The formal dedication of the Monument, including bronze plaques with the names of all the TF Ironhorse Soldiers killed in action was held on 2 September 2004.)

Other Welcome Home Ceremonies and Events
Not only were Welcome Home ceremonies held at Fort Hood, they were also held in other locations where TF Ironhorse Soldiers returned. Two of the larger ceremonies were in Vicenza, Italy, held on March 12, 2004 to honor Soldiers of the 173rd Airborne Brigade and in Colorado Springs, CO on June 5, 2004 to honor all Fort Carson Soldiers who had served in Iraq.

173rd Soldiers Welcomed Home
The United States Army Europe Public Affairs Office described the 173rd Airborne Brigade homecoming:
Story by Diana Bahr
CASERMA EDERLE, VICENZA, Italy—In what seemed like a never-ending line of desert camouflage uniforms and tan boots, the Soldiers of the 173rd Infantry Brigade (Airborne) (part of TF Ironhorse in Iraq) filed onto a muddy football field Friday afternoon, formed ranks and faced the audience and visiting dignitaries.

Crowds of family members, friends and co-workers jammed the bleachers and lined up along the running track, cheered and waved flags as each unit was announced.

The ceremony opened with brigade commander, Col. William Mayville, assisted by brigade Command Sgt. Maj. William Gunter, uncasing the brigade's colors and attaching the newest battle

340

streamer—representing the brigade's participation in Operation Iraqi Freedom I.

After opening remarks by U.S. Ambassador Mel Sembler, who congratulated the Soldiers for their efforts, U.S. Army Europe commander, General B.B. Bell took the podium, followed by Southern European Task Force (Airborne) commander, Major General Thomas Turner.

"Soldiers of the 173rd Airborne Brigade served with valor and distinction during Operation Iraqi Freedom. They made a lasting contribution to bringing stability to Kirkuk and surrounding areas. The 173rd Soldiers helped establish an independent civilian government, a new police force, and they restored basic services to the people of Kirkuk, improving their daily lives," said Turner. "We will not forget our Soldiers who made the ultimate sacrifice in Iraq, nor will we forget the shared sacrifices of our Italian allies..."

At the conclusion of his speech, it was time for Turner, accompanied by Mayville and Bell to end the ceremony with a pass in review of the Soldiers. As the troops marched off the field, the crowd moved over to a fest tent where the celebrations continued. There was something for everyone—from a 'Kid's Korner' where clowns entertained and children could have their faces painted, paint pictures, jump rope and have fun—to concerts from Joan Jett and the Blackhearts for the rock-n-rollers to Italian group, Hill Billy Soul for the country-lovers to the U2 Tribute band, Elevation, to the Washington Redskins Cheerleaders—who everyone seemed to adore...

Joan Jett didn't let her fans down as she sang and sweated through an hour and a half performance. Saving the best for last, she played her signature song, "I Love Rock 'n Roll' and bringing the crowd to their feet and singing along. A couple of songs later, "Crimson and Clover" found the crowd surging toward the stage, swaying to the beat. At the end of her set, SETAF Chief of Staff, Col. Blair Ross, presented Jett with a plaque. Not content with just a plaque, Jett requested—and received—an airborne beret...

In addition to the 173rd Airborne event, other activities marked the return of the TF Ironhorse Soldiers. COL Don Campbell, 4ID/TF Ironhorse Chief of Staff, along with sixty-three members of the TF, including fifteen recipients of the Purple Heart, were honored at the home baseball opener of the Texas Rangers on 9 April. COL Campbell threw out the first pitch, a job that was repeated by MG Ray Odierno, along with another group of TF Ironhorse Soldiers, at a home game of the Houston Astros a few weeks later.

Continuing honors given to returning Soldiers of the 4ID and TF Ironhorse, fifty members of the 4ID, led by MG Odierno and CSM Charles Fuss, provided the Honor unit at the 60th anniversary of the D-Day landing in Normandy, France. After the ceremony on Utah Beach, the 4ID Soldiers mixed with several of the 4ID veterans who had stormed ashore on the beach on 6 June 1944. Soldiers of the 173rd Airborne Brigade participated in the annual parachute jump outside St. Mere Eglise on 5 June.

4ID/TF Ironhorse "Lessons Learned" Conference – San Antonio, Texas

MG Ray Odierno hosted the "Lessons Learned" conference with former commanding general, LTG Ben Griffin, and future commanding general, MG J.D. Thurman in attendance along with the Battalion and Brigade Commanders and Command Sergeants Major and spouses. In three intensive work days, wrapped up with social events in the evenings, attendees studied and reported on six subject areas: Training for Operation Iraqi Freedom, Soldier Issues, Combat Operations, Logistics, Deployment Planning, and Rear Detachment/Family Readiness Groups. Findings of these study groups are not included in this document but they were forwarded to appropriate Army commands for action. Informal evening dinner meetings gave the command group time to reflect on the accomplishments of the Task Force and enjoy some well-earned relaxation.

4ID Change of Command Ceremony – June 18, 2004

Under a brilliantly blue Texas sky, MG Ray Odierno relinquished command of the 4th Infantry Division to the 54th Commanding General, MG James D. Thurman. In his last speech as Commanding General of the 4th Infantry Division, MG Odierno spoke of his pride in the Soldiers and of the job they had done so well. He remembered the TF Ironhorse Soldiers who had made the supreme sacrifice for our country. He thanked all who had supported the Soldiers during their deployment.

As the troops passed in review, the commanding officers and command sergeants major of each unit peeled off from the formation as they left the parade field and assembled behind MG Odierno on the reviewing stand.

When the final unit left the field, the assembled officers and command sergeants major joined MG Ray Odierno and the audience in singing the 4th Infantry Division song:

Steadfast and Loyal
We're Fit to fight!
The Nation's Finest Soldiers
Keep Liberty's Light
Our Soldiers ROAR for Freedom
We're Fit for any Test
The Mighty 4th Division
AMERICA'S BEST!

As the Soldiers left the reviewing stand, they all knew that the 4th Infantry Division, under MG J.D. Thurman, the new commanding general, is "fit to fight" and is "fit for any test". One chapter of the 4th Infantry Division's history had ended but many more proud chapters stand ahead of the Mighty 4th Division, America's Best!

SSG Terrance Mack welcomed home all 4ID troops at ceremonies in Starker and Abrams gyms - February through April 2004

4ID Leaders and Colors from Iraq at the 4ID Utah Beach Monument on the 60th anniversary of the D-Day landing - 6 June 2004

Change of Command - MG J.D. Thurman, left, after assumption of command from MG Ray Odierno, right. FORSCOM Commanding General GEN Daniel McNeill is in center - 18 June 2004

4ID Soldiers, freshly arrived home, salute during playing of National Anthem before being dismissed to join their families in Starker Gym

Bob Babcock, right, talking with Max Rudolph on live KNCT-TV broadcast from the 4ID Parade field - Fort Hood - 22 April 2004

TF Ironhorse Monument dedication at Fort Hood, Texas - 2 September 2004

August 2003, November 2003, January 2004

Throughout the deployment to Iraq, the TF Ironhorse organization changed frequently to meet mission requirements. Included here are representative samples of the TF Ironhorse organization as of August 2003, November 2003, and January 2004.

TF Ironhorse Organization—August 2003

1st Bde Combat Team
- 1-22 Infantry
- 3-66 Armor
- 299 Engineers
- 4-42 Field Artillery (-)
- 4th Forward Support Battalion
- A/1-4 Aviation
- 720th MP Battalion (-)
- 1st Platoon, 4th MP Company
- A/104 Military Intelligence (-)
- A/124th Signal
- Infantry platoon (-) - Georgia

2nd Bde Combat Team
- 2-8 Infantry
- 1-67 Armor
- 3-67 Armor
- 588 Engineers
- 3-16 Field Artillery (-)
- 204th Forward Support Battalion
- 1-10 Cavalry
- 1-17 Field Artillery
- 978th MP Company (-)
- 2nd Platoon, 4th MP Company
- B/104 Military Intelligence (+)
- B/124th Signal
- UAV Platoon

3rd Bde Combat Team
- 1-8 Infantry
- 1-68 Armor (+)
- 1-66 Armor
- 4th Engineers
- 3-29 Field Artillery
- 64th Forward Support Battalion
- C/1-4 Aviation
- 64th MP Company (-)
- 3rd Platoon, 4th MP Company
- C/104 Military Intelligence (+)
- C/124 Signal
- UAV Platoon

4th Bde Combat Team
- 1-4 Aviation (-)
- 2-4 Aviation (+)
- 404th Aviation Support Bn
- C/1-44 Air Defense Artillery
- B/1-4 Aviation

173rd Airborne Brigade
- 1-508 Airborne Infantry
- 2-503 Airborne Infantry
- 1-12 Infantry
- 1-63 Armor (-)
- C/1-68 Armor
- D/319 Field Artillery
- 201st Forward Support Bn
- B/1-101 Aviation
- 1st Platoon, 554 MP Company
- B/110 Military Intelligence (-)

TF Gunner
- DivArty HQ
- 2-20 Field Artillery (-)
- 5th Engineer Battalion
- B/1-44 Air Defense Artillery
- 44th Chemical Company
- 46th Chemical Company
- 47th EOD Company
- Infantry platoon – Macedonia

TF Able
- 555th Engineer Group
- 223 Engineer Battalion (-)
- 244 Engineer Battalion (-)
- 14th Engineer Battalion (-)

DISCOM
- 704th Direct Support Bn
- 64th Corps Support Group

4ID HQ Troops
- 1-44 Air Defense Artillery (-)
- 124 Signal Battalion (-)
- 418 Civil Affairs Battalion (+)

TF Ironhorse Organization—August 2003

4ID HQ Troops - Continued
104 Military Intelligence Bn (-)
502nd Personnel Services Bn
230th Finance Battalion
4th MP Company (-)
502nd Psychological Ops Co (-)
C/1-101 Aviation

TF Ironhorse Organization—November 2003

1st Bde Combat Team
1-22 Infantry
3-66 Armor
299 Engineers
4-42 Field Artillery (-)
4th Forward Support Bn
1-10 Cavalry (-)
A/1-4 Aviation
720th MP Battalion (-)
1st Platoon, 4th MP Co
A/104 Military Intelligence (-)
A/124th Signal
Infantry platoon (-) - Georgia

2nd Bde Combat Team
2-8 Infantry
1-67 Armor
3-67 Armor
588 Engineers
3-16 Field Artillery (-)
1-17 Field Artillery
204th Forward Support Bn
C/1-10 Cavalry
978th MP Company (-)
323rd MP Company
2nd Platoon, 4th MP Company
B/104 Military Intelligence (+)
B/124th Signal
UAV Platoon
Infantry Battalion - Nigeria

3rd Bde Combat Team
1-8 Infantry
A/2-124 Infantry
1-68 Armor (+)
1-66 Armor
4th Engineers (+)
3-29 Field Artillery

64th Forward Support Battalion
C/1-4 Aviation
64th MP Company (-)
3rd Platoon, 4th MP Company
C/104 Military Intelligence (+)
534th Signal Company
C/124 Signal
UAV Platoon
Rifle Platoon (+) - Moldova

4th Bde Combat Team
1-4 Aviation (-)
2-4 Aviation (+)
404th Aviation Support Bn
C/1-44 Air Defense Artillery
B/5-101 Aviation

173rd Airborne Brigade
1-508 Airborne Infantry
2-503 Airborne Infantry
1-12 Infantry
1-63 Armor (-)
C/1-68 Armor
D/319 Field Artillery
201st Forward Support Bn
B/1-101 Aviation
1st Platoon, 554 MP Company
B/110 Military Intelligence (-)
B/404 Civil Affairs (+)

TF Gunner
DivArty HQ
2-20 Field Artillery (-)
5th Engineers
B/1-44 Air Defense Artillery
44th Chemical Company
46th Chemical Company
47th EOD Company
Infantry platoon – Macedonia

TF Ironhorse Organization—November 2003

TF Able
555th Engineer Group
223 Engineer Battalion (-)
244 Engineer Battalion (-)
14th Engineer Battalion (-)

DISCOM
704th Direct Support Bn
64th Corps Support Group

4ID HQ Troops
1-44 Air Defense Artillery (-)
124 Signal Battalion (-)
418 Civil Affairs Battalion (+)
358 Civil Affairs Brigade (-)
402 Civil Affairs Battalion
104 Military Intelligence Bn (-)
502nd Personnel Services Bn
230th Finance Battalion
4th MP Company (-)
502nd Psychological Ops Co (-)
C/1-101 Aviation

TF Ironhorse Organization—January 2004

1st Bde Combat Team
1-22 Infantry
3-66 Armor
299 Engineers
4-42 Field Artillery (-)
4th Forward Support Bn
A/1-4 Aviation
1st Platoon, 4th MP Company
A/104 Military Intelligence (-)
A/124th Signal
Infantry platoon (-) - Georgia

2nd Bde Combat Team
2-8 Infantry (-)
1-67 Armor
3-67 Armor
588 Engineers (+)
3-16 Field Artillery
1-17 Field Artillery
204th Forward Support Bn
C/1-10 Cavalry
978th MP Company (-)
323rd MP Company
2nd Platoon, 4th MP Co
B/104 Military Intelligence (+)
B/124th Signal
UAV Platoon
Infantry Battalion - Nigeria

3rd Bde Combat Team
1-8 Infantry
A/2-124 Infantry
1-68 Armor (+)

1-66 Armor
1-10 Cavalry (-)
4th Engineers (+)
3-29 Field Artillery
64th Forward Support Bn
C/1-4 Aviation
4th Platoon, 64th MP Co
3rd Platoon, 4th MP Co
C/104 Military Intelligence (+)
534th Signal Company
C/124 Signal
UAV Platoon
Rifle Platoon (+) - Moldova

4th Bde Combat Team
1-4 Aviation (-)
2-4 Aviation (+)
404th Aviation Support Bn
C/1-44 Air Defense Artillery

173rd Airborne Brigade
1-508 Airborne Infantry
2-503 Airborne Infantry
1-12 Infantry
1-63 Armor (-)
C/1-68 Armor
D/319 Field Artillery
201st Forward Support Battalion
B/1-101 Aviation
3rd Platoon, 554 MP Company
B/110 Military Intelligence (-)
B/404 Civil Affairs (+)

TF Ironhorse Organization—January 2004

2nd Brigade, 25th Inf Division
1-21 Infantry
1-27 Infantry
1-14 Infantry
2-11 Field Artillery
225th Forward Support Battalion
A/125 Military Intelligence
25th MP Company

TF Gunner
DivArty HQ
2-20 Field Artillery (-)
5th Engineers
B/1-44 Air Defense Artillery
44th Chemical Company
46th Chemical Company
745th EOD Company
Infantry platoon - Macedonia

TF Able
555th Engineer Group
223 Engineer Battalion (-)
244 Engineer Battalion (-)
14th Engineer Battalion (-)

DISCOM
704th Direct Support Battalion
64th Corps Support Group
180th Transportation Battalion
553rd Corps Support Battalion
544 Maintenance Battalion

4ID HQ Troops
1-44 Air Defense Artillery (-)
124 Signal Battalion (-)
418 Civil Affairs Battalion (+)
358 Civil Affairs Brigade (-)
402 Civil Affairs Battalion
104 Military Intelligence Bn (-)
502nd Personnel Services Bn
230th Finance Battalion
720th MP Battalion (-)
4th MP Company (-)
502nd Psychological Ops Co (-)
C/1-101 Aviation

4ID/TF Ironhorse Headquarters

Commanding General – MG Raymond T. Odierno
Command Sergeant Major – CSM Charles Fuss
Assistant Division Commander (Support) – BG (P) Steve Speakes, COL (P) Albert Bryant, Jr. (July 2003)
Assistant Division Commander (Maneuver) – BG David Rodriguez, BG Mike Barbero (May 2003)
Chief of Staff – COL James Barclay, COL Donald M. Campbell, Jr. (June 2003)
G1 – LTC Steven Shea
G2 – LTC Natalie Lee, LTC Todd Megill (June 2003)
G3 – LTC J. B. Burton, LTC Theodore Martin (June 2003)
G4 – LTC Victor Maccagnan, LTC Terry Hermans (June 2003)
G5 – LTC Donald Jackson, LTC Donald Hick (July 2003)
G6 – LTC Ed West, LTC John Schleifer (July 2003)
Staff Judge Advocate - LTC Flora Darpino, LTC Tracy Barnes (August 2003)
Division Engineer - COL Bobby Nicholson
Division Surgeon - LTC Kirk Eggleston
Division Chaplain - LTC Gilbert Richardson
Provost Marshall - LTC Doug Ingros
Public Affairs Officer - LTC William McDonald
Information Operations - MAJ Joe Cox
Effects Coordination Cell - LTC Richard Richardson, MAJ Tim Bush (June 2003)

1st Brigade – COL Donald M. Campbell, Jr., COL James B. Hickey (June 2003)
CSM Lawrence Wilson

1-22 Infantry – LTC Mark Woempner, LTC Steven Russell (June 2003)
CSM Salvadore Martinez

1-66 Armor – LTC Ryan Gonsalves
CSM John Moody

3-66 Armor – LTC Larry Jackson
CSM Willie Keeler

299 Engineers – LTC Doug McNeese, LTC Mark Huron (June 2003)
CSM Robert Wells

2nd Brigade – COL Dennis Rogers, COL David R. Hogg (June 2003)
CSM Frederick Johnson

2-8 Infantry – LTC John Miller
CSM Lonnie Rawles, CSM Gabriel Cervantes (November 2003)

1-67 Armor – LTC Robert Valdivia, LTC Joseph Martin (June 2003)
CSM Ernest Barnett

3-67 Armor – LTC Mark Young
CSM David Roberson

588th Engineers – LTC William Adamson
CSM Macarthur Edmundson

3rd Brigade – COL Fred Rudesheim
CSM Dennis Johnson

1-8 Infantry – LTC Philip Battaglia, LTC Nathan Sassaman (June 2003)
CSM Jesse Topasna

1-12 Infantry – LTC Tim Parks, LTC William Schafer (June 2003)
CSM Eli Thomas III

1-68 Armor – LTC Richard Piskel, LTC Aubrey Garner (June 2003)
CSM Gary Cheesebrew

4th Engineers – LTC Brian Stevens, LTC Laura Loftus (June 2003)
CSM Gerald Kinloch

4th Brigade – COL Michael Moody
CSM Joseph Tainatongo

1-4 Aviation – LTC Jim Muskopf
CSM Wagdi Mabrouk

2-4 Aviation – LTC Jack Frost
CSM Willie Tart

1-10 Cavalry – LTC Theodore Martin, LTC Reginald Allen (June 2003)
CSM David List

DivArty – COL Kevin Stramara
CSM James Sherill

2-20 Field Artillery – LTC Allen West, LTC Richard French (October 2003)
CSM Henry Burns

4-42 Field Artillery – LTC Dominic Pompelia
CSM James Howell

3-16 Field Artillery – LTC Michael Mahoney
CSM Elijah King

3-29 Field Artillery – LTC Jeffrey Springman
CSM Cornelius Speed

DISCOM – COL Jim Rentz, COL James Moore (July 2003)
CSM Charles Henry

4th Forward Support Battalion – LTC Mike Minyard, LTC Daryl Gore (June 2003)
CSM Milton Jones

204th Forward Support Battalion – LTC Rosa McNeely, LTC Douglas Tostrud (May 2003)
CSM Trent Ellis

64th Forward Support Battalion – LTC Joseph Lofgren
CSM Dwight Morrison

404th Direct Aviation Support Battalion – LTC Richard Evans
CSM Gordon Murray

704th Division Support Battalion – LTC Terry Hermans, LTC Catherine Reese (June 2003)
CSM Deidra Jones

Separate Battalions
1-44 Air Defense Artillery – LTC Richard Starkey
CSM Randy Leatherwood

124th Signal Battalion – LTC John Schliefer, LTC John Baker (July 2003)
CSM Michael Davis

104th Military Intelligence Battalion – LTC Todd Megill, LTC Conrad Christman (June 2003)
CSM John Pegues

502nd Personnel Support Battalion – LTC David Tighe
CSM Curtis Blankenship

720th Military Police Battalion – LTC David Poirier
CSM William Generali

418th Civil Affairs Battalion – LTC Kenneth Bean, LTC James Suriano (August 2003)
CSM Gary McElligott

230th Finance Battalion – LTC Scott Schmidt
CSM Lautenschlager

173rd Airborne Brigade – COL William C. Mayville, Jr.
CSM William W. Gunter

1-508 IN – LTC Harry Tunnell, LTC Randy George (October 2003), LTC Timothy McGuire (November 2003)
CSM Willie Peoples, CSM Arthur J. McCann III (November 2003)

2-503 IN – LTC Dominic Caraccilo
CSM Earl Rice

1-63 AR (-) – LTC Kenneth Riddle
CSM Michael Peters, SGM Gregory L. Baugh, CSM Ansley Harris

1-12 IN – LTC Timothy Parks, LTC William J. Schafer (June 2003)
CSM Eli Thomas

1-101 AVN (-) – LTC Douglas Gabram
CSM Joe Moodt

64th Corps Support Group – COL Mike Terry, COL Tom Richardson (June 2003)
CSM Shirley Pharris

180th Transportation Battalion – LTC Dave Cotter, LTC Glenn Grothe (June 2003)
CSM Richard Adams

553rd Combat Support Battalion – LTC Mark Kormos, LTC Patrick Gaston (June 2003)
CSM Donald Harris

544th Maintenance Battalion – LTC Ricky Sherman, LTC Christopher Wicker (June 2003)
CSM Edwardo Garcia, Jr.

44th Combat Support Battalion - LTC Michael Holmes
CSM Benjamin Ramos II

555th Engineer Group – COL James Vosler, COL Christopher Toomey (July 2003)
CSM Gregory Glen

5th Engineer Battalion – LTC Robert Sinkler, LTC Anthony Funkhouser (June 2003)
CSM Michael Cline

244th Engineer Battalion – LTC Jeffrey Jerome
CSM Hiron Frazier

14th Engineer Battalion – LTC Clarence D. Turner
CSM Bernard Mabini

223rd Engineer Battalion – LTC Rubel West
CSM Thomas Ales

1092nd Engineer Battalion – LTC Ashley Campers
CSM Terry Lee

565th Engineer Battalion – LTC Richard Hornack
1SG Arthur Hart

In Memory of the
Task Force Ironhorse Soldiers who Died in Iraq

I'll Think of You

Written and Sung by LTC Steve Russell at
Memorial statue dedication on 2 Sept 2004

I wait for your face, to return from a distant place
I seek your words, mental speeches that are never heard

Refrain:
And today I thought of you;
Of the full life that you never knew;
Of the world that passed you by;
Of your loved ones you never told good bye;
So today, I'll think of you, of you.

Free souls; steep price; proud flags draped on sacrifice
Of youth now gone, but their memories carry on

Repeat Refrain

1LT Osbaldo Orozco
C CO 1-22 IN

SGT Sean C. Reynolds
74 LRS 173 ABN BDE

SGT Richard P. Carl
571st MED

CW2 Hans N. Gukeisen
571st MED

CW3 Brian K. Van Dusen
571st MED

PFC Rasheed Sahib
HHB 2-20 FA

SPC Nathaniel A. Caldwell, Jr.
B CO 404 ASB

SGT Keman L. Mitchell
C CO 4 EN

SSG Kenneth R. Bradley
B CO 588 EN

SGT Atanacio Haro-Marin
C BTRY 3-16 FA

PVT Jesse M. Halling
401st MP CO - 720 MP

SFC Dan H. Gabrielson
652 EN CO - 588 EN

SGT Melissa N. Valles
B CO 64 FSB

CPL Christian C. Schulz
C CO 3-67 AR

SPC Jonathan P. Barnes
HHC 1-67 AR

SGT Daniel K. Methvin
HHC 1-67 AR

PFC Wilfredo Perez Jr.
HHC 1-67 AR

CPT Leif E. Nott
A TRP 1-10 CAV

CPL Justin W. Hebert
D BTRY 319 FA

PVT Matthew D. Bush
F TRP 1-10 CAV

SSG David S. Perry
649 MP - 588 EN BN

SGT Steven W. White
HHB 4-42 FA

CPL Craig S. Ivory
501 FSC

SPC Ronald D. Allen, Jr.
C DET 502 PSB

SGT Sean K. Cataudella
H TRP 10th Cav

SSG Mark A. Lawton
A CO 244 EN

CPL Richard S. Arriaga
HHB 4-42 FA

CPT Brian R. Faunce
HHC 3BCT

SGT Anthony O. Thompson
HHB 4-42 FA

SPC James C. Wright
HHB 4-42 FA

CPT Robert L. Lucero
ROC HHC, 4ID

CPL Kyle G. Thomas
A CO 2-503 IN

CSM James D. Blankenbecler
HHB 1-44 ADA

PFC Analaura Esparza-Gutierrez
A CO 4 FSB

CPL James H. Pirtle
C CO 2-8 IN

CPL Joseph C. Norquist
HHC 588 EN

SPC James E. Powell
B CO 1-22 IN

SPC Donald L. Wheeler, Jr.
A CO 1-22 IN

PFC Stephen E. Wyatt
C BTRY 1-17 FA

1LT David R. Bernstein
C CO 1-508 IN

PFC John D. Hart
C CO 1-508 IN

CPT John R. Teal
HHC 2D BDE

SPC Artimus D. Brassfield
HHC 1-66 AR

SPC Jose L. Mora, Jr.
C CO 1-12 IN

PFC Steven Acosta
C CO 3-67 AR

SGT Michael P. Barrera
A CO 3-67 AR

Memoriam

CPL Isaac Campoy
A CO 3-67 AR

PFC Rayshawn S. Johnson
C CO 299 EN

CPL Genaro Acosta
B BTRY 1-44 ADA

PFC Jacob S. Fletcher
C CO 2-503 IN

SGT Joseph Minucci, II
C CO 2-503 IN

CW2 Alexander S. Coulter
HHC 4ID

Mr. Brent A. McJennett
Proactive Communication Inc.

SSG Dale A. Panchot
B CO 1-8 IN

PFC Scott M. Tyrrell
C CO 299 EN

CPT George A. Wood
B CO 1-67 AR

CPL Gary B. Coleman
B CO 1-68 AR

SSG Eddie E. Menyweather
C CO 588 EN

CW4 Clarence E. Boone
HHC DISCOM

SPC Raphael S. Davis
B CO 233 EN

SPC Joseph M. Blickenstaff
B CO 1-23 IN

SSG Steven H. Bridges
B CO 1-23 IN

SPC Christopher J. Wesley
B CO 1-23 IN

SPC Charles E. Bush, Jr.
HHC 402 CA

SGT Benjamin W. Biskie
HHC 5 EN

CPT Christopher F. Soelzer
HHC 5 EN

MAJ Christopher J. Splinter
HHC 5 EN

SGT Michael E. Yashinski
501 FSC 173 ABN BDE

SSG Thomas W. Christensen
652 EN CO 588 EN

SSG Stephen C. Hattamer
652 EN CO 588 EN

SPC Charles G. Haight
HHC 14 EN

SSG Michael J. Sutter
745 OD CO 79 OD BN

SGT Curt E. Jordan, Jr.
A CO 14 EN

CPT Eric T. Paliwoda
B CO 4 EN

PFC Cody J. Orr
B BTRY 1-44 ADA

CPL Larry E. Polley, Jr.
B BTRY 2-20 FA

SGT Edmond L. Randle
B BTRY 2-20 FA

CPL Gabriel T. Palacios
HHC 588 EN

PFC James D. Parker
HHC 588 EN

PF Ervin N. Dervishi
B CO 1-22 IN

SGT Juan C. Cabral
A CO 4 FSB

SPC Holly J. McGeogh
A CO 4 FSB

SGT Eliu A. Mier
A CO 4 FSB

SSG Roger C. Turner, Jr.
HHT 1-10 CAV

CPL Nichole M. Frye
A CO 415th CA BN

SFC Henry A. Bacon
HHT 1-10 CAV

CPL Bert E. Hoyer
652 EN 588 - EN BN

Steadfast And Loyal

Chapter I
4ID Museum archives

Chapter II
From *War Stories – Utah Beach to Pleiku,* Robert O. Babcock, St. John's Press, Baton Rouge, LA, 2001

Chapter III
TF Ironhorse Operations Order for entry through Turkey; Interviews: MG Ray Odierno, CG, 4ID; COL Don Campbell, CO, 1BCT Bde; COL Mike Moody, CO, 4BCT Bde; COL Bobby Nicholson, DIV ENG; LTC Phil Battaglia, CO, 1-8 IN; LTC Todd Megill, G-2. Newspaper article from Washington Times

Chapter IV
Embedded media information came from an interview with MAJ Josslyn Aberle and LTC Bill MacDonald at Fort Hood, TX on April 15, 2004, conducted by a military history detachment. Other input was from interviews of LTC Phil Battaglia, CO of 1-8 IN and LTC Mark Woempner, CO of 1-22 IN, conducted by Bob Babcock in July 2004, and from interviews with Brigade Commanders and 4ID General Staff during weeks of April 20-23 and June 14-18, 2004

Chapter V
Op Order from 4ID; Interviews: MAJ Brian Reed, 1-22 IN XO; MAJ Bill Ostlund, 173rd Airborne Brigade S-3; MG Ray Odierno, 4ID CG; LTC Ted Martin, CO 1-10 Cav; LTC Phil Battaglia, CO 1-8 IN; LTC Mark Woempner CO 1-22 IN; COL Don Campbell, CO 1BCT Brigade

Chapter VI
Interviews with COL Don Campbell, CO 1BCT; COL Kevin Stramara, CO, DIVARTY; COL Fred Rudesheim, CO 3BCT; LTC Phil Battaglia, CO 1-8 IN; LTC Ted Martin, CO 1-10 CAV; LTC Mark Woempner, CO 1-22 IN; MAJ Brian Reed, XO 1-22 IN; MAJ Ed Chesney, XO 3-66 AR; LTC John Miller, CO 2-8 IN; MAJ Tom Boccardi, S-3 1-12 IN; CPT Joel Dillon, CO C/1-12 IN

Chapter VII
"History of the 555th Combat Engineer Group and Task Force Able during Operation Iraqi Freedom.", produced by the 555th EN GRP; Interviews: COL Kevin Stramara, DIVARTY CO; COL Fred Rudesheim, 3BCT CO; COL Christopher Toomey, 555 EN GRP CO; LTC Phil Battaglia, 1-8 IN CO; MAJ Josslyn Aberle, TF Ironhorse Deputy PAO; MAJ Brian Reed, 1-22 IN XO; CPT Joel Dillon, C/1-12 IN CO; Press releases from TF Ironhorse PAO; Briefing Presentations from TF Ironhorse G-3; 1BCT, 2BCT, 3BCT, 173rd Airborne After Action Reports

Chapter VIII
TF Ironhorse PAO Press Releases; After Action Reports from all BCTs; Gunner Gazette newsletter articles; LTC Steve Russell journal and interview; Stories written by 4ID PAO team for posting on 4ID web page and inclusion in Ironhorse Desert News; 4ID Update from Iraq electronic newsletter by Bob Babcock

Chapter IX

TF Ironhorse PAO Press Releases; After Action Reports from all BCTs; Interviews: COL Dan Shanahan, Rear Detachment CO; Chaplain DeWayne Brewer, Rear Detachment Chaplain; Mrs. Linda Odierno, FRG leader; COL Don Campbell, Chief of Staff; COL Jim Hickey, 1BCT CO; LTC John Miller, 2-8 IN CO; LTC Steve Russell, 1-22 IN CO, LTC James Suriano, 418 CA BN; Electronic diary of LTC Steve Russell, 1-22 IN CO; Gunner Gazette; 4ID Update from Iraq electronic newsletter - Bob Babcock

Chapter X

TF Ironhorse PAO Press Releases; After Action Reports from all BCTs; Interviews: LTC Scott Schmidt, 230 FIN BN; COL James Hickey, 1BCT CO; COL Don Campbell, Chief of Staff; LTC Doug Ingros, Provost Marshall; COL David Hogg, 2BCT CO; COL Kevin Stramara, DIVARTY CO; COL Fred Rudesheim, 3BCT CO; LTC Anthony Funkhouser, 5 EN BN CO; COL Mike Moody, 4BCT CO; LTC Steve Russell, 1-22 IN CO; LTC John Miller, 2-8 IN CO; CPT Joel Dillon, C/1-12 IN CO; Electronic diary of LTC Steve Russell, 1-22 IN CO; 4ID Update from Iraq electronic newsletter by Bob Babcock

Chapter XI

TF Ironhorse PAO Press Releases; Operation Red Dawn Press Release and After Action Report; Interviews: COL James Hickey, 1BCT CO; MAJ Brian Reed, 1BCT S-3; MAJ Josslyn Aberle, TF Ironhorse Deputy PAO; CPT Desmond Bailey, G TRP 10 Cav CO

Chapter XII

TF Ironhorse PAO Press Releases; After Action Reports from all BCTs; Interviews: LTC Gil Richardson, TF Ironhorse Chaplain; Chaplains Jim Caraway, Klon Kitchen, Steve Maglio, Oscar Arauco; COL Fred Rudesheim, 3BCT CO; LTC Joe Martin, 1-67 AR; LTC Kirk Eggleston, Division Surgeon; CSM Charles Fuss, TF Ironhorse CSM; LTC Donald Hick, G-5; Electronic diary of LTC Steve Russell, 1-22 IN CO; Mike Hedges, Houston Chronicle; 4ID Update from Iraq electronic newsletter by Bob Babcock

Chapter XIII

TF Ironhorse PAO Press Releases; After Action Reports from all BCTs; Interviews: LTC John Miller, 2-8 IN CO; COL Kevin Stramara, DIVARTY CO; COL James Moore, DISCOM CO; COL Tom Richardson, 64 CSG CO; MAJ Bill Ostlund, 173rd ABN BDE S-3; COL David Hogg, 2BCT CO; MAJ Joe Cox, TF Ironhorse Information Operations; 4ID Update from Iraq electronic newsletter by Bob Babcock

Chapter XIV

Unit highlights submitted by COL James Hickey, 1BCT CO; COL David Hogg, 2BCT CO; COL Fred Rudesheim, 3BCT CO; COL William Mayville, Jr., 173 ABN BDE CO; COL Mike Moody, 4BCT CO; COL Christopher Toomey, 555 EN GRP CO; COL Kevin Stramara, DIVARTY CO; COL James Moore, DISCOM CO; COL Tom Richardson, 64 CSG CO; COL Dan Shanahan, Rear Detachment CO; ECC article submitted by MAJ Tim Bush; TF Ironhorse overall highlights from PAO press release

Chapter XV

TF Ironhorse PAO Press Releases; Interview: COL Dan Shanahan, Rear Detachment CO; MAJ Charles Armstrong, Welcome Home Project Officer; COL (Ret) Ted Kostich, Project Officer for Monument; 4ID Update from Iraq electronic newsletter by Bob Babcock

10th MTN DIV: 10th Mountain Division
1BCT: 1st Brigade Combat Team
2BCT: 2nd Brigade Combat Team
3BCT: 3rd Brigade Combat Team
4BCT: 4th Brigade Combat Team
2LT: Second Lieutenant
1LT: First Lieutenant
1SG: First Sergeant
55 most wanted list: Most wanted Saddam supporters - shown on playing cards
AAFES: Army Air Force Exchange System
ADA: Air Defense Artillery
ADA Linebackers: Bradley Fighting Vehicle modified to an ADA weapons system
ADC: Assistant Division Commander
AFB: Assault Float Bridge
AH-64: Apache Helicopter
AH-64D: Longbow Apache Helicopter
AHR: Attack Helicopter Regiment
AO: Area of Operations
AOE: Army of Excellence
AOR: Area of Operational Responsibility
APC: Armored Personnel Carriers
AR: Armor
ASB: Aviation Support Battalion
ASOG: Army Special Operations Group
ASR: Alternate Supply Routes
Assyrians: Ethnic group in No.Iraq, predominantly Christian, (appx. 2% of pop.)
AT: Antitank
ATK: Attack
AVN: Aviation
Baath party: Political party of Saddam Hussein
BCT: Brigade Combat Team
BG: Brigadier General (One star)
Black List #1: Reference to Saddam Hussein
BN: Battalion
Bradley chain gun: The 30mm gun on the Bradley Fighting Vehicle
Bradley Fighting Vehicles: Primary armored infantry vehicle in the Army
BRT: Brigade Reconnaissance Troop
Buffalo Soldiers: Nickname for Soldiers of 1-10 CAV, dates to 1800s
BWI: Baltimore-Washington International airport
C-17: Cargo airplane
C2: Command and Control
C-4: Plastic Explosive
C4I network: Command, Control, Communication, Computer and Intelligence
CA: Civilian Affairs

CAS: Close Air Support, provided by USAF in support of ground forces
CAV: Cavalry
CEA: Captured enemy ammunition
CEM: Captured enemy material
CENTCOM: Central Command - HQ for all Middle East operations
CG: Commanding General
CHEM BN: Chemical Battalion
CHU: Containerized Housing Unit
CJTF-7: Combined Joint Task Force 7 - in command of all ground units in Iraq
CMIC: Civil Military Information Center
CMO: Civil Military Operations
CMOC: Civil Military Operations Center
CNN: Cable News Network
CO: Commanding Officer
Coalition: The United States and our Allies in Iraq
COL: Colonel
Conexes: Metal shipping containers
CONUS: Continental United States
CP: Command Post
CPA: Coalition Provisional Authority
CPT: Captain
CSB: Corps Support Battalion
CSG: Corps Support Group
CSM: Command Sergeant Major
DAO: Division Ammunition Office
DCU: Desert Camouflage Uniforms
DFAC: Dining facility
Digital division: Name 4ID was called after their Force XXI work was complete
Dinar: Iraqi Money
DISCOM: Division Support Command
DIVARTY: Division Artillery
DMAIN: Main 4ID Headquarters
DMC: Distribution Management Center
DRF: Deployment Ready Facility
DSB: Division Support Battalion
DTOC: Division Tactical Operations Center
ECC: Effects Coordination Cell
Embedded media: Reporters who lived with and reported from a military unit
EN: Engineer
EN GRP: Engineer Group
End state: The desired results after an action or series of actions were taken
EOD: Explosives, Ordnance, Demolition
EPW: Enemy Prisoner of War
FA: Field Artillery

FBCB2: Force XXI Battle Command Brigade and Below

Fedayeen: Suicidal supporters of Saddam Hussein, called Saddam Fedayeen

LE: Logistics Element

FN BN: Finance Battalion

FOB: Forward Operating Base

FORSCOM: Forces Command

Fratricide: Friendly Fire that killed our personnel

FRG: Family Readiness Group

FSB: Forward Support Battalion

FSE: Fire Support Element

G-1: Personnel officer in Division HQ

G-2: Intelligence officer in Division HQ

G-3: Operations officer in Division HQ

G-4: Support officer in Division HQ

G-5: Civil affairs officer in Division HQ

G-6: Signal Officer in Division HQ

Governorates: Provinces

H&I - Harassment and Interdictory artillery fire

H-58: Kiowa observation helicopter

Hellfire: Anti-tank missile

HESCO bastions: Concrete barrier walls

HET: Heavy Equipment Transport

HHB: Headquarters and Headquarters Battery

HHC: Headquarters and Headquarters Company

HHS/B: Headquarters and Headquarters Service Battery

Hooah: Army expression meaning many positive things: yes, awesome, tough, etc.

HUMINT: Human Intelligence

Humvee: HMMWV, High Mobility Multi-Wheeled Vehicle, also called Hummer

HVT: High Value Target

IBAS: Interceptor Body Armor System

ICDC: Iraqi Civil Defense Corps

ID: Infantry Division, as in 4ID for 4th Infantry Division

IED: Improvised explosive device

IN: Infantry

IO: Information Operations

IPF: Iraqi Police Force

IPTIP: Iraqi Police Transition and Integration Program

Ironhorse: nickname for the 4ID and attached units

Judge Advocate: Legal officer in Division HQ

KDP: Kurdish Democratic Party

Kevlar: Protective helmet worn by American Soldiers

KIA: Killed In Action

Kurds: Ethnic group mostly in Northern Iraq, persecuted under Saddam, 10-20% of population

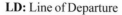

LD: Line of Departure
LOC: Line of Communication
LRS: Long Range Surveillance
LSA: Logistics Support Area
LTC: Lieutenant Colonel
LTG: Lieutenant General (Three Stars)
M1 Abrams tank: Main battle tank of US Army
M1A2 SEP: Main battle tank with more advanced electronics
MAJ: Major
MANPAD: Man Portable Air Defense Weapons
MCO: Movement Control Office
MEK: Mujaheddin Al Khalq
MG: Major General (Two Stars)
MI: Military Intelligence
Milvan: Military Van
MLRS: Multi-Launch Rocket System
mm: Millimeter
MOS: Military Occupation Specialty
MOUT: Military Operations in Urban Terrain
MSG: Master Sergeant
MSR: Main Supply Route
MWR: Morale, Welfare, and Recreation
NBC: Nuclear, Biological, Chemical
NCO: Non-Commissioned Officer
NCOIC: Non-Commissioned Officer in Charge
NOD: Night optical device
Non-compliant enemy forces: The bad guys, called by several names
NVG: Night Vision Goggles
OBJ: Objective
OGA: Other Government Agencies
OH-58D: Kiowa Warrior helicopters
OPCON: Operational Control
Operation ICE: Iraqi Currency Exchange Operation
OPTEMPO: Operational Tempo
ORHA: Office of Reconstruction and Humanitarian Assistance
PAO: Public Affairs Office
PBO: Property Book Office
PFC: Private First Class
PIR: Parachute Infantry Regiment
PUK: Patriotic Union of Kurdistan (one of two major Kurdish parties)
QRF: Quick Reaction Force
R&R: Rest and Recuperation
Ramadan: Muslim holy month
RAOC: Rear Area Operations Center

Recon: Reconnaissance Platoon
Red Crescent: Iraq equivalent of Red Cross
Redlegs: Artillerymen
Regulars: Nickname of 22nd Infantry Regiment
RGT: Regiment
RPG: Rocket Propelled Grenade
RSOI: Reception, Staging, Onward Movement, and Integration
S-1: Personnel officer in brigade and battalion HQ
S-2: Intelligence officer in brigade and battalion HQ
S-3: Operations officer in brigade and battalion HQ
S-4: Support officer in brigade and battalion HQ
S-5: Civil affairs officer in brigade and battalion HQ
SAPI: Small arms protective insert - goes inside IBAS
SETAF: Southern European Task Force
SF: Special Forces
SFC: Sergeant First Class
SGM: Sergeant Major
Shadow 200 RQ-7A: Spy drone unmanned aircraft
Shia: Muslim religious sect, primarily in the south, 60% of Iraq population
Shiite: Same as Shia, often used interchangeably
SIGINT: Signal Intelligence
SKS: Soviet rifle
SMG: Soviet Machine Gun
SOF: Special Operations Forces
SPC: Specialist
SPOE: Sea Port of Embarkation
Spy drone: Unmanned aircraft
SSG: Staff Sergeant
SSO: Saddam Hussein's Special Security Organization
Sunni Arabs: Muslim sect, made up about 30% of population. Saddam was Sunni
TAA: Tactical Assembly Area
TF: Task Force
TF Ironhorse: All the units working together under a single command, 4ID was primary element of TF Ironhorse but many others were included - see page 335
TOC: Tactical Operations Center
TOW missile: Wire guided anti-tank missile
TRAN BN: Transportation Battalion
Turkomen: Ethnic group, about 5% of population. Ethnically related to Turks
UAV: Unmanned Aerial Vehicles
UH-60: Blackhawk Helicopter
USAID: United States Agency for International Development
UXO: Unexploded Ordnance

The Story Continues...

With the return from Iraq, TF Ironhorse ceased to exist as a combined arms fighting force, but the units involved continued to prepare for the next time they would be called forward in the Global War on Terror. After a well deserved 30-day leave in May and June 2004, the leaders and Soldiers began to prepare for certain future deployments.

The way ahead for the 4ID was defined in five steps—reset, reorganize, retrain, prepare, and deploy. Reset included recovering the vehicles and equipment that had been shipped back from Iraq, bringing them back up to standards, and repairing or replacing them as required. The year in Iraq had been one of high usage for all 4ID equipment.

Reorganization included building a totally new modular organization to adapt to the lessons learned in Iraq and the Global War on Terror. From the three traditional maneuver brigades of infantry, armor, engineer, artillery, and support battalions, the 4ID changed to four Units of Action, or Brigade Combat Teams, and grew in strength to almost 20,000 Soldiers. The purpose of the new BCTs was to be modular and to allow "plug and play"— each BCT would fit interchangeably into any situation that our nation required, working either with other 4ID units or as a stand-alone and self sustaining unit, or, with another division or task force.

There were many personnel changes during the summer of 2004. New leaders and new Soldiers had to retrain to become the cohesive teams that had been the norm during the previous deployment. Constant field training exercises, live fire gunnery, and basic skills enhancement filled the training days of the 4ID in the second half of 2004 and in 2005.

In early December 2004, the Pentagon gave the orders to 4ID to be prepared to deploy back to Iraq sometime in 2005. As the first chapter of the 4ID's history in the Global War on Terror closed, the second chapter has already begun. Once again, the "Steadfast and Loyal" 4th Infantry Division will be called into action to support our nation's interests and the leaders and Soldiers are eager to write the next chapter in our history.

About the Author

Robert O. (Bob) Babcock was born and raised in Heavener, Oklahoma. He received his ROTC commission at Kansas State College (now Pittsburg State University) in Pittsburg, Kansas in 1965. He served with Company B, 1st Battalion, 22nd Infantry Regiment, 4th Infantry Division from November 1965 through July 1967, including one year in Vietnam. From 1968 to 2002, Bob worked as a sales and marketing executive with IBM.

In 2003, Bob formed Americans Remembered, Inc., a non-profit corporation and an official partner of the Veterans History Project. He is past president, historian, and archivist of the National 4th Infantry Division Association, president of the 22nd Infantry Regiment Society, and a member of Vietnam Veterans of America, Atlanta Vietnam Veterans Business Association, Veterans of Foreign Wars, and American Legion. He is the author of another 4ID history, *War Stories - Utah Beach to Pleiku* and his own personal account of his service with 4ID in Vietnam, *What Now, Lieutenant?* He and his wife, Jan, live in Marietta, Georgia.

VETERANS HISTORY PROJECT

Americans Remembered, Inc.
Official Partner of Veterans History Project
"Preserving Memories of America's War Veterans and Those Who Supported Them"

The American Folklife Center of the Library of Congress and Americans Remembered, Inc. invite you to join us in an important national project—the Veterans History Project. The project honors our nation's war veterans and those who served in support of them by creating a lasting legacy of recorded video interviews and other documents chronicling their wartime experiences.

The U.S. Congress voted unanimously for legislation to create the Veterans History Project on October 27, 2000. Congress also saw the value of engaging the American public in its own history. Bob Babcock founded Americans Remembered and has been an official partner of the VHP since December 2002. Hundreds of interviews have been contributed to the National Archives, and given to veterans for their family archives. Gary Swanson, one of our volunteers, has personally completed over 500 interviews of WWII veterans in two years.

Our primary focus is on first-hand accounts of U.S. veterans from World War II, Korean War, Cold War, Vietnam War, Persian Gulf War, and the Global War on Terror. In addition, those civilians who were actively involved in supporting war efforts (such as war industry workers, USO workers, flight instructors, medical volunteers, etc.) are also invited to share their valuable stories.

How can you help?

We would like you to join us as a member of our Volunteer Corps. Seldom have you had an opportunity to do work that future generations will learn so much from. We owe a debt of gratitude to our veterans and those who supported them in preserving our freedom. Regardless of the role you play—interviewer or interviewee or financial contributor—you will be able to say: "I did my part, did you?"

For more information:

Visit our website at www.americansremembered.org or contact us at: Americans Remembered, Inc., PO Box 682232, Marietta, GA 30068. Americans Remembered is a non-profit 501 (c)(3) corporation and all contributions are tax deductible.

Other Books by Bob Babcock

War Stories, Utah Beach to Pleiku by Robert O. Babcock - ISBN 0-9710551-0-6. Soft cover. Cover Price $29.95. Your Price $28.00 including shipping. Second printing available, October 2005. 450 war stories written by 4th Infantry Division veterans from World War II, the Cold War, and Vietnam.

What Now, Lieutenant? by Robert. O. Babcock - Soft cover. Your price is $22.00, including shipping. Available October 2005. The personal account of Bob Babcock's experiences as a platoon leader and executive officer with Bravo Company, 1st Battalion, 22nd Infantry Regiment, 4th Infantry Division in Vietnam in 1966 and 1967.

Orders should be sent to Bob Babcock, PO Box 682222, Marietta, GA 30068